The Negro in Sports

Edwin Bancroft Henderson

3d Edition

Edited by Daryl Michael Scott
With an Introduction by Al-Tony Gilmore

The ASALH Press
Washington DC

"To set the cause above renown,
   To love the game beyond the prize,
   To honor as you strike him down,
   The foe that comes with fearless eyes,
   To count the life of battle good,
   And dear the land that gave you birth,
   But dearer yet the Brotherhood,
   That binds the brave of all the earth."

                              —— *Sir Henry Newbolt.*

This book Is Dedicated to My Sons,
Dr. Edwin Meriwether Henderson and
Dr. James Henry Meriwether Henderson

EDITOR'S PREFACE TO THIRD EDITION

The Association for the Study of African American Life and History (ASALH) is gratified to republish one of the works that our founder, Carter G. Woodson, initially selected to put before the public. Edwin B. Henderson's *The Negro in Sports* is among the most important books in the history of the Associated Publisher.

This new edition, the 3rd, retains Henderson's revision and expansion of his original manuscript. The text has been altered only by the addition of an introduction by the historian Al-Tony Gilmore. A former member of the ASALH Executive Council and a pioneer in the field of sports history, Gilmore contributes an introduction that places the relationship of Henderson, Woodson, and the Association in the proper light. His attention to detail and accuracy is in keeping with both the original author and director of the Associated Publishers. Additionally, whenever the project stalled, and it did for several years, Al-Tony kept pressing the issue.

In working on this project, I came to appreciate the intellectual conviction that motivated the author. Henderson's effort to record the achievements of African American athletes reflected his belief that black athleticism would play a vital role in transforming the position of blacks in America. He nurtured this belief for the first four decades of the twentieth century and watched it come to fruition by the close of his life. He had imagined the effects of a Jesse Owens, a Joe Louis, a Jackie Robinson, and a Bill Russell while others before and since have seen black athleticism as a false, even harmful path. Even with the examples of a Paul Robeson or a Charles Drew—perhaps the ultimate scholar athletes—many believed the Greek ideal of a strong mind and body did not and would not apply to blacks. In going against the intellectual grain, Henderson had a lot in common with Woodson whose idea that the study black history, by blacks or whites, would advance the cause of the race. The majority of educated blacks, rejected that view. The project brought together two dissenters whose views proved right.

Given the intellectual richness of this project, *The Negro in Sport* deserves better than the second generation copy that this edition represents. Yet, without the original plates or photographs, we were left to enhance the images published in the 2nd edition to the best of our ability. Perhaps at some future date, readily available technology will allow ASALH to produce a better edition.

Daryl Michael Scott

Upper Marlboro, MD
December, 2014

CONTENTS

INTRODUCTION

Edwin Bancroft Henderson, Carter G. Woodson and the Making of *The Negro in Sports*

In the spring of 1996, the National Archives invited Sam Lacy, the venerable sportswriter for the *Baltimore Afro-American* newspaper, to participate in a seminar based on his life. At the twilight of a career spanning more than six decades of commentary on the exploits of black athletes, coaches, teams, and sports organizations, and on the challenges to racial barriers in sports, two events combined to cause a resurrection of interest in Lacy: the fiftieth anniversary of Jackie Robinson breaking baseball's color-line, and Lacy's own induction into baseball's Hall of Fame as a writer. As an influential journalist, he had been one of the most important forces in the integration of baseball, and as early as 1948, he had been elected the first black member of the Baseball Writers' Association of America.

Walter Hill, a historian at the Archives, coordinated the event. He asked me to serve as moderator, and to develop a set of questions that would enable Lacy to provide a retrospective on his distinguished career. Being a writer of sports history, developer of the first college course on The History and Politics of Black Athletes in America, and admirer and regular reader of his legendary, "Lacy's A to Z", sports column – beginning in high school and continuing through college – without comment, question or reticence, I agreed. My delight with the request was secondary only to the pride and honor I felt it bestowed. Three generations of my family were readers of Lacy's writings, and now I was on the prelude of an unrivaled personal and professional experience to share with the fourth. In preparation, I methodically re-examined my well-worn copy of Edwin Bancroft Henderson's *The Negro in Sports*, confident that it would be a trustworthy source for establishing historical perspective, framing pertinent questions, making insightful comments, and probing elusive and controversial issues.

The seminar was subscribed beyond capacity with a diverse audience of scholars, government employees, sports enthusiasts, and the general public. At the time, the nonagenarian Lacy still wrote his popular column, and was as comfortable discussing current sporting events as he was those of more than a half-century earlier. His relaxed and introspective style, the rapid-fire precision of his memory, his eloquent language, and his humorous personal anecdotes made for a memorable afternoon. All of those in attendance were mesmerized, recognizing that the moment was special. Afterwards, his curiosity about the content and sequence of my questions prompted him to ask if I had ever read *The Negro in Sports*, pointing out that it was the definitive account of much of what we had discussed, and then proceeding quietly to inform me that Henderson, his close friend, had consulted with him during the writing of the book. With my preparation validated, I breathed a sigh of relief and summoned the courage to place one hand on the shoulder of Lacy's diminutive frame. With the other I produced from my briefcase a copy of the book. A brief silence followed; then he smiled and winked at me, while firmly shaking my hand and thanking me for doing "your homework."

Henderson's book, *The Negro in Sports*, first appeared in 1939, and may be best appreciated against the backdrop of the early years of the As-sociation for the Study of Negro (African American) Life and History (ASALH), and the work of its immortalized founder, Carter G. Wood-son. Receiving a Ph.D. in history from Harvard in 1912, Woodson soon earned a well- deserved dual reputation that followed him throughout his life. On the purely professional side, he was a tenacious and unrelenting advocate of African American history; and on the lighter, personal side, he was a stubborn and intractable personality, particularly on matters relating to the operation of the Association, which he and several others organized in 1915.[1]

Totally absorbed in the teaching, writing, researching, and publishing of African American history, he founded The *Journal of Negro History* in 1916, incorporated the Associated Publishers in 1921, initiated Negro History Week in 1926, and introduced the *Negro History Bulletin* in 1937. Woodson cultivated black pride while demanding white respect for black historical contributions. In recognition of the volume of work he produced through the Association and for demonstrating the role of black history as a weapon in the struggle for racial equality, in 1926 the NAACP selected him for its Spingarn Medal, awarded annually for outstanding achievement by a member of the race.[2] Among blacks, the award confirmed his stature as a historian, coming as it did at the peak of the Harlem Renaissance, a literary and cultural movement among African Americans led by intellectuals, writers, and artists stressing black contributions to culture, literature, history, and the arts. More than anyone else, Woodson and the Association were the source of an outpouring of publications consumed by the market of readers – black and white – identifying with the Renaissance. Appearing during and after the Great Migration and coinciding with the rise of the 1920s "New Negro", all of the Association's publications countered images and interpretations of blacks in textbooks, periodicals, and popular culture, infamous for casually and routinely denigrating and lampooning black life.[3]

Based in Washington, D.C., Woodson enjoyed the success of the Association, but generally avoided the aura of his fame, other than when it assisted him in soliciting funds from philanthropists and foundations, originating new book projects, expanding the Associations membership and programs and selling books. Much of his time was also invested in mentoring and publishing a budding generation of black scholars, including Charles Wesley, Alrutheus Taylor, Lorenzo Greene, James Hugo Johnston, Lawrence Reddick, Rayford Logan, Mercer Cook, Ira De Augustine Reid, W. Sherman Savage, Luther Porter Jackson, and Rufus Clement, all of whom would ultimately receive doctoral degrees from the nation's most prestigious institutions of higher education. Through the Association Woodson was able to monitor the training of blacks in the graduate-school pipelines, recruit them for projects of his own design, provide exposure at the Association's annual meetings, expand networks with other scholars, and publish their work with the Associated Publishers – over which he exercised dictatorial authority and absolute administrative control.[4] Though Woodson was partial to younger scholars of his own race, only those with impeccable academic credentials and the greatest potential were able to secure his confidence and earn his tutelage. Those of lesser ability could not find entry into his inner circle. Youthful brilliance notwithstanding, when differences of opinion on research and writing arose, Woodson insisted on having the final word.[5] Publishing in the 1920s and '30s was a formidable task for young black scholars writing of black life and history. With mainstream publishers extremely reluctant to accept non-fiction manuscripts on black topics, especially during the dismal economic climate of the Great Depression, the Associated Publishers was often the only outlet for book-length works by black academic authors.

Woodson, the Associated Publishers, and ASALH all came in one package, and the young scholars, who frequently felt isolated in the professional organizations of their disciplines, accepted it as the most reliable option for continued growth and development. In their autobiographies, memoirs, and writings, the dislike of Woodson's dogmatic personality is a recurring theme, generally offset by reverence and respect for his contributions. Historian Lorenzo Greene worked for Woodson in the early 1930s, traveling by car throughout the country selling Association books. In his meticulous diary, he recorded his displeasure and often intense anger over disagreements emanating from Woodson's domineering and demanding personality and the fierce confrontations resulting from questions about Greene's loyalty and integrity. The frequency of those acrimonious episodes was not unusual for those who worked under Woodson's authority and crossed the rough edges of his temperament.[6]

A classic Victorian, Woodson refrained from smoking, alcoholic beverages, and popular dancing, and he rarely attended purely social, recreational, or sporting events. He rejected the music idiom of jazz, hugely popular with black audiences throughout the 1920s and '30s, because of his belief that it was too erotic for the cause of social progress.[7] Taking enormous pride in, and generous self-credit for, his work with the Association, without restraint he allowed his personal life to capitulate to his professional work. Perhaps nothing exemplified this more than the residence he purchased in Washington, which doubled as the Association's national headquarters. Operating out of a modest brick row house in a largely segregated neighborhood, Woodson orchestrated a movement that produced a body of scholarship sufficient enough to make his name synonymous with African-American history, and academically sound enough to leave an indelible imprint on the craft of history. Still, he was arrogant, indifferent to criticism, and personally removed from many important events in the daily lives of average black people.

Something changed in Woodson's outlook in the late 1930s when, according to his biographer, Jacqueline Goggin, he became "more tolerant of Black working class culture".[8] No single factor can responsibly account for the shift she observed, which likely can be credited to a confluence of social and cultural forces in black life. Writers, social scientists, and historians were beginning to place more value on ordinary lives, and Woodson needed to be on the frontier of this trend. Further, the decade of the 1930s witnessed the influence of black athletes and sporting events on black life and culture in ways unimaginable since Jack Johnson became boxing's champion in 1908. Cutting across social classes, black sports united the "talented tenth" with the remainder of the race, and proved to be a common denominator for pride, dignity, and respect in ways that could not be accomplished with other activities.

As much as Woodson was an elite intellectual whose cultural and social preferences did not originate in black working-class culture, he was not isolated from what black athletes were doing to undermine segregation and white supremacy in the minds of most black people. As recently as the 1932 and 1936 Olympics, Eddie Tolan and Jesse Owens respectively had earned the title of "the world's fastest human", and Owens' four gold medals in Berlin destroyed Hitler's presumption of Aryan physical supremacy. Equally dramatic was Joe Louis' reign as world boxing champion, when black pride and American nationalism were evoked by his defeat of Max Schmeling of Nazi Germany.[9] Even in segregated settings, the culture of black sports was a phenomenon. The stadium-filling crowds attended black college football clashes such as the Florida A&M sponsored Orange Blossom Classic, Howard-Lincoln and Tuskegee-Wilberforce games, and the annual East-West All-Star baseball game in Chicago all of which became major black social and sporting events. What the Drake and Penn Relays were to integrated track and field, the Tuskegee Relays became to black colleges. Coaches like Eddie Hurt of Morgan State, Henry Kean of Kentucky State, Billy Nicks of Morris Brown, Fred Long of Wiley, and Gideon Smith of Hampton Institute had more public name recognition among blacks than the presidents of their institutions. In fact, the excitement over black sports reached such intensity at black colleges that administrators conceded that athletics were "an inherent and permanent part of the educational scheme." In predominantly white intercollegiate athletics, black athletes were integrating teams and making their marks, demonstrating the potential of the race when allowed to compete on an equal basis, something denied in the larger society. The "New Negro" students at Howard University wrote in the student newspaper, *The Hilltop*, that athletics was a universal language. "By it and through it", they declared in 1924, "we hope to foster a better and more fraternal spirit between the races in America and so to destroy prejudices; to learn and to be taught; to facilitate a universal brotherhood." Because of the records they were setting and dominance in the sprints, Black track and field athletes were credited, by Literary Digest in 1935, with being agents of better race relations, enabling "the American Negro to prove his ability."[10]

Soon Woodson and other intellectuals began to make some sense of the extensive media coverage of black athletes relative to that given to leaders of the race. The public visibility of black athletes exceeded that of all the other professions combined. At first glance, it seemed to minimize the more important issues of racial inequality, but a closer examination disclosed that subliminally it actually emphasized the issue of race. Black athletes by their nature were agents advancing the image of the race. Much of America determined blacks to be at the rear end of the procession of mental competency and deficient in the qualities of courage, stamina, skill, and physical prowess. Those myths exploded in the heat of athletic competition when black athletes successfully competed against whites and they were weakened further, even in segregated events like black college track and field, in which time and distance were universal measurements of performance. Champion and gifted black sports figures were exceptionally popular and competed with traditional leaders for status among blacks. This caused much consternation among those educated and middle-class aspiring blacks, who consciously sought distance from elements of black culture associated with ordinary poor and uneducated black people. The idea of athletes dominating the media and being paraded as "race representatives" was unsettling at best, and embarrassing at worst. During the 1930s athletes like Louis, Owens, Henry Armstrong, and Satchel Paige were better known than race leaders such as Walter White, A. Phillip Randolph, and Mordecai Johnson, and marquee black sporting events were drawing larger numbers of people than the annual conventions of the NAACP, the American Teachers Association, and the National Urban League. All of this spoke volumes about new paradigms and black popular culture, whose complex value systems were generated from the bottom up, rather than top down, and whose expressions could no longer be suppressed or ignored. No one appreciated this dynamic more than Edwin Bancroft Henderson, who wrote in the *Crisis* magazine, "Those who maintain that a Negro historian, or editor, or philosopher, or scientist, or composer, or singer, or poet, or painter is more important than a black athlete are on sound ground, but they would be foolish to maintain that these worthy individuals have more powerful influence than the athletes." However much the reality of the statement may have been deplored, it could not be denied, and the evidence was compelling.

Reported incidents of racism and discrimination were not in short supply for the black press and advocacy organizations, and when black athletes were victims, reporting was widespread often maximizing outrage in ways more difficult to achieve with lesser- known persons. It is implausible that Woodson would have been unaware of a racially motivated incident that occurred in the fall of 1937, when undefeated Syracuse University decided not to play its star quarterback, Wilmeth Sadat-Singh, after Lacy wrote in his column that Singh - despite his fair complexion, East Indian name, and Hindu stepfather - was born to black parents. The opposing team, University of Maryland, upon learning that information, threatened to withdraw from the game if Singh was allowed to compete on its home field. Syracuse officials complied with Maryland in a "gentleman's agreement", and Maryland won the game. It was not the first, nor would it be the last, of such arrangements when integrated teams played segregated teams from segregated schools. The following year with the much-anticipated game scheduled at Syracuse, Singh played and, to the satisfaction of blacks throughout America, Maryland was throttled. Athletic and social justice could not have been more rewarding. Duke also traveled to Syracuse for a game that year and anticipating that the issue of Singh would arise, inserted a "no Negro" clause in the game contract. However, with Rose Bowl ambitions being jeopardized by a possible embarrassing game cancellation should Syracuse not comply, Duke had second thoughts and decided not to invoke the race restrictive clause. Crisis magazine found the turn of events to be of such redeeming value that it decided to grace the cover of its November 1938 issue with a full page photograph of Singh, making its readers aware that racism in sports was as relevant, intolerable, and reprehensible as it was in any other aspect of American life. North Carolina's leading black newspaper, the

Carolina Times of Durham, closely followed the Duke-Syracuse episode, applauding the sportsmanship of Duke's decision and noting its implications for larger society, without commenting on the school's self-serving motives. No doubt the outcome was bitter-sweet and justice by default, but it was much more defensible than no justice at all. Encouraged by the prospects of the NAACP's recent legal challenges to segregation in Maryland, Missouri, and North Carolina, as well the moderate though changing attitudes towards interracial athletic competition, the Carolina Times sustained the faith to believe that the "day is not very far away" when "Duke University and the University of North Carolina, too, will admit Negroes to their graduate schools."11

All of these major media incidents and more, led Woodson to begin to understand the crucial intersection of sports and race, and seizing the fertile moment, he decided to initiate a book project unlike any other published by the Associated Publishers. It would be a book on black sports history, one he desperately hoped would reach new readers and revitalize the sagging book sales and revenue caused by the economic pressures of the Great Depression. When he determined the person best able to research and write the book, it is unlikely that Woodson considered any of the prominent black sportswriters of the era – Chester Washington and Wendell Smith of the *Pittsburgh Courier*, Fay Young of the *Chicago Defender*, St. Clair Bourne of the *New York Amsterdam News*, Lucious Jones of the Atlanta Daily World, Sam Lacy of the *Afro-American*, or Romeo Daugherty of the *New York News*, all known for probing journalism and skillful writing. He overlooked them, not because any one among that capable group of journalists was a writer he judged inadequate, but probably because he was not intimately familiar with the sports pages of the black press. He was also aware that no scholar, white or black, had written or demonstrated a research interest in black sports. In fact, no paper on the topic had ever been presented at a scholarly gathering, or published in an academic journal, including those of the Association.

No scholar or contemporary of Woodson has ever indicated that he regularly followed sporting events, or frequently engaged in recreational activity. However Woodson would have known the editors and writers for the periodicals of advocacy organizations and political persuasion, such as the NAACP's *Crisis*, the National Urban League's *Opportunity*, the socialist and Harlem based *The Messenger,* and related early 20th century periodicals such as *The Voice of the Negro* and *The Colored American Magazine.* By the late 1930s, Edwin Bancroft Henderson had developed a national reputation for more than two decades of writing on black sports in those respected publications.[12] It was a niche he carved for himself, editors recognized the unique appeal of his articles and their inherent value in widening readership in an America that was becoming obsessed with sports. Henderson's writings fell into several categories: historical firsts, individual and team accomplishments, and integrated sports opportunity. His articles also filled a vacuum, satisfying the reading appetites of those who preferred to celebrate their own athletic heroes, and those who simply enjoyed learning more about black sports. Those articles resonated with readers of the advocacy and civil rights publications, and were consistent with Woodson's work, hopes, and core beliefs. Also, aside from that body of sportswriting, beginning around 1920, Henderson became actively engaged in writing letters to newspapers protesting discrimination.[13] Many appeared in newspapers in the North and Southeast, including the widely circulated *Washington Post, Washington Star,* and *Baltimore Sun,* all papers that Woodson read. Therefore, it is reasonable to surmise that Woodson had Henderson in mind when he decided to move forward with the book project.

When Woodson first met Henderson is uncertain, but their meeting may have occurred in the early 20th century when both were employed in the segregated schools of Washington, D.C., Henderson's hometown. Both were assigned to M Street High School (later Dunbar) and they eventually worked together at Armstrong, where Woodson served a brief stint as principal in 1918 and Henderson worked one day each week. Their Harvard credentials were exceptionally rare for black educators in public schools, though not unusual for the faculty of M Street, where many were Ivy League graduates, several holding doctorates. It was America's first and best black public high school -- for more than fifty years, a significant contingent of its students were the progeny of some of black America's most esteemed families, and went on to matriculate at the nation's finest institutions of higher education. Regardless of background, however, all students were accountable to high standards in that competitive college preparatory environment. Few teaching positions for blacks in America's schools conveyed the cachet of an appointment at M Street. That special status, coupled with their education, cemented Henderson and Woodson as certified members of the "talented tenth" in the early decades of the 20th. Century.

Henderson had begun his career in 1904, following his graduation from Miner Normal School, a two-year teachers' college in Washington, from which he had graduated first in his class. That summer and for the next two he enrolled in the Dudley Sargent School of Physical Education at Harvard, where he was introduced to the concepts of organized school sports, and the pedagogy and administration of physical education. Beginning as an elementary teacher, he soon passed the examination in physical training, becoming the first black male certified for physical training in the nation's public schools. Those credentials set Henderson on his career journey, though his initial goal was to become a physician, he studied at the Howard University Medical School for a brief period after each school day, until its evening program was terminated.

In the early years of the 20th. Century, organized team sports in black public schools were virtually non-existent. Even at black colleges before 1890 all sports were intramural, with the first football game between Livingstone and Biddle (Johnson C. Smith) being played in North Carolina in 1892.[14] Introducing to black Washington in 1907 the relatively new game of basketball, which he had learned at Harvard, Henderson led undefeated black YMCA teams to national championships in 1909 and 1910. In his school assignments, he taught the basics of boxing, wrestling, gymnastics, fencing, and track and field, while organizing the nation's first black secondary school athletic conference, and co-editing the *Spaulding Official Handbook* on that conference from 1910 to 1913. With unlimited energy and passion for youth participation in sports, and improved understanding and appreciation for the rules of athletic competition, he founded the Public Schools Athletic League and the Eastern Board of Officials, which provided instruction for black trainers, coaches, and referees. Institutionalizing rules, structure, and integrity to athletic competition, both organizations were the first of their kind for blacks. Though restricted to segregated sporting venues, he was relentless in his campaigns against racial restrictions, and resolute in his advocacy for interracial athletic competition. Sports, he reasoned, could be linked to the struggles for racial equality and self dignity, and sportsmanship would prevail over prejudice. This became his guiding philosophy and the message he confided with aspiring black athletes.[15] To the numerous students he coached and taught, he promoted wholesome recreation, the spirit of teamwork, the discipline of training, and the virtues of fair play. "I owe you", wrote former student athlete Dr. Charles Drew, world-renowned surgeon noted for his pioneering work in preserving blood plasma, "for setting most of the standards that I have felt worthwhile, the things I have lived by and for and where possible have attempted to pass on." It was not just what Henderson taught that was memorable, noted Drew, it was what he "stood for" and the way he lived.[16]

More well- educated, financially secure, and elite blacks resided in Washington than anywhere else in America when Henderson began his career in the public schools. Acceptance into those social circles was not easy, but early on the public started to take notice of his work, making him a highly visible personality. Oliver Randolph, a writer for The Indianapolis Recorder, a black newspaper, penned an article in 1910 on Washington's black power brokers, including front page photos of Robert Terrell ---the first black federal judge – and Henderson, who recently had been appointed by the Board of Education "to organize an athletic league of colored schools." He was credited with being "the originator of the movement" for organized sports in schools, and "one of the best known colored athletes among promoters in the country." Written during the Progressive Era, what must have appealed in that article to reformers and race leaders, who did not fully comprehend the social implications of Henderson's work for race progress, were Henderson's remarks about how his program would promote a culture of discipline, character building, wholesome recreation, teamwork in pursuit of collective goals, and mitigate juvenile delinquency. Since 1925, Henderson had served as Director of Physical Education for D.C.'s black schools, and subsequently improved his education credentials with bachelor's and master's degrees from Howard, and a doctorate in athletic training from Central Chiropractic College in Washington. "E.B. was known by everyone in Washington, from the black upper class to the working class", remembered a Howard student from Henderson's suburban Falls Church, Virginia neighborhood, who often rode the streetcar with him to the city. "He was a gentleman, race man, and was respected by all for his work in sports and campaigns for an integrated society", she recalled with admiration.[17]

Once Woodson decided to proceed with the book, Henderson was the most logical choice as author, given his background, even though his academic training was in the field of physical education. Woodson was pragmatic and dismissed any concerns about how the scholarly community might react to Henderson, or the topic of the book. He knew he had the right person --perhaps the only person of that time with the requisite skill-set --and the strength of the book would reside in its capacity to appeal to non- traditional academic audiences, especially teachers, recreation professionals, sports fans, and average working-class black people; the latter a huge untapped population whose culture Woodson was coming to appreciate. He must also have had a good feeling that the book would make a profit.

On the surface, Woodson, the Harvard-trained historian, and Henderson, the public school physical education administrator, made an odd couple, but what they shared in common was much more than at first appeared. Both were from the same Washington social world, rubbing shoulders and maintaining friendships with the close network of black elites. In 1938 Henderson became a charter member of The Pigskin Club, still one of the leading sports organizations in America, a group whose original roster of 51 members included college professors, judges, lawyers, doctors, dentists, government officials, businessmen, school administrators, and others representing black Washington's most well-known, best educated, and financially secure families. Henderson's property investments, based on 47 acres in Falls Church, where he had lived since 1911, provided him with enough wealth to build a summer cottage during the Great Depression in Highland Beach, Maryland, the resort enclave exclusive to Washington's most prominent black families. Both he and Woodson were active members of the NAACP and Omega Psi Phi fraternity, and had been colleagues at M Street School when the positions they held were among the most coveted and prestigious among black teachers in America. Moreover, they were among the few who shared the early 20th. century experience at Harvard . Woodson prided himself on researching, writing, and promoting black history, while Henderson's exemplary track record in organizing and promoting black sports was matched only by his unparalleled knowledge of its history. Another important commonality was a willingness to entertain new approaches to racial uplift. In 1920 they were among those attending the founding conference of the short-lived organization, Friends of Negro Freedom, created by A. Philip Randolph and Chandler Owens, editors of the socialist leaning The Messenger magazine. In addition to questioning the wisdom of disproportionate white leadership in the NAACP, its central goals were to garner support for black owned businesses, and to provide black workers with training in labor unions and organizing techniques -- programs the NAACP had not incorporated.[18] This sort of affiliation likely contributed to building community and mutual respect among the relatively small though influential persons attending that gathering. If confidence is sustained by common experiences, shared values, and personal relationships, then Woodson's trust in Henderson's capabilities for delivering a good manuscript was secured on a sound foundation.

Though only eight years younger than Woodson and a well-known figure in his own domain, Henderson's obsequiousness to Woodson was owed to the latter's stature as the best-known black historian. Henderson had no pretensions to being in the academic leagues of Woodson's protégées such as Wesley, Logan, and Greene, but Woodson clearly saw the intellectual distance between Henderson and most physical educators, coaches, trainers, and recreation personnel. Without question, in that regard, Henderson was *sui generis*. The culminating reasons for Woodson's confidence in Henderson may have been best summarized by a frequent and admiring reader of Henderson's broad-ranging letters-to-the-editor, who was surprised upon learning of his profession. "I probably assumed you were a professor of literature or history or perhaps an exceptionally articulate lawyer", the admirer wrote, "who just happened to be a knowledgeable athletic buff on the side." What was misleading, he continued, was the rarity of encountering "any athlete, coach or athletic director" who possessed "such a wide background in the liberal arts" and who "hurdles the English language with clarity, distinction and style."[19]

"One day in 1937", Henderson recalled in describing the initial discussion of his book, "Dr. Carter G. Woodson sent for me and asked me to write the story of the colored athlete in sport." At first, Henderson demurred, having doubts about his ability to take on the formidable

assignment, but cautiously agreed and saw his confidence soar when
Woodson "promised to guide me through the intricacies of the work."[20]
From the outset, sportswriters from the black newspapers were dependable
sources for his research, and he could consult the files and clippings on
black athletes he had maintained over the years. He would not find much
assistance in the ivory towers because there were no scholars exploring
the black experience in sports. But on the black college campuses, where
Henderson had cultivated meaningful relationships with coaches, athletic
directors, and officials, he found invaluable resources that paid dividends
on his efforts. The major repository for his research was the Library of
Congress, where he spent days on end "going through bound volumes of
colored newspapers and other daily papers."[21] Henderson was no stranger
to the Library of Congress; a place he had visited regularly in high school
and later, when writing articles on black athletes.

   As the research progressed and the outline of the book took shape,
Woodson and Henderson generally found themselves in consensus. But
when Henderson produced drafts for Woodson to review, he soon discovered that Woodson pushed back with reservations over his writing. "We
had many arguments as to style. He wanted to use only precise English in
describing a football game or boxing event."[22] At some point it must have
dawned on Henderson that Woodson knew almost nothing about sports
nomenclature, forcing him to stiffen his resolve to overrule Woodson's
language preferences which were not apt for athletics and would ultimately
"prove dull reading for those who knew sports." Felicitous writing and
lucid prose were not Woodson's trademarks, and to have employed an
academic style of writing would have handicapped Henderson's "serious
effort" to reach black youth.[23] Out of those disagreements and back-and-
forth exchanges, a popular journalistic style with strong academic accents
emerged. For Woodson to have compromised an inch on this contentious
issue, confirms that the book sought an untapped market beyond that
traditionally identified by the Associated Publishers. It was also indicative
of the trust Woodson had in Henderson, and the value he placed on his
opinions. Though Woodson, like most other historians of the era, was
not well versed in sports history, he was a disciple of historical integrity
and academic credibility and was intolerant of any transgressions in those
areas. He dedicated himself to proofreading the draft, the edited man-

uscript and the revisions "day after day and late at night", remembered Henderson, until the tandem "whipped the book in shape."[24]

First released in 1939, with a modest publicity campaign consisting of advertisements in a few journals and complimentary review copies to journals and newspapers, *The Negro in Sports* reportedly sold out of the first printing within two months. For a while, Henderson later recalled, "it was the best seller" of Woodson's publications, though there are no existing records of the numbers of copies sold.[25] Across the board it was lauded as a pioneering work, receiving scores of brilliant notices and reviews in periodicals throughout the segregated nation. Though slighted by the academic journals that refused to provide reviews, outside of those circles it reached an audience broader than that of any other books of the Associated Publishers.

Some readers of this reissued book may find the propagandistic style of Henderson's writing somewhat outdated and unusual. Others may view it as a document frozen in a time capsule, though one which provides for insights into both the mind of Henderson, and the progress of race relations for the decade between 1939 and 1949 when the initial and revised editions were written. First and foremost, it was a Carter G. Woodson publication, meaning it had the multi-purposes of informing and changing opinions about black people, promoting race pride, and meeting the standards of scholarly credibility. In retrospect, at that time, few thought serious academicians --- black or white --- would find substantial usefulness or research potential in the subject matter. During the entire period of the 1930's and 1940's-- and considerably afterwards – it was possible to obtain a high school diploma and college degree without having a single lesson plan devoted to black history or having any knowledge about black abolitionists, slave insurrectionists, black participation in any of America's wars, or organized black protest against segregation or discrimination. Black history, by and large, did not exist outside of ASNLH, black secondary schools, colleges, social, religious and community groups, institutions, and concerned families. Of those college professors and school teachers who taught black history, none promoted a curriculum or had literature that dared to explore the significance of black sports on society. Black athletes were appearing for the first time on the covers of the NAACP's Crisis and the Urban League's Opportunity magazines, and articles on black athletes were beginning to appear more regularly in those publications, but none of that was making its way into the classrooms. All of this, of course, would change dramatically a generation later, in no small measure because of *The Negro in Sports*, ironically written a generation earlier.

Whatever readers of *The Negro in Sports* may have expected, the panoramic scope of its coverage could not be ignored. Appropriately, the major sports were provided more coverage, though Henderson's sense of fairness and his recreation background prompted him to include a chapter on women's athletics, and commentary on less popular sports such as wrestling, crew, weight lifting, horseshoes, fencing, bowling, swimming, and skeet shooting. Maintaining accurate sports records and statistics was something Henderson encouraged because they were the most lasting indicators of athletic achievement, objective assessments of performance, and useful for athletic comparisons. In order to impress upon black athletic officials and administrators the need to keep records, he included an appendix. One purpose of the appendix was to provide examples of templates for records keeping in secondary schools, particularly track and field; another was to affirm and document selected past black performances in the major sports. The reissuing of this book reminds us that memory is fragile, though when passed from one generation to another it relays dimensions of athletic performances elusive for records keeping. *The Negro in Sports* contains profiles of numerous athletes who now exist much more in memory and oral history than in subsequent historical narrative. For example, Ora Washington, a club athlete and non-collegian from Philadelphia and Inez Patterson of Temple University, by lore and word-of-mouth from those of that 1930's generation, were by consensus the most dominant female athletes to have ever appeared. Washington completely controlled tennis and basketball, while Patterson made a record breaking six all-collegiate teams in basketball, track, hockey, swimming, volleyball, and dancing. This book rescues those once household names and athletic heroines from virtual anonymity, reviving their exploits for a new generation of readers. The civil rights activist in Henderson was core to his existence, obliging him to include women in his research and writing during a period when historians routinely excluded or marginalized women in their scholarly dialogue. Early in his career, when he first introduced an organized sports league in the black schools of Washington, he made clear that "the girls will not be discriminated against and will engage in competition under the supervision of a female member of the physical education staff." Also in making that statement, he was making a clean break from many who believed that the rigors and physical exertion demanded in sports did not comport with established notions of femininity and the roles of women in society.

Written in less than two years without the advantages of financial grants or leave from the administrative responsibilities of his employment in the D.C. public school system, what Henderson delivered was nothing short of remarkable. The sweeping range of his research on black sports at the interscholastic, intercollegiate, recreational, and professional levels, must have silenced those who may have questioned the propriety of Woodson's involvement in the venture. Sociologists, historians, and other scholars would later come to agree that Henderson was the first to place black sports in a historical context, and for directing scholars to the intellectual junction of black sports and society.[26] It proved to be a multi-purposed masterpiece of scholarship, intricately interwoven into the struggle for racial equality. The profusely illustrated book, containing more photos than any other Associated Publishers work, was also inspirational to black youth, instructional to black athletic organizations and officials, enlightening and entertaining to the general public, and useful to advocates for race progress.

The first edition (1939) of 371 pages contained 17 chapters and an appendix, and the second edition (1949) of 507 pages – also a best seller – revised and updated those chapters and appendix while including two new chapters reflecting the accelerated changes that had occurred in black sports and society. "Athletes in World War II" and "A New Era in Baseball" were the titles of the added chapters, with the latter capitalizing on the bandwagon of media frenzy surrounding Jackie Robinson's breaking of baseball's color line, and the symbolic power of that event for integration and democracy in America.

The artwork for the dust jacket of the first edition was centered on a photograph of Joe Louis. In clockwise rotation around him was a constellation of photos of Wilmeth Sadat-Singh, quarterback of Syracuse ; Inez Patterson, a versatile female athlete from Philadelphia; track stars

Jesse Owens of Ohio State and Olympic fame; Edward Smith, world record- holding hurdler of Wisconsin; William Lacewell of UCLA; Ben Johnson of Columbia; and William Watson of Michigan. Inside the book both Johnson and Watson were noted for being captains of their respective teams, an unusual honor for black athletes on integrated intercollegiate teams during the 1930s. On the rear cover were All-American college football players Jerome "Brud" Holland of Cornell, Fritz Pollard of Brown, Paul Robeson of Rutgers and Kenny Washington of UCLA ; boxers Henry Armstrong, George Dixon, and Joe Gans ; Renaissance basketball player William "Wee Willie" Smith ; perennial American Tennis Association champion, Talley Holmes; and track stars John Woodruff of Pittsburgh, Dave Albritton of Ohio State, Mack Robinson of UCLA; Lula Hymes of Tuskegee Institute; and Ivy Wilson of the Mercury Track Club of New York City. The spine of the book was fittingly reserved for a photograph of Ralph Metcalfe of Marquette, who finished second in the 100 meters race in both the 1932 and 1936 Olympics to Eddie Tolan and Jesse Owens, twice denied by an eyelash the coveted title of the world's fastest human. The dominant number of track athletes on the cover suggests several things: the national excitement and pride over black performers in the 1936 Olympics had not subsided; no other sport was as integrated or provided more opportunities for blacks to represent America; and the objective nature of measuring track performances served as indisputable evidence of the possibilities for the race to compete and win in a true democracy. When both the first and second editions appeared, it is not hyperbole to argue that the only places in America where fairness and democracy for blacks were regularly on public display were stadiums, ball-fields, and athletic arenas. Across the board, in educational institutions, public accommodations, employment and housing opportunities, the administration of justice, the distribution of public funds, and at the ballot boxes, blacks were in high-stakes litigation for justice denied.

Surprisingly, the choice for the central image of the dust jacket of the second edition was Joe Louis, again, and not Jackie Robinson whose integration of major league baseball represented the best example of race progress in the post-World War II era. Pointing to the possibilities of the future with every swing of his bat, every run of the bases, and play in the field, Robinson's cracking of the color-line in what was called "the national game" pointed to new vistas for race progress, opportunities, and pride. By 1949, Louis' boxing career was on the decline and, in the decade since 1939, track and field had lost some of its national appeal with the cessation of the Olympics until 1948, by which time the revised edition was substantially near completion. Undeniably, however, Robinson and the re-integration of professional football and were among the primary reasons for publishing the second edition. Henderson did include a photograph of Robinson with Brooklyn Dodger manager Leo Durocher on the rear cover, and a similar one on the front cover of baseball star Larry Doby of the Cleveland Indians in a victory celebrating embrace with a white teammate Steve Gromek. Those two interracial images were iconic for Henderson's vision of an integrated America. Others on the front cover were Don Newcombe, Robinson's teammate and the first dominant black pitcher in Major League Baseball; Owens, whose track records and victories had grown to mythic proportions; Marion Motely, of the Cleveland Browns, the most celebrated black football player of the late 1940's ; Eulace Peacock of Temple, the most outstanding track sprinter between the 1936 and 48 Olympics; Sugar Ray Robinson, the reigning welterweight champion; and the immortal pitcher, Satchel Paige, of Negro League fame, and more recently a member of the Cleveland Indians. Jerome "Brud" Holland, Fritz Pollard, Paul Robeson, Joe Gans, George Dixon, and Henry Armstrong were included again on the second edition's cover, along with 1948 Olympic sprint champion Harrison Dillard of Baldwin-Wallace; silver medalist, Herb McKenley of Jamaica; lightweight boxing champion, Ike Williams; and Levi Jackson of Yale who was named the first black captain of its football team. The 1949 edition also repeated the photograph of Ralph Metcalfe on the spine, making it one of the most distinguishable ASALH publications on any bookshelf.

African Americans became increasingly impatient for change in the post-World II climate. The status quo was being challenged on every front and long standing racial barriers were beginning to show deterioration. Organized protests for a race-blind democracy were buttressed by Harry Truman's courageous support for civil rights. Demands for equality were surging, and sport was leading the way. Based on the success of the 1939 edition, the prospect for a welcoming market and good sales of the revised edition was without much risk. The first edition also received an endorsement from the influential National Education Association in 1946, when it commissioned Ambrose Calliver, the black Specialist for Higher Education of Negroes in the U.S. Office of Education, to produce a booklet, Sources for Instructional Materials on Negroes, which was widely circulated to its membership. *The Negro in Sports* was listed with 47 other books in the high school section of the publication, broadening the market for the book among educators, and resulting in a resurgence in sales some seven years after the initial publication. Additionally, the integration of baseball and football; black athletes becoming fixtures in intercollegiate sports and international track and field; the success of the Harlem Renaissance, Washington Bears, and Harlem Globetrotters in the integrated World Championship basketball series; the on-going proliferation of black boxing champions ; and Sam Lacy being admitted to the Baseball Writers' Association of America, all pointed to sustained interest and progress in black sports, and led Henderson to write in the preface to the second edition that he did not believe "that the future will necessitate another edition since integration and the growth of democracy seem nearer."[27]

Oddly, for a book with the depth of original research of *The Negro in Sports*, it fails to document its sources with citations. Such trust in sources has never been a viable commodity in the scholarly community, which indicates that Woodson completely planned the book for a different audience. Much like the *Negro History Bulletin*, its goal was to translate research into a reader-friendly style and format. In retrospect, the decision to publish without detailed documentation coupled with the advocacy of the writing may have been a miscalculation that cost Henderson an audience among the scholars of the era who were altogether too predisposed to dismiss the topic as one more suited for journalists and writers of popular literature . A generation later, however, scholars of sports history would come to embrace Henderson's book as a foundational *opus magnum* for the study of black sports. Had Woodson or Henderson known what the influence of the book would be for the next generation of sports scholars, it is inconceivable that they would have omitted documentation. At the times of the release of both editions, sports as a field of academic inquiry resided on the outer perimeters of the scholarly enterprise.[28]

Throughout the book Henderson demonstrates an inability or reluctance to conform to the obligatory restraints of detached, neutral, and objective scholarship. In numerous sections he makes no effort to conceal his personal joy and jubilation when commenting on players, teams, and coaches, and in other places he seems to be the coach on the sidelines, exhorting his team to victory. Because he was as much an observer, participant and booster as he was a researcher and writer about black sports, his subjectivity and propaganda efforts are transparent, though his integrity is never compromised. In no way, however, does his cheerleading interfere with his obsession with meticulous detail. The sports statistics cited in both volumes are impeccable, and have never been charged with inaccuracies. As for the intangibles ---which can never be proven without direct competition --- such as who were the better teams and athletes, Henderson was provocative, and unafraid to push his envelope. Never once did he retreat from his belief that black athletes with adequate preparation and resources could compete in any sport. Throughout his entire professional life --- with the exception one year --- he worked and lived under the segregated realities of Plessy v. Ferguson, but he never accepted the premise of that law, maintaining that the sports comparison with whites was also applicable to intellectual life. Like the highly educated black persons of his era and significant others, he knew nothing was wrong with or inferior about blacks, and that much was corrupt with the American system of segregation and notions of white supremacy.

Shirley Povich of the *Washington Post* who was in the forefront of those who clamored for the integration of baseball, thought Henderson had gone too far in comparing Negro League players, with "immortals such as Ty Cobb, Babe Ruth and Walter Johnson", though he was impressed that Henderson did "not gloat" over the triumphs of blacks in baseball, and lauded him for paying homage to the spirit of American sportsmanship and its capacity for opening doors to equal opportunity. Phillip Graham, publisher of the *Washington Post* who, after being pressured by Henderson in 1947, stopped sponsorship of the Golden Gloves Boxing Tournament until it was integrated, wrote a letter to Henderson thanking him for a copy of the book. Graham was anxious to note a rising generational change in racial attitudes, pointing out that his children and few of the "younger generation seem to be at all interested in the pigmentation of

Jackie Robinson."[29] Never separating and never apologizing for linking his scholarship to the cause of social justice, Henderson hoped his book would provoke precisely the type of reaction. A complimentary copy was sent to Harry Truman at the White House; Henderson had visited the Oval Office a year earlier with Tuskegee Institute's female track and field athletes who had participated in the 1948 Olympics.[30]

Reviewers, especially the black press, spoke to the social significance of the book. From the segregated and acutely race-conscious South, the *Tampa Bulletin, Norfolk Journal and Guide*, and *Dallas Express*, among others, praised the first edition for its historical resurrection of the proud images of many largely forgotten athletic pioneers. James Nabrit, a young law professor at Howard University, who would soon join NAACP lawyers to argue several of the cases culminating in Brown v. Board of Education, and would later become president of Howard, must have pleased Henderson when he noted, in The Journal of Negro Education, that the book was "the first time a broad picture" of blacks in sports had been produced, and expressed satisfaction that it offered insightful commentary on "the social significance of black contributions to athletics." The *Washington Tribune* and the *Afro-American* argued that it deserved space in the bookcases of black families, where it would inspire youth with athletic inclinations. Favorably comparing the book to an American classic, black sports writer Randy Dixon exercised hyperbole when he opined it to be "the most important reflector of the true status of a phase of racial activity since Harriet Beecher Stowe wrote *Uncle Tom's Cabin*." *The Journal of Health and Physical Education* reminded its readers of Henderson's years of achievement in physical education "with members of his race in the field of sports." Perhaps no review, however, was more satisfying to Henderson and Woodson than that of the *Springfield* [Massachusetts] *Union* when it concluded that blacks would "find plenty of ammunition for their cause" of equality and justice in the book. Other white publications including the *New Haven Journal Courier, The Scholastic-Coach* and the *Cincinnati Enquirer* gave it high marks.[31]

Echoing the reviews of a decade earlier, the number for the second edition grew and some evidence suggests that it sold more copies. Woodson, for example, offered 1,000 copies at a discount to one distributor because it regularly sent orders for what he boasted was "one of the most popular books before the public today." Fred Leigh of the *Washington Afro-American* anticipated that it would be as much in high demand as the "flurry of books" on baseball players Robinson, Larry Doby, and Satchel Paige. Near the time of the book's release, Frank Menke was working on a revision of *The All Sports Records Book* and wrote to Henderson for the sources of some of the records cited, to which Henderson replied, "Sam Lacy has all the facts at his finger tips." Sharing the credit he was receiving with others who contributed to the research, Henderson forwarded to Woodson a letter from Buster Miller of *The New York Amsterdam News* who was "the one who gave me the splendid account of Afro-American jockeys."[32] Had Henderson cited those and other sources in footnotes, one can only speculate how the academic community might have received the book, or may have recognized it as opening an entire new field of study.

One consistent theme throughout the book is that segregation was an affront to freedom in America, and its effects generally resulted in blacks receiving inferior facilities, training, equipment, and athletic instruction. Integrated athletics, Henderson maintained, was the best determinant for true champions and legitimate athletic success, though his fascination with and respect for black college sports prompted him to urge the prospects for black teams competing against white or integrated teams. "When athletes are allowed to compete against each other, representing different racial or social groups",asserts Henderson",and when they observe the rules of sportsmanlike play in the contests, the reaction upon them and those who witness the competitions almost invariably results in more toleration, greater respect, and appreciation of the oneness of the human race." In March of 1944, a secret sporting event was staged by others who valued the spirit of interracial competition, John B. McLendon, the basketball coach at North Carolina College for Negroes, courageously defied Jim Crow laws prohibiting interracial sports contests, when his team defeated the Duke University Navy Medical School in a private, unpublicized, unsanctioned, no-spectators-allowed, early Sunday morning game on the black college campus. Two years before, McLendon had an undefeated basketball team that he believed was equal to any in the nation., and he sought to prove it by issuing a challenge to several white colleges to play a game in Washington, D.C. where laws did not forbid such competition. Only one school, Brooklyn College, responded favorably. The game had two purposes: to provide a wartime example of democracy in society, and to prove that black teams could compete with white teams on a level playing field. An invitation to the game was extended to First Lady Eleanor Roosevelt - the nation's most visible and vocal white advocate for black equality. She could not attend the game, but understood the stakes enough to send Interior Secretary Harold Ickes, as her official representative. Earlier in 1916, well before basketball gained acceptance as a major sport, Ohio State scheduled a regular season basketball game against the black Scholastic Athletic Association Club of Pittsburgh. Both games – a quarter of a century apart - were won by the black teams and played without incident. 33 Interracial sports evoked strong emotional feelings closely associated with race pride, just as international sports had the same effect on national pride. Both were tightly tethered to those paradigms, though the latter was something less of a potential powder-keg in the context of American race relations that the former. Americans had not forgotten the national race-riots of 1910, which followed Jack Johnson's defeat of Jim Jeffries, the Great White Hope. Henderson did not reference any of those games in his book, though he expressed hope that such exceedingly rare athletic team competition would become more common, with the emphasis gradually more on team abilities and sportsmanship, rather than race.

Intra-racial sport, to the contrary was a different dynamic, and was removed from those filters; black college athletics ---similar to segregated black professional sports teams --- created an opportunity for relaxation and enjoyment based purely on athletic competition and the more subtle variables of loyalties associated with the local, state and regional geography of the teams and sports personalities. During segregation, sports at black colleges had more practical meaning to African Americans than did athletics at white schools. The exploits of black athletes at white schools manifested racial pride, and they were lauded as agents for the changing of racial attitudes. Still, the physical and psychological distance of those schools from black communities made black college sports a more viable alternative. Black interest in black college sporting events during the 1930's and 1940's proportionately rivaled that of white schools, and Henderson's comprehensive treatment of those athletic programs remains the best single athletic reporting on the schools of that era. No one since

Henderson has done more credible work in chronicling the conferences, teams, players, and coaches at black colleges, and it remains one of the more under-represented areas of sport historiography. For certain he had a race and academic obligation to include those schools, but that obligation was not a burden, nor was it patronizing. For his entire professional life, he was personally involved and profoundly instrumental in the development of black college sport as an official, writer, and organizer. While he found satisfaction with the publicity generated from black athletes matriculating at white colleges and excelling in sports, and recognized them as ambassadors of good-will for race relations, he was unwilling to concede they were any more gifted athletically than their counterparts at black schools. Only after the wide scale integration of intercollegiate sport in the late 1960's and early 1970's did black sports followers in the South begin the newer practice of patronizing the historically white schools in their states more than those of the respective black colleges. This pattern of transferred sports loyalty occurred for two complimenting reasons: the growth of black student enrollment and alumni at those institutions, and the recruitment of undeniably better athletes to those schools. When the second edition of *The Negro in Sports* was published, at least 99 percent of black college athletes attended black schools, not because they could not compete at white schools, but because only a small number of white schools were actively recruiting black athletes. Of those, Michigan, UCLA, Iowa, Indiana, Penn State, Illinois and a handful of others had ever dared to have more than two starting black players on an athletic team. In fact, when UCLA fielded the football stars Kenny Washington, Woody Strode, and Jackie Robinson in 1938, blacks from around the country adopted the Bruins as their team. In a short period of time, that trio built a winning tradition at what was then a small white school, placing UCLA on the sports map. Black schools during that era had their choice of black athletes, and those who followed black sports would never have questioned their ability to compete had the opportunity presented itself. In sports, there was never a feeling of inferiority, only lack of occasion, and Henderson's methodical coverage of those schools mirror those beliefs. Since the publication of the 1939 edition, athletes from black colleges have maintained a remarkable record of competing in every Olympic Games, though the general quality of athletes has precipitously declined at those schools due

to integration and vastly superior resources at historically white schools.
But sports still has a tendency to level the playing fields, sometimes making
school pedigree secondary to pure athletic ability. By the first decade of
the 21st. century, to make the case, four graduates of black colleges are
enshrined in the NBA's Hall of Fame, and twenty-three are in the NFL's
Hall of Fame. More will undoubtedly follow.

Up to the publication of the 1949 volume, only one college football
game, the Angel Bowl of 1947 in Los Angeles, had dared to pair an all-
black team, the Texas All Stars against an all-white one, the San Pedro All
Stars -- though a team of black college players, selected by the Pittsburgh
Courier, had faced the 1938 Chicago Bears in an exhibition game at
Soldiers Field in Chicago. The mis-match was transparent, even though
the Pittsburgh Courier and others hoped for a competitive game. Some
black sports writers lamented the loss, having felt that a victory would
have hastened the opening of the NFL door to blacks. While it was a
bitter set-back, described by William Nunn of the Courier as "the most
disappointing sports spectacle of the decade", black fans were reported
to have taken the loss in stride. No one, including the Chicago Defender
and Baltimore Afro-American pushed for a rematch considering that the
cohesive, well-conditioned professional team easily trounced the hastily
assembled, poorly conditioned, and disorganized black collegians by a
51-0 score. George Halas, coach and owner of the Bears, decided not to
extend the experiment beyond that one game. The NFL was to remain
segregated for nearly another decade without a formal policy of segregation. Despite the unfavorable conditions for black athletes in segregated
settings, Henderson's view that integration would enhance black athletic capabilities, fell short in his explanation of how black athletes from
segregated backgrounds often triumphed over white athletes in boxing,
track and field, and other non-team-oriented sports. Perhaps, his understanding of the relationship between athletic resources and success in
sports would not permit him to exempt superior black athletes, whom he
logically reasoned would have enhanced their performances with access
to better resources and athletic environments. In the 1930s Henderson
flirted with "Darwinian" theory and the slippery slope of racial anatomy in explaining black athletic success. In one controversial article, he

wrote that American blacks descended from the one in five slaves who were physically strong enough to survive the Middle Passage. Further, he suggested "there is just a likelihood that some vital elements persist in the histological tissues of the glands or muscles of Negro Athletes." More than any other reason, the exploits of Joe Louis and Jesse Owens instigated the nonsense conversation of the era.[34] Conveniently missing from that discussion were the historical forces that had largely confined conspicuous black achievement to sports, and the uncelebrated fact that blacks were achieving in all other fields proportionate to preparation and opportunity. To accept black physical superiority was as dangerous and illogical as accepting black mental inferiority. On one side of the color-line, black success in sports fueled hopes for a changing world. On the other side, however, it had to be explained and rationalized in the context of practices of white supremacy in a largely and legally segregated nation.

The Darwinian knife was razor sharp and it cut both ways. By the time the book was published, Henderson was drifting away from social Darwinism and tilting toward the scientific research of his former student W. Montague Cobb, an anatomy professor at Howard University Medical School, whose research argued that racial types did not correspond to various levels of athletic skills and abilities. The physical anatomy of black athletic champions, Cobb revealed, defied any attempts to designate black athletes categorically to a single physical type. "Genetically we know they are not constituted alike. There is not one single physical feature, including skin color, which all Negro champions have in common which would identify them as Negroes", Cobb concluded.[35]

Since then, social scientists have continued to revisit notions of black physical superiority and mental inferiority, in providing explanations for the dominance of blacks in some fields of sports, and for lower test scores on standardized examinations. Henderson, who early in his career advised black schools to promote debating teams as much as sports, preceded Arthur Ashe's often-cited essay of the 1970s, "Send Your Children to the Libraries." Both men admonished that a more balanced approach to developing brain and brawn advanced the causes of racial uplift while eliminating self-acceptance of racial stereotypes.[36] Nonetheless, Henderson never completely abandoned his belief in the innate physiological attributes of black athletes and continued to proffer those suggestions throughout his life. "By offering this theory", sports scholar David Wiggins has observed, "Henderson inadvertently provided corroboration for the racialists whose arguments for innate physiological differences have served to maintain the stereotypical notion that African Americans could not excel in the life of the mind and that their outstanding sport performances came naturally and not through hard work, dedication, and other character traits so admired in American society."[37] In a nation and in a life where for generations all of the laws, customs, and traditions of the ruling class define and treat one race as inferior, members of that race often find solace in any evidence suggesting the contrary, even when it reverses the logic of oppression to the other side. It constituted an intellectual and personal contradiction that Henderson never fully reconciled.

Within four months following the second edition, Woodson died, making it the last book that he shepherded into publication. After his death in April of 1950, Mary McLeod Bethune, president of ASNLH, appointed Rayford Logan as editor of the *Negro History Bulletin*, and he, along with Charles Wesley, who would be elected president in 1952, seized an opportunity in 1951 to point the way for a brighter future for sports history with a special edition of the *Bulletin*, edited by Henderson. Since its founding, the market of the *Bulletin remained one* of teachers, students, and Association members. The scholarship was sound though less rigorous, and the language more relaxed than that of *Journal of Negro History*. Both Harvard trained -- Logan, a diplomatic historian, and Wesley, a labor historian -- found merit in sports history for the audience of the *Bulletin*, though neither likely saw Henderson's work as meeting the standards of the articles in the more prestigious *Journal of Negro History*. Nonetheless, in the early 1950's, with the integration of college and professional sports dominating media coverage of blacks, as well as providing examples of race success in integrated settings, the sociology of sports and society was difficult to ignore. Also, with the original and revised editions of *The Negro in Sports* being published, both having argued that race progress in society would mirror progress in sports, Henderson's work and its prophecy of sport serving as a catalyst for social change took on new meaning, gaining acceptance from some black scholars and social scientists. Howard University professor Sterling A. Brown, an insider with the Woodson mentored historians, opined in 1951 that Henderson was "the leading historian of the Negro in sports", a statement that was little more than an insight into the obvious for two reasons: Henderson was the only scholar of black sports at that time, and he had researched and written on the topic for five decades. Still, black sports history as a field of study was summarily dismissed to the *Negro History Bulletin*. Another 21 years would pass before the *JNH* would publish its first article on sports history, and it would be 1995 before the *NHB* would have another issue devoted exclusively to black athletes. It would be tennis champion Arthur Ashe, rather than a scholar, to later write that "black historians never deemed sports serious enough for their scarce time, and these same historians … underestimated the socio-historical impact of the black athlete in black American life. But the truth", he continued, "is the psychic value of success in sports was and is higher in the black community than among any other American subculture."[38] Fortunately, since Ashe made those remarks in 1988 with the publication of his own three volumes on black athletes, A Hard Road to Glory, the historiography on black sports has matured. It has been credited with first-rate books and articles, and produced by enough capable scholars, that it is no longer a neglected field of study. To the contrary, it now thrives. Among academics, the North American Society for Sport History founded in 1974, and its publication The Journal of Sport History, leads the way in promoting, stimulating and encouraging the study of black sport history. The reissuing of *The Negro in Sports* by The ASALH Press indicates a formal second coming-of-age for ASALH (Association for the Study of African American Life and History) on black sports, one that may inspire other scholars to pursue research in the field. What Henderson set in motion with Woodson in 1939 and 1949, has come to intellectual fruition more than a half century later. Both were visionaries, far ahead of their contemporaries in expanding and challenging the frontiers of African American history.

After serving D.C. public schools for 50 years, Henderson retired in 1955, and for a considerable period of time wrote nothing on sports. Then in 1968 – in the midst of the revolt of black athletes led by Muhammad Ali, John Carlos, Tommy Smith, Curt Flood, and Bill Russell– at the urging of Charles Wesley, then president of ASALH, Henderson collaborated with the editors of *Sport Magazine* to write *The Black Athlete: Emergence And Arrival*, a popular book that built on the model of *The Negro in Sports*, extending the encyclopedic and reference book coverage of black athletes through the 1960s. Henderson was honored when baseball great Jackie Robinson paid homage by contributing an introduction to the book. In the 1970s, Henderson once again wrote articles on black athletes for *Crisis* magazine, and contributed chapters in two books.[39] In1973, he was elected president of the North American Society for Sport History, and in 1974 he became an inaugural member of the Black Athlete's Hall of Fame. Henderson died in 1977, a celebrated scholar, trailblazer in black sports, leading civil rights activist, respected mentor and coach, and esteemed public school administrator.

Out of sheer respect for Carter G. Woodson, there should be only one Father of Black History. To ceremoniously use "Father" for sub-specialty areas unnecessarily detracts from Woodson's singular prominence and enduring meaning. And while that term may be inappropriate for Henderson, he indisputably deserves the title of founder and primary architect of black sports history, an interdisciplinary field that has grown exponentially since the 1980s, and one that curiously claims in its ranks more physical educators, like Henderson and scholars from other disciplines, than professionally trained historians. Nonetheless, the quantity and quality of work in the field have been promising and impressive. All owe a debt to Henderson's book as the first and most influential of its genre and a limitless source of themes, topics, conceptual frameworks, new ideas, and research direction. It remains the holy grail of black sports historiography.

Sadly, the field of study for which Henderson labored as midwife had not gained the unfettered respect of the historical profession during his life, though physical educators accorded him proper stature as a leading figure in his field with an array of honors and recognition. Even the historian John Hope Franklin, strangely failed to mention *The Negro in Sports*, in his letter to the national basketball hall of fame committee endorsing Henderson for induction, though he commented on his contributions as once being "the premier health educator", for blacks "in Washington. D.C. and throughout the United States." That omission aside, when looking back over his illustrious life and innumerable contributions, Edwin Bancroft Henderson once said, "If I am remembered for very long after I am gone, it will be because I wrote *The Negro in Sports*."[40] The reissuing of the book confirms his prophecy, allowing it to become more accessible to those interested in black sports history and continuing his legacy. All readers should be careful to remember that this reissued book is far removed from the America in which it was written. More recent generations may have no lasting personal experiences with segregation ---de jure or de facto --- and may struggle to understand how sports changed attitudes and improved race relations. Black athletes have now become so prominent and common-place, that race alone is no longer a determinant for black loyalty in team sports. This stands in contrast to the major sports of the late 1940's and early 1950's, for example, when the Cleveland Browns, Los Angeles Rams, and Baltimore Colts in football; the Brooklyn Dodgers, Cleveland Indians, and New York Giants in baseball; and the Boston Celtics, Syracuse Nationals, New York Knicks, and Rochester Royals in basketball, were the favorite teams nationwide for blacks, simply because they were courageous enough to have multiple black players. Teams like the Washington Redskins, Boston Red Sox and New York Yankees, among others, had no base of support among blacks because of their resistance to pressures to sign black players. For at least a decade following the 1949 version of *The Negro in Sports*, it would not have been unusual for black sports followers to recite from memory the names of every black player in integrated major professional sports. Racial progress in modern sports has been so sweeping that a once common feat is now virtually impossible for anyone. It was a different world, one where segregation in most of America was official, compulsory, and nearly complete. Under those conditions, psychologically many blacks felt the burden to prove the capacity of the race to compete with whites. In the process, blacks developed unique vicarious relationships with black athletes, and sports became a legitimate vehicle for that goal. Henderson's book was the first to place black sports in the context of race in America, and its theme resonated with black and progressive reading audiences of that era unlike any other published by Woodson under the auspices of the ASALH.

The Negro in Sports eludes classification because it cast such a broad net. At once, it is a sports history narrative and several different types of reference works: a mini-encyclopedia, biographical dictionary, collection of photojournalistic essays, and record source. Considering the progress of blacks in the intervening years since its publication, its initial goal to inspire black youth may not be as relevant today as at its first publication. Since the last quarter of the 20th century, however, its impact on scholarship has been inestimable, and continues to expand. Nearly every scholarly book on black sports has revisited some theme, personality, event, or issue first examined by Henderson. It is unimaginable that the influence of the book on new scholarship will ever be exhausted, given the limitless possibilities for research. For writers of black sports history, it has become a common denominator, and it is unanimously considered to be the most pioneering and enduring work in the field.

Henderson's life spanned several generations of the black saga in America. In his lifetime, he witnessed and experienced the transition of his race designation from Freedmen to Colored, to Negro to Black, and to African-American. As a barometer of his on-going growth and consciousness, he never used the designation "Negro" in his later life and writings. He was born in a nation where the majority of the African-American population were former slaves; he was 13 when the U.S. Supreme Court declared the Plessy v. Ferguson decision; 25 when Jack Johnson won boxing's heavyweight championship; 53 when Jesse Owens and Joe Louis became world celebrities; 64 when Jackie Robinson broke baseball's color-line; 71 when the Brown v. Board of Education decision was rendered; 76 when John B. McClendon, then coach at black Tennessee State, won the NAIA championship for a record-breaking third consecutive season, in the first integrated basketball intercollegiate tournament; 80 when Martin Luther King, Jr. led the March on Washington; 82 when an all- black team at Texas Western College defeated an all-white Kentucky team for basketball's NCAA title; 83 when Bill Russell became the first basketball coach in the NBA; 85 when John Carlos and Tommy Smith gave the Black Power protest salute at the Mexico City Olympic Games; and 92 when Frank Robinson became Major League Baseball's first black manager. Though he never ventured to write a third edition of *The Negro in Sports*, what Henderson observed in American sport since the era of the first and second editions, must have been one of the more vindicating experiences of his lifetime. The rise of mainstream black referees, umpires, judges, timekeepers, and others on the officiating side of sport; the proliferation of black coaches and managers on the athletic side of sport; the increase of black writers, journalists, and broadcasters in the major media side of sport; the appointment of black general managers, front office person-nel, and athletic directors on the administrative side of sport; the entry of black owners and investors on the entrepreneurial side of sport; and the increasing volume of literature and development of scholars of all backgrounds in the field of black sport history, would have been virtually unimaginable to the generation of the first edition. In each of those sports related capacities, Henderson is best appreciated as an early leader among those who never questioned the ability of his race to succeed if provided opportunities, and for advancing his bedrock belief that sports would lead the way for improving race relations, and ultimately the integration of America. On that score alone, history will note his foresight and vision, and judge him benevolently for his contributions.

In February 2013, 130 years after his birth, Henderson was selected for induction into the James B. Naismith Basketball Hall of Fame in recognition for his role in introducing the sport of organized basketball to black Washington, D.C. and Black America in the early 1900's. He was hailed by the selection committee as the grandfather of basketball in the African American community. Gentleman, scholar, athlete, coach, sports administrator, civil rights activist, and physical educator, he was all of that, and will now – contrary to his belief – be remembered for more than the author of *The Negro in Sports*.

Al-Tony Gilmore

Bethesda, Maryland
June 2013

Al-Tony Gilmore, Ph.D Historian and Archivist Emeritus of the
National Education Association and Visiting Scholar of History,
The Estelle and Melvin Gelman Research Center
Special Collections Division
The George Washington University

agil6108@aol.com

NOTES

1. Jacqueline Goggin, *Carter G. Woodson: A Life in Black History* (Baton Rouge: Louisiana State University Press, 1993), 31-65.

2. Goggin, *Carter G. Woodson*, 70.

3. One of the best accounts of the pejorative images which Woodson sought to reject through scholarship is Rayford W. Logan, *The Betrayal of the Negro: From Rutherford B. Hayes to Woodrow Wilson* (New York: Collier Books, 1965).

4. Goggin, *Carter G. Woodson*, 55, 66-68, 76-78, 109, 138-39.

5. *Ibid*, 126.

6. Arvarh E. Strickland (ed.), *Selling Black History for Carter G. Woodson: A Diary, 1930-1933, Lorenzo J. Greene*, (Columbia: University of Missouri Press, 1996); Arvarh E. Strickland (ed.), *Working With Carter G. Woodson, The Father of Black History: A Diary, 1928-30, Lorenzo J. Greene*, (Baton Rouge: Louisiana State University Press, 1989). Also see: Kenneth Robert Janken, *Rayford W. Logan and the Dilemma of the African American Intellectual* (Amherst: University of Massachusetts Press, 1993); Pero Gaglo Dagbovie, *The Early Black History Movement: Carter G. Woodson and Lorenzo Johnston Greene* (Champaign-Urbana: University of Illinois Press, 2007). My personal conversations with Rayford Logan, Willie Miles, Charles Walker Thomas, Arnette Lindsay and Charles Wesley – ASALH stalwarts – all confirm the recent writings on Woodson that address his unusually difficult personality.

7. Goggin, *Carter G. Woodson*, 161.

8. *Ibid*.

9. Al-Tony Gilmore, "The Myth, Legend, and Folklore of Joe Louis: The Impression of Spirit on Society", *The South Atlantic Quarterly*, Vol. 82, No. 3 (Summer 1983), 256-68; Al-Tony Gilmore, "Black Athletes in Historical Context: The Issue of Race", *Negro History Bulletin*, Vol. 58, No. 3-4 (October-December 1995), 7-14.

10. Quoted in John Milton Hoberman, *Darwin's Athletes: How Sports Has Damaged Black Americans and Preserved the Myth of Race*, (New York: Houghton-Mifflin Company, 1997), 25. See also Edwin Bancroft Henderson's "The Season's Football", *Crisis*, No. 9, (February 1915), and "The Season's Basket Ball", *Crisis*, No. 12, (June 1916); "Negro Stars on the Playing-Fields of America", Literary Digest, March 2, 1935, 32.

11. Hoberman, *Darwin's Athletes*, 27. During the 1930s and early 1940s, at the state and regional levels, college athletes, including LeRoy "Po Belly" Walker of Benedict, the Brewer twins, John and James of Virginia State, "Big Ben" Stevenson and Mozelle "Mule" Ellerbee of Tuskegee, Jerome "Brud" Holland of Cornell, Duke Slater and Ozzie Simmons of Iowa, Kenny Washington of UCLA, John "Big Train" Moody of Morris Brown, "Big" John Brown of North Carolina College for Negroes, Bill "Dolly" King of Long Island, Clarence "Big House" Gaines of Morgan, George "Big Bertha" Edwards of Kentucky State and others, all resonated with impressionable black youths and adults more than conventional black advocacy leaders. Also during this period, women athletes, such as Alice Coachman of Tuskegee, Tydie Pickett of Chicago, Louise Stokes of Malden, Massachusetts – all Olympians – and the indomitable multi-sport star Ora Washington of Philadelphia, were better-known names than those of the majority of black women professionals. This does not necessarily suggest, however, that the exploits of black athletes were considered more important than the work of black leaders and organizations. Rather, it implies that personal identification with celebrated athletes and local heroes struck a strong emotional chord with average black working people, often evoking expressions markedly different from those of higher social, financial, and educational standing. See:

Al-Tony Gilmore, "The Black Southerner's Response to the Southern System of Race Relations: 1900 to Post-World War II", in Robert Haws (ed.), *The Age of Segregation: Race Relations in the South, 1890-1945*, (Jackson: University Press of Mississippi, 1978), 67-88; Charles H. Martin, Benching Jim Crow: The Rise and Fall of the Color-Line in Southern College Sports, 1890-1980, (Champaign-Urbana: University of Illinois Press,2010), 34-35.

12. Henderson was a prolific writer for black advocacy publications. The best summary and analysis of those writings is contained in David K. Wiggins' "Edwin Bancroft Henderson, African American Athletes and the Writing of History", in Patrick Miller and David K. Wiggins, *Sport and the Color Line: Black Athletes and Race Relations in Twentieth Century America* (New York: Routledge, 2004), 271-88. Representative examples of those writings include: Henderson, "Athletics", *The Messenger* (March 1926), 91; "Zenith of Negro Sport", *Colored American Magazine*, No. 16 (May 1909), 295-300.

13. James H. M. Henderson and Betty F. Henderson, *Molder of Men: Portrait of a Grand Old Man – Edwin Bancroft Henderson* (New York: Vantage Press, 1985), 18.

14. *Ibid*, 4-9; Edwin Bancroft Henderson, "Looking Back on Fifty Years", *Washington Afro-American*, July 24, 31, August 7, 10, 28, and 31, September 11, 1954; Michael Hurd, *Black College Football, 1892-1992: One Hundred Years of History, Education, and Pride,* (Virginia Beach, Virginia: The Donning Company, Publishers, 1993), 27-31.

15. Henderson and Henderson, *Molder of Men*, 6-9; E. B. Henderson, II, "The Grandfather of Black Hoops", http://www.ivyleaguesports,com/ article; Eddy Lentz, "Agents of Change: Edwin B. Henderson", http:// www.ivyleaguesports.com/documents.

16. Drew to Henderson, May 31, 1940, Edwin B. Henderson Papers, Moorland-Spingarn Research Center, Founders Library, Howard University, Washington, D.C. (hereafter cited as MSRC). Also quoted

in Henderson and Henderson, *Molder of Men,* 27. Drew was captain of the 1922 Dunbar High School championship basketball team coached by Henderson.

17. The Indianapolis Recorder, December 3, 1910, 1. Interview with Patricia Robinson Gray by author, Washington, D.C., April 10, 2010. In speaking of Henderson, Gray stated that though he was respected for his own accomplishments, he was a member of Washington's black elite because of the socially prominent background of the family of his wife, Mary Ellen Meriwether Bancroft. Both were active in civil rights causes for over 50 years, and were active leaders in the NAACP.

18. Henderson and Henderson, *Molder of Men*, 10, 37-40; William B. Gatewood, *Aristocrats of Color, the Black Elite, 1880-1920* (Bloomington: Indiana University Press, 1990), 258-63; Lawrence Otis Graham, *The Senator and the Socialite: The True Story of America's First Black Dynasty* (New York: Harper-Collins Publishers, 2006), 268-87; Rodney P. Savoy, Jr., "Brief History of the Pigskin Club of Washington, D.C. Incorporated", (www.pigskinclub.com); Mary Gibson Hundley, The Dunbar Story (New York: Vantage Press, 1967); Thomas Sowell, "The Education of Minority Children", The Public Interest, Spring, 1974, 8; Constance Green, The Secret City: A History of Race Relations in the Nation's Capital (Princeton: Princeton University Press, 1967), The Black Washingtonians: The Anacostia Museum Illustrated Chronology, (Hoboken, New Jersey: Wiley Publishers, 20050, 171-72.

19. Henderson and Henderson, *Molder of Men*, 24.

20. *Washington Afro-American*, August 24, 1954. Benjamin Brawley of Shaw University and Morehouse College and Lorenzo Dow Turner of Fisk University teamed with Woodson in the late 1930s to make publishing decisions for the Associated Publishers. There is no indication that either Brawley or Turner had any involvement in the decision to publish Henderson's book. See Goggin, *Carter G. Woodson*, 126.

21. *Washington Afro-American*, August 24, 1954.

22. *Ibid.*

23. *Ibid.*

24. *Ibid.*

25. *Ibid*; Woodson wrote a number of letters to bookstores boasting of the sales potential of the book. For example, see Woodson to Mary Ebel, July 25, 1950; Woodson to N.E. Williams, December 14, 1949. Carter G. Woodson Papers, Library of Congress, Manuscript Division, Reel 2, Series 2: Correspondence (hereafter cited as Woodson Papers); Wiggins, "Edwin Bancroft Henderson", 282-85.

26. The Indianapolis Recorder, December 3, 1910, p1. Representative of sports scholars influenced by *The Negro in Sports* are Harry Edwards, Donald Spivey, Jeffrey T. Sammons, Jules Tygiel, Susan Cahn, Bruce Chadwick, John Behee, Charles K. Ross, James A. Riley, Dawn Knight, Anthony O. Edmonds, Janet Bruce, John B. Holway, Rita Liberti, Art Rust, Lane Demas, Thomas Hietala, William H. Wiggins, Charles Martin, and David K. Wiggins. The list is longer. Black sport history is a field that has been researched by scholars from a range of disciplines, and since the 1970's has gained acceptance by respected academic journals and organizations. During the prime of his long career, Henderson was slighted by historians for a number of reasons, some of which may have had to do with his book being undocumented, his training as a physical educator, personal rejection of some of the negative stereotypes associated with black images in sports, and the concentration of the historical profession on social, intellectual, political, economic, and military history.

27. Henderson, *The Negro in Sports* (Washington: Associated Publishers, 1949), x; Ambrose Calliver, Sources of Instructional Materials on Negroes, (Washington: National Education Association, 1946), in NEA Archives Ms.2266,Series 2, Subseries 6, Box 1097, folder 23.

28. Historian Jeffrey T. Sammons writes that my dissertation, "America's

Reaction to Jack Johnson: 1908-1915", University of Toledo, 1972, was the first to be written on black sports by a trained historian, more that 30 years after the first publication of *The Negro in Sports*. See Sammons, "Race and Sport: A Critical Historical Examination", *Journal of Sport History*, Vol. 21, No. 3 (Fall 1994), 213. Sammons' article is a seminal piece on the topic, running 75 pages in length.

29. Phillip Graham to Henderson, December 29, 1949; clipping of Povich article, "A Happy Decade for the Negro in Sport", *Washington Post*, January 22, 1950; Woodson Papers.

30. Henderson's request to Truman to write a comment on the book was denied. Eben Ayers, Assistant Press Secretary of the White House to Henderson, December 23, 1949; Woodson Papers.

31. Henderson and Henderson, *Molder of Men*, 81-85. Of the leading black protest and advocacy organizations, only the Urban League reviewed *The Negro in Sports*, in *Opportunity* No. 18 (March 1940), 77; Journal of Negro Education, Volume 10, Number 1, January, 1941.

32. Clipping of Leigh article from "Capital Spotlight" column in *Afro-American*; Menke to Henderson, January 4, 1950; Henderson to Woodson, December 20, 1948; Woodson Papers. For Lacy, see Sam Lacy, *Fighting For Fairness: The Life Story of Hall of Fame Sportswriter Sam Lacy* (Centreville, Maryland: Tidewater Publishers, 1998).

33. Henderson, *The Negro in Sports*, 302, 310, 328-48; Milton Katz, Breaking Through: John B. McLendon, Basketball Legend and Civil Rights Pioneer, (Fayetteville, Arkansas: University of Arkansas Press, 2007); Eric Ferreri, "The Secret Game United What Law Divided", Raleigh News and Observer, April 16, 2010, C1. After the game, in a display of sportsmanship, taking their camaraderie a step further, the players divided into mixed teams to play again, shirts versus skins. Basketball program of 1916, "Scholastic Athletic Association Club of Pittsburgh versus Ohio State College" in Al-Tony Gilmore's sports and black memorabilia collection, Bethesda, Maryland. Also see: Rob Ruck,

"Sport and Black Pittsburgh, 1900-1930" in Miller and Wiggins, Sport and the Color-Line, 12.

34. Davarian L. Baldwin, *Chicago's New Negroes: Modernity, The Great Migration, and Black Urban Life, (Chapel Hill: University of North Carolina Press, 2007), 237; Neal Rozendaal, Duke Slater: Pioneering NFL Player and Judge, (Jefferson, North Carolina: McFarland and Company Publishers, 2012), 144-145; Ruck, "Sport and Black Pittsburgh, 1900-1930"*, 362-64; Henderson, "The Negro Athlete and Race Prejudice", Opportunity, No. 14 (March 1936), 77-79; Darren Ivy and Jeff Upshaw, Untold Stories: Black Sports Heroes Before Integration, (Little Rock: Arkansas Democrat-Gazette, Wehco Publishing Company, 2002), 23.

35. Henderson, *The Negro in Sports*, 363.

36. V. D. Johnston and E. B. Henderson, "Debating and Athletes in Colored Colleges", *Crisis*, No. 14 (July 1917), 129; Arthur Ashe, "Send Your Children to the Libraries: An Open Letter to Black Parents", *The New York Times*, February 6, 1977, Section 5, 2.

37. Wiggins, "Edwin Bancroft Henderson", 278-79.

38. Sterling A. Brown, "Athletics and the Arts", in E. Franklin Frazier, (ed.), The Integration of the Negro in American Society, reprinted in marl A. Sanders, (ed.), A Son's return, Selected Essays of Sterling A. brown, (Boston: Northeastern University Press, 1996), 107-108. Al-Tony Gilmore, "Jack Johnson and White Women: The National Impact, 1912-1913", *Journal of Negro History*, Vol. 58, No. 1 (January 1973), 18-38; *Negro History Bulletin*, Vol. 58, No. 3-4 (October-December 1995); Arthur Ashe", Views of Sport: Taking the Hard Road with Black Athletes", New York Times, November 12, 1988.

39. See Wiggins, "Edwin Bancroft Henderson", 282-83; Edwin B. Henderson, "The Negro as Athlete", *Crisis*, No. 77 (February 1970), 51-56; Edwin B. Henderson, "Physical Education and Athletics Among Negroes", in Bruce L. Bennett (ed.) *Proceedings of the Big Ten Symposium*

on the *History of Physical Education and Sport* (Chicago: Athletic Institute, 1972), 67-83; Edwin B. Henderson, "The Black American in Sports", in Mabel M. Smythe (ed.), *The Black American Reference Book* (Englewood Cliffs, N.J.: Prentice-Hall, 1976), 927-63.

40. Edwin B. Henderson, "Looking Back on Fifty Years", *Afro-American*, August 1954; letter from John Hope Franklin to John L. Dolova, president and CEO of the Basketball Hall of Fame, November 3, 2006, in Edwin Bancroft Henderson papers, Collection of E.B. Henderson II, Falls Church, Virginia. While revered by writers of black sport and physical education scholars as the founder of the field, historians and scholars of African-American historiography have failed to acknowledge the foundational influence of *The Negro in Sports*. Even Earl E. Thorpe's *Negro Historians in the United States* (Baton Route: Fraternal Press, 1958), later revised and reissued as *Black Historians: A Critique* (New York: William Morrow Press, 1971), fails to cite Henderson though Thorpe crafted a chapter, "Historians Without Portfolio", for such writers as Henderson. Moreover, one category of historians he labels as the "Negro History School of Scholars", is defined as those who emphasized black luminaries of the American saga whose contributions were equal to those of comparable whites. In retrospect, no single non-reference book had ever listed more blacks who contributed to an area of the American experience than *The Negro in Sports*. Inexplicably, Henderson's name has not appeared in important reviews such as Darlene Clark Hines (ed.), *The Status of Afro-American History* (Baton Rouge: Louisiana State University Press, 1986); August Meier and Elliott Rudwick, *Black History and the Historical Profession, 1915-1980* (Champaign-Urbana: University of Illinois Press, 1986); and Pero Gaglo Dagbovie, *African American History Reconsidered* (Champaign-Urbana: University of Illinois Press, 2010). To the contrary, physical educators consider Henderson to have been one of the leading figures in his profession. See Leon Coursey, "The Life of Edwin Bancroft Henderson and His Professional Contributions to Physical Education", Doctoral Dissertation, Department of Physical Education, Ohio State University, 1971. Coursey covers Henderson's long career as a civil rights activist, physical educator, and chronicler

of black athletes. Though not focused exclusively on black sports history, an instructive overview of the rise of the field of sports history, despite initial intellectual snobbery from the history profession, and its applicability for history curricula can be found in Stephen A. Riess, "The Historiography of American Sport", *OAH Magazine of History* (Organization of American Historians) 7 (Summer 1992).

CHAPTER I

Athletics from the Past to Our Times

The Decline in Greece and Rome. Passing rapidly through
the dark ages to athletic beginnings in America, this first chapter
revives the names and feats of men and athletes whose records
seldom are seen while we worship the galaxy of present-day heroes
of track, court and field.   Here we wish to orient the reader from
past to present.

The decline of Rome was coincident with the professionalism
of her athletics and games.   The populace saved from the wars
became enervated through luxurious living and effeminate manners.
The people became easy prey for the northern European barbarians
full of the vigor and vitality of a race bred in hostile environment
in which only the physically fit and mentally alert could survive.
The world needed a young vital humanity to replace the Romans,
but it took a thousand years for the conquerors to achieve a culture
that approached that of the Romans.

Unfortunately, the Christians springing up in the midst of a
pagan Rome molded a theology that led to the idealism of the
spirit and the degradation of the physical body.   The cultivation
of the mind and soul and the subjection of all things physical became
the culture of the dark ages.   In the dark ages the feudalist society
that promoted chivalry found a place for athletics, and these games
were mainly adjunctive training events for battle.   None of the
ancient Greek ideals of harmonious cultivation of a sane mind in
a healthy body motivated the feudalist tournaments and sports.

A New Interest in Athletics. During the Renaissance, or
the period beginning roughly around the fifteenth century, there
began a revolt against the narrow spiritual discipline of the preceding dark ages, and something of a revival of the development

1

of the whole man, akin to the philosophy of ancient Athenian Greece, was seen. From then on down through modern times liberal education has struggled to educate man as a physical, mental, and spiritual entity.

Early in the history of America, sports and games and systems of physical training and athletics became a part of our national life. In Colonial days, play and some athletic events were common to practically all settlers with the exception of limitations set upon enjoyment of life by the Puritans. Many are the anecdotes concerning sports engaged in by George Washington and men of his time. Early in the school history of the United States, it was discovered that the health of students was seriously affected by the cloistered life of study without recourse to recreational interest and activity, and many colleges instituted gardening, and various utilitarian exercise features of the manual labor schools to absorb the energies of students in a profitable manner.

Physical education, then called physical training or culture, began in some schools early in the eighteenth century. It consisted at first of gymnastic systems of exercise introduced by refugees from Europe where physical training had become a valuable means of training a populace in preparation for defensive or aggressive warfare.

Soon after the war between the northern and southern states, the German Turnverein and the several European systems of physical education made great headway. As a means of physical education of children the schools and school systems in many places adopted one or more of the systems of physical culture or physical training.

Before the Civil War, the only noteworthy incident of truly athletic development was the origin of our great American game, when in 1839 Abner Doubleday of Cooperstown, N. Y., is supposed to have started the ball and base running combination which we now call baseball.

Baseball a Century Ago. During the Civil War, baseball was a popular game among the soldiers. In 1869 the first professional

JACKIE ROBINSON, BROOKLYN DODGERS, 1947, 1948, 1949

team, the Cincinnati Red Stockings, toured the country. The growth of amateur and professional baseball and the decline of the former is of contemporary history. Tennis came to America in 1879. It was in its early history considered a fit game only for weaklings and women. Golf became an American game in 1888 and was played largely by older men. A distinctly American game is basketball. It was originated by James Naismith, a student of the Young Men's Christian Association Training School at Springfield, Massachusetts, who invented the game and lived long to see its maturity as the leading winter sport.

Negroes among the Pioneers. The part American Negroes have taken in the play and games of America is the burden of this effort. From time to time there will be discovered new records and instances of Negro participation in athletics that are hidden away in obscure volumes or letters. We do know, however, that early in the annals of athletic endeavor, colored athletes played a noteworthy part, and their performances and their contacts have gone far to liberalize popular conceptions of some of the capacities and abilities of this minority of our citizenry.

The Negro athlete has loomed large as a contender in the field of college athletics which cover but a brief span in American life. Prior to 1870, college athletics consisted largely of boating. There was some baseball, less football and little interest in track and field. The popularity of football began as an organized game in the colleges about 1880, played only by colleges of the Eastern States. As early as 1872, there are records of organized track and field days, but until recent decades these games were of less interest than football, baseball and boating. Now in some colleges, track and field athletics rank above baseball, rowing, and possibly basketball.

The First College Physical Director, a Negro. Negro athletes appeared on the college scene early. There may have been some unnamed heroes in the very early days whose identity never reached national notice. Although no outstanding competing athletes of color are recorded prior to the early nineties, it is significant and noteworthy that the first director of Harvard University physical education was a colored man. He was employed as an instructor and director of the first gymnasium built in 1859, and remained in charge until 1871, when he died. He deserves honorable mention, for his work was second to none of the pioneers in the field of gymnastics and physical education in America. That he was a man of ability, of character, and worthy of his position at the University is attested to by the several accounts. Said a writer in the *Harvard Magazine* of October, 1859,[1] "It is with feelings of pleasure and pride that we record the completion of the Harvard Gymnasium; of pleasure, in anticipation of the good effects of regular and varied exercise; of pride, that 'Conservative Harvard' should be the first of the colleges in this country to incorporate into its course of education an organized system of physical training. For several years the subject has attracted attention, and the students had been loud in their demands for better accommodations than were afforded by the small, though well-conducted gymnasiums of Professor Stewart. But no means of satisfying these demands were afforded till about a year ago, when, through the medium of Dr. Huntington, eight thousand dollars were given for the erection of a Gymnasium. The spot selected for the building was the little Delta at the junction of Cambridge Street and Broadway. The expense of the building and fixtures exceeded ten thousand dollars. The Gymnasium was opened for use on Wednesday, September 14.

A. Molineaux Hewlett. "Meanwhile, most fortunately, the services of Professor A. Molineaux Hewlett had been secured. He came with an experience in gymnastic training of fourteen years, the last five of which had been devoted most acceptably to the citizens of Worcester. By the fine accommodations of the new building, and under the admirable system of the new Professor, a fresh impulse was given to physical training, which, contrary to prediction, has been on the increase. The uniform courtesy of

---

[1] *The Harvard Magazine*, Volume VI, October, 1859, p. 38.

the Professor, and the personal interest which he takes in the exercises, keep alive the interest of his pupils and make the hours spent in the Gymnasium among the pleasantest."

In 1875, T. W. Higginson, writing in the *Harvard Book*, referred to the fact that, "The first teacher of gymnastics in Harvard College was Abram Molineaux Hewlett. He was a professional teacher of boxing, and had established a gymnasium of his own in Worcester, Massachusetts, where he was highly esteemed. He was a mulatto, of very fine physique, and of respectable and estimable character. He was moreover a fair gymnast and a remarkably good teacher of boxing. In the first years of his term of service there was a good deal of activity in the Gymnasium and regular class-exercises went on. After a few years the interest fell off, in some degree, or concentrated itself chiefly on the 'rowing weights.' Mr. Hewlett died December 6, 1871, and the present teacher, Mr. Frederic Williams Lister, was appointed in 1872."

Here then lived a Molineaux affecting favorably the athletic careers of Harvard men for over a decade, and the youth of New England for nearly a generation, just as a half century before another Molineaux—Tom—had achieved a reputation for physical prowess as a representative of America in the boxing circles of England.

Early Negro College Athletes. About 1890 we began to hear of colored athletes on the college scene. From Alexandria and Norfolk, Virginia, two Negro youths went to the Virginia Normal and Collegiate Institute, at Petersburg, and from that institution to Amherst College as a result of recommendations of John M. Langston and Senator Hoar. Their exploits on the gridiron and on the track of Amherst and Harvard made headline copy for the press of their day. These boys, W. T. S. Jackson and W. H. Lewis, made enviable athletic history. Jackson was known for his track and football career, whereas Lewis created undying fame as one of the great football centers of the game. At Amherst, these players were teammates. As evidence of the reputation they had, the New York *Times* of October 11, 1891, reported, "Harvard resorted to few tricks, but Amherst worked hers with fair success. Jackson,

AMHERST TRACK TEAM, 1892

Extreme left, Dwight Newport, trainer of all Amherst teams for 40 years; died in 1937. Front center, with emblem, W. T. S. Jackson.

a young colored fellow, played half-back for Amherst, and was by
all odds the best man on the field.   His tackling was clean and sure,
he made some phenomenal runs and was well guarded by the rest
of the team.   Lewis, the colored center, also played a phenomenal
game."   Undoubtedly Jackson was far the more spectacular of
the two players when they were at Amherst.   The *Harvard Crimson*,
reporting the annual game with Amherst the year prior, 1890, said,
"For almost all his effective rushing, though his tackles gained
some ground with the ball, he—Captain Lewis—had to rely on
halfback Jackson, whose play all around was as skillful as any on
the field."

Jackson was also a track star.   His half mile record of 2:05.4
seconds withstood the attacks at Amherst for many years.   One
of his outstanding races evoked from the Worcester, Massachusetts,
Telegram of May 29, 1890, most flattering comment.   "A determined field answered the call of the Marshall for this event," said
the paper.   "In it were an even dozen fliers, among them the men
who had in the past been easy winners.   But it remained for a new
man to carry off the honors.   W. W. Rowe, Dartmouth; J. N. Nawa-
more, Wesleyan; L. W. Griswold, Amherst; E. R. Lampson, Jr.,
Trinity; L. B. Bacon, Williams; R. H. Hutchins, Trinity; E. A. Taylor, Worcester; S. W. Allen, Amherst; E. B. Merriman, Williams,
and W. T. S. Jackson, Amherst, came for the word.   The last is a
Negro and an athlete of speed and stamina.   'Be easy, gentlemen,
until you get the word' and as the line wavered but slightly, the
report came.   There was a flash for the turn.   Wells simply left
the mark and dropped out.   Griswold at once cut to the pole and
set the pace.   The others were content to follow, until as the turn
was rounded, Bacon and Jackson shot out after the leader.   It
was an awful race up the stretch, and as the line was neared Bacon
fell heavily and Jackson forged ahead, winning in the remarkable
time of 2.08 1/5.   Considering the track and the wind it was one
of the biggest efforts of the day."

William H. Lewis, of Harvard.   As for Lewis, after his football
at Amherst, he became the most talked about football man of his

WILLIAM H. LEWIS, All-American Football Center, One of the Great
Centers of All-Time.   Former Asst. U. S. Attorney-General.
Died, 1948

day. Walter Camp picked him as center-rush on his All-American teams for the years 1892 and 1893. In 1904, the All-Time All-American team published in the New York Evening *World*, gave Lewis the center berth, along with such celebrities as the great end Hinkey of Yale; guard Heffelfinger of Yale; and Daly of Harvard, and later of the Army. For years, Lewis was a graduate coach of Harvard's line players. His presence each fall was a great stimulus to Harvard's teams. His illustrated book on *How to Play Football* was an authoritative demonstration of the techniques and fundamentals of the old game, and one of the few books published on football for many years. After a successful career as a practicing attorney in Boston, and a public servant of the state of Massachusetts, he was appointed to the post of Assistant Attorney-General of the United States in the administration of President Taft.

William Tecumseh Sherman Jackson. William Tecumseh Sherman Jackson became a teacher, and then principal of the M Street High School—now Dunbar—of Washington, D. C. He always was an ardent disciple of sport, and through his influence many boys went to New England colleges to star in athletics. Both men had close contacts with Presidents of the United States. Lewis became a prominent political figure under President Taft. When Coolidge was president, he invited Mr. Jackson to spend many pleasant informal evenings to revive the memories of the days when the colored lad was the college hero, and the President just a plodding freshman.

Others of note also deserve honorable mention. Among the early athletic heroes was Dr. George A. Flippin, now deceased, a formidable half-back on the University of Nebraska's teams of 1892, 1893, and 1894. The Rev. Mr. William L. Washington, deceased, a teacher and preacher of Washington, D. C., was one of Oberlin's football heroes during 1897, 1898, 1899. Before the turn of the century in the east and west, other college athletes were receiving good will plaudits by college crowds. At Illinois, G. C. H. Burleigh was a hurdler with a good record for that day of 16 3/5 seconds. George M. Chadwell played left end on Williams College football team during the seasons 1897, 1898, 1899.

AMHERST FOOTBALL TEAM, 1889

Second from left, W. T. S. Jackson; extreme right front, seated, W. H. Lewis.

Spencer Dickerson, of the University of Chicago, in 1896, was running the quarter mile in fast time.

Today when we marvel at the record smashing feats of Negro and other athletes we must not forget the illustrious performances of these pioneer and past greats who did their stunts where good fields, tracks, and guidance were scarce. Much of the wonder work of our boys of this age rests on the trials of the boys of the nineties for inspiration and motivation.

CHAPTER II

Past Heroes of the Prize Ring

Boxing is an ancient sport. Striking with the hand as a weapon of defense or offense goes back far into antiquity. Homer records boxing as one of the events of the celebration at the fall of Troy. Boxing was one of the cruelest of sports in the calendar of Greek and Roman games. Not much is in the record after the decline of Greece and Rome until the early part of the 18th century when in 1716, John Figg announced himself "A teacher of boxing, fencing and singlestick to the nobility of the British Empire."

Boxing Stirs Human Emotions. From then down to today, boxing has made a strong appeal to the emotions of man and to his appreciation of the skill involved in physical combat between man and man. Other nations had their swords, foils, rapiers, daggers and stilettos. The English, however, sought in their contests to disable, but not too seriously to wound or kill antagonists. Fair play, though crude in the beginning, began its tradition in the prize ring. Under the veneer of the culture that present civilizations have wrought for man, there still lies the dormant capacity for the thrills of the fight. So great is the rush of adrenalin or so powerful the hormones generated by seeing or listening to a pugilistic encounter that many weak hearts crack under the strain, while many other humans find themselves limp and exhausted after the exhibition of primitive brawn and brain is done. Much of the brutality of the age old sport has been eliminated by modern rules of the game, training and practices, and boxing will make its appeal to mankind for many generations yet to come.

Code of the Ring. Figg was a champion of the staff as well as of the fist. There were no standardized rules. The opponent must be so disabled as not to continue. The fight ended thus. Shrewd antagonists took all sorts of advantages in the melee. In 1740, John Broughton won his title as champion of England and held it for ten years. During this decade he evolved a boxing code that established some semblance of a standard procedure. Broughton's code was followed until 1838 when the British Pugilists Protective Association promulgated the London Prize Ring Rules. Under these rules no gloves were used. A round ended only when one or both contestants were down. Wrestling holds were allowed. At the end of each round, thirty seconds of rest followed. Each man, thereafter, was expected to meet his opponent in the middle of the ring. If he did not he was disqualified.

About 1860, the Marquis of Queensberry promoted the new rules that provided for the use of gloves, and are used with modifications today, although both bare knuckles and glove fighting continued until James J. Corbett fought John L. Sullivan in 1892. No championship with bare knuckles was fought after the Sullivan-Kilrain fight in 1889. The Marquis of Queensberry rules provided for five-ounce gloves, for rounds of three minutes with a minute rest, and barred the pivot blow, rabbit and kidney punches.

Today the number of rounds of a fight are limited. For many years fighting was on a par with cock-fighting and not recognized legally. At present boxing is legalized in all of our states and in most countries. Whereas many boxers died following fights in the old days, medical examinations of contestants, scientific training, and stricter observance of fighters in the ring prevent much of the fatal aftermath of pugilistic encounters.

A great deal of the opposition to boxing lies in the bad repute of many of the managers and followers of the game. Some people are still sensitive to the shock of clashing bodies and fists, and the bruising and cutting of skin and flesh. More serious, however, are the "rackets" involved in the ring business. A few race disturbances following bi-racial fights have given excuse for rowdy reactions on the part of normally prejudiced individuals, but on the whole these contests have helped breed a finer appreciation of good sportsmanship and a broader tolerance for different peoples and especially minorities. Except for a few states in the Union, boxing is making headway. Bi-racial bouts are increasing, for these matches add the color of emotional tone as well as of pigment. Golden Glove and similar tournaments motivate boxing in boys' clubs and other athletic units, and the international bouts add interest to the game.

Negro Champions. For 1938, Negro boxers were rated by the National Boxing Association as heading the lists in all of the classes except the middleweight, bantamweight, featherweight and flyweight. Joe Louis led the heavyweight. John Henry Lewis topped the light heavies. Solly Krieger held the title in the middleweight class and Sixto Escobar, of Puerto Rico in the bantamweight class. The flyweight class was vacant, but the featherweight class title was won by Armstrong, who refused to defend it. Henry Armstrong smashed all honor records by winning the titles in three classes in the same year. He won the featherweight from Sarron, the lightweight from Ambers, and the welterweight from Barney Ross. Without doubt the Negro boxers also ruled the world in 1939. Boxing in America began with Negroes.

It was not until 1816 that the first prize fight between white men in America took place. So weak was the competition for years that in 1839 "Sailor" Burke, champion of England, could find no real contender in America and returned to England. A recognized white man as titleholder did not appear until 1849. His name was Tom Hyer. This was over a hundred years after Figg, and a half century after "Bill" Richmond and Tom Molyneux.

"Bill" Richmond. The first Negro American to claim pugilistic honors was "Bill" Richmond. Richmond, born on Staten Island, was taken when a boy to England by Lord Percy, Duke of Northumberland in 1777. There he worked as a cabinetmaker. Because of his physique and fighting capacities, he became valet to and greatly attached to Lord Camelford, a nobleman, who had great likeness for sports of the turf, pit and ring. Richmond weighed only 168 pounds. He fought many highly chronicled battles between 1800 and 1818. During this time he lost to the heavyweight champion Tom Cribb by a decision.

His last recognized fight was in 1815, but until he died he was idolized by all classes of his day. His rooms and hotel in Whitcomb Street, Haymarket, were highly patronized by the nobility and gentry. That he was well known to Lord Byron is attested by the references to him in the *Life and Journals of Lord Byron*, edited by Thomas Moore.

Richmond's athletic form, his civility, self-control and temperate habits made him respected by all who knew him; even a king had invited him to the court, the story goes. One of the first writers of *Fistiana* says, "Richmond may be pointed to as one of the men who never lost sight of the situation in which he was placed in society. In the elevation of the moment, he always bore in mind that, however the Corinthian fancier may connect himself with milling, there are times when he has a different character to support, and must not be intruded upon. Would that many of our white-faced boxers would take a hint on this point from Bill Richmond, the Black."

Respected in life he was greatly mourned at death, which overtook him in the 66th year of his age in the house since occupied by Owen Swift (The Horseshoe Tavern), Titchbourne Street, Haymarket, London, England.

The first American champion to fight in an international bout was Tom Molyneux in December, 1810, in England. Molyneux was born in Georgetown, D. C., in 1784. Later he lived with the Molyneux family in Virginia. Stories of that day give some evidence for the belief that Molyneux's father and grandfather had been notable boxers among the plantation slaves. The story of how boxing as a sport began in America is worth telling. Many of the sons of wealthy planters of our Southland were accustomed to travel and to the pursuit of education in England. There they found time to frequent the sporting places in that country. On return to America it was only natural that the putting of one plantation's Negro against a fighter of some reputation of a neighboring owner became a pastime.   Rumor has it that Tom Molyneux was rewarded for his pugilistic feats by being granted liberty.

Molyneux Fights Cribb.   In 1809 we find him about the old Catherine Markets in New York City challenging and defeating all comers.   Going on a merchant ship to England where the fight game was flourishing, he was taken in tow by "Bill" Richmond. Molyneux won several battles against some of the best in England and soon after his arrival he was matched with the redoubtable Tom Cribb.   This was the first great fistic battle of the centuries. The fight was fought under the "London Prize Ring Rules."   It was a masterful struggle, and had it not been for the trickery of Cribb's seconds Molyneux would have been the winner.   In the twenty-third round, Cribb was unable to return in the time limit, but his seconds made a claim of "foul," whereupon time was extended beyond the 30 seconds and Cribb was able to return. Later Molyneux became so weakened that at the end of the 40th round he could not return, and Cribb was declared victor.   Molyneux fought Cribb again in 1811, but was defeated in 11 rounds. He never recovered from the effects of his first fight with Cribb. He died in Scotland after an eventful career.

The name of Molyneux or Molineaux occurs several times in the history of the ring.   One of the early boxers was Jim Wharton, "Molineaux, the Morocco Prince."   Born in Virginia in 1813, he reached England in 1820 aboard a merchant steamer.   He was a skillful boxer of great strength and stamina.   He fought nine battles of repute and was never defeated.   One notable event was the 200 round contest with Tom Britton on February 9, in 1836. It lasted four hours and seven minutes and was declared a draw. Wharton died April 26, 1856, at Liverpool, England.

"Bob" Smith and Travers.   "Bob" Smith, born in 1840 in Washington, D. C., lived in Liverpool, England, and won many important ring contests of his day.   "Bob" Travers was one of the most prominent of all pugilists.   He lived and fought in the latter half of the 19th century.   During his life he fought more battles in the squared ring than any fighters who preceded him. In his life there were more acknowledged great fighters than at any other time before the age of Sullivan, Jackson, Corbett, and Kilrain.

It is said that Travers's career of fighting is worth a volume. Two of his most noted encounters were with Jem Mace and Patsy Reardon. He lost to Reardon after four hours and five minutes of fighting in a heavy rain storm. He died in 1890.

George Godfrey. George Godfrey, of Boston, Massachusetts, was the first colored heavyweight champion of America. He was born on Prince Edward Island, March 20, 1853. Fighting at 170 pounds, he defeated all the better colored boxers. He was once matched to fight John L. Sullivan, but here as always Sullivan's reluctance to risk his crown in contest with a colored pugilist, caused him to decline the offer. Godfrey lost to Peter Jackson in 19 rounds of fighting on August 24, 1888, at the California Athletic Club.

Charles Hadley. About 1882, "Professor" Charles Hadley, of Bridgeport, Connecticut, was a startling scientific boxer. During his career he was awarded the *Police Gazette* Champion Medal emblematic of the colored boxing championship of America. At Cleveland, Mervine Thompson, "The Cleveland Thunderbolt," was prominent in 1884. He weighed 190 pounds and was a magnificent physical specimen of manhood. He was a sensation in his day and won many competitions with white and colored boxers. Here again Sullivan was allowed to draw the color line and would not meet Thompson's challenge.

Peter Jackson, the Great Heavyweight. It was during this era there appeared the prince of fighters, Peter Jackson. He was born in the West Indies in 1861. He stood six feet one inch high and weighed 212 pounds. Commentators of his day considered Jackson the most marvelous of fighting men of all times. The Rt. Hon. Earl of Lonsdale, K.C., in the foreword to *Kings of the Ring*, by James Butler, wrote, "Personally, I always think that the best man—the quickest, most scientific and the hardest hitter—

that I have ever seen was Peter Jackson, whom as you know, I originally found in San Francisco, in a boxing competition, when I arrived there on my return from the Arctic. But you well know that, and a good deal of his training was done here at Barley Thorpe. The same with little George Dixon, whom I brought home at the same time. . . ."

PETER JACKSON

Although Lonsdale, like other supporters of artists and celebrities, claimed credit for discovery of Jackson, this sailor lad had won honors as the champion of Australia in 1886 from Tom Lees. One writer aboard a sea-going schooner, and, growing fanciful in dealing with Jackson commented, "There was something of the lazy, indolent strength of a great cat about him. The lithe grace of his sprawling limbs, their loose suppleness, the easy way big muscles rippled and ran under the satiny skin as he moved—these things suggested it.

"And then, too, there was the proud challenging poise of the kinky-haired, handsome head on the massive neck, set like a column in the wide shoulders, chocolate brown, and just now, shining with a faint sweat induced by the hot noonday sun.

"A bronzed giant of a fellow, he was stretched full-length along the snowy whiteness of the little schooner's spotless deck, softly crooning one of those plaintive negro blue melodies that are old as times.

"But not by the wildest flight of fancy with which that West Indian negro deck-hand whiled away the hours could he have foreseen the amazing future that a smiling Destiny had already planned for him. How, indeed could this Peter Jackson, this big and unspoiled colored seaman, guess that he was to become one of the greatest and most scientific boxers in the world, hailed everywhere as the Black Prince of the Ring?"

Peter Jackson landed at Sydney, Australia, and was taught boxing by Larry Foley. In three years after meeting his first opponent, he won the championship of Australia by defeating Tom Lees in 30 rounds. In 1888, Peter Jackson arrived in San Francisco. At this time nearly all American heavyweights drew the color line very conveniently when Jackson hurled defies at them, especially John L. Sullivan. Soon after arrival, Jackson fought George Godfrey, of Boston, and won in 19 rounds. The California Athletic Club practically forced Joe McAuliffe, who was considered a coming champion, to meet Jackson, who won the purse of $3,000 in 24 rounds. Jackson tried hard to get matches in 1889. Finally he was matched to meet Patsy Cardiff in San Francisco. Cardiff had a six-round draw with John L. Sullivan to his credit. After an easy bout, Jackson knocked Cardiff out in ten rounds. Jackson then went to England and knocked out the highly publicized Jem Smith in two rounds. In 1891, James J. Corbett met Peter Jackson on May 21, at the California Athletic Club. Corbett weighed 168 pounds and Jackson 204 pounds. A purse of $10,000 was posted. Corbett was a young man of few battles, Jackson was 30 years old and had weathered the blows of a hundred grueling fights. Corbett was beginning his career as a masterful boxer and excellent ring strategist. He skillfully managed to evade the powerful blows of the more ancient giant, and stayed in the ring by his ability to side-step, block, clinch and retreat, not unlike the Bob Pastor whom Joe Louis fought. After 60 rounds, both men were so exhausted they could hardly meet at the center of the ring; the referee called the fight "no contest" at the end of the 61st round —four hours of boxing.

In estimation of the personal worth of Peter Jackson, an English contemporary wrote, "I came to know Peter Jackson intimately. I knew him in the days of his greatness, when, sitting on top of the

GEORGE DIXON

pugilistic world, feted and lionized, he might well have been excused some slight vanity, yet all my memories of him are of a pleasant, softly spoken, modest fellow, utterly unspoiled . . . He was a charming rarity, unassuming, intelligent, cultured, something of a Paul Robeson of the fighting business, who never made a single enemy."

George Dixon. The next attractive figure in this sphere was George Dixon. He fought as a bantam and featherweight champion. Dixon was 5 feet, 3 inches tall. He was a champion in one or the other classes for eleven years, fighting continuously. He fought two drawn battles with Joe Gans, in 1895 and in 1897. Dixon was one of the few Americans to win in England. In 1890 he challenged the English featherweight champion Nunc Wallace. The fight for a purse of 400 pounds took place at the Pelican Club, in London, on June 27, 1890. Dixon knocked out Wallace in 18 rounds. During his stay in London he put up at the best hotels and trained in the beautiful countryside of Oakham, Rutlandshire, England. Much comment was made upon the stylish dress and cultured sportsmanly manner of Dixon, and the cordial relations existing between the two rivals before the Wallace-Dixon fight—quite a new pattern for fighters.

One of the greatest fights Dixon ever engaged in was his earliest battle with Cal McCarthy. They met in Boston in February, 1890. In seventy rounds these two boys matched skill and strength. McCarthy was stronger, Dixon cleverer and more agile at defense. At the end of the 67th round neither boxer was able to deliver a punch with sting. The referee then announced that if either lad were on his feet at the end of the 70th round, he would call it a draw, and thus it ended.

Finally, after a number of record-making fights, including the bout in England with Nunc Wallace, little George was matched again with Cal McCarthy for the championship of the featherweight division, although both lads were really bantams. They met in Troy, New York, on March 31, 1891. McCarthy was the favorite. Unlike the first non-championship melee in which these two engaged, it took but 22 rounds for the fight to end. McCarthy had lost some of his former stamina, so it was said, by letting up in training, and Dixon was able to meet his wild charges and out-punch him. Only once, in the twenty-first round, did McCarthy battle as he did in earlier fights. He swarmed all over Dixon with rights and lefts and really hurt the coming champion. However, the brown boy's ring generalship and his well conditioned body staved off the dying attack. In the next round Dixon came up fresh, measured his opponent carefully and knocked him out to gain the featherweight crown.

In his one autobiography published in 1893, when Dixon was in his prime, he wrote, "I was born in Halifax, Nova Scotia, in 1870, and when about eight years of age my parents moved to Boston, where I still reside. I received a public school education, having attended a Halifax school for two years and a Boston school for three years. When about fourteen years of age I secured employ-ment with a Boston photographer, and while there engaged, I first began to learn how to spar. I witnessed an exhibition one night at the Boston Music Hall which was given by two local athletes, and the next day I purchased a book on boxing from which I gained much valuable information. It would require too much space to give the name of each opponent and the result of each contest in which I have figured during my career, so I shall endeavor to give an idea of my record by stating that I have won or drawn every contest in which I have engaged with two exceptions. The first, which was to have been to a finish, was with George Wright, of Canada, whom I met at Boston about six years ago, and he was declared winner on a foul—the other bout, which was decided against me, was with Billy Plimmer, of England, who was given a decision on points in a four-round glove contest which took place at Madison Square Garden, New York City, a few nights after I defeated Eddie Pierce. . . . During my career I have won more than one hundred thousand dollars in stakes, purses and gate receipts. I have taken part in more than five hundred four-round bouts and about forty contests to a finish."

Dixon's last great fight was with "Terrible" Terry McGovern.

Despite the fact that Dixon was an old man, having kept the championship for the greater part of eight years, he fought a losing but memorable battle with McGovern on January 9th, 1900, in the old Broadway Athletic Club. McGovern had a stiff fight for eight rounds when he dropped George. McGovern from the first kept boring in trying to land a telling blow, but the skill of the old Master prevented him until that eighth round. It seemed until then that Dixon might be able to last through and win on points, but the savage continuous attack of fresh young Terry told when a blow went to Dixon's mid-section. He sank to the canvas, rose on the count of nine, but a crashing left and right took his championship for ever. He fought occasionally until 1903, but never was the fighter of old. To this day, there never has been an equal to George Dixon, who was for so long a time the king of the featherweight and bantam divisions. Dixon was widely popular. He married a white girl, from which came no untoward comment. He carried himself always in a manner to merit the respect of all who knew him.

Joe Gans. The next to make history in the ring was the lightweight Joe Gans. The early fighters in history fought without regard to weight. In 1876, the lightweight class was established. The first limit was 133 pounds, but in 1909 it was raised to 135 pounds. Among the lightweights, Joe Gans, of Baltimore, is reputed to be king of them all. Even Benny Leonard dubbed Joe to be the Old Master. Some of the authors of *Fistiana* believe that for his weight, Joe Gans was the greatest boxer who has ever lived. He was king of the lightweights from 1901 to 1908. He fought anyone at any weight.

In 1899, Gans defeated George McFadden in 25 rounds at the Broadway Athletic Club. This fight brought Gans into the limelight, for McFadden had ended the fighting career of Kid Lavigne, who was a terror to lightweights. In 1901, Gans sought a chance at Erne for the lightweight title. Erne tried to evade the contest, but finally at Fort Erie, Ontario, on May 12, 1901, Gans knocked Erne out in the first round. Gans won battles from Willie Fitz-

JOE GANS

gerald, Jimmy Britt, and a host of others. He outpointed in two fights Jack Sullivan, a middleweight of some reputation.

Two of the never-to-be-forgotten fights in the battling career of the Old Master, Joe Gans, were those with his final conqueror, Battling Nelson. Gans does not need an alibi, yet it is a fact that when Gans met Nelson in the evening of his career, his system was pretty well weakened by the infection that has stopped so many athletes in their stride. In 1906, September 3, at Goldfield, Nevada, Nelson, the young, vigorous, rugged Dane met Gans in a battle. For many rounds the "Old Master" side-stepped, jabbed, and countered. His blows were clean. But the tow-headed Dane kept coming in, swinging wildly and continuously, not unlike "Henry" of the lightweight class of his day. Some of the blows of Nelson had Gans in trouble, but the ring strategy and the use of a lightning left kept the Battler at bay. The most outstanding incident of the fight that reeked of unfairness was the refusal of the referee, George Siler, to end the fight much earlier than he did. At least three fouls occurred prior to the end of the fight that justified the grant of victory to Gans. Nelson committed fouls in most categories.

In the 18th, 26th, and 34th rounds Gans had Nelson athwart the ropes, but in each instance the bell saved the durable Dane. Youth and vigor brought Nelson back at the beginning of each round. Finally, in the 42nd round, Gans had Nelson troubled. A flurry of jabs and hooks were putting an end to Nelson when he committed so palpable a foul that Siler motioned him back to his corner and awarded the fight to Gans. Competent observers claim that Gans had won every round on points. Thus as late as 1906, Gans was the world's lightweight champion. In 1907 Gans knocked out both Kid Herman and Jimmy Britt.

Two years before he received his summons after a losing fight to the Grim Reaper, Gans fought Nelson again. This time they met in San Francisco on July 4, 1908. It took the rugged yellow-headed boy but 17 rounds to register a knockout of a shell of Gans of old. In 1910, trying to recover from the dreaded scourge of disease, Gans went to Prescott, Arizona, but returned to Baltimore and died, August 13, 1910.

Andy Bowen. One of the most remarkable lightweights was Andy Bowen, of New Orleans. Bowen established a record for lengthy fights. On April 6, 1893, he fought a 110 round draw with Jack Burke, which lasted 7 hours and 19 minutes. In 1891, he fought 217 rounds in three fights. He beat Jack Everhardt, one of the outstanding lightweights of the day. Lavigne, one of the fearless, ready-to-meet all comers, lightweight champion, travelled from Boston to New Orleans to meet Bowen. The fight went 14 rounds; when weakened by the exhausting fights of the preceding year, Bowen was knocked out and died the following day.

"Kid" Chocolate and Al Brown. Two of the later day lightweight pugilists of fame were Kid Chocolate and Panama Al Brown. In 1928, following a tournament under the auspices of the New York Boxing Commission to arrive at a championship in the featherweight division, Kid Chocolate came to the top. He won a long string of fights in the featherweight class before becoming a lightweight.

Al Brown won the American bantamweight title by defeating Vidal Gregario in New York City in 1929. He defeated Huat, the French champion in France in 1932. Since he failed to return home, his American title was declared vacant in 1935. He was beaten by Baltazar Sangchili in Spain in June 1936. Georgie Pace, the colored boy from Cleveland was a challenger for the bantam title.

Joe Walcott as Champion. Earlier in the century Joe Walcott of Toronto emerged as champion. He won the welterweight championship in 1901 by defeating Rube Fern in Toronto, Canada, in five rounds. Walcott was a short, powerfully built native of Barbados. He had tremendous hitting strength and was a good boxer. He met middleweights and heavyweights. He beat Dan Creedon, the Australian, four times in a year. He knocked out Joe Choynski in seven rounds on February 22, 1900, in New York City. Walcott was welterweight champion from 1901 to 1904, losing by a foul to Dixie Kid in San Francisco. Dixie Kid held the welterweight championship from 1904 to 1908.   There were few good contenders until Ted Lewis met Dixie Kid in London and knocked him out.

On May 9, 1930, young Jack Thompson took the title from Jackie Fields in a fifteen round decision bout.   Thompson was outpointed by Tommy Freeman in September, 1930, but Thompson regained the championship in April, 1931.   He finally lost to Brouillard in October, 1931.

Jack Johnson, First Negro Heavyweight Champion.   The first Negro to win the world's heavyweight championship was Jack Johnson.   He was born in Galveston, Texas, March 31, 1878.   After a career that stamped him as contender of consequence, it seemed that the fate of Peter Jackson and other aspirants for the throne would be his.   The champions gave him the run-around.   In 1907, Tommy Burns held the world's championship and began a tour of the world with Jack right behind him issuing defies wherever he landed.   Finally, near Sydney, Australia, on December 26, 1908, Johnson met Burns.   The fight was a bitter one in which the verbal battle in the ring was as intense as the physical contest.   It did not take long for Johnson to find that Burns could not get through his defense and throughout the gruelling fight Jack was the master. Burns was knocked out in the 14th round.   Johnson returned triumphant to the United States.   He fought three no-decision bouts with Tony Ross, of Pittsburgh, Jack O'Brien, of Philadelphia, and Al Kaufman.   Then Johnson was challenged by Stanley Ketchell, the middleweight champion.   They met on October 16, 1909. Ketchell weighed 160 pounds and Jack tipped at 209.   It was a great fight.   Some believe it was intended mainly as an exhibition. However that may be, Stanley made the mistake of trying to slip over a hay-maker in the twelfth round, and knocked the astonished heavyweight champion down.   Johnson arose slowly, met the rushing Stanley with a wicked left, right and left which left Ketchell lying on his back out cold for some time.

Jack Knocks Out Jim Jeffries.   No one was left in the world thought capable of defeating this ebony superman, so the pressure

JACK JOHNSON

was put upon Jim Jeffries to come from retirement and his western ranch. Jeffries, who ruled the roost after Corbett met his Waterloo, left the ring with a glorious tradition. He engaged Corbett and Choynski and a host of other past heroes to train him for this fight. Jeff had abundant weight to dispose of but finally got down to 225 pounds, and seemed in good condition. Johnson weighed 212 and was never better. On a clear hot day, July 4, 1910, under a blazing sun, the "white hope" sought to win back his honor from the black son of Africa. For a couple of rounds Jack felt out his opponent. Jeff was not able to lead through Jack's defense. In the third round Johnson, a smiling "kidder" in all his bouts, began to tease the ex-champion, and chatter with the ring side seaters, especially Corbett. Then Jack began shooting in those long snake-like left jabs, mixing in some swift uppercuts and found Jeffries had no counter attack. Jeff's blows were steam-less. In the 7th round Johnson was boxing masterfully and slamming Jeffries with a sizzling array of jabs, hooks and swings. Throughout the 8th, 9th, and 10th, with closing eyes, Jeff was boxing badly and finding it powerless to put his boiler-making strength into his blows. From the 12th to the 15th, Jeffries tried, with the desperation of an undefeated fighter, to stave off defeat and fought fiercely. Coming up for the 15th Jack shuffled toward Jeff, sent a burning left to Jeff's jaw and knocked him down for the first time in his career. He arose at the count of ten. Jack met him with the same blow in the same place. Jeffries went down and was counted out sitting on the floor in a deep daze.

Johnson Falls. Then followed a spree of world-wide celebration for Johnson. He was feted by white and black all around the world. The smashing of the idol of white physical supremacy upset the calculation of many of both races. Sportsmanship had not arrived to the heights it attained when Joe Louis met and defeated the white champions of his day. So bitter was the feeling that Congress was easily persuaded to make it a federal offense to transport the fight pictures in commerce. Johnson became involved in events that made him a target for judicial proceedings. He left the United

States in 1914 for France, where he fought Frank Morgan, who really gave him a fight. Johnson was given a 20-round decision. Carpentier was the referee.

He then went to Barcelona, and opened a café. He was soon "broke," and when offered $30,000 and expenses to fight Jess Willard in Havana, Cuba, he took it. The fight with the gigantic Willard showed that Jack was not the same well conditioned fighter who met Jeffries and the others. He showed much of the same skill and generalship but lacked stamina and force. Near the close of 25 rounds trying to reach Willard, Jack succumbed to a blow in the mid-section, slowly went to the canvas and lay there with his left hand and forearm raised to keep the hot Havana sun out of his eyes.

Johnson was the first Negro heavyweight to win a world's championship. It was claimed that Johnson held the title longer than any other heavyweight champion. He is also credited with having fought more heavyweight battles from the beginning to the end of his career than any other fighter in history. It is also remarkable that Johnson, although meeting some of the hardest hitters and greatest fighters of his day, left the ring unmarked and unscarred. This is largely due to his masterful boxing.

Johnson was a most colorful character. He won the championship in an era when because of his race he was the target of persecution and prosecution. After winning the championship he was forced to defend it more often in France and Spain than in America. Johnson indicates in his book that, "This desire to wipe out prejudices against me and to still criticism of my conduct included my willingness to permit Willard to acquire the heavyweight championship of the world." [1] Jack Johnson died Jan. 10, 1946, following an automobile accident at Franktown, N. C.

Tiger Flowers and Battling Siki. In 1926, a sensational praying welterweight known as Tiger Flowers was challenging for a fight with Harry Greb, the titleholder. They finally met in New York

---

[1] *Jack Johnson The Man*, Copyrighted by J. J. and Bill Sims.

on February 26, 1926. The bout was close, but Flowers received the nod from the judges. On August 19, 1926, Flowers and Greb met again and Flowers won handily at the end of 15 rounds. Flowers lost his title to Mickey Walker by a questionable decision in Chicago, and never regained it, for a major operation shortly afterward ended the life of this colorful fighter.

Louis Phall, the Battling Siki, born in a West African jungle, won the French Croix de Guerre in the Great War and began a pugilistic career by defeating several French boxers of note. His most remarkable fight was that with the idol of France, Georges Carpentier.

Jeannette, McVey, Langford and Wills. This chapter cannot close without drawing upon the records of four as valiant boxers as the world has seen. America's hateful color line prevented some of them from basking in the sun-light of fame that many less able warriors have earned. Joe Jeannette, Sam McVey, Sam Langford, and Harry Wills deserve high honors. These men champions feared. Most of their celebrated fights were with each other. They were contemporaneous. Joe Jeannette was born in 1881, stood 6 feet, 1 inch and weighed 195 pounds. Sam McVey was born in California in 1885 and died in 1921. He weighed 205 pounds and was 5 feet, 11 inches tall. Harry Wills was born in 1892, was 6 feet, 3 inches tall, and weighed 215 pounds. Sam Langford was born in Nova Scotia, March 4, 1886. He was but 5 feet, 6½ inches in height and weighed 200 pounds.

Langford was a "killer." He fought over 250 battles, winning over 145 of his contests. He did his spectacular fighting between 1902 and 1923. Jeannette won 74 fights, fought 56 no-decision fights, and lost 6. He fought ten with Langford, six with Jack Johnson and others with McVey and Harry Wills. McVey won 47 fights, including battles with Sam Langford and Joe Jeannette. He was knocked out by Jack Johnson, Sam Langford, and Harry Wills as late as the year 1918.

Harry Wills was the masterful boxer of his day. He fought Sam Langford 14 times. He won over Langford, McVey and Jeannette

SAM LANGFORD

and was once knocked out by Sam Langford. He had 31 knockouts to his record. Saddest of all his memories must be the thought
that Dempsey would not meet him. The color line was always

EZZARD CHARLES
Heavyweight Champion of the World —1949

convenient. America had not yet grown, nor even New York, to
be the tolerant real American metropolis it has reached since the
days of Franklin D. Roosevelt, Governor Lehman, Mayor La
Guardia, and a democratic boxing board.

CHAPTER III

Boxers of Later Days

Joe Louis. Seldom in ring history has there been a fighter of greater reputation than Joe Louis, or Joe Louis Barrow. The story of Joe Louis matches the exploits of any national hero in the hearts of young America. Joe Louis was born on a farm near Lafayette, Alabama, May 13, 1914. Early in his career his mother and the Barrow children found their way to Detroit, Michigan. As with Owens, and many of the great and past-great athletes of today, the trek of Negro dwellers from the land of few privileges, the South, to the freer country of the North, gave them their great opportunity. Proving in the boxing circles of Detroit his might and skill, Joe began to attract attention as an amateur boxer. In 1933, we find him a runner-up to Max Marek in the light-heavyweight national American Athletic Union championship. In April, 1934, Joe won the A.A.U. light-heavyweight championship in Boston. In two years, as an amateur, he won 43 fights by knockouts, and seven by decision. He lost four.

Joe became a professional on July 4, 1934. By 1939 he had engaged in forty fights, winning 33 by knockouts, and six by decisions. He lost by a knockout to Max Schmeling on June 19, 1936, in 12 rounds. His present record includes the defeat of five former heavyweight champions.

Sports page columns devoted to comments and stories about Joe would probably weigh more than a year's bound volume of the New York *Times*. Every prominent commentator of public events has found something to say about Louis. Since the day of Peter Jackson, few have found a more colorful fighter to write about. Joe has the physique of a Greek god. His color appears to be a golden-bronze. Few Negro fighters have shaded lighter than he. His courage is unquestioned. Knowing that nearly a hundred

JOE LOUIS

thousand pairs of eyes were on him, and that many, many millions over the world were listening in, yet no whit of trepidation unnerved his neuro-muscular mechanism when he engaged in the primal business of outsmarting to beat the most worthy contenders who faced him under the lights.

Despite the fame and wealth that have come to the uneducated Negro lad, he still remains at heart an unassuming boy. He conducts himself as a gentleman in all situations. A "killer" in the business of the ring, yet he finds fun in dancing, playing golf, attending movies, and cheering the less fortunate in life. He is noted for his willingness to visit the sick. He plays a remarkable game of softball and is an attraction at games. He dresses immaculately. He rides and owns pure-bred horses. He is unspoiled by women, cares bountifully for his mother and sisters, and is loyal to his friends and business associates. He talks little, and has invested wisely. Joe inspires the youth of all races and is worshipped by his own young people. Unlike so many athletes, he trained faithfully, and neither smokes nor drinks. He is religious. His management, John Roxborough, Julian Black and Jack Blackburn, had his explicit, unalloyed confidence and loyalty.

Carnera Falls. His battles with former champions were the highlights of his career. Although he came along through the amateur and early professional bouts, like a portending comet, few knew how he would meet the champions. Under the blaze of lights he shook hands with the mighty Carnera, the huge giant from Italy. The bronze boy stepped around and shot his dynamite fists into the mid-section of his gigantic adversary. He stepped away from or ducked under the whizzing swings of the slow-thinking Italian for a round or two, and at the same time found a way to bring down Carnera's guard. From then on until the 6th and last round, Louis' opponent was a beaten man. The power of Joe's fists tottered the massive form, and in the 6th round the losing gladiator was a much battered and beaten man.

Max Baer Succumbs. Then Joe met Max Baer on September 24, 1935. Max was a very scared fighter after he sampled a few of

Joe's hooks and jabs. Baer clowned throughout the fight even when his face was bruised blue and leaked blood. In less than four rounds, Max's pugilistic destiny had been ruined by the skill and power of the brain and brawn of the boy from Alabama.

Joe was scheduled next to meet Max Schmeling. By June 19, 1936, Louis was considered invincible. He probably inwardly felt he was every man's master. Some say he trained carelessly. Other rumors had it that the ring followers were due a clean-up in the betting. Whatever the reason, Louis discovered it did not pay to lead a left hook or jab and have his jaw open for a countering right swing. Early in the fight Max Schmeling took the leads of Louis and gambled on hay-making right swings, and then another and another. One landed and Max grew confident. Louis fought bravely but could not stop the right that came with stunning rapidity until in the 12th round Louis ended on the canvas for the first knockout of his professional career.

Jack Sharkey Goes Down. Then came old Jack Sharkey, who had once been great with the glory of the title. This was a repetition of the Carnera fight. Sharkey was famed for boxing skill. However, Sharkey was a toy in the hands of the young master. Joe showed he could lose a fight and come back nothing daunted, and prove his march to destiny. Sharkey went out in three rounds on the night of August 17, 1936. The boxing czars made Louis fight through a list of a half dozen contenders, all of whom went out in a total of fifteen rounds, except Bob Pastor, who by an excellent assortment of sprints, ducking, weaving and dodging kept in the ring for ten rounds. Louis hardly landed a punch. Of course Pastor was only there to stay, not to fight.

Joe Wins World Championship. In due time Louis met Braddock, the champion, on June 22, 1937. International repercussions helped Louis land this match. Coming from the Aryan stronghold of Herr Hitler, Max Schmeling was given a pretty runaround by the financial wizards of the fight game. Some say lovers of democracy and opponents of the anti-Semitic persecution programs abroad were influential in denying to Schmeling the chance to fight Braddock. Whatever the reason, Louis was given the opportunity to fight for the championship. Braddock was certainly fearless. He fought a great fight. Bruised and cut by the smashing hooks and counter blows of Louis, Braddock did not retreat at all. He got to Louis many times but not before most of the steam of his blows had been dissipated by the cutting-down tactics of Louis. With both knees wobbling, Braddock came out gamely in the 8th round. Louis, who always respected and liked Braddock, mercifully crashed his powerful left and right to Braddock's jaw and the great come-back champion reeled to the canvas for the count, and to Louis went the first heavyweight championship since Jack Johnson gave it up under the glare of the afternoon sun in Havana years before.

Schmeling Knocked Out. Then for Louis remained only the lustful desire to meet Schmeling again. The stage was set. All of Aryan conscious Europe looked to Max to cut down again the conqueror of America's champion white hope. The spiritual weight and morale of the Germanic nation supported Max. Max himself budded exuberantly with racial and personal confidence. Louis went to training viciously. Only one thought was his—to beat the Teuton. The world stood expectantly on the outcome of the fight. The night came. Joe distinctly outwitted the soothsayers and those who knew how the fight would be fought. Instead of showing respect or fear for the vaunted right of Max, which had been so deadly on their first meeting, Joe shot to the center of the ring and nailed Max at the opening. Never a chance did Max have. The power of youth cracked on the bearded jaw of the German. Cries of anguish were registered from Max as the blows of Louis fell. His face took on the anguish of the dying wild boars that Max so often had hunted and killed in the black forest of his homeland. The pictures of the fight show the pain and torture he suffered, as he was hurled into the ropes by a blow. Louis smashed into the ribs with a right and followed up with a lightning-like hook that bereft Max of conscious life. The fight was over in a little over two minutes of the first round. Max spent a few weeks in the hospital. Joe could afford to retire, for there were, as with Alexander of Macedon, no more pugilistic worlds to encounter, at least during 1938.

The Greatest Heavyweight of All Time. In the beginning of his career it was too early to evaluate Joe Louis properly. Today in 1948 we can confidently say that the combination of Joe Louis, sportsman, boxer, American, has never been equalled. As a sportsman he has never been accused of unfair tactics. In his responses at the "Mike" following a gruelling fight in the midst of turmoil and emotion his comments to the world have been models for modesty and in tribute to his opponents. True to the instincts of gentlemen boxers everywhere, after unleashing his most savage attacks upon an adversary within the rules, he has never failed to become a generous and considerate victor at the end.

As a boxer he excelled them all. He had 15 predecessors as heavyweight champion. He held the title eleven years, longer than any other heavyweight champion. He successfully defended his championship 25 times, a record in the annals of boxing history. The gate receipts he attracted topped all with a grand total of over $10,000,000. Had he been living in a day of lesser income taxation he could have retired many times a millionaire. Some would place Jeffries a No. 1 ranking choice over the years, but Louis defended his title more times than Jeffries fought. Jack Dempsey was a harder hitter and could take more punishment it is claimed but this is but speculation. Jack Johnson, it is claimed, was a harder hitter and a cleverer boxer, while Jim Corbett was a great boxer and an excellent ring general, but Joe fought 62 fights, losing only one. He knocked out 52 of his opponents and won 9 contests by decisions. Only Carnera knocked out more opponents, many of the setups abroad. Joe was the youngest fighter to attain the championship, winning the coveted crown at 23 years old.

As an American, although handicapped by a lack of formal education for having lived in a section where little was done to educate Negroes, he was a model for emulation. There was nothing subversive in his make-up, and he never displayed the vices of an Uncle Tom. He always resented the segregation of and discrimination against his race. His contributions to the morale of our fighting forces during the war, and his efforts to raise money for the relief funds of army and navy have never been equalled. When he fought Buddy Baer in New York's Madison Square he gave his share of 40% of the profits which with Mike Jacobs' share and 2½% of Baer's end of the net amounted to $89,092.01. Until this time the total in the coffers of the Navy Relief fund was a paltry $6,000. He fought Abe Simons in March, 1942, and earned $64,980.02 for the Army Relief fund. No single individual has ever produced so much for a charitable cause.

At the close of his army career the Brown Bomber had travelled over 30,000 miles all over the globe giving exhibitions, cheering the sick and wounded in the hospitals, and performing this duty under the usual hazards of war. He engaged in 196 exhibitions before millions of GIs. His courage under fire was undaunted. Twelve nights and continuous buzz-bombing in London failed to discourage him. One day after pulling the lanyard on a big gun of the 92nd division aimed against the German Gothic line, this same gun exploded killing several Negro artillerymen. He escaped death or injury several times when travelling by train, bus, truck or airplane. We are justified in repeating that no truer ideal American athlete ever lived than this greatest of all heavyweight boxers, Joe Louis.

Armstrong Defeats Sarron. Of all but equal status was Henry Armstrong known as "Homicide Hank," and "Hammering Hank." According to Grantland Rice, he was probably "pound for pound, close to being the greatest fighter" the commentator had ever known. Henry achieved the most remarkable feat of winning three titles in a year. On October 29, 1938, he won the featherweight title by a knockout in six rounds from Peter Sarron, the scrappy little Syrian who had fought winning battles all around the world. On May 31, 1938, Armstrong passed by the lightweight field and took the welterweight crown from the head of Barney Ross by a decision at the end of fifteen rounds. Then doubling back on August 17, he won from Lou Ambers the lightweight title by a decision after fifteen rounds of the most gruelling fighting he had ever engaged in.

This most remarkable of pugilistic athletes was born in St. Louis, Missouri, December 12, 1912. He migrated from St. Louis to Los Angeles about 1931. He was flat "broke." His first night was spent in a Mission Flop House. He began the hard way, battling himself into the hearts of promoters and well wishers. The records of his fights until 1936 are not fully known. In 1936 he lost three fights and won eleven, six by knockouts. In 1937 he earned his reputation as "Homicide Hank" by blasting 26 fighters via the knockout route, and by decision. In October he became the featherweight king. By 1938 he had annexed three crowns, and won more than a dozen major engagements. Both of his championship fights went the long way. He fared better in defeating Ross than in his engagement with Ambers.

John Henry.   Honorable mention is due also John Henry Lewis, one of the great champions of our times and one of the finest gentlemen in the ring game. John Henry has claimed distant kinship to Tom Molineaux, the first American heavyweight champion. Lewis was born in Los Angeles, California, on May 6, 1914. He was brought up in Phoenix, Arizona. His father was a fighter of some merit and trained John Henry.

Unlike his last competitor, Joseph Louis Barrow, John Henry was unlucky enough not to be born to become a heavyweight. Americans have always shown an inferiority complex in the matter of weight. To the heavies in boxing, wrestling, and football sports we pay greatest tribute and most money even though the lighter weight performers are often more skillful and more colorful.

Until John Henry Lewis met Joe Louis he had never been knocked out in 99 fights. He had won 48 by knockouts, 39 by decision, lost 7, and fought 5 to draw decisions. His one-hundredth fight, an essay to wrest the heavyweight title from his good friend Joe,

HENRY ARMSTRONG

led to his first knockout.   Lewis had been boxing since 1930 as a
light-heavyweight.   Once he beat Jim Braddock who later became
heavyweight champion and lost to Joe Louis.

Lewis's fight with Joe Louis was the first in which two colored
fighters had met for the heavyweight championship of the world
since Jim Johnson met Jack Johnson in 1913 in Paris.   John Henry
managed to make 180 pounds while Joe scaled 200 pounds.   It
was generally conceded that John Henry could only hope to win
if he could avoid Joe's lethal punches and outbox him.   But unlike
Bob Pastor, John Henry met a more experienced Joe who did not
risk any rounds for the picture industry.   Joe slammed a straight
left into John Henry's face and followed up with a flurry of right
hooks that connected for three knock downs; and, in a little more
of a round than it took Joe to send Schmeling away, he had John
Henry recorded for a technical knockout.   The fight fought in
Madison Square Garden netted Louis about $40,000 and John
Henry Lewis about $17,000.

Later Boxers.   Hundreds of Negro professional boxers have
been entertaining the boxing crowds in the big cities all around the
nation.   From their ranks have come several world champions.   In
1948, Negro boxers held four of the eight world championships.
Ray Robinson was without a peer in the welterweight class.   Ike
Williams was king of the lightweights and Joe (Sandy) Saddler
dethroned Willie Pep for the world championship in the featherweight division.

Probably the most confused championship was in the lightweight
division.   Beau Jack, one of the most colorful of boxers was the
little caddy hailing from Augusta, Georgia.   He came north and
after a long string of victories won the lightweight championship.
Beau Jack fought six times in Madison Square Garden in 1943,
grossing $481,415, an average of $80,236 a show.   Even colorful
Henry Armstrong could not match Beau Jack as a box office attraction.   Beau Jack won the championship on May 21, 1943 by defeating Bob Montgomery.   Montgomery regained on November 19,
1943, the New York phase of the world championship.

JOHN HENRY LEWIS

Ike Williams of Trenton defeated the National Boxing Association champion, Juan Zurita, on April 18, 1945. Then on August 4, 1947, Ike Williams defeated Bob Montgomery who held the New York title, for the undisputed world lightweight championship.

CHALKY WRIGHT, FORMER WORLD LIGHTWEIGHT CHAMPION   BOB MONTGOMERY, FORMER WORLD LIGHTWEIGHT CHAMPION

On December 20, 1946, Ray Robinson who had been knocking at the door of championship honors for several years was awarded the welterweight championship after Marty Servo, title holder, would not meet Ray Robinson and the Boxing authorities agreed that the winner of the Bell-Robinson fight would be acknowledged the world champion. Ray defeated Tommy Bell. Robinson had

Ike Williams—World Lightweight Champion, 1947, 1948, 1949

RAY ROBINSON, WELTERWEIGHT CHAMPION OF THE WORLD

difficulty getting recognition and matches because he retained a
colored manager and refused to submit his contract to exploiting
managers. George Gainsford was recognized as Robinson's manager in March, 1946. Robinson met defeat only once in his boxing career, when on February 5 he lost to Jake LaMotta, but on

February 28, Ray won over
LaMotta.

The lightweight division has
had a number of fighters to
follow in the class in which
the immortal Joe Gans led off.
Henry Armstrong defeated Lou
Ambers for the title August 17,
1948; Chalky Wright held the
title from Sept. 25, 1942 to
Nov. 20, 1943; then came Beau
Jack, Bob Montgomery and Ike
Williams. In the featherweight
division, George Dixon was
champion from 1890 to 1900.
Kid Chocolate won the New
York version of the world
championship on October 13,
1932. Henry Armstrong beat
Petey Sarron for the championship on October 29, 1938.
Jackie Wilson was champion
from November 18, 1940 until
January 18, 1943. On October
28, 1948, Joe (Sandy) Saddler
of Harlem lifted the crown from
Willie Pep by a knockout in
four rounds in New York.

George Dixon claimed the
bantamweight title until he
outgrew that class. Only one
colored boxer has held it since.
Al Brown of Panama was champion of the bantams from 1929
to 1935. No colored American
boxer has been at the top of the
flyweight division.

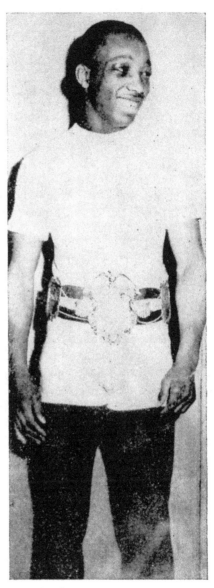

SANDY SADDLER, FEATHERWEIGHT
BOXING CHAMPION, 1948

CHAPTER IV

Our Sprinters

Howard P. Drew. The earliest colored lad to break into the "fastest human" class, a category illumined up to that time by the speed records of Arthur Duffey and Bernie Wefers, was Howard P. Drew. He began his noteworthy career as an athlete at the Springfield High School in Massachusetts. In 1912 and 1913, he won the national Amateur Athletic Union 100 yard championship. In 1913 he won the 220 yard title. In 1914, representing the University of Southern California, Drew became co-holder with Arthur Duffey of Georgetown of the world's record, 9.6 seconds, in the 100 yard sprint. This, Drew held alone for many years after Duffey's record was taken away from him because of his admitted professional status. Drew was never an in-and-out performer. He was consistent. He seldom broke prematurely from his mark; he was a fast starter and came through the century race in his drive with a remarkable burst of speed.

In his day the press comments were beginning to take on the colorful character of present day commentary concerning Negro athletes. From the New York *Tribune* we read, "It seems incredible that a man running without fear of life and not the slightest desire to catch a train can impel himself to such prodigious speed. The sight of Drew hurtling along inevitably suggests a concealed motor. Anybody who saw Drew run last night cannot doubt his supremacy among American sprinters."

The New York *Gazette* said, "Alvah Meyer of the Irish-American Athletic Club was once credited with running 100 yards on a board floor in Buffalo in 9 4/5 seconds, but no one believes he ever did it. He doesn't believe so himself. After seeing Drew perform last night he said, 'That beat my performance all hollow. Drew is the greatest sprinter in the world. He's in a class by himself.'"

Meredith and Drew ran their wonderful races without spiked shoes and both were assured by the Amateur Athletic Union that their records would pass muster. The New York *Times* reported, "The colored sprinter placed himself once more on the top of the athletic ladder by winning the seventy-yard invitation race, which brought together four of the best sprinters in the world.

"So great was the crowd which witnessed the sports (in the Twenty-second Regiment Armory in New York) that the doors of the Garden were closed by order of the Fire Department long before 9 o'clock."

The late "Mike" Murphy, American coach of the 1912 Olympics at Stockholm, said of Drew, "Never in all my life have I seen any sprinter with such wonderful leg action as Drew. Why, his legs fly back and forth just like pistons. He gets away as fast as any man I ever saw, and he has a wonderful finish. Trainers and experts say that he has the quickest start of any man ever seen upon the track. Yet he is so cool and collected that he never beats the gun."

HOWARD P. DREW
University of Southern California—
Sprint Champion

After Howard Drew, colored "speed merchants" began to appear here and there in the college meets. In the track meets staged by colored institutions, a very fast boy in the scholastic or college circle would occasionally make a record run, but the lack of good tracks, scientifically built or measured and authoritatively certified, the scarcity of authenticated officials and the weak program of track athletes at most schools served to prevent sprinters from developing or receiving nationally accredited records. In later years, however, athletes like Singletary of St. Augustine, John Borican of Virginia State, Ellerbee of Tuskegee and others have proved their merit in record making company.

De Hart Hubbard. At Michigan University, in 1920, a closely knit, splendidly built speedster of color, De Hart Hubbard, opened a new era. Better known for his broad jumping, he began to cheer colored Americans whenever the Big Ten track games were heralded. For the first time the radio waves began to crackle with thrilling references by the early broadcasters to the dark lad who led his light-skinned contenders to the tape.

At that time, one commentator said, "De Hart Hubbard of Michigan is by all odds the greatest all-round track athlete ever produced. He ran 100 yards in 9.6 seconds; hopped, skipped and jumped 43 feet, 10¾ inches, and held the world's record for the broad jump in 1925, doing 25 feet 10⅞ inches." At Chicago in 1928, he jumped 26 feet 2 inches, but the record was disallowed because the level of the take-off was one inch higher than the surface of the landing pit.

Edward Gourdin. At about the same time another record breaking broad jumper, Edward Gourdin, began to start at sprint distances. At Harvard he won many a sprint race but will always be remembered as the first athlete to broad jump over 25 feet. He was the first human to jump to a record of twenty-five feet or more. He performed this feat in a perfect dramatic setting in the Oxford-Cambridge Harvard-Yale international meet at Cambridge, Massachusetts, in July, 1921.

Not until the coming of another star in 1929, did Negro sprinters begin to take up record breaking again. Since then, there has been a parade of sterling Negro "speedsters"; and records in the

Mozelle Ellerbee, Tuskegee

100 and 220 yards, and the 100 and 200 meters, official and unofficial, have been hung up by these boys in scholastic, college and amateur circles from the Atlantic to the Pacific, and abroad.

Eddie Tolan. In August, 1932, a Negro's name crashed front page head lines of the New York *Times* and those of a thousand journals around the world. Eddie Tolan, the phantom flier of Detroit, Michigan, raced his colored American, Ralph Metcalfe of Marquette University, to a photo-finish in the finals of the Olympic 100 meter dash at Los Angeles, California. Black America and men of color around the world were never before so stirred emotionally. It was the first time a Negro had won the premier event. Howard Drew made a bid for it in the 1912 Olympics but a pulled tendon prevented him from winning. Again, a day later, Toland and Metcalfe ran a thrilling race to top the best sprinters of the world in the 200 meter race, and again it was the Detroit flier, Eddie Tolan, who electrified America by winning.

A current journal of the age, describing the running of the premier event of the Olympic Games in 1932 said, "The 100-meter race in the 1932 Olympics was about to be run in the Los Angeles Municipal Stadium before 60,000 expectant lovers of track athletics. Of the six entrants in the finals of this event, three represented America; Eddie Tolan, formerly of the University of Michigan, Ralph Metcalfe, of Marquette; and George Simpson, white, once crack dash star of Ohio State, completed the home trio. These six human rockets toed the mark; one of them was nervous, he broke, and the tension was momentarily relieved. The start was made again. The sharp bark of the gun! Six human forms catapulted toward their objective like bats from a cave. Metcalfe was last and seemingly out of it. At 50 meters, little Tolan's piston-like legs brought him into the lead. In the next split-second, a huge brown form, gaining momentum like a falling body, came out of the ruck. The Marquette meteor, slower starter than Tolan, caught him at 90 meters and it seemed as though he would flash across the finish first. But the end of this epochal dash was as nice a dead heat between America's two premier track stars as was ever run. The

Courtesy of the "Afro"

BEATTY, WARD AND TOLAN

timer's electric clock, however, caught the Michigan marvel's chest a hair's breadth ahead of Metcalfe at the end.

"In the winning of this race, Tolan not only brought the 100-meter title back to America after a lapse of twelve years, but he also established a new Olympic record of 10.3 seconds, which lowered the world mark set by Percy Williams, white, of Canada. The little runner from Detroit went on to win the 200-meter race and to establish a new Olympic record of 21.2 seconds."

Prior to the Olympics, from high school days on, when Metcalfe was in the Tilden Technical High School of Chicago and Tolan was in the Cass High School of Detroit, each scored victories in race after race. The walls of one room of Tolan's home today are covered with medals, and great trophies adorn the furniture. The same wealth of merit tokens abounds among the possessions of Metcalfe. In more than 300 races Tolan was defeated only seven times. With no more amateur laurels to covet, Tolan entered the professional field and showed his flying heels to all competitors here and abroad. Not only did he contend in athletics but he battled prejudices all along the way. On a trip to Europe with some of the white runners he was insulted repeatedly, but he never let the slights and insults keep him from training carefully and running in victory form.

He later served the city department of Detroit in an efficient, modest way. He had one chief regret. His early ambition was to become a physician, but the strenuous work of glorifying his college (Michigan), his race, and America made the attainment of his cherished hope impossible. After all, however, few men in modern times could have brought more satisfaction to the hearts of Americans than did Eddie Tolan, one of the most modest and best loved heroes of the cinder path.

Ralph Metcalfe.   Another of this type is Ralph Metcalfe. He was born on May 20, 1910, at Atlanta, Georgia. As a child he went with his mother to Chicago. He was graduated from Tilden Technical High School in 1930 and entered Marquette. He was an earnest student, and despite his success as runner, he retained

RALPH METCALFE, MARQUETTE UNIVERSITY

an attractive modesty in speech and manners.   His popularity and
ability merited him the enviable honor of being elected to the captaincy of his track team, and to membership in Alpha Sigma Mu,
the only All-University Honor Society at Marquette.   His name
is listed often as a record holder on the Amateur Athletic Union
and the National Collegiate Athletic Association honor rolls.
Formerly he was connected with the physical education department of Xavier College for Negroes in Louisiana, and found and
developed boys who have achieved national fame.   He studied
later at the University of Southern California to equip himself
better to perpetuate for the race in the youth of today the skills
and arts that made him an honor to the land of his birth.

A writer of standing in the athletic world, reporting of Metcalfe
in 1932, remarked, "This South Side Chicago collegian first gained
note as a budding track immortal in the Junior National Championship meet held in Pittsburgh during August, 1930.   After two years
of unbroken triumphs in school boy competition, he came to the
National Junior Championship in 1930 as a member of the Chase
Athletic Club of Chicago.   In his first day of competition, he won
the 100-yard dash in 0:9.7 seconds, setting a new record.   The
next day, competing in the 220-yard Senior National Championship,
he placed fourth among the cream of America's sprinting crop.
From this moment on, Metcalfe's track career has been dazzling.
He has run and won great races against the best competition in the
world; he has carried his challenge to the enemy by going abroad
and defeating the best European track stars."

In the National Collegiate meet in Chicago on June 11, 1932,
two months before the Olympics, Metcalfe—in one of the most
sensational individual performances in track history—shattered the
world's records for 220 yards, 100 and 200 meters, and tied Tolan's
accepted world's record for that year of 9.5 seconds for 100 yards.
The same writer pays this tribute to this sprint hero, Metcalfe,
saying concerning him, "A good student, a fine fellow, this 180-
pound human rocket has carved his name forever in the sports-
world hall of fame."

Following the startling performances of Tolan and Metcalfe

in the 1932 Olympics, there arose much speculation as to which was the greater sprinter of the two. One commentator pays tribute to Metcalfe thus, saying, "Tolan and Metcalfe are the two greatest sprinters ever to drive spikes into cinders. It is impossible to determine which one is the better. In spite of bespectacled Eddie's two victories over Metcalfe in the Olympics, the latter is hailed by many of the experts and legions of track-lovers as Tolan's superior."

Ralph Metcalfe came down from the 1932 to the 1936 Olympics equalling and breaking sprint records in college and amateur circles. Physically, in form, Metcalfe was comparable to statues of Greek gods. It was a most inspiring sight to witness the powerfully built bronze human machine striding through the 220 yards with the smoothness of a twelve cylinder motor car. Whereas, the redoubtable Jesse would seemingly glide along the furlong with the grace and satin strength of a gazelle, Ralph would pound along with power emanating, almost visibly, with his every stride. Going into the 1936 Olympics with most of his running career behind him, Ralph made a comeback that many experts hardly thought possible.

Jesse Owens. Never before in the recorded history of the oldest forms of athletic games, the track and field events, has a meteor so colorful, so wonderful in performance as Jesse Owens, ever blazed across the great athletic firmament. A climax to the galaxy of stellar sprinters was reached when Jesse Owens appeared in the East Technical High School of Cleveland. As with the enthusiasm that greets some great composer, conductor, or opera star, the emotions of millions who witnessed some of the artistic achievements of Owens were restrained only by the physical limitations of the seating space. The few brief seconds between the report of the gun that sent him and his competitors hurtling through space over a cinder track, to the break of the taut yarn by his flying body, sufficed to bring to spectators a thrill, second only to nerve gland responses of the highest type.

In 1935, the press reported the one man feat of record-breaking by Jesse Owens as being without a close parallel in the annals of track. One article went on to say, "Briefly, what Owens has done

JESSE OWENS

in the past fortnight is this: Twice equalled Frank Wykoff's world record of 0:09.4 for the 100-yard dash; shattered all listed standards for the 220 with a 0:20.3 mark, and leaped farther than any other human being with a broad jump of 26 feet 8¼ inches." So astounding were the performances the writer proceeded, "A record of such commanding excellence demands explanation. A theory has been advanced that through some physical characteristic of the race involving the bone and muscle construction of the foot and leg the Negro is ideally adapted to the sprints and jumping events. The feats of Howard Drew, Sol Butler, Ned Gourdin, De Hart Hubbard, Eddie Tolan and Ed Gordon of the recent past and Ralph Metcalfe, Willis Ward, Eulace Peacock and Ben Johnson, who now on occasion share a place in the sun with Owens, constitute evidence for this hypothesis."

However, from his earliest competitive days, Owens possessed a world of natural ability. It is said that as a junior high school student he could jump more than 23 feet and sprint 100 yards in 10 seconds flat. But it was not until 1933 that Owens gained more than a local reputation. He scored an unprecedented triple in the 1933 national interscholastic championships of the University of Chicago at Stagg Field. Then wearing the colors of East Technical High School of Cleveland, he ran the 100 yards in 0:09.4, the 220 in 0:20.7 and broadjumped 24 feet 9½ inches.

These performances were received with skepticism in some quarters, but when he followed them by taking the National Amateur Athletic Union broad jump title with a leap of 24 feet 6⅜ inches and placing third to Metcalfe in the 100 meters, his status as a national luminary was assured. As a freshman at Ohio State, Owens came East to the National Amateur Athletic Union indoor championships, set a world's mark of 25 feet 3½ inches for the broad jump and placed third in the dash. Outdoors he gained the broad jump crown and was a close second to Metcalfe in the sprint.

Owens signalized his entrance into varsity competition by raising his indoor broad-jump mark to 25 feet 9¾ inches and taking second to Johnson in the indoor national sprint. Then he went on to win the Big Ten dash title.

He opened his outdoor campaign by becoming the first American ever to jump 26 feet, exceeding that mark by 1¾ inches, and ran the 100 in 0:09.5 at the Drake relays. Then came the spectacular quadruple triumphs in the quadrangular meet with Wisconsin, Northwestern and Chicago, and in the Big Ten championships.

Thus, after breaking record after record that had defied the efforts of thousands before him, and accomplishing series of victories in the dashes, broad jump, and low hurdles, Jesse went on to accomplish a feat that for its social import will, like a great wave breaking on countless shores, affect human thinking and human behavior for many, many years.

When in August, 1936, before the Fuhrer Hitler in Berlin, the mighty Jesse led that long line of American Negroes to victory after victory in events that many men would have died willingly to achieve, he not only won praise for America and his race, but he spiked many heavy guns of Nazi-Nietsche philosophy of race. Thrice Jesse mounted to the rostrum of individual victory; thrice the American flag topped all others and the American anthem resounded in the ears of a hundred and ten thousand spectators at the games; and then again, as one of the four members of the sprint (400 meters) relay team which included Metcalfe, he helped establish a new record of forty seconds.

A great deal of credit for the performances of Jesse must be given to his coach, Charles Riley, of his high school team, and coach Larry Snyder of Ohio State University. Much also was done by public-spirited alumni and citizens to help him secure work and to keep him in school with an amateur status.

When he returned from his triumphant Olympic feat most of America paid tribute to him. Ticker-tape showers and stately reception by Mayor La Guardia met his entry to New York and America. All sorts of exploitation schemes were suggested to him. Naturally, he knew he must soon earn a living. In old Greece, many an Olympic winner entered his home city through a specially made breach in the walls and his statue was copied in marble, and frequently he was given a pension. For some reason, Jesse was not called to Washington on his return to be greeted by the President, a tribute that in the belief of many, he justly deserved.

Seeking to gain by his fame and publicity, the Republican Party exploited his success as an athlete and used him in the political campaign. Soon after the oak trees won by Jesse at Berlin were planted on the Ohio State campus, he forsook his amateur competition, and engaged in several money-making ventures. Today he lives with his wife and mother in the city he has helped to make famous. It is yet too soon to predict his future in the ranks of the plain citizenry. His fame will doubtless go on as the years pass. His records are high. Even though these are record breaking days, it may be many generations before one man will chalk up so many record breaking achievements.

Ben Johnson. Although Tolan, Metcalfe and Owens have passed beyond amateur ranks, sprinters of color still march on. Overshadowed only by these three all-time great sprinters, two Negro ace runners began their careers. Ben Johnson, elected twice as captain of the blue and white team of Columbia, led a world of sprinters to the tape indoors and outdoors in America and Europe. A written estimate of his day says,

"Ben Johnson, Columbia's Negro captain, stamped himself as the newest 'fastest human' with a new world record for 60 yards. . . . Johnson obliterated such famous names as Jesse Owens, Eulace Peacock, Emmett Toppino, Chester Bowman and Loren Murchison from the record books as he stepped down the straightway in 6 seconds flat.[1] He gave warning of what was to come by tying the record of 0:6.2 in the trial heats and then clipping one-tenth second off that in the semi-finals."

The performance gave Johnson ranking as the outstanding performer of the meet. A committee of sports writers placed the Columbia ace ahead of Cunningham and New York University's sophomore, Jimmy Herbert, who remained unbeaten that year in the 600 yard run.

Eulace Peacock. The other speed ace of outstanding ability who, although eclipsed by that great contemporary, Jesse Owens,

---

[1] This record of 60 yards in 6 seconds has not been allowed despite the vigor of insistence by the starter and most of the officials at the meet.

CAPTAIN BEN JOHNSON, COLUMBIA UNIVERSITY TRACK TEAM

Eulace Peacock, Temple University's Star Athlete

yet, holding some of the few victories over the redoubtable Jesse
was Eulace Peacock.   Peacock has had an unusual amount of hard
luck due to an injured tendon.   Peacock, one of the best track
athletes ever to come from the East, was a product of Temple University.   His records in the sprints, jumps, and pentathlon events
are high on the lists.   As late as 1939 he was still a victorious
athlete, running under the colors of the Shore Athletic Club of
Elberon, New Jersey.   One of his great days was described in 1935,
in an article saying:

"Blinding speed set the tempo for track and field in 1935 as Jesse
Owens and Eulace Peacock, sprinters extraordinary, engaged in
a series of magnificent duels on straightways and in jumping pit.
After long years of dominance by the milers, track turned to the
dash men for its most thrilling and startling performances.

"On May 25, the lithe and sinewy Owens, satin smooth in his
running, broke three world's records and tied another in one of
the most astounding exploits in the annals of the sport.   He fled
over the black cinders in 0:09 for 100 yards, 0:20.3 for 220 yards
flat and 0:22.9 for the 220-yard low hurdles.   Then to top it all
off, Owens went catapulting 26 feet 8¼ inches for a new broad
jump mark.

"Apparently, there was no question about the world's fastest
human after that.   The 21-year old Ohio State sophomore was
hailed as the greatest of all time.   He added to his stature in the
National Collegiate Amateur Athletic championships.   Then came
the National Amateur Athletic Union title games in the sun-drenched
stadium at Lincoln, Nebraska, in July.   And another Negro sensation went rocketing right past him.   Peacock, a sophomore at
Temple University, had seen the flaming scarlet jersey of the Brown
Bombshell lead him to victory all season long.   Peacock rode the
wings of a breeze to an upset victory in the 100 meter dash, clocked
in the world's record time of 0:10.2."

Referring to "A Magnificent Leap," the commentator said
further, "The spectators gasped in wonder, only to have Peacock
pull them out of their seats once more by beating the 'unconquer-
able' Owens in the broad jump as well, with a magnificent leap of

26 feet 3 inches, also better than the accepted universal figures. And a few days later Peacock proved that his sprint triumph was no freak by vanquishing again the Buckeye Bullet in another sprint race.

Left—Billy Mathis, National A.A.U. Sprint Champion, Outdoor, 1947. Right—Barney (Norwood) Ewell, The Most Consistent Sprint Champion since Jesse Owens; Lost the Olympic 100 Meters by an Eye-Lash to Harrison Dillard in 1948.

"There they are, then, Owens and Peacock or Peacock and Owens, whichever is the correct order. And these two disciples of speed led the advance of America's track and field athletes into the Olympic year with the United States as well fortified as it ever was for stirring deeds at Berlin next August." Unfortunately for Peacock, his temperamental tendon kept him from winning a berth on the 1936 Olympic team.

Others of Later Years. During the years following these great feats colored lads have continued their winning ways. Mathis, Dillard, Carey, Conwell, Ewell, La Beach, Beckett, Lorenzo Wright, Elmore Harris, McDonald Bailey of Great Britain, William Carter, Herbert Douglass, Buddy Young, McKenley, and many others have won stellar honors on the sprint lanes in meets all about the nation and over the world.

One of the most versatile sprinters of the period was Buddy Young. After starring as an athlete in high school in Chicago, Young entered the University of Illinois and along with other colored track men brought many sectional and national honors to the midwest school. In 1945 he was a triple winner on a soggy NCAA track, scoring victories in the 100 yard dash in 9.7 seconds; the 220 yard dash in 21.3 seconds; and the broad jump with a leap of 22 feet 10 inches. Because of a slippery track he tripped over a hurdle and thus was unable to duplicate the feat of Jesse Owens in 1935.

Why colored boys have been without peers in the sprints has incited great curiosity among the sports commentators. Sprinting is not an expensive sport and requires less in the way of facilities than most of the other events on the calendar of track. As colored boys enter institutions with good coaching, the best in the way of facilities and equipment, and stout competition, there will be more of these boys qualifying in the varied events instead of having so many sprinters but few Dillards, Duggers, Dixons or Fonvilles.

CHAPTER V

Versatility in Track and Field

Beginners. Except for the exploits of W. T. S. Jackson, running the half-mile at Amherst in the 'nineties, Napoleon Marshall the 440 at Harvard in 1895, and Spencer Dickerson of Chicago in 1896, there were few noteworthy track and field athletes in the colleges in those days. The first Negro track and field entrant in the modern Olympics was George Poage of Milwaukee and Wisconsin University in 1904. Poage was a remarkable hurdler and quarter-miler. He held a college record of 49 seconds for the 440, 25 seconds for the low hurdles, and in the St. Louis Olympics forced his competitor, Hillman, to new Olympic records in the 400 meter flat and 400 meter hurdle races. About the same time, in the East, that inimitable runner, John B. Taylor of the University of Pennsylvania, was winning inter-collegiate 440 yard championships. At the same institution Howard Smith and Dewey Rogers were winning races. Ted Cable of Harvard with the weights, and the great Howard Drew at the sprints and broad jump, were among the luminaries in the first decade of the century.

Then came that long almost unbroken string of broad jumpers, beginning with Sol Butler of Dubuque in 1920, and continuing down through the present. Later as Negro boys got the chance to practice over the hurdles, in high jumping, pole-vaulting, and in weight throwing, they eclipsed many American and some world records.

Only in the distance records have Negro boys been poorly represented. When one recalled the performances of Earl Johnson of the Thomson Steel Works Athletic Club, Augustus Moore of St. Bonaventure College, and James T. Smith of Indiana, he had about exhausted the great distance runners among Negroes.

69

John B. Taylor.   In addition to the work of Negro sprinters a big contribution to running fame has been through the medium of

the 440 yards or 400 meters runs.   The first great quarter-milers of the race were the two runners mentioned earlier in this chapter, John B. Taylor of Pennsylvania and George Poage of Wisconsin.   Taylor is credited with a mark of 48.8 seconds. He was the inter-collegiate champion quarter-miler in 1904, 1907 and 1908.   He was America's hope in the Olympic games in London in 1908, but a squabble in a re-run race and interference by a spectator may have accounted for his failure to show his ability in the games of that year.

JOHN B. TAYLOR,
University of Pennsylvania, 1906–08

Binga Dismond.   Then in 1915, that wonder-runner, Binga Dismond of the University of Chicago, raced the double-furlong distance to equal the world record made by that peerless runner, Ted Meredith.   This record of 47.4 seconds was never applied for, but the observers of that race describe Binga as turning his head to see his outdistanced competitor and letting up when a new world record might have been his.   Dismond, now a physician in New York City, started his running career in the games held at Howard University under the auspices of the old Inter-Scholastic Athletic Association. There it was that he proved to himself that he had record-making possibilities.

Champions in the Quarter-Mile. After the First World War, quarter-milers began to appear with more regularity. William Hastie of Amherst, Charles West of Washington and Jefferson, Orthel Roberts of Iowa, Richard Moody of Marquette, Ivan Johnson of California, Harold Jewell of Northeastern, and Cecil Cooke of Syracuse made reputations in this event. Cooke became inter-collegiate champion of the Inter-Collegiate Association of Amateur Athletes of America and had a best mark of 48.8 seconds in 1926. Robert Webb of Drake with a record of 49.4 seconds, Herman Carr of Marquette with 48.2 seconds, Theodore Graham of Syracuse with 48.4 seconds, William Exum of Wisconsin with a mark of 49.1 and Ricardo Ruiz with 49.8 seconds were all good performers during those years. Out of the West came "Blazing Ben Eastman" who set a mark in 1932 of 46.4 seconds that for many years defied the world for the 440 yards run.

Archie Williams and Luvalle. In June, 1936, in Chicago, however, another wonder runner of the age, a Negro boy, Archie Williams, cracked the record for the metric counterpart of the 440 by hanging up a world record of 46.1 seconds for the 400 meters race. Along with Williams, also from the West, Jimmy Luvalle, who once attended the Garnet-Patterson school in Washington, D. C., attracted the attention of the sports loving world by consistently winning over the 400 meter distance, and when losing, failing only before his fellow-countryman, Williams. Luvalle was the only Phi Beta Kappa man on the Olympic Team. In the Olympic Games in Berlin in 1936, Archie was the lad who proved the best man in the world at his distance. In the same race, Luvalle registered the third best in the world. Twice during his stay at the University of California at Los Angeles James E. Luvalle came East in 1933 and in 1935 and carried back the 400 meters championship of the I.C.A.A.A.A. as well as several quarter-mile races garnered during his stay on the Atlantic coast.

John Woodruff. Hardly had the world begun to praise these western wonder-runners than from Pittsburgh a tall lanky long-striding athlete by the name of John Woodruff came to the fore. Although his specialty was probably the 880, yet Woodruff in 1937 won the I.C.A.A.A.A. championship 440 yards race in 47 seconds flat.

In colored college spheres quarter-milers have been coming fast. When track and field athletics develop to the place that these events should hold with other sports in these colleges, and when the tracks are more scientifically constructed and more accurately measured, there will be found many boys who will be able to duplicate the feats of Dismond, Williams, Luvalle, Woodruff and others. During the Penn Relay games, where more Negro boys from the colleges in the South are showing up from year to year, the relay teams are holding their own with the best quartets of quarter-milers in the East.

Jimmy Herbert. Before entering the half-mile division, we must refer to another sterling athlete who held a world record, James Herbert, a student of New York University who ran the premier indoor distance, 600 yards, in the world record time of 1 minute, 11 seconds. During the 1938 indoor season, Herbert was unable to win at the 600 yards distance largely because he trained for and was running anchor on his school's champion indoor relay team.

Phillip Edwards. The Negro runner has made enviable marks in the 880 run. Back in 1891, that pioneer half-miler, Jackson of Amherst, established a college record of 2 minutes, 5.4 seconds. Today the record for the 880 yards is 1 minute, 49.6 seconds. Among the earlier mid-distance runners there were Howard Smith at Pennsylvania, Cecil Lewis at Chicago, and Randolph Granger at Dartmouth. One of the best half-milers in the game was Phillip Edwards of New York University and of Canada. Until "Long" John Woodruff appeared in 1937, Phillip Edwards held the I.C.A.A.A.A. half-mile record of 1 minute 52.2 seconds. Edwards was always a strong contender representing Great Britain in the Olympic

"Jimmy" Herbert, New York University

Games. In the 1936 Games in Berlin, Edwards ran third in the 800 meters.

John Woodruff proved to be the find of the season in the 1935 pre-Olympic year. With a powerful and over-long stride, John would often have to run around a wide field of competitors to pull through the stretch to victory. There was probably no one in the world who could defeat Woodruff at this distance if given an even break at the start, unless it was Borican. Woodruff climaxed his sophomore college year by going to Berlin and, in the presence of Headmaster Hitler, defeating the best middle distance runners of the entire world in the 1936 Olympics. Another good half-miler was J. Arthur Wieseger of Minnesota who held the Minnesota record of 1 minute 56.8 seconds.

John Borican. In the midst of these events another middle distance runner was playing havoc with the indoor records in the 1,000 yards. Most significant is the fact that this athlete, John Borican, a graduate of Virginia State College at Petersburg, was one of the few runners to come out of the Colored Inter-Collegiate Athletic Association to crack a world record. Twice that season Borican defeated at the 1,000 yards race the king of all middle distance runners of that day, Glenn Cunningham. In his last race, he ran the distance in 2 minutes 8 seconds, which was better than the accepted outdoor time of 2 minutes 9.7 seconds by Elroy Robinson of Fresno, California, and the indoor record of 2 minutes 10.1 seconds by Cunningham. John Borican was a capable performer in all of the pentathlon events and held the American record in this feature.

Smith of Indiana. The race had never had an outstanding miler. There had been fewer good two-milers. James T. Smith of Indiana, although in a college that had contemporaneously three other stars, put a 4 minute 11 seconds mile to his credit. Smith was the fastest member of the four-mile quartet that set a new American record at the Penn Relays on April 23, 1937. The team consisted of M. Truitt, J. Smith, T. Deckard and D. Lash. The record made was 17 minutes 21.7 seconds. In that race Smith completely lapped his competitor in his mile lap, and 20,000 people stood and waved him on to his share of a record that loomed up. Augustus Moore of St. Bonaventure and the University of Pittsburgh was a fairly good miler. He was a better cross-country runner. His best time was a 4 minute 23 seconds mile. Dan Ferguson of Ohio State and Andrew Harvey of Temple were good milers. James Smith, Ferguson and Harvey have performed capably at the two mile distance. Smith had a mark of 9 minutes 10 seconds for this distance. He was co-captain of his University track team in his senior year.

Earl Johnson. Negro distance athletes have done more remarkably in the cross-country events. The most renowned distance runner of this group was R. Earl Johnson. Johnson was national five-miler for 1921, 1922, and 1923. He was a member of S. W. Thomson Steel Works Athletic Association near Pittsburgh. His best five-mile time was 25 minutes 23 seconds. Johnson was national senior cross-country champion in 1921. Johnson also captured the national ten-mile title in 1924. In the distances Gus Moore should be nominated second only to that splendid runner, Johnson. As a member of the Brooklyn Harriers Athletic Association, Moore won the national ten mile A.A.U. championship in 1930. For 1928 and 1929, "Gus" was the national cross-country champion in the senior cross-country events. Dr. Montague Cobb was a good long distance man when at Amherst. In 1930, John Enoch of Colgate captained the cross-country team. There were a few other athletes here and there who won places in the longer distance races but none had as yet gone to the record heights. One of the best prospects looming on the horizon was the young James Monroe High School star of New York, Frank Dixon. During the 1938 season he won two cross-country races from a field representing the pick of the high schools in the greater New York area. On October 15, 1938, Frank won the two and one-half mile cross-country race in which 300 runners followed him across the tape. A week before, Dixon had won a race over the same distance in the good school-boy time of 12 minutes 10 seconds.

Phenomenal Leapers. Negro jumpers have been the wonder athletes of the world. In every year from 1920 to 1937, Negro athletes have monopolized the records and championships in the broad jump. With the exception of victories by Bates of the Meadow-Brook Club in Philadelphia in 1930 and 1931 and E. B. Hamm of Georgia Technical College in 1928, the colored lads earned most of the championships after 1920. Hamm reached a record jump, for him, of 25 feet 3 inches. Four non-white athletes reached the 26 foot mark and beyond. Sol Butler's leap in 1920 was 24 feet 8 inches. Later Negro boys extended the mark to that inconceivable measurement of 26 feet 8¼ inches, set by the famous Jesse Owens in 1935. The first human to reach the 25 foot spot in the jump pit was Edward O. Gourdin of Harvard University. Just when it was being predicted that human powers had reached a limit in the long jump, Ned Gourdin astounded the world with his leap of 25 feet 3 inches in July, 1921.

De Hart Hubbard a Champion. Shortly after, that doughty, bronzed lad of Michigan, De Hart Hubbard, became the cynosure of sport's eyes around the Mid-West. Year after year, beginning with 1921, the radio crackled with the thrilling descriptions of the running and jumping of the lad from Michigan in the Big Ten and other meets. Hubbard was national title holder in this event from 1922 to 1927 inclusive. Patenting his style after the world record holder Gourdin, Hubbard achieved the record in 1925 by leaping 25 feet 4⅜ inches, and in 1927 the record books credit him with 25 feet 8¾ inches. In 1924 Hubbard took Olympic honors in this event.

Ed Gordon. After Hubbard, the white boy from Georgia, Hamm, broke the Negro ranks in 1928, but in the following year Edward Gordon of Iowa University jumped 24 feet 4¼ inches to win the national title. In 1932, after two years of winning by Bates, Gordon jumped 25 feet 3⅜ inches to regain the national honor, and in the Olympics of that year Gordon won with 25 feet ¾ inch.

Peerless Jesse Owens. At the East Technical High School of Cleveland, a smooth running, smiling lad, Jesse Owens, yet in his senior year in 1933, won the senior National A.A.U. championship with a jump of 24 feet 6⅜ inches. The next year found him in Ohio State University. His climb to an undying fame began. He won the national title again as a representative of Ohio State by registering 25 feet ⅞ inch. May 24–25, 1935, will never pass from memory of lovers of the games of the track and field when this peer of sprinters and broad jumpers for all time established the most sensational achievement of breaking three world records and equalling a fourth. On one of these days, Jesse Owens jumped 26 feet 8¼ inches, a mark that many believed would hold a long time. Going into the 1936 Olympics, Owens smashed the Olympic running broad jump record by leaping 26 feet 5 5/16 inches.

Kermit King and Bill Lacefield. With Owens out of the amateur setting, another Negro, Kermit King of the Pittsburg, Kansas, Teachers College, took over the task of maintaining supremacy for Negro jumpers, and won national A.A.U. honors with a record jump of 25 feet 1½ inches. In 1938, another Negro kept up the procession. That time from out of the West, William Lacefield of the University of California at Los Angeles won the national A.A.U. championship in the running broad jump.

There were many excellent broad jumpers beyond this list of national meet winners, but have we or can we dwell on all of the accepted or recorded great jumps attributed to some of these performers? Among some of the performers whose jumps were as good as some we have registered, were those of three great athletes, William Watson and Willis Ward of Michigan, and Edward Brooks of Chicago. Some of the other good broad jumpers were Ted Smith of Syracuse, James Clark of Indiana, Johnson and Pollard of North Dakota, and Joe Batiste of Tucson High.

Eulace Peacock. In 1935, a great Negro athlete, Eulace Peacock of Temple University and the Shore Athletic Club, beat the redoubtable Jesse at Owens' specialty, the broad jump. Eulace is one of the few men in the world to go over 26 feet, and in defeating Owens in 1935, he scored 26 feet 3 inches for his feat. His record for the Amateur Athletic Union championship that year was 26 feet, 3 inches. The success of the Negro in the broad jump occasioned no small amount of bewilderment among the observers and students of athletic events.

A few decades ago, in the college meets, high jumps at less than six feet were won. Occasionally some un-orthodox jumper would top the bar at a few inches higher. After the development of the various lay-out styles and the advent of colored jumpers the height of six and a half feet was reached. In 1932, Spitz of New York, Orsdel of California and a colored high school boy, Cornelius Johnson out on the Pacific Coast, all jumped 6 feet 6⅝ inches for the Amateur Athletic Union record for that year.

High Jump Stars. In 1939, three Negroes were credited with having leaped over a bar at 6 feet 9¾ inches, to which height no white man had then reached. At Randall's Island, on the eve of the embarkation for the German Olympics, Cornelius Johnson and David Albritton went over the bar at 6 feet 9¾ inches for a world's record. After that time Melvin Walker reached this mark in the Butler Relays in Indianapolis on March 20, 1937. Melvin and David were of Ohio State University.

Among Negroes who achieved athletic fame in this event, Edward Burke of Marquette was national indoor champion with a record indoor jump from wood of 6 feet 9½ inches. Albert Threadgill of Temple, another excellent jumper in the East, claimed an indoor record of 6 feet 7¾ inches from a wooden floor without the use of spikes. Gilbert Cruter of Colorado University had a mark of 6 feet 8¾ inches to his reputation. William Watson and Willis Ward of Michigan went well over 6 feet. Joe Batiste of Tucson High, Perry Stanley Simmons of Wayne, Pollard of North Dakota, Lacey of Loyola, Allen Wesley of Michigan were all beyond 6 feet. From a Negro institution, Lloyd Thompson of Xavier College of New Orleans had jumped 6 feet 7¼ inches. From 1932 to 1939 but one white man had been able even to tie with Negroes for the national Amateur Athletic Union annual title event of leaping over the bar. Johnson, Melvin Walker, and Albritton had monopolized the honors.

CAPTAIN WILLIAM WATSON OF MICHIGAN'S TRACK TEAM

Weight Throwing.   As late as 1939 only one Negro claimed a
national Amateur Athletic Union championship in weight throwing.
Thomas Anderson, representing the St. Christopher Club of New York
in 1919, threw the 56 pound weight 30 feet and 11¾ inches to win
the junior A.A.U. championship.   In 1938, Lilburn D. Williams
of Xavier University won the junior national A.A.U. 16 pound
shot-putting championship with a put of 48 feet 11¼ inches which
mark was exceeded by Strode of the University of California at
Los Angeles, and William Watson of Michigan.   Woodrow Strode
in 1938 put the lead ball 51 feet 6 inches.   In 1921 John Shelburne won the Inter-Collegiate Amateur Association of Athletes
of America championship with 45 feet 3½ inches.   Watson had
hurled the lead sphere 54 feet 1¾ inches.   As excellent as this
mark was it was still short of the world record of 57 feet 1 inch by
that southern giant, Jack Torrance.   Watson during the spring, 1939,
threw the discus 161 feet 4 inches.   Charley Jones of New York
University was the first Easterner, white or colored, to better 50
feet with the shot.

Theodore Cable.   The first colored boy to win an inter-collegiate
weight championship was Ted Cable of Indianapolis in 1912 and
1913.   He won the hammer throw with distance marks of 162 feet
4½ inches, and 156 feet.   The world record today is 193 feet 7½
inches.   In his day he was highly lauded by the press and honored
by Harvard.

The Javelin and Discus.   Although not reaching so high a
place in the annals of sport yet many of our throwing athletes performed meritoriously in several field events.   Back in 1911, Pinkett
of Amherst was a capable weight thrower.   Charles Drew was
also a fair shot-putter of note at Amherst.   Fred Slater of Iowa
was an outstanding weight putter in his day at Iowa.   Among other
good shot-putters were Howard of Drake, Hansbary of Oberlin,
and Marshall of Williams.   In the javelin throw, G. Murdock
Wharton of Dartmouth hurled the shaft over 180 feet, Peacock
181 feet, and David Myers of New York University put the
javelin 206 feet 9 inches.   In 1932 George Williams of Hampton

FONVILLE, MICHIGAN, WORLD RECORD HOLDER, SHOT PUT

Institute won the javelin throw at the Penn Relay Games with a throw of 205 feet 2⅜ in., and threw the spear 215 feet in the N.C.A.A. championships.

Discus throwers have been scarce among Negroes. Woodrow Strode of the University of California at Los Angeles in 1938 sent the discus 161 feet 10 inches. Howard of Drake and Brooks of Michigan were good performers. Here the record is 180 feet 2¾ inches, set by Bob Fitch of the United States in 1946. Bill Watson of Michigan bettered 161 feet, Booker Brooks registered 158 feet, Claude Walton had 151 feet 8¼ inches to his credit, Archie Harris of Indiana was the best shot-putter and discus thrower at his institution. He won the 1941 A.A.U. Championship with a throw of 167 feet 9½ inches and holds the N.C.A.A. record of 174 feet 8¾ inches.

Pole Vaulters. Pole vaulting requires excellent equipment, good poles, well built approaches and pits and standards. These things for many years were possible in only the best colleges. Colored pole vaulters were only mediocre athletes. Later, however, some Negro boys showed promise. At the Penn Relay games in 1936 Howard Jones of Virginia Union went over the bar at 13 feet 3 inches. Another lad, Ulysses Wharton of Dartmouth consistently did over 13 feet and reached 13 feet 3 inches.

Hurdlers. Negro hurdlers were scarce, but they were good. Jesse Owens over the 220 yard hurdles had the world record of 22.6 seconds. Owens did not possess the finished form of a Brookins, or any of the noted low hurdlers, but his great speed and ability to take the hurdle in stride made him invincible. For three years, Alexander L. Jackson represented Harvard over the sticks during 1912, '13, and '14, and won many points for the Crimson. One of the fine Negro hurdlers over the 400 meter distance was Eugene Beatty, formerly of Michigan Normal. Had he not fallen in the last of the hurdle races prior to the 1932 Olympics he probably would have scored in that Olympic event. John Brooks of Chicago was good. Track captain Ben Franklin, of

Courtesy of " Flash "

EDWARD SMITH, UNIVERSITY OF WISCONSIN STAR HURDLER, AND
CO-HOLDER OF THREE WORLD'S RECORDS.

In February, 1939, Smith won the 40 yard high hurdle race in 5.2 seconds, equalling the accepted world's record on a dirt track. Smith has run the 120 yard hurdles in close to 14 seconds. Wisconsin increased its reputation for liberal democracy by refusing to engage in track competition with the University of Missouri when that university drew the color line on Smith.

Boston University, was one of the best hurdlers in New England. Ed Smith was a fine hurdler at Wisconsin.

Fritz Pollard, an Olympic Star. A great hurdler of the '30's was Fritz Pollard, son of the illustrious athlete of a generation ago. The son was considered the greatest all-round athlete that North Dakota had ever had. Pollard went in to the Olympics in 1936 with the noted Forrest Towns, who held the world's record. In Berlin, Pollard was the third best in the world. He ran the high hurdle race in the fine time of 14.1 seconds.

The Negro athlete De Hart Hubbard also distinguished himself in the running hop, step and jump event, the championship of which he won in 1922 and 1923. This is not an orthodox event.

Pentathlon Winners. The five-event athletic competition, known as the pentathlon, found several of our Negro athletes leading all of the contenders in America. In 1921 and 1922 Ned Gourdin, of Harvard University, the first athlete to jump over 25 feet, won the national pentathlon championship. In 1933 and 1934 Eulace Peacock of the Shore Athletic Club annexed the championship in this event. The 1938 athletic almanac credits to John Borican the American record with a total of 3,304 points and the championship of 1938.

Triple Champions. Among the noteworthy incidents of Negro participation in track and field were the triple and succession wins during college competition. Bill Watson of Michigan, captain of the track team, competing in Big Ten games for the last time, set three records. Not only did Watson smash the 23-year old discus throw mark, but he set records in points—48—the highest number scored in Big Ten competition and became the first athlete in the history of the Conference to win three events in each of three years.

Watson's series of wins in one year was eclipsed only by Jesse Owens in 1935, when he broke three world's records and equalled another. Owens however had a record of seven wins in his competition in the Big Ten. Watson scored nine first places in three years, winning the same events in 1937, 1938 and 1939.

"Long" John Woodruff. In the east at the I.C.A.A.A.A. games, John Woodruff, in 1939 at Randall's Island, won the 440 and 880 yards races for the third consecutive year. Only once before, in 1884, had this happened. For the third time Woodruff won

the 440 in 47 seconds, the record that Carr set in 1932. In these same games, Woodruff went on to win the 880 in the I.C.A.A.A.A. record time of 1:51.2, which mark displaced the old record of 1:51.9, set by Ben E. Eastman of Stanford in 1932.

Woodruff retired from college as one of the great runners of all time. Only twice after his unorthodox striding brought him fame on the track did Long John meet defeat. In 1936 he was beaten by Charlie Beetham in the National A.A.U. 880-

DAVE ALBRITTON   JOHN WOODRUFF

yard race.　Once afterwards he essayed to run the mile, but finished in the ruck.　He was clocked in a half mile race at Dallas, Texas, in 1:47.8, but measurement of the track after the race showed it to be two feet short.　The world's record of Elroy Robinson, established at Randall's Island in 1937, is 1:49.6.　Clearly that part of a stride of Woodruff's was not more than 2 seconds long which means John completed the distance in at least 1:48, a good second and a half better than any runner had ever done.

Eddie Dugger.　Eddie Dugger at Tufts College won highest praise in several New England track seasons.　A sophomore, this well built athlete led Tuft's teams to victory seven consecutive times in the 1939 outdoor season.　He was excelled in the sprints only by the track sensation of Brown University, Kenneth Clapp.　He ran the 100 and 220-yard dashes in record time for the New England Inter-Collegiates, did better than 14.8 seconds over the high, and forced Kenneth Clapp to a new record of 23.8 seconds in the 220 hurdles.

Later Achievements in Track and Field.　After 1939 colored track and field athletes extended their domain in many branches of sports.　In the pole vault and the distance runs they did not make much headway although on scholastic levels some brilliant prospects were in the making.　In the death of John Borican was lost one of the most versatile and great middle distance runners of all time.　Beginning his college work at Virginia State and continuing at Columbia University, Borican was fast over the hurdles and a master at distances from the 600 to the mile.　He was also a pentathlon winner for 1938, 1939, and 1941, and a decathlon victor in 1941.　His pentathlon performance of 3,304 points is still an American record.　John Borican died at his home in Bridgeton, New Jersey on January 4, 1947.

Following the 1936 Olympics when Jesse Owens and fellow Americans shocked the late and unlamented Hitler, colored track and field athletes have incited the envy of the world.　In the hurdles, Harrison Dillard of Baldwin-Wallace College surprised the world

HARRISON DILLARD OF BALDWIN–WALLACE COLLEGE, Winner 100 Meter
Dash, 1948 Olympics; Holder, World High Hurdle Record

with his record-making performances. He held the unofficial world record in the 220 yard low hurdles, and was an unbeatable hurdler over the high sticks until on the occasion of the Olympic tryouts he essayed to qualify for both the 100 yards and the 120 hurdles in a close series of heats. Before this loss, Dillard had won 82 straight victories, 20 more than any other American had done previously. Dillard compensated for his failure to represent America in the hurdle event by astounding the world with the premier victory in the 100 meter sprint event in the 1948 London Olympics.

Elmore Harris, formerly of Morgan State College and the Shore A.C. of New Jersey, was a capable hurdler as well as a sterling quarter miler. Edward Dugger formerly of Tufts College was a consistent winner over the sticks until the coming of Dillard. One of the greatest 440 men in the world in the person of Herbert McKenley came to the United States from Jamaica. Running under the colors of Boston College and the University of Illinois, he became a consistent winner in distances between 220 and 440. It was claimed that he had a world's record of 46.3 seconds. He had lowered the accepted world mark of 46.4 seconds on two occasions, once in 1946 and again in 1947. The International Amateur Athletic Association has accredited him with a record af 29 seconds for the 300 yards sprint. In the great galaxy of middle distance runners of that day were John Woodruff, James Herbert, Robert Kelly of Illinois, Lewis Smith of Virginia-Union and Prairie View, Roscoe Brown of Lincoln University, Stan and Maurice Callendar and Reginald Pearman of New York University. Elmore Harris was almost unbeatable in the 440, even by the great McKenley, until he gave up track to become a professional football player.

As out of a blue sky came Mal Whitfield of Ohio State who won both the 400 and 800 meter runs to qualify for the Olympics where he won the 400 from the best runners of the world and lost to Wint, a great colored middle distance runner from Great Britain, in the 800 meter race.

Champion broad jumpers, as sprinters, still come from the Negro group. Jesse Owens' leap is still the world's best, but after Jesse came William Lacefield of Los Angeles, Herbert Douglass of Pittsburgh, William Steele of San Diego College, Barney Ewell, Eulace Peacock, Fred Johnson of Michigan State and a host of others who jumped well enough to win honors in most national meets. Steele also jumped over 26 feet. He did that in a trial for the Olympics and then went on to win the world's title in the 1948 Olympics.

CHARLES FONVILLE, UNIVERSITY OF MICHIGAN, WORLD RECORD HOLDER
IN THE SHOT PUT 1948

Negro high jumpers are still with the winners. Dave Albritton and Joshua Williamson became perennial place winners after 1936. Since the Olympic winning feat of Cornelius Johnson in 1936 have appeared Ed Burke, Lloyd Thompson, Mel Walker, Adam Berry, Don Barksdale, Paul Robeson Jr. and others who won many championships during their careers. Cornelius Johnson, like Borican, died in the prime of life.

For the first time in track and field competition a colored athlete has established a world record in shot putting. Charley Fonville representing the University of Michigan track team at 20 years of age and weighing only 194 pounds, put the shot 58 feet and $\frac{1}{4}$ inch for a new world record. This amazing feat accomplished in the spring of 1948 eclipsed the American record of Al Blozis of Georgetown whose best was 56 feet and $\frac{1}{2}$ inch, and the world record of Jack Torrance of Louisiana State of 57 feet, 1 inch. Blozis and Torrance were truly giants weighing over 250 pounds each. Like Dillard, Fonville was to be disappointed in trying out for the Olympics. A strained back prevented him from making the mark necessary to qualify.

A few of Negro athletes earned top rating in some other events. Don Barksdale, besides being a great high jumper and a basketball star, was also probably one of the best Hop-Step and Jump contenders in America and would undoubtedly have qualified for the Olympics in this event had he not been top man in basketball. Archie Harris in 1941 was a great discus hurler, and Frank Dixon in 1943 won the national indoor A.A.U. mile title.

One of the controversial issues in track and field of the decade, was the national A.A.U. outdoor championships held in San Antonio, Texas, in 1946. Interest centered around these games because they were held in the South. A national argument arose as to whether colored boys should compete in that section of the Nation where tradition maintained a complete Jim Crow pattern of life. Some of the best athletes, notably of the Pioneer Club of New York, refused to go. The great majority, however, went. Fortunately, a most hospitable atmosphere obtained in San Antonio, except that hotel accommodations were not available. Every effort

HERBERT MCKENLEY, 1949, 440 YARD WORLD RECORD HOLDER

was made to insure fair play and sportsmanship. At least 36 colored athletes competed.

The senior colored contestants in the San Antonio championships won seven first places, four seconds, six thirds, three fourth places and two fifths. In the junior events, 30 points were received by five colored athletes. The seven first places were won by: Dillard, who took both hurdles in 14.2 seconds and 23.3 seconds; Billy Mathis, the 100 meters in 10.7 seconds; Barney Ewell, the 200 meters in 21.2 seconds; Willie Steele, the broad jump with 24 feet; Dave Albritton, the high jump with 6 feet, 6 7/8 inches; and Elmore Harris, the 400 meters in 46.3 seconds.

The first indoor track meet open to all registered amateurs regardless of race was held in the new spacious National Guard building in Washington, D. C. on January 3, 1947. Nearly 5,000 spectators saw colored and white boys compete across race lines for the first time in the first annual meet of the Washington Evening Star, which might herald the opening of a new day in sport in the Nation's Capital and points south.

This brief recital of some of the notable work done by Negro boys in competition with the best athletes of the world is not only a tribute to athletic ability but to lack of inferiority feeling and to the possession of courage and other worth-while traits of character. Often training alone, practicing under great difficulties, frequently depressed, yet they persevered until they reached their goals. Their achievements marked for them and for their race the possession of characteristics of sportsmanship, courage and ability second to those of no other people. By their exhibitions these boys wrested good will from millions of persons who formerly were at least indifferent to the race. They created for Negroes a healthier and more favorable environment by reason of the appeal they made to the fair-minded, sports-loving citizens of America and the world on a hundred fields.

CHAPTER VI

Football and Its Heroes of Yore

From Past to Present. Football in some form has been played for many ages. Several centuries before the coming of Christ, the Spartans of Greece played a game called "Harpaston" which involved kicking a ball. Early in the 10th century football came to England. At first, kicking alone was allowed, and a goal was simply an end boundary of a field. Goal posts originated during that century. So popular a pastime did football prove to be that it caused Englishmen to forego much practice at archery. Since archery was so vital an arm of offense and defense in warfare, King Henry II of England (1154–1189) abolished football. This ban endured for 400 years. Then James I of England lifted the ban against football.

Until 1823 football was a kicking game only. In that year one William Webb Ellis deliberately, or "pulling a boner," picked the ball up and ran with it. Someone tackled him and the sportswriters had something new. Carved on a stone at Rugby College is an inscription that commemorates the exploit of William Webb Ellis, "who with a fine disregard for the rules first took the ball in his arms and ran with it." However, it was not until 1860 that some of the professional teams experimented with this play originated by Ellis. The battle was on between the soccer and the Rugby boys.

In the United States football did not amount to much of a game until about 1868 when Princeton and Rutgers adopted a set of rules for a kicking game on a large field, with 25 players on a team, and goal posts 20 feet apart. The first inter-collegiate game took place between these teams in 1869 at Brunswick, New Jersey. Columbia had a team in 1870, Yale in 1872, Michigan and Cornell in 1873 and Harvard in 1874.

97

Harvard and Yale designated "Rugby" rules for their game in 1875. About this time Yale, Rutgers, Columbia and Harvard organized the American Intercollegiate Football Association with Rugby rules modified to permit the scoring of a field goal to count for more than four touchdowns.

The player of the modern game hardly realizes the travail of football in its years of development during the past century. Until 1882 there was no such thing as a distance requirement in a definite number of tries or downs. A team gave up the ball only when it had scored, lost the ball, or kicked it. In 1882 the rules were changed to require a team to gain five or lose ten yards in three consecutive downs or give up the ball. The number of players was reduced from 25 men to 15, and to 11 men on a side. Safeties, touchdowns, goals after a touchdown and field goals had various values until 1909 when the field goal was reduced from 5 to 3 points as a last change.

In 1905, the country was aroused by the death toll and crippling injuries occasioned by football. Following the season in 1905, the solons met and revised the rules to make a safer game. These rules abolished the old guards-back and tandem plays, prohibited hurdling, introduced a forward pass and other innovations. In 1912 the yardage to be gained was ten yards in four tries or downs, thus superseding the five yards in three downs play of earlier days. Most of the changes since then have been to emphasize open play, make wider appeal to spectators, speed up the game, and impose safeguards against health or accident hazards.

Biddle Plays Livingstone, the First Game. A few Negroes were playing football on white college teams as early as 1890. About the same time colored boys in the Negro schools of the South were beginning to kick the ball around. Biddle University and Livingstone College in North Carolina are said to have played the first Negro college game on Thanksgiving Day, November, 1892. The game was won by Biddle, now Johnson C. Smith, by a score of 4 to 0. Six of the men who played on the Biddle team were still living in 1939, namely, the Rev. L. B. Ellerson, D. D., of Newark, New Jersey;

HOWARD UNIVERSITY FOOTBALL TEAM, 1893, WITH PROF. C. C. COOK
(THIRD FROM LEFT) AS COACH

HOWARD UNIVERSITY FOOTBALL TEAM, 1894

J. H. Hutton, M. D., Omaha, Nebraska; S. M. Plair, Phar. D.,
Rock Hill, South Carolina; Professor C. H. Shute, D. D., Johnson
C. Smith University; Rev. G. E. Caesar, Little Rock, Arkansas; and
W. L. Metz, A. M., D. D., of Edisto Island, South Carolina. Of
the Livingstone players, only W. J. Trent, president of Livingstone
College, Salisbury, North Carolina, still lives. The umpire of that
famous game was the late Mr. Murphy, white, a law student of the
University of North Carolina, who later became a legislator in that
state's assembly. A building at the Agricultural and Technical
College of Greensboro bears his name.

Howard and Lincoln, Tuskegee and Atlanta University began
to play in 1894. Since that time this game has become the great
fall sport of Negro colleges. In the first two decades the spotlight
was on the Lincoln-Howard and Shaw-Union games. During this
period, there was much non-conference activity in football in the
South, Southwest, and Midwest. Great teams and spectacular
players were developed at Tuskegee, Morehouse, Fisk, Atlanta,
Meharry, Talladega, Knoxville, West Virginia State and
Wilberforce.

Very few football games were played during a season in the
younger days of football. As late as 1912 Lincoln University in
Pennsylvania played only three games, one with Hampton, a club
team, and one with Howard. Hampton played Howard, Lincoln
and Shaw and two club teams. West Virginia State played Kentucky State at Louisville, Wilberforce University, and a club team
that season. Tuskegee played Fisk, Talladega, Jackson College
and Atlanta Baptist College (Morehouse). Livingstone College
played six games in 1911. Today, colleges play seven to nine
games each season.

William H. Lewis and Sherman Jackson. Negro football
players on white teams appeared first on the liberal college teams
of New England. The two gridiron athletes who claimed the
attention of earliest writers were William H. Lewis and W. T. S.
Jackson, who were team mates on the Amherst College elevens of
1890 and 1891. Since those first days, many colored boys have

CHARLES DREW, CAPT. OF AMHERST TRACK TEAM

thrilled the hearts of thousands at Eastern and Western college games.

At Amherst, following Lewis and Jackson, came Edward Gray in 1908, who merited a selection on one of Walter Camp's third honor teams for 1908. Around 1920 George Gilmer and Elvin H. Wanzo earned the Amherst letter. From 1923 to 1925, Charlie Drew of Arlington, Virginia, stood out as the best all-around athlete at Amherst. He not only played stellar football and basketball but was elected captain of the track team.

Harvard University has had two eminent football players of the Negro group. The Boston *Globe* of November 21, 1929, in a feature article referred to Lewis thus, "Perhaps the first great Harvard center was William H. Lewis, the colored star of the 1892 and '93 teams. He was so good that in 1900 he was chosen by Walter Camp as All-Time All-America center. Lewis weighed around 175 pounds in the days when a center was supposed to tip the scales at 200. He made up for this, however, with his head work and fighting spirit. Lewis was a wizard at fathoming plays and was a deadly tackler."

Another player who made varsity in football at Harvard was Clarence Matthews, playing end. Matthews was a greater baseball player, but played a sterling game on the gridiron winning his letter in 1904. Howard Lee played tackle at Harvard in 1896.

Tufts College has had some famous colored football players. Among these players were Edward Morrison and William F. Brown in 1914, '15, and '16; Otis E. Galloway in '18, '19, '20, and '23; and C. R. Taylor in '25 and '26.

Far up in Vermont at the University, Victor Crawford in '23 and '24, and Harry Payne in '24, won football letters. At Williams College, George M. Chadwell at end, in '97, '98, and '99, and Ernest Marshall at tackle in 1906 and 1907 were the early players at the old line college. In later years, Boston University gave opportunity for prominence in football to Jesse Chase in 1934, Moreland Forte as end in 1935–1936, Chester Smith and Roland Bernard in 1938. A Boston University coach expressed the opinion that Chester Smith would have been All-American caliber had he played on a

Frederick (Fritz) Pollard, All-American, 1916

more prominent team. At Boston College, Lou Montgomery was marked an ace football star at his college. Montgomery was the backbone of 1939 season's Boston College team.

Fritz Pollard. Brown University's outstanding contribution to football was Fritz Pollard. No more brilliant comet ever streaked across a turfed gridiron than the flashy Fritz. He was nominated All-American by Walter Camp on the 1916 aggregation of stellar players. Young Fritz, the son of the All-American Fritz Pollard, mentioned below, proved to be a greater luminary in track, and almost as spectacular in football as was his athletically illustrious sire. Other notable athletes performed for fame and glory about the fields at Brown. In 1912, Hugh Shippley made Eastern scribes take notice of his end play in a great game with Carlisle. J. Mayo Williams and Joseph Carter gained respect of Brunonians during athletic careers from 1918 to 1923, Williams starred in football and the sprints while Carter was better known as New England's champion dash man. Bruce Green, for three years, gained plaudits and letters as a leading half back on the Brown eleven.

The exploits of some of these athletes will bear presentation in detail. The New York *Times*, reporting Brown's defeat of Rutgers 21 to 3 on Saturday, October 27, 1916, said, "In the last half of the game, however, the heavy work began to tell on Rutgers men, and they naturally weakened, after which Murphy went in at half back for Brown, and with Pollard, the colored star of the local team, began an attack which seemed to take the heart out of the Rutgers players.

"With the third period half over, Captain Scarr fumbled after catching a punt on his own thirty-yard line and the ball rolled to Rutgers' two-yard line, where Brown recovered. It took Pollard three trips at the line before he carried the ball over and gave Brown its first score of the game.

"This play seemed to make the Rutgers players lose heart and a short time later Murphy and Pollard worked a fake play, and the colored lad raced across the Rutgers line for his team's second touchdown."

Pollard's great day was the afternoon he beat Yale. The score was, Brown, 21; Yale, 6. It was this game that catapulted him to fame. The New York *Times* on Sunday said:

"Brown's clean-cut victory will stand among football critics as a victory for a superior attack, executed by a superbly coached and perfectly conditioned eleven.

"Individually, Fritz Pollard, a lithe, dusky, six-foot half back, displayed the cleverest all around back field success attained on a Yale field this season. In end running, forward passing, in executing a bewildering criss-cross and delayed pass run, which was Brown's trump card, in running back punts, in side stepping and dodging Yale tacklers in a broken field, Pollard gave a peerless performance. His head-line exhibition brought the crowd of 25,000 spectators up with a roar in the opening minutes of the final playing period.

"Catching a punt hoisted aloft to mid-field by the toe of Harry Legore, Pollard dexterously threw off the Yale ends, started toward the right, drawing the entire pack of the Yale tacklers in that direction, then using a puzzling side step, switched to the left, where he outstripped every Yale pursuer in a desperate sprint for the Yale goal line, sailing across with the second touchdown for the visitors. This heartbreaking performance nailed the lid down on Yale hopes and the Elis were never dangerous thereafter.

"Brown sent a delegation of 1,000, forming the largest cheering section ever seated in the Yale bowl, with the exception of Harvard and Princeton delegations. The Brown crowd had a merry field day, the brass band which accompanied them filling the Yale bowl with the Brown melody."

On the following Saturday, Brown met Harvard, and in one of the leading Sunday papers we read:

"Brown realized the football ambition of years today and defeated Harvard. The score, 21–0, was the most decisive defeat that a Haughton-coached eleven ever received, a fact which should not detract from Haughton's prowess. . . . In view of the fact that Brown has not been defeated this year, it will have an excellent claim to the college championship, and Pollard, its star dusky little half back should be unanimous choice for a position on the mythical All-American eleven.

"Besides scoring two of Brown's touchdowns, Pollard contributed largely to a third, and in addition prevented Harvard from scoring in the one flash of offensive play that the Crimson displayed during the game. From the spectacular point of view the game was all Pollard, but Brown had other excellent backs and a line and ends which outplayed Harvards to a fare-ye-well. . . .

"At times he (Pollard) advanced from five to ten yards with a half a dozen Crimson Jerseys in front, back and at either side of him. The interference for Pollard was excellent, and his five feet six, 155 pounds of dark humanity was speedy and strong enough for the rest. And he never failed to catch a punt in his backfield and run it back. Harvard was penalized 15 yards once for roughing Pollard."

Matthew Bullock and New England Stars. At Dartmouth, the mountain-college at Hanover, three of the great players in the college game rose to stardom. In the years of 1901, 1902, and 1903, Matthew Bullock was a famous end. Why Bullock did not receive All-American selection has never been understood. Bullock was one of the brainiest men of football ability the game has had. Leslie Pollard, 1908, brother of the great "Fritz," and John H. Shelburne, 1919, and 1920, also made great records for themselves and for the race on Dartmouth's teams.

Back in the early times, perhaps the first colored captain of a New England college football team was William H. Craighead, of Massachusetts State, who was elected leader of the 1905 eleven. Craighead's reputation still holds in the annals of his school. Other players who were noted on the State team were William H. Williams, 1905, 1906, Charles Elliott Roberts, Gerald N. Lew in 1911, and Benjamin Hubert in 1912. Colby College can boast of two football players of imposing stature on the gridiron in Edward Niles, '19, '20, and Joseph Washington. Bates College had the two Ray brothers, Charles and Dave, from 1924 to 1926. Charles Ray was captain of the team in 1926.

ED WILLIAMS, NEW YORK UNIVERSITY

The Young Men's Christian Association College at Springfield has for many years had colored athletes on its roll of fame. Leading among the commanding players who have made respected football history are William Kindle, Leonard Gibson, Arthur Wheeler, Joseph Bolden, Mack Greene, Arthur Neilson, and Louis Watson. The earliest footballer at Springfield was Robert Hamlin, who played at tackle in 1904, and who later became a zealous international secretary of the Young Men's Christian Association.

In 1913, '15, and '16, at Syracuse, Joseph Edward Trigg, a graduate of the M Street High School, now Dunbar, of Washington, D. C., started athletic history at this New York college. He became a traditional hero of the gridiron. Not only did Trigg star in football but was the only Negro to earn a place on a college crew. Since then McRae of Boston University rowed on his college crew. Chester Jackson in 1928 came into football prominence at Syracuse. In 1937, 1938, a flash from Syracuse illumined the football horizon in the person of Wilmeth Sidat-Singh. It will be a long time before the glory of his feats will pass from the memory of football fans in the East.

Colgate's Red Raiders seldom had a player worthy of more respect than Ray Vaughn, full-back of '26, '27 and '28. D. B. Crosby was a good end on the 1929 eleven. B. T. Harvey, notable coach at Morehouse, was a fine athlete at Colgate.

New York's Gridiron Warriors. In other colleges in New York State there have been some scintillating colored football stars. At New York University Dave Myers, '28, '29 and '30, and Edward Williams, '36, '37 and '38, upheld the traditions of Negro players on the gridiron. In 1938 Williams was a star of great magnitude on a weak team. In 1920 and 1921, George Calloway played a sterling game on Columbia University's team. The most colorful player who boasted luminous recognition at Columbia was Manuel Riviero, an American Negro of Cuban extraction. Riviero had no difficulty in playing on the gridiron of the Annapolis Service eleven. Accepted for a Cuban, Riviero found no obstacle in meeting the requirements of the snobbish athletic management of the

PAUL ROBESON, RUTGER'S ALL-AMERICAN

United States Naval Academy.   During his years on Coach Little's
team Riviero was always a spotlight player.   "Bill" King, the limelight performer on Long Island's basketball quint, starred at fullback for two seasons.

The Magnificent Robeson.   Rutgers University will always be
known for two important happenings.   Rutgers and Princeton
played the first football game in American history, and it was at
Rutgers that Paul Robeson won four sports letters, and helped to
build one of the greatest teams in the history of his school.   He
also was elected by Camp and the Press to gridiron honors on the
1917 and 1918 All-American.   Of Robeson, the director of athletics
at Rutgers writes:

"Paul Leroy Robeson is regarded as the greatest living All-
American football player.   In the opinion of most people, he, of
all the All-Americans who have been chosen, has gained the greatest
and most merited fame since his graduation.   Undoubtedly, he rates
as one of the five most prominent living Rutgers alumni, and by
many people connected with the University is regarded as the most
distinguished alumnus now living.   He is one of ten men in the
University's history who won four varsity letters as an undergraduate.
He was an outstanding debater while in college and was a member
of Phi Beta Kappa, honorary scholastic society, and of Cap and
Skull, senior honorary society.   Strangely enough, he never was a
member of the University glee club, despite the fact that it is his
magnificent voice that has brought him his greatest fame."

Unfortunately, Rutgers did not have a schedule that called for
contests with many of the more prominent football colleges, hence,
not many metropolitan newspapers carried the spirited comment
other less deserving stars received.   Also the war in Europe was
taking a toll of athletics.   Fewer colleges were playing in 1917 and
fewer still in 1918.   The public at that time was more interested in
the reports of battles won than in games on the gridiron.   It was
during these trying days that Robeson was in the midst of his
athletic career.   Accounts of the game with Fordham and with
Service teams will depict the style of our hero's play.

The New York *Times* of Sunday, October 28, 1917, printed a thrilling picturization of the Fordham-Rutgers game:

"It can hardly be said that one player stood out on the Rutgers' aggregation, unless it was Robeson, the giant Negro, at left end. He was a tower of strength both in the offense and defense, and it was his receiving of forward passes which shattered any hopes of glory which might have arisen in Fordham ranks during the game. Twice the big Rutgers Negro raced down the field after receiving a perfect toss from Whitehill. The first time Robeson was not downed until he had covered thirty-five yards and placed the ball on Fordham's five-yard line. On the other occasion Robeson raced twenty-four yards before being brought to earth again close to the Fordham goal line. Each of these passes gave Rutgers a chance to score, and Rutgers did not throw away the opportunity. . . .

"Both the wings of Rutgers have been taught an excellent offense. Robeson invariably spilled two men and several times three or four were dropped to the ground, even before the play was well under way. The vicious playing of Robeson was costly to Fordham, not only in the outcome of the game but in players, since no less than three Fordham men were sent into the game at different times to take the place of those who had been battered and bruised by Robeson. McGrath, the former Exeter and Yale guard, was the first opposition placed in front of Robeson, but he did not last long. On the first play of the game time was taken out while McGrath recovered from the effects of a bruised jaw and eye."

Among the few sports items in the New York *Times* for 1918, was the description of the game Rutgers played against a Service eleven:

"Whitehill dropped back and took the ball on a long pass from center, while Robeson in the meantime had rushed through the Newport players and was waiting at the goal line. He reached up and grasped the ball as the naval men were upon him, and all went down in a great heap. When the pile of players was unraveled, the ball was about six inches from the goal line, but the officials ruled that the ball had gone over and Rutgers got another touchdown. The score was 14 to 0 in favor of Rutgers."

On Wednesday, November 5, 1918 another Service game occurred with this comment resulting:

"The Scarlet football team which Foster Sanford has developed at Rutgers swept Nielson Field this afternoon with Charley Brickley's Navy transport eleven and ran up a score of 40 to 0 with just as much ease as if it had been having an afternoon practice with the scrub. . . .

"Sanford showed a brand-new play yesterday in the form of a double pass. He sent in the regular quarterback, Baker, for this one play, just to try it out. Baker fell far back of the line to take a long direct pass from center. In the meantime, Paul Robeson, the giant end, raced over behind Baker and received a backward pass from Baker. Standing deep in the backfield, with no one near him, Robeson hurled the ball on a 40-yard forward pass through the air to Captain Feitner, who was down in the Transport territory waiting for it. The play is spectacular and worked perfectly.

"The Navy lads had the ball only a few times during the game. Brickley once made five yards through the line, but he was so badly shaken up when big Robeson stopped the play that Charley tarried in the background after that."

In Pennsylvania not many Negro athletes have made football teams. Neither the University of Pennsylvania nor Pittsburgh can name a Negro star. At Washington and Jefferson two colored boys won letters, one creating a national reputation in football and in track. Charles F. West played halfback for four years, 1920–1923, and was in the national eye. Charles F. West, now a physician in Alexandria, Virginia, was one of three Negroes to get into a Rose Bowl game.[1] During his stay in college, a southern college, Washington and Lee, refused to play the Pennsylvania school unless West was benched. This was refused and athletic relations between the two institutions were broken. West was also a pentathlon winner. He hurt his leg after being selected for the Olympic team and

---

[1] In 1916, Fritz Pollard played Stanford in the Rose Bowl; in 1929 Brice Taylor of Southern California played in the same place. West, from halfback position called signals and directed plays.

another athlete was substituted. Subsequently, in a try-out in France West easily beat his American team mates, but the French would not allow a change in entry. West was one of the best athletes in his generation, regardless of race. In 1937–38, John Ore, playing end, was a marked player at Washington and Jefferson.

Oberlin and Mid-West. The records of the West also show colored gridironers of eminence. At Oberlin, beginning with the late William Washington in the seasons of 1897, '98 and '99, colored football heroes appeared more regularly there than at any other college. In 1901 and 1902, Samuel D. Morrell won his letters; in 1908 and 1909, Nathaniel P. Brown won honors; Leon Taylor earned letters in 1919 and 1920; T. D. Hansbary in 1925, 1926; S. Jamison in 1927; James D. Barnes in 1934, 1935, and 1936; Carlos E. Berry in 1932 and 1935, and Samuel E. Barnes in 1934, 1935, and 1936. This great college of liberal traditions records more colored football letter men than any other northern or western college.

Other athletes who made Ohio's football fields glorious by their deeds are Frank (Doc) Kelker, 1936–1937, and Robert A. Brooks, of Western Reserve. Kelker was one of Western Reserve's greatest all-round athletes. He was a strapping fellow weighing one hundred ninety pounds and standing six feet two inches. As end, he was the spark-plug of Reserve's great team which lost but one or two games in twenty-nine starts. Kelker "prepped" at the Dover (Ohio) High School, where he played on the undefeated football team for three years. Kelker was also a crack basketball player on a strong Western Reserve team. He played center and was one of the high scorers on this quint, which defeated some of the best known fives in the country. Kelker specialized in the sprints on the track and was clocked under 49 seconds in the 440. He was very popular with the students, who honored him in many ways. He became a physical director of one of Cleveland's large high schools.

At Ohio State, "Bill" Bell, 1929–1931, was another athlete who experienced a "bench-warming" because of a southern institution, probably the most intolerant in the land, the United States Naval Academy. It refused to let him play at the Naval Academy field. However, an agreement was forced that obligated the Navy to play against Bell in 1931 in Ohio. Bell was one of the finest football players ever to represent the race on Ohio teams. Later he became one of the leading athletic directors in the South at the Florida Agricultural and Mechanical College, where his athletes took high rank.

At Illinois University two colored lads were prominent players in the first decade of the century. Roy M. Young earned a letter playing tackle in 1904 and 1905. In the next year, H. H. Wheeler won his letter. Since then many colored players have reached first rank.

Butler University, Indiana, produced an outstanding player in 1937 in the person of Thomas Harding. In 1923, John Southern, and in 1928, Alonzo Watford were football players of note at this institution.

Archie Harris, of Atlantic City, a sophomore, as 1938 end of the Indiana team, was an excellent player. Harris had also shown significant promise as a discus-thrower and shot-putter. In practice he had hurled the discus beyond many record throws. Also at Indiana, Fitzhugh Lyons as end in 1931–1933, and Jesse Babb as end in 1932–1933 were noteworthy football players.

Iowa will always be remembered in football by that imposing star of the gridiron, Fred "Duke" Slater. At the University of Iowa for four years, 1918 to 1921, he achieved a national reputation. Not only was he accorded the honor of receiving the choice of most of the western authorities for All-Western tackle, but was selected in 1919 for third All-American and in 1921 for second All-American. About ten years before Slater was at Iowa, A. A. Alexander had won honors on the football team. In 1927 Ledrue Galloway, now deceased, won his letter in football at Iowa.

The two Simmons boys from Texas made colorful gridiron history during their stay at Iowa University. "Ossie" Simmons was considered by many observers to be the "flashiest" backfield man in the game during his day at Iowa. He was fleet of foot, a high knee

CAPT. HOMER HARRIS—IOWA, 1938
The only colored Athlete to be Captain of a Big Ten Football Team

runner, a wonderful sidestepper and a triple threat. On a team not over strong in blockers or linemen, and which at times showed signs of team-friction, "Ossie" attracted the attention of the country even when his team was losing. At one time there were five colored players on the Iowa team throughout the season. "Don" Simmons was a good end and frequently was on the receiving end of a pass from his brother. Homer Harris is one of the few colored boys to win a berth as captain of a major football eleven. Iowa thus honored Harris in 1938.

Theatrice Gibbs, of Dubuque, starred on the striped field for four years, '35, '36, '37, and '38. His schoolmates dubbed him a fine player and splendid sportsman.

Willis Ward was the first Negro athlete to make the University of Michigan football team. It is known that one of the coaches, although of national stature in his capacity, had been little inclined to use or be tolerantly fair to colored football candidates. Ward, however, was a boy hard to discourage, as was evidenced by those who knew him. Ward not only was a good football player, but was one of the best all-round athletes the University ever had.

At Michigan State there were in those days three colored players whose memory for gridiron feats will long be revered by their generations. Gideon Smith in 1913, 1914, 1915; Harry C. Graves in 1918, 1921, 1922; and Benjamin Goode in 1924, were the boys who made good at Michigan State. Incidentally, all three have done outstanding work as leaders in the field of physical education and coaching at colored schools and colleges. Graves was at Wilberforce and later was coach and health education teacher at Armstrong High School, in Washington, D. C. Smith became identified pre-eminently with football and good sportsmanship in the department of health and physical education at Hampton Institute, while Goode was on the coaching line at West Virginia State for several years. Later McCrary played at Michigan State.

Bell and Jefferson. The University of Minnesota with its power teams in the Big Ten sampled the playing of two Negro stalwarts, Horace Bell (a brother of William, of Ohio State) and "Bob"

HORACE BELL, MINNESOTA

Marshall, of the teams from 1901 to 1904. Marshall received the honor of being selected as All-Western end. Bell's fame lasted through the seasons of 1936 to 1938. It was he who started games with the kick-off. It was he who crashed into the scoring columns with his long and accurate goals from the field. It is seldom a lineman gets so much publicity. In one of the great game broadcasts of the 1938 season, when Minnesota played Northwestern, the announcer seemed to be describing a duel between Bell and Bernie Jefferson. Both boys scored for their teams. Frequently the clashes between these two Negro opponents led the radio recorder to ascribe personal enmity to these two opposing brothers in black. Throughout the write-ups of Gopher games we read, "The extra point was made from placement by Bell, giant Negro guard." Bell contributed to the much sought for honor of being named Western Conference champion that was the glory of the 1937 Minnesota team. Ellsworth Harpole, at guard in '31 and '33, and Dwight Reed, an extraordinary end of '35, '36 and '37, made memorable their football exploits at Minnesota.

At Northwestern University at least four Negro players made inspiring contributions to the football history of the school. In 1922, Sam Taylor, renowned in baseball, made his debut as a hero. Then came Tom Verdell, a scintillating end of the 1927 and 1928 teams. Verdell served later as a coach at Virginia State College for Negroes. Clarence Hinton was a halfback of ability during the years of 1935, '36, and '37. Beginning with 1936 and throughout 1937 and 1938, Bernard Jefferson, the great Negro halfback in those years played for Northwestern University. His coach and many others regarded Jefferson as one of the best halfbacks of the Big Ten.

Nebraska had her share of Negro players. W. N. Johnson played end on a stout Nebraska eleven from 1900 to 1904. Robert Taylor played on the same team. The late George A. Flippin was one of the very early players of color in the game. He was playing halfback at Nebraska when William H. Lewis was starring at Harvard. Clinton Ross was a good tackle in 1913.

Negroes created highly favorable situations for other race athletes at the University of North Dakota and Coe College in the Mid-West, and became consequential performers in football on the coast at Loyola and the University of Washington. Here and there football luminaries showed up momentously at other Western colleges.

Fritz Pollard, Jr., son of the great "Fritz" of old days at Brown, commanded the attention of the Nation for his track and football career at the University of North Dakota. Pollard as halfback in '36, '37, and '38, was key player on his team. He was mentioned for several All-American honors. A team mate of Pollard's, sharing in the glory of North Dakota's football, was Horace Johnson, an impressive halfback during 1936, 1937, and 1938.

Joseph Collins, left half at Coe College in 1920, 1921, and 1922, elicited the highest commendation from his coach, Moray L. Eby, of twenty-five years' tenure. Eby said, "Collins is one of the best football players ever developed in the State of Iowa and I consider him on my all-time Coe College eleven."

Charles Russell, '37, and Hamilton Greene, represented the University of Washington capably on the gridiron.

Loyola College, on the coast, has had some players of consequence in Edward Atkinson in '31, Walter McCowen in '36, '37, and '38, and Al Duvall, a tackle of the 1933, '34, and '35 teams, who received mention by at least two selectors of dream teams for All-American honors.

Walter A. Gordon, once line coach of the Bears, held the enviable position as chief scout for the 1937 Rose Bowl champions and freshman squad mentor. He is former Golden Bear (California) player and was a highly regarded figure in football circles of the Pacific Conference.

In the 1929 Tournament of Roses, Georgia Tech sought to bar Brice Taylor, sepia flash of the California University squad, from the Rose Bowl. In reply to the demand that Taylor be kept on the side-lines, college officials told the Dixie crew that if California University played, Taylor played. The authorities are reported as saying to the Georgians that "the University of California team had been invited to play and that Taylor was a member of that

Walter Gordon, Scout and Coach, University of California

team." Taylor played and was a star despite the fact the Georgians won, 8–7.

Racial Intolerance on the Gridiron. The bar sinister has operated many times to satisfy the caste or class prejudice of Southern schools when matched with football teams with colored players. Bell, of Ohio, was not allowed to play against the Navy. Sidat-Singh was benched at the University of Maryland's game with Syracuse in Maryland. Dave Meyer, of New York University, was not allowed to play against a Southern team. Charles West was a cause of loss of athletic relations between Washington and Jefferson and Washington and Lee. However, some of the Southern teams did not insist on the gentleman's agreement which bound Northern colleges not to use colored players when teams from the South played in the North. North Carolina willingly played New York University's team on which was Williams. Coach Wade's Duke team did not ask that Sidat-Singh be barred. Maryland played Syracuse with Sidat-Singh at Syracuse. The Southwest is fast growing more American. Southern Methodist did not ask to bar Woodrow Strode and Kenny Washington of the University of California team at Los Angeles.

Few coaches seem to have the fortitude to treat their colored players with the regard due them in cases of this sort. Usually the colored lad is up against an option of withdrawal from the team with the loss of his athletic scholarship, or of permitting himself to be benched when playing a Southern team. Yet with the increasing number of colored lads on northern teams and the more tolerant attitude of broader trained educators and coaches, this line of separation is doomed to pass. In truth, one of the most poignant justifications or objectives of school or college athletics is vitiated when snobbery or racial prejudice prevents youth from developing a tolerance for all contestants regardless of race on the play field here in America.

Honor Teams. The culminating and highest glory in the career of a football player is to earn the honor of selection by competent or responsible agencies for position on an All-American team. Walter Camp, in collaboration with Caspar Whitney, began selecting such teams as far back as 1889. Until his death, except for the Great War year, Camp selected All-American teams. Since his departure various individuals or groups have claimed the descent of the mantle from Camp.

When Walter Camp essayed the role of making decision as to the season's best players, football was in the main a Northeastern United States game. Most of the players could be seen in action during one season. Now, every week-end in the fall finds hundreds of games played about the entire country. A consensus of opinion is sought by many agencies. Of the various polls taken, that of the Associated Press seems to represent the most competent source. Other institutions or individuals assume authority to pick All-American selections in various jurisdictions about this country.

All-Americans. Negroes who have weathered the conflicting opinions and judgments and who were honored by Walter Camp during his years of selecting All-Americans are the following:

William H. Lewis, Harvard; center—1892 and 1893
Fritz Pollard, Brown; halfback—1916
Paul Robeson, Rutgers; end—1917 and 1918.

Matthew Bullock, who went from a highly successful football career at Dartmouth to teach and coach at Atlanta Baptist College (Morehouse), and the writer were among the first to select all-college teams. In 1911, Bullock published the following All-Southern team: Ends, Brock of Atlanta Baptist College (Morehouse), and Kendall, of Fisk; tackles, Harmon and Savage of Atlanta Baptist College (Morehouse); guards, Goodgame of Atlanta Baptist College (Morehouse), and Kirksey of Talladega; center, Bass of Meharry; halfbacks, Gibson of Atlanta Baptist College (Morehouse), and Hendley of Tuskegee; full back, Emerson of Tuskegee; quarterback, Lewis of Fisk. For the same season, the writer selected for the All-Middle Atlantic Colleges: Ends, Oliver and Slaughter of Howard; tackles, Aiken of Hampton, and Goss of Lincoln; guards, Johns of Shaw, and Clelland of Howard; center, Warner of Hampton; halfbacks, Pollard of Lincoln, and Gray of Howard; full back, Brown of Shaw; quarterback, Collins of Lincoln. Yearly thereafter honor selections were made.

Not from Robeson's day until the coming of Jerome Holland of Cornell has a Negro player been so universally honored as the latter. Among others mentioned for honors in some years were Edward Gray, who in 1908, at Amherst College, was selected by Camp for his third honor team, and "Duke" Slater, who was so honored on the third team for 1919, and the second team for 1921. Robert Marshall, of Minnesota, was mentioned for the second team in 1905 and 1906. In later years, Julius Franks of Michigan and Bill Willis of Ohio State were All-American selectees.

Wherever the alumni of many of our universities are gathered, the name and fame of many of our colored athletes will be recalled and remembered with emotion. The millions of Americans who have witnessed colored heroes of the gridiron striving to carry their hopes to fruition in victorious contests cannot but grow more tolerant towards a minority element with which their heroes are identified. With the same traits of courage, of self-denial, and of fighting for a cause that mark the valiant militarist, these Negro boys battling on the striped gridirons are rendering a social service not to be overlooked as a force of great power in establishing the Negro in the hearts of his brother Americans.

CHAPTER VII

Later Day Gridiron Heroes

Sidat-Singh. The feats of colored boys on gridirons in the past few years have occasioned syndicated feature stories rich in the descriptive language of the noted sports scribes. Pages of comment followed the gridiron feats of Holland, Bell, Jefferson, Strode, Kenny Washington, and Sidat-Singh, during the season of 1938. On October 18, 1938, the Sunday *Star* of Washington published Grantland Rice's laudation of Sidat-Singh in the Cornell game. In part, Rice said, "And then a rather dull game suddenly turned into a panoramic pageant of startling episodes as Sidat-Singh, adopted son of a Hindu, turned himself into a human machine gun with a touch of the howitzer on the side.

"In less than nine minutes Sidat-Singh fed seven passes to Ruth and Allen, his two receivers, for a total of nearly 200 yards and three Syracuse touchdowns. Each pass, thrown accurately and unhurriedly to Cornell's right side, traveled exactly along the same route.

"This was a great game between Syracuse and the Cornell team with Brud Holland and Sidat-Singh in starring roles. Coach Ossie Solem, anticipating a hard game, is reported to have said, 'Our only chance was backfield speed, headed by Glickman and Sidat-Singh's passing arm. Singh is an exceptionally good passer. When you can complete five in a row for 162 yards and three touchdowns under pressure, you can't be fluking.' Coach Solem continued, 'There wasn't time enough left to keep on with our running game. We had to go to the air all the way. When Brown ran back their kick-off by 92 yards to give Cornell a 17 to 6 lead, I couldn't see where we had a chance. The clock was running out.'

"Singh was in a spot where he couldn't afford to miss a shot against a really fine football team, one of the best in the country. Singh's coolness, accuracy and perfect timing under these conditions

WILMETH SIDAT-SINGH OF SYRACUSE

was something you seldom see. To collect 19 points against such a team as Cornell has—all in less than nine minutes when you've been outplayed for 51 minutes is just one of those things that rarely happen on any field."

Grantland Rice wrote in a special dispatch to the New York *Times* anent the Syracuse-Cornell game of 1938, "A new forward pass hero slipped in front of the great white spotlight of fame at Syracuse today. The phenomenon of the rifle shot event went on beyond Sid Luckman and Sammy Baugh. His name is Wilmeth Sidat-Singh, a Negro boy from Harlem wearing an East Indian name with the deadly aim of Davy Crockett and Kit Carson." Further, Rice commented, "Sidat-Singh promptly faded back for the eighth time in this last period and whipped a bullet pass to Allen, who was waiting for the ball. The pass led to another touchdown and the ball game. In the course of this exterminating rifle fire Sidat-Singh completed five passes in succession for a total of 158 yards and three touchdowns. If there is any passer who has surpassed this record, coming from behind, I can't recall it in the ancient annals of the game. It was one of the most amazing exhibitions of machine gun fire I've ever seen where the odds were all the other way."

In 1937, Maryland University refused to let Sidat-Singh play when it was learned he was a colored boy, and Syracuse lost. But in October, 1938, at Syracuse, the Marylanders were swamped by Sidat-Singh's crew to a tune of 53–0, thus avenging a defeat of the previous year when its ace footballer was benched.

The year before Sidat-Singh justified the statement that he was the most deadly passer in the game, Baugh, O'Brien, *et al.*, notwithstanding. On November 7, 1937, the following was written:

"Sidat-Singh, passing star of Syracuse University's aerial minded team, led his mates to a 27–6 triumph over Western Reserve before 15,000 fans in Archbold Stadium today.

"For the second week in a row the fans saw the 175-pound star from New York City supply the spark that fired his team to victory. His accurate tosses gave his receivers little to do but grab the ball and run.

"After making a ten-yard run in the second period, Sidat-Singh passed ten yards to Quarterback Bill Hoffman. . . . And Fullback Vic Baylock scored on a fake line plunge.

"The second tally came a few minutes later on some razzle-dazzle that caught every one napping. Sidat-Singh, on the Reserve 40, passed to Hoffman, who lateralled to Walt Rekstis. Rekstis fumbled but Adam Markowski swept in to grab the ball in the air and romp 25 yards to score.

"In the third quarter, another 40-yard lateral with Sidat on the firing end brought a third marker. Sidat flipped a bull's-eye toss over the center to Markowski, who made a basketball toss to his partner at end, Rekstis, who dashed 25 yards to the goal to score. The fourth and final score was one of the most spectacular. Singh faded back to the Reserve 35 and tossed to Markowski standing almost on his goal line. Harold Ruth went over on the next play on a cut back from an end sweep." This was the game that broke the Western Reserve streak of 28 undefeated games.

Holland. Until 1939 Cornell boasted only one Negro football player. But what a player "Brud" Holland was! A volume could scarcely contain the commentary complimentary to the skill, strength, endurance and sportsmanship of Holland. On Cornell's teams with some of the foremost players in the East, Holland stood shoulders above his team mates and their opponents. Holland was the first Negro to make Cornell's "Big Red football team." He entered Cornell in 1935 as a graduate from the Auburn High School, where his career had already been spectacular. His famous end-around play was a consistent yardage gainer. He was good on the receiving end of passes. He was blasting to plays hurled around his end. He was one of the modern game's sixty-minute players. With Holland on the team Cornell rose to higher heights than the Ithacan eleven ever had reached before. Only when Holland's eleven in the 1938 series met that Orange threat from Syracuse fronting, the great Sidat-Singh, did Cornell fail. The battle on the day these two power teams met was a classic for the book of all time great games. One of the contemporary journals of 1938, commenting on Holland, said: "Jerome 'Brud' Holland, who played his last intercollegiate game here Thursday on Franklin Field against the University of Pennsylvania football team, was named in a Cornell Manual as a member of the University's All-Time football team. Holland is undoubtedly one of the greatest ends ever seen at the school and will long be remembered as the player who made the end-around play famous. Cornell's splendid record during the 1938 season has caused the Big Red to be invited to participate in several post season games, but the athletic council has refused all bids since it is against the school's policy to participate in post games."

Alison Danzig, writing in the New York *Times* of October 3, 1937, in an article headed, "Cornell Crushes Colgate As Great Line Play Aids," said, "Cornell hasn't had a team comparable to this 1937 machine since the halcyon days when Eddie Kaw and George Pfann were running riot in the early Twenties. Brud Holland, the great Negro end, who scored three touchdowns in the last quarter, two of them on end-around runs, was almost mobbed by his team-mates when he came off the field; George Peck, as comparably the finest running back on the field, . . . Whit Baker, . . . and Elliot Hooper . . . were the figures who arrested the eye."

Randy Dixon, in his column in the Pittsburgh *Courier*, describing several Holland moments in one of the annual Penn-Cornell Thanksgiving day games wrote, "Holland, a rugged child of nature, 6 feet 1 inch, 207 pounds, was the cynosure of 70,000 pairs of eyes. Those who banked the stadium, and there were approximately 4,000 of Holland's racial ilk, had come in expectancy of seeing 'Brud' enact his famous end-around play, and to glean a peep-full of his immobile defensive genius and his heralded art as a diagnostician. At the end of each game he has played in the Penn stadium, Holland has achieved the plaudits of the thousands of spectators, many of whom lined the walk-way to shake his hand as he left after playing practically the entire game."

Dixon, at the close of his commentary, says, "Holland's exit was a meritorious salaam. As the premature dusk settled over historic Franklin Field, and the biting mist that sent its emissaries of hail, rain and snow churning the field into a quagmire, Jerome E. Hol-

"Brud" Holland, Cornell's All-American

land—who by dint of superior ability, ingratiating personality and God-given courage, has surmounted all barriers and gained the highest fame that can befall a college athlete—wrote the last chapter in his saga of modern-day Negro youth.   He'll go on and complete his course in social service work at Cornell in June.   They have already named a gymnasium after him.   Fellow students are supplying the necessary gold.   He won't be forgotten."

That Holland would repeat for All-American honors was doubted by many.   He was a marked man from the beginning of the season. His end-around speciality was drilled against by every coach whose team was to meet Holland's.   But he could not be stopped.   On the defense he was bowling over the offensive play before it could get started.   Uncannily he would adopt unorthodox blocking to stop a quickly diagnosed threat.   Offensively he was equally good at running, blocking, tackling, or receiving passes.

Despite opposing great players like Sid Luckman of Columbia and Bob McLeod of Dartmouth, this dark boy from Cornell stole the spotlight throughout the 1938 season.   Not only did Holland make All-American on the Associated Press' team, the Nation's most representative selection, but he was so honored in the selections made by the New York *Daily News* polled from among 115 of the nation's best sports writers, by *Life Magazine*, by Kate Smith's radio hour, by the New York *World Telegram*, and many others.

Kenny Washington and Woodrow Wilson Strode.   On the Pacific Coast, two colored boys at the University of California at Los Angeles were in the limelight of football comment and opinion nearly every week during 1938.   Kenny Washington was heralded as one of the wonder halfbacks of the year, while Strode received frequent mention for fine work as an end.   In every game Ken Washington's sensational ball carrying made the big story of the day.   He was easily the choice of the Associated Press' 14th annual All-Pacific Coast football team.

Even the Eastern press carried word pictures of the sterling worth of Kenny Washington, and occasionally of his teammate Strode. After the game with Idaho, one press comment said, "The Univer-

Courtesy of the " Afro ".

"KENNY" WASHINGTON, UNIVERSITY OF CALIFORNIA AT LOS ANGELES
An All-Pacific Coast Halfback, and "Spark-Plug" of the Football Team
of that College, much heralded in the comment of the Sports Writers of
the Current Day Press.

sity of California at Los Angeles jolted Idaho out of its Rose Bowl
dream today by swamping the erstwhile unbeaten Vandals, 33 to 0,
before 25,000 fans.   In the worst walloping ever handed Idaho by

Courtesy of " Flash "

BERNARD JEFFERSON, NORTHWESTERN UNIVERSITY

the Ulans, Kenny Washington broke loose for 46 yards on one dash
to set the stage for a touchdown, tore down the field for 47 yards
for another score and drove 7 yards for still another tally."

In the University of Washington affray, Kenny was responsible in large measure for the victory of the University of California at Los Angeles in the game played on October 9, 1938.

"Ken Washington's team," said the New York *Times*, October 10, 1938, "rose to one of its greatest gridiron triumphs today when it defeated highly favored Washington 13 to 0, in a Pacific Coast Conference battle. It was the first time the Ulans had been able to score on the Huskies in the four games played since 1932. Battling the Huskies to a standstill in the first quarter, the Bruins turned a Washington fumble into a spectacular touchdown play, with Kenny Washington, big Negro back, taking a lateral pass that was good for 45 yards and the first score. . . ."

Again Washington was the star. Again on October 2, 1938, the University of California at Los Angeles defeated Stanford by a score of 6–0.

The comment of the same writer was: "The University of California at Los Angeles, staving off a last minute aerial attack that had the Bruin rooters' hair standing on end, knocked over Stanford for the first time since 1935 today by a score of 6 to 0. A crowd of 37,000 saw the game.

"The Belligerent Bruins drove the Indians all over the field, but were able to score only once, in a second quarter sprint by Halfback Kenny Washington and Fullback Buster Sutherland.

"Fighting for their coach, William H. Spaulding, who flew to Melrose, Wisconsin, two days ago at the death of his mother, the Ulans turned a Stanford fumble into a touchdown on a drive that began on the Indians' 24 yard line. Sutherland crashed over after alternating with Washington in carrying the pigskin. . . ."

Bernard Jefferson. Right halfback on the Northwestern University varsity, Jefferson rose from the ranks, beginning at Ottawa High School where he had starred in football, basketball, and track. He is an inch less than six feet and weighed 185 pounds. "Big Jeff" was one of the game's iron men and the most dependable man on the Northwestern team. He was a most deceptive "triple threat" protagonist. He bore the brunt of running and punting attacks and passed well. Frequently he played the entire game without substitution. Jefferson was ranked one of the best all-around backs in the Big Ten, the toughest single group of teams in the country.

Reporting on October 30, 1938, the game between Northwestern and Minnesota, in which the former defeated the latter by a score of 6 to 3, the New York *Times* referring to this master player, said, "Then Bernard Jefferson, husky halfback, took the ball on a play that used Hahnenstein for a decoy. Jefferson ripped through left tackle, was checked for an instant on the 3, and with sheer running speed and form blasted over the goal line with three tacklers hanging on him. The 185 pound Negro simply would not be stopped.

"That furious touchdown charge crushed Minnesota's hopes. Jefferson's drive stood out in bold relief and won the praise of the Northwestern homecomers. The Wildcats might have won in the first three plays of the opening period on a tricky triple pass, which ended with Jefferson throwing a 45-yard pass to Captain Diehl, running across the Gopher goal. He reached for the ball with one hand, but it bounced off his fingertips.

"Minnesota's only display of power came late in the second period, after Jefferson had punted to Minnesota's 44. Van Every passed to Manucci, who was run out of bounds on Northwestern's 34. Another Van Every pass was good for a first down on the 20. With 48 seconds to go, Horace Bell, giant Negro guard, booted a 34-yard goal from placement, the first score made against Northwestern this year."

Commenting later on the game with Michigan, the New York *Times* said, "80,000 people saw Jefferson and his teammates hold Michigan to a scoreless tie on Saturday, November 12, 1938, at Ann Arbor. The crowd that filled the Michigan Stadium alternately gasped and cheered as the two big teams battled back and forth seeking the break that never came. Each team reached the shadow of its opponents' goal posts in the thrill-packed second half, but lacked a winning punch.

"A fifty-one yard run by Bernie Jefferson, Northwestern's Negro halfback, on a pass from Halfback Hahnenstein gave the Wolverine defense its most gruelling test early in the third period. Jefferson's run put the ball on Michigan's 11. . . ."

In the Notre Dame game, Bernie Jefferson crowned himself with glory, but the Irish were not to be denied. Notre Dame started the second period with a tally for six points. Then, "With Bernie Jefferson, Northwestern Negro half, Ollie Hahnenstein and Jack McGurn smashing and passing, the Wildcats led 7 to 6." In the third period the Notre Dame specialist Hofer was called to the game and from placement in the 20 yard line registered three points and the top score. "After that a tight Notre Dame defense checked and baffled all attempts of the Wildcats to score. Outstanding in the losing battle was Jefferson, playing his last intercollegiate game, who gained more ground than any other back. He played brilliantly on defense and punted sensationally. . . ."

In the game between Wisconsin and Northwestern, Jefferson was a star even in the loss of the game. The New York *Times* reported on November 6, 1938, "Wisconsin fired its bolt today and the explosion shattered the dream of a Western Conference championship which Northwestern had prayed for after its conquest of Minnesota a week ago. A crowd of 37,000, filling both sides of Dyche Stadium and trickling into the end stands, watched the Badgers, out-score the Wildcats in a sensational second half to register a stirring upset."

In the last quarter of the game, "Jefferson, Northwestern Negro halfback, took Howland's kick-off and ran ninety-two yards down the side line for a touchdown. He got the ball on the 8-yard line and behind perfect interference reached mid-field. Then he cut into the open, with Madsen, a sophomore backfield man, putting a terrific block on the last tackler. Another Badger, Gavre, tried to overtake Jefferson, but lunged and fell flat on his face. Jefferson crossed standing up. . . ."

The outstanding 1939 football star who had difficulty in being named on many selected All-American teams was Kenny Washington. After a poll conducted by the *Liberty Magazine*, an All-American team was selected by players from ninety-one major football schools and 1,659 football players. Of the eleven players chosen

LEVI JACKSON, FIRST VARSITY FOOTBALL PLAYER AT YALE UNIVERSITY—
CAPTAIN YALE'S 1949 TEAM

for the first team, "only one player of the 664 named received the vote of every player who opposed him.   He was Kenny Washington, U.C.L.A.'s great halfback.   One hundred and three players who competed against the Negro star agreed in their returns that he was the outstanding man they met."   The *Liberty* account further reads, "A glance at the records and we find that this almost-perfect player

"WALLY" TRIPLETT, GREAT HALF- DENNIS HOGGARD, END ON PENN
BACK ON PENN STATE'S 1947 AND STATE'S 1947 AND 1948 TEAMS
1948 TEAM

was greatly responsible for the success of U.C.L.A.'s best football season in its history.   In yardage gained by ground plays at this writing, he totaled 863 yards in 141 tries.   He threw 76 passes in 9 games, and had completed 32 for gains that totaled 497 yards. All told, he was directly responsible for 1,360 yards.   He received the highest combined percentage of any one player in the country."

More Recent Records. During the decade from 1938 to 1948, so many football players appeared on the major college and professional teams, outside the Mason and Dixon line, that space prohibits naming them all.   In 1940, Lou Montgomery of Boston

College was denied participation on some of his team's games to satisfy southern prejudice. Although given the highest citizenship award by the Veterans of Foreign Wars in Boston for his example of sportsmanship and gentlemanly qualities, he was kept from playing in the Cotton Bowl game in Dallas, Texas, on New Year's Day. Yet, in 1947, Wally Triplett and Dennis Hoggard of Penn State, one of the three unbeaten, untied teams in the nation, played against Southern Methodist University's football team in the Cotton Bowl in Dallas, Texas, before thousands of cheering southerners.

In October 1947, Chester Pierce of Harvard University, stopped in the dormitories at the University of Virginia as a member of the Harvard University squad and played on Cavalier Field on the Charlottesville campus. On the following Sunday, in Charlotte, N. C., Bill Williams and other colored players of the Staten Island Stapletons, a professional team, played before 16,000 spectators against the North Carolina Clippers.

Possibly the first interracial football game in Dixie on a college level, was the contest between the Camp Lee team and the University of North Carolina eleven. Paul Zuba, a colored boy, played on the Camp Lee team practically the entire game. Levi Jackson, who later became Yale's star, was also in the game. The spectators were a "mixed" group, seated without any separation and a "mixed" band furnished the music throughout. In New York City, Wilberforce State played against Bergen College in November 1947, which was heralded as the first all-colored *vs.* all-white college football game in New York, but in 1946 the A. & T. College of Greensboro, N. C., playing the New London Submarine Base team, was reported to have played the first interracial football game in New York City.

Many of the college stars of the 1938-1948 decade went into professional ranks. Some of the older star players, like Woody Strode of Loyola of California, and "Big Train" Moody of Morris Brown began to fade out, but a host of sepia gridiron artists seemed destined to loom large on pro-gridirons. Kenny Washington, former great player of U.C.L.A. was signed by the Los Angeles

CHESTER PIERCE, HARVARD UNIVERSITY PLAYER, First Colored Player to
Play on Southern College Campus. Played Against University of Virginia on
Charlottesville Campus in 1947. Marshal of Graduating Harvard Class

"BILL" WILLIS, ALL-AMERICAN PRO-GUARD, 1948
Member, Cleveland Brown's 1948 Champion Team; Former Guard on
Ohio State's Team

MARION MOTLEY, CLEVELAND BROWN'S STERLING FULLBACK; ALL-
AMERICAN PROFESSIONAL FULLBACK, 1948

Rams in the National Professional League and thus became the first outstanding pro-player since Joe Lillard of Oregon a dozen years prior.

With the coming of the new All-America League, the color line receded in professional football ranks. Beginning with a precarious financial foothold the new league in 1947 began drawing huge crowds wherever the teams studded with colored stars appeared. In 1947, the Cleveland Browns of the All-America League with Marion Motley, Bill Willis, and Horace Gillom starring, played "Buddy" Young's New York Yankees before more than 70,000 in New York City, with the Cleveland Browns on the winning end of the score. A record crowd greeted the Los Angeles "Dons" with John Brown, Ezzert Anderson and Bert Piggot against the Baltimore Colts in the Monumental City. Bill Bass was a tower of strength for the Chicago Rockets. Many other colored players saw action in the professional football game.

On the major college gridirons about the nation, colored players since 1939 have become too numerous to mention. As the 1947 season came to a close, three colored players had been named to some of the All-American selections. The Associated Press All-American had three colored ends on the second and third teams. Bob Mann of the Michigan champion big nine eleven and Ike Owens of Illinois covered both ends of the second mythical eleven, while Leonard Ford of the University of Michigan, a defensive end, was given a glory spot on the third All-American. For honorable mention, Gene Derricotte of Michigan; Emlen Tunnell of Iowa; Levi Jackson of Yale and others were named. One of the players in the Mid-West heralded as one of the most brilliant was Linwood Sexton, who closed four years of sensational football on University of Wichita's team. Sexton was selected on the All-Missouri Valley Conference team for three consecutive years. His play, spirit and courage as a member of the "Shocker" team was so remarkable that his number "66" will be retired and never again worn by a Shocker player. He later signed with a professional team.

Among the other college players who incited great praise through radio and press, during those years were the following: Sam Pierce

Left—Buddy Young, National A.A.U. Sprint Champion, Star back on University of Illinois Team, Halfback on New York Yankee Professional Football Team, 1948

87—Len Ford of Michigan, 1948; 81, Bob Mann of Michigan, 1948

of Cornell who broke a tradition by playing against the Navy at Baltimore in 1940. Julius Franks, a guard at Michigan, received plaudits by some All-American selectors. "Bill" Willis was a terrific tackle at Ohio State. Homer Mitchell was a star at Boston

GENE DERRICOTTE, MICHIGAN, 1947, 1948   GEORGE TALIAFERRO, INDIANA, 1947, 1948

University. Charley Bentley played quarterback at Brown, Norman Houston was a halfback, and Henry Thomas, end. Garrett Hill and Emlen Tunnell, halfbacks, were widely acclaimed in the Hawkeye (Iowa) State. With Sam Pierce, halfback at Cornell, was Charlie Robinson. Marion Motley hailed from Nevada University. Martin Chapman was a great player from Akron University and Ted Hanson starred at Western Reserve. In late years, Paul Robeson, Jr. played with Cornell; Paul Patterson along with Ike Owens and Buddy Young were at Illinois. At Indiana, George

HORACE GILLOM, END ON CLEVELAND BROWN'S PROFESSIONAL
TEAM

Taliaferro was the outstanding back.   Levi Jackson, the first colored player, at Yale became a great factor in victories over Harvard and other rivals.   Melvin Murchison, a V–12 student, was the first player to make Princeton's varsity team.

In addition to those mentioned the 1948 crop of colored football stars on the many teams of the nation were: Bernie Custis and Horace Morris at Syracuse, Fritz Alexander at Dartmouth, Al Bishop at Brooklyn College, Elmo Jackson at Muhlenburg, Dan Tower and Walt Cooper at Washington and Jefferson, Bucky Hatchell and Harvey Grimsley at Rutgers, Al Cannon and Ken Moses at Columbia, Jim Robinson and Bob Lee at Pittsburgh, Bill Payne at New York University and Campbell Johnson of Rensselaer.

In the Midwest, Glen Pullens was at Minnesota; Cal Vernon and Bob Teague were at Wisconsin; Jim Clark, Stan Dixon and Bob Dorsey at Ohio State; Earl Banks at Iowa; Horace Smith at Michigan State; and Wilfred Rawl, Buckner, Brooks and Carter at Indiana.

In the Far West Staten Webster, Tom Tryon and Len Jones were on the University of California team. Harry Thompson, Bill Duffy, and Henry Daniels at University of California at Los Angeles; Woody Lewis, Chet Daniels and Winn Wright at Oregon; and Alva Tabor and Sherman Howard at Nevada also starred.

With the trend of colored boys towards colleges all over the nation at the present rate it is not possible to do more than mention the names of the heroes of the gridiron sport.   Many of the players now on college teams will be bid for by the professional clubs. Nineteen forty-eight has begun with a galaxy of colored boys on pro-teams.   Mann, Ford, Sexton, Owens and a host of others of the 1947 college teams have signed up for the big salaries.   One of the few boys to make pro-grade coming up from colored conference circles in the 1948 season was Tom Casey of Hampton's '47 squad.

CHAPTER VIII

The Great Indoor Game, Basketball

The Origin. Basketball is one of few invented popular sports. Most boys know that Dr. James A. Naismith, while instructor at the Springfield Young Men's Christian Association in 1891, used two peach baskets and had his boys play the first game of basketball. Today millions in the United States and in more than two score countries play basketball.

When the first colored boys began to play, is not definitely known. The writer learned the game in his physical education classes in 1904 at the Harvard University Summer school, and taught it to boys in Washington, D. C., in the winter of that year. It was at first considered a "sissy" game as was tennis in the rugged days of football. By 1906, a league of teams had developed in Washington, D. C., and by 1911 nearly every elementary school and high school had teams.

In New York, Brooklyn, and Jersey City, club teams were playing basketball as early as 1906. The Smart Set Athletic Club of Brooklyn and the St. Christopher Club of New York were the first to establish basketball teams. Shortly afterwards, the Alpha Physical Culture Club, the Jersey City Athletic Club (later merged to form the Mozart Athletic Club), the Laetitia Athletic Club, the Indian Athletic Club, the Williamsbridge Colored Men's Association, the St. Cyprian Athletic Club, and the Salem Crescent Athletic Club organized basketball teams. Prominent among the promoters of this new club activity were George Lattimore of the Smart Set Athletic Club, Conrad and Gerald Norman of the Alpha, the Rev. F. A. Cullen of the Salem Club, and sports-writer Romeo L. Dougherty.

In Philadelphia, two clubs did pioneer work in the field of basketball—the Stentonworth Athletic Club and the Wissahickon Boys'

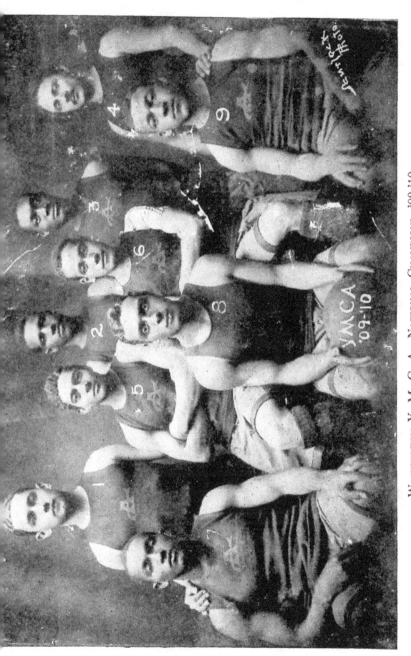

Washington Y. M. C. A., National Champions, '09-'10

Seated—Gray, Oliver, Henderson, Clifford, Curtis. Standing—Chestnut, Nixon, Anderson, Johnson.

Club. The Wissahickon Club had the first colored basketball team in the city. The Stentonworth Club comprising former high school boys was piloted by Harry Duplessis in the early days of Quaker City basketball.

Baltimore, because of lack of indoor playing space, provided little club activity in basketball in the beginning. The one club, the Dunbar Athletic Association, developed most interest in track. Among the early sponsors of the club were James Callis, Ralph Cook, and Dwight O. W. Holmes.

Development of the Game. Big time basketball began with the inception of inter-city games among the club teams of Brooklyn, New York City, and Washington, D. C. The meeting of the Smart Set Club, the Metropolitan champion and the winning team of the Inter-Scholastic Athletic Association of Washington, D. C., in 1908, was the first important inter-city game. The Washington team, the Crescent Athletic Club, was defeated in Washington and in Brooklyn. In 1909, the writer organized and was captain of the Washington Young Men's Christian Association team which defeated, in Washington and in New York, all of its opponents including Alpha, the Smart Set, and the St. Christopher clubs. For two years the Washington "Y" team was undefeated. In December, 1910, the captain of the "Y" team substituted George Gilmore for himself at center in a game in New York against the Alpha Physical Culture team. Soon thereafter the Young Men's Christian Association team disbanded, and the "Y" team became the Howard University team which enjoyed a winning reputation for several years.

Among the eminent players occupying the sporting mind of the public during this period were Hudson Oliver, Edward Gray, Arthur L. Curtis, Conrad Norman, Gerald Norman, Archie Thomas, Sing Goode, Accooe, R. Lattimore and Bradford.

Outside of New York in the first days there were few courts that offered much opportunity for playing the regulation game with or without assembly room for spectators. The games in New York and Brooklyn were played on the spacious floors of the Manhattan

Casino, the Fourteenth Regiment Armory or other ample courts. About 3,000 spectators were present when the Washington "Y" defeated the Smart Set team in Brooklyn.

Cumberland Posey. About this time, 1911, Cumberland Posey and his associates in western Pennsylvania were trying to place basketball on a firm footing. As in Washington and Baltimore, there were few indoor courts available. During this period, Posey and his Monticello lads, the Independents, and the Scholastics were being heard from around the winter indoor circuits. Howard University's Big Five, the former championship "Y" team, continued its winning streak in 1911, and then met Cumberland Posey's Loendi outfit and lost. So also did the rest of the former greats among the New York and Brooklyn leaders. This Loendi team, consisting originally of players like Posey, Clarke, Norris, Hall, Richmond, and the Bell boys, was the big attraction in the East for a decade.

For a while, in New York, Will Madden, formerly the guiding hand of the St. Christopher team, took the best of the players from the St. Christopher and formed the "Incorporators." By this time the amateur spirit was on the decline among the clubs. Players were traded around, and big money began to attract the best players to one or two big aggregations. This was the beginning of the decline of the original clubs, the Alpha, the Smart Set, and others. Gilmore, Holland, and Jenkins were among the players who began thus to shift about.

In Pittsburgh, in the meantime, a team of white players climbed to National fame. This was the great Coffey Club named after a Jewish Rabbi Coffey. Realizing the powerful gate attraction a Loendi-Coffey game would be, the strategy board of the Loendi Club sought the best basketball talent possible, and consolidated a team comprising some of the best court players the race has seen on one team. There were in 1919 and until 1924 on the Loendi team from time to time Gilmore, Posey, the Young Brothers, Sessoms and Betts, Ricks, Fiall, Gayle, Moten, and others. The battles over the years between the Loendi and Coffey quints were remarkable for the closeness of the contests, all of which, but two, were won by the Coffey team, but the margin of victory on either side was by one point in nearly every game.

Some of the club teams which flashed with brilliance for short periods of time after World War I were the Spartans and St. Christopher of New York; the Homestead Steel, the Edgar Thomson Steel, the Young Men's Christian Association and the Holy Cross of Pittsburgh; the Vandals of Atlantic City, the Arctic Avenue "Y" of the same place; the big "Y" of Quaker City; the Athenians of Baltimore, and the Borough Athletic Club of Brooklyn.

The Game in Negro Colleges. Actual basketball in Negro colleges began about 1909 or 1910. Until then, the brief basketball scene was dominated by the clubs. Prior to 1910 there were but few Negro colleges engaging in the sport. Hampton Institute was probably the only college that had a gymnasium large enough to accommodate a game on a regulation court and seat a thousand spectators. Howard University had the strongest team of the collegiate class after the disbanding of the champion Young Men's Christian Association team of Washington.

Lincoln University, Union University, Hampton Institute and Wilberforce University were among the few colleges to have teams prior to 1911. From then on, however, college basketball developed. At first the games were played in stuffy city halls, with crowds packed in, hanging from every conceivable vantage point, crowding on to courts that frequently resembled an ellipse instead of a rectangle during the game. In some places, the game was played in rooms not much larger than goodly-sized handball courts. Even today when many new gymnasia are spacious enough for playing the game, but few are yet large enough to seat the student population along with an outside crowd. The modern game and its fans require field houses. Some of the college gymnasia are headed that way.

The college game in Negro colleges compares favorably with the amateur club game and the play in the majority of white colleges. In the few colored college tilts with the good or very good

Howard University Basketball Champions, 1933-1934

white teams in 1938, the colored teams played well enough to win some games. This measure of strength between white and colored teams has led to improvement of the game. It is an excellent move and should be encouraged. During the 1939 season Union University and Kentucky State College won games from the celebrated Long Island University aggregation of players, although the "Blackbird's" team was not always recognized by the college as the University representative team.

Professional Basketball. The outstanding professional basketball club was the Renaissance team of New York. This team (1923–1939) was the peer of all teams playing the court game for several seasons. There were very few teams that could beat the "Rens" when this team really got going. So uneven was much of its competition, that few people saw the team perform at its best. The general feeling is that the players were instructed not to run up a large score against weak opponents. Frequently the team gave an exhibition of fancy and trick passing that for machine-like precision beggars description.

There never was a basketball team among white players that excelled, for individual and team contribution, the playing of the old Celtic aggregation consisting of "Nat" Holman, Beckman, Haggerty, Barry, Lapschick and Banks. They were the marvels of the time. However, in 1928, the Renaissance team, made up of Ricks, Fiall, Slocum, Sanders, Mayer and Captain Jenkins easily defeated the Celtics in a crucial seasonal test. Since then the "Rens" beat all the best professional teams. Under the leadership of the owner and manager, "Bob" Douglas, and the captaincy of Jenkins, the Renaissance floor machine made an enviable record for basketball and sportsmanship. In two games with their famous rival, the Celtics, in 1938 over 25,000 people witnessed the contest. At one game in Kansas City, over 15,000 people watched the performance. In Cleveland in 1932, 11,000 people saw the game on a Saturday and 15,000 on Sunday.

The Rens and Their Record. Over a period of nearly sixteen years the Renaissance players won 1,588 games and lost 239. In

Left to right: Wm. "Willie" Smith, Charles "Tarzan" Cooper, John Isaacs, Wm. "Pop" Gates, Clarence "Puggy" Bell, Eyrie Saitch, Zack Clayton, Clarence "Fats" Jenkins.

the season ending—1939—they won 112 and lost 7 games. In the following fourteen years, they never failed to win at least 100 games every season. In Chicago, they swept through the toughest opposition in the country to win the first world's professional basketball championship tourney on record.[1] Add it up and you have the Renaissance Big Five, the most amazing court aggregation ever to cut loose at the referee's whistle. The world's championship, undisputed title which they won in the Chicago tourney, was not a new honor to the Rens. For the subsequent decade followers of the game have been forced to admit that no outfit could rightfully claim any such distinction without first mastering the powerful Harlem quintet.

Robert J. Douglas, the well known Harlemite, genial founder and manager of the team, returned from his flying trip to the Windy City for the tournament with the broadest of smiles that week-end because in this their greatest achievement, the Rens had brought to concrete realization the dream he had cherished ever·since he sent the first quint out on the floor. The victory in Chicago marked not only concrete realization of the honors which the team had long deserved but vindication of the unswerving faith which the manager had so long placed in it.

It was in October, 1923, that Bob Douglas organized the Rens. An ardent follower of the game which he had played himself for more than a dozen years, Douglas watched the amateur game sink lower and lower during 1921 and 1922 and conceived the idea that putting out a professional team might prove a worthwhile enterprise. On that first team, Bob had such men as Hilton Slocum, Frank Forbes, Leon Monde, Hy Monte, Zack Anderson, Harold Mayers. Slocum was made captain from the beginning and retained that post until his connection with the team was severed in 1932.

Spartans Become "Rens." The naming of the team the Renaissance Big Five was purely accidental, or perhaps it would be better

---

[1] The Renaissance Team won the world's professional title and a $1,000 purse March 28, 1939, in Chicago.

to call it a result of circumstances. Douglas himself admits that he did not care for the name at all; he had intended to call the team the Spartans after his old club. In seeking to procure as a home court, the Renaissance Casino, which had just been built, however, Bob offered to use that name for the team and thus gave the place itself additional publicity when the aggregation played elsewhere. The proposition was accepted and the name stuck. Outside of Harlem, though, the team is seldom if ever known by the full name Renaissance. To the countless thousands of fans all over the country who await their visits annually, the crack New Yorkers are known as the "Rens" or the "Rennies."

The second season of its existence saw the entry into its roster of the perennial "Fats" Jenkins, the revered George Fiall, "Clix" Garcia and the one and only "Pappy" Ricks. Forbes, Monde, Monte, Anderson, Harold Jenkins, and Wardell dropped out. The replacement of Garcia by Walter Saunders in 1925 and the addition, the next year, of Eyre "Bruiser" Saitch were the only changes until 1930 when Fiall was replaced by Charles "Tarzan" Cooper. Saunders was dropped in 1930, to be replaced by Bill Yancey, and the team went on until 1932 when Johnny "Casey" Holt made the grade, replacing Harold Mayers. In the same year William "Wee Willie" Smith came in to take the place of Slocum, and the team that wore the "Rens" color from then until 1935 has been rated by Bob Douglas himself as one of the best that ever trod the hardwood.

It was that team of Cooper, Smith, Saitch, Yancey, Holt, "Fats" Jenkins and "Pappy" Ricks that doubled the Celtics' 1925 professional record of 44 straight wins by racking up 88 consecutive victories and capped that performance by beating the Celtics themselves 7 out of 8 games. That was the second season in which the Rens had a legitimate claim to the world's title, the first being in 1929 when they defeated the Celtics and every team in the American Pro court league in a number of series.

In 1935, Ricks and the Rens parted. Johnny Isaacs, another recruit, succeeded Jackie Bethards in 1936, and at the same time, Al Johnson replaced Yancey. When the team assembled in October,

1939, in preparation for the following season, Johnny Holt, now a member of the police department, Al Johnson and Lou Badger were among the missing, the latter being a bit too light in weight for the professional circuit in which the Rens move.   In their places, accordingly, when the season started, were William "Pop" Gates, who made high school basketball history at Benjamin Franklin, Clarence "Puggy" Bell, whose name still is uttered in reverence by fans of the Harlem Young Men's Christian Association, and Jack Clayton, a crack defensive player, alumnus of Central High School in Philadelphia.   These three, along with Jenkins, Isaacs, Cooper, Smith and Saitch, comprised the later team.   Jenkins, who assumed the captaincy after Slocum's departure in 1932 and held it long thereafter, was the best known.   Coming originally from the Commerce High of New York City, he played longer and was better than at least 90 per cent of the present day court performers.

Next in point of service comes Saitch.   Admired by the feminine fans as the handsomest man on the team, "Bruiser" as he was known, was a DeWitt Clinton man, and was the crack floor man of the outfit. Bill "Tarzan" Cooper, with the team more than 10 years, was regarded as one of the best center men in the game.   "Tarzan" was the focal point around which all of the Rens' plays revolved, and when he got "in the bucket," the storm was on.   Cooper was another Philadelphia lad, from Central High School.   "Wee Willie" Smith, who stood 6 feet, 5 inches, hailed from Cleveland, where Bob Douglas spotted him playing in a preliminary game and signed him up immediately.   In the 1937–38 season "Smitty" was the Rens' outstanding player.   Johnny Isaacs is still remembered as the Textile High School star who was the unanimous choice of every local sports writer for All-Scholastic center of Greater New York during the 1936–37 season.   Isaacs was signed up after one workout with the Rens.[1]

---

[1] "The fame of the Rens brings a couple of dozen ambitious young players to New York every October in hopes of winning a berth on the team.   Manager Douglas, always on the lookout for choice material, has made it a custom to encourage every youngster in whom he sees any promise.   'Every one of the boys I bring here to try out for the team,' he remarked, 'has his

Basketeers in The Big Colleges. Only a few colored boys prior to 1945 made good in the court game among the larger colleges. The pull of colored colleges on high school basketball players of ability, and the difficulty of breaking through the prejudices and discriminations in most of the larger conferences have served to prevent a greater number of Negro players from becoming members of college teams. Few coaches care to have the trouble of providing accommodations for colored players when on trips. If the train goes south, the colored player is left behind. The team may find itself separated when there are hotel accommodations to be considered. Seldom do coaches or school authorities make use of or plan to use this situation to develop greater tolerance through sport. Recently, the athletic teams from the South are playing teams on which there are Negroes, when they come North. It may not be long before color lines will disappear in this sport in many more states.

Of the early college basketeers who have achieved fame and glory on teams with white players, there have been a few who deserve honorable mention. Two of the players recorded on these earlier college teams were Wilbur S. Woods who played at Nebraska,

fare paid and all his living expenses while he's making his bid. And if he does not make it, I pay his fare back home.'

"All the living expenses of the members of the team are paid while they are on the road "even down to their chewing gum," Bob also revealed. The team covered about 38,000 miles this season, traveling in the handsome bus which Douglas has provided. The bus is driven by Tex Burnett, himself a crack baseball catcher at one time, and in four years he has had but one minor accident, grazing a truck on the highway out west while travelling in a heavy snowstorm. The team is also accompanied by Eric Illidge, the club secretary, and Vincent 'Doc' Bryant, the trainer. During the past season they appeared in such places as New Orleans, Wyoming, Iowa and other far sections of the country.

"Manager Douglas does not travel with the team, remaining in New York from where he arranges the bookings and maps out the itinerary. His assistant, Frank Richards, handles the enormous job of publicity, getting out releases, mats and posters. Richards estimates that he has sent out some 200,000 posters for the team. For the past fifteen years, they have been treating cage fans to some of the classiest basketball in the world. For at least ten of these years they have had a strong claim to the world's championship."—With permission of Cyril Bourne, sports writer, from the New York *Amsterdam News*, April 18, 1939.

and won his letter in 1908, 1909, and 1910.   In the East, in New
York City two excellent college players were seen on the metropolitan
courts.   The Rev. John Johnson was the first colored basketball
player at Columbia University in 1919, and Dr. Dash was an eminent performer at the City College of New York.   Maynard Garner
of Washington, D. C., entered Hamilton College in New York.   He
played center on the college team and was elected captain of the
Hamilton varsity in his senior year.   In 1923, Charley Drew was
starring at Amherst in football, basketball, and track.   In addition
to being elected captain of the track team, Drew won the Ashley
Memorial trophy awarded to the best all-round athlete at college.
In Ohio, at Oberlin, where colored athletes have always been free
to go out for teams, the two Barnes boys, the late James D. and
Samuel E., were representative of the college on the basketball
team during the years 1928, 1929, 1930.   Fenwick H. Watkins
was captain of the University of Vermont team in 1908.

In this sport too, Paul Leroy Robeson, who while earning a
Phi Beta Kappa key and winning four college letters, gained the
acclaim of the followers of the indoor court game.   Robeson was
center for three years, 1917, 1918, and 1919, on the Rutgers University quint.

Negroes not Represented in Big Ten.   Colored players have
never been welcomed on the basketball courts of the Big-Ten colleges.   But Cleveland Abbott, Tuskegee's physical director, and
Owen Ross were stars on the South Dakota State team during the
years before World War I.   Horace Johnson was a basketball
player at the Dakota College during '36, '37 and '38.   Along
about 1920 Ralph J. Bunche crashed into the Pacific Conference
games.   His coach wrote that Ralph was one of the best he had
coached.   He was probably the only colored player who had played
on conference teams on the Pacific Coast.   At Dartmouth, Forest
C. Whittaker made the varsity team.   Boston University in 1937
had two good players on its teams, Bob Yancy and Ben
Franklin.   Larry Bleach, Detroit, 1937, and Coward of Brooklyn
College, 1938, were outstanding.   Probably two of the best college

basketball players of all times, regardless of race, were George Gregory of Columbia and Wilmeth Sidat Singh of Syracuse.

Sidat Singh. A star in football, Wilmeth Sidat Singh of Syracuse was one of the best basketball players on the court in his day. In the Palestra Gymnasium at Pennsylvania during the following winter, a columnist thus wrote of his feats, "Sidat Singh scored twenty points to aid the Syracuse team in defeating the University of Pennsylvania quintet by a 49–38 score before 3,000 spectators. Sidat Singh, a marked man from the beginning, racked up eight field goals and four out of seven free throws for the twenty points, equaling the season's top mark, and coming within one point of equaling the all time high score of 21, for one player, in the Pennsylvania Palestra. Singh did not play in the Navy game but was a star performer in his team's sensational play of the season, 1939, when Syracuse won fourteen straight games."

Singh was a natural athlete. His court work, one writer says, does not show the "silky finesse of the born court strategist but he has the canny sense of out-guessing his opponents which enables him to get a greater number of shots than do most forwards in the game." Singh's name received more special notice in the write-ups of Syracuse's games than any other player.

On December 31, 1938, from the New York *Times* we read, "With its gridiron hero, Wilmeth Sidat Singh, heading the attack with 18 points, Syracuse's five subdued Pennsylvania State tonight before 16,000 fans, 43 to 23. The victory gave the Orange ample revenge for a previous set back. Sidat Singh collected 11 points in the first half to help Syracuse to a 21–8 advantage at intermission."

George Gregory. George Gregory's memory at Columbia University will long be revered for his sterling work on the courts at the Morningside institution. Gregory's career was eventful and shows how athletic ability may serve. Gregory had dropped from school and was a member of the 135th Street "Y." In a game with the DeWitt Clinton five the coach of the high school was struck with the playing of Gregory, and soon thereafter George was induced to enter DeWitt Clinton. He became captain of a famous high school team, and his team won the New York City championship in 1926 and 1927. He was graduated and entered Columbia. There he attracted the attention of critics all about the Eastern circuit. In his senior year he became captain of one of the greatest basketball teams in the history of Columbia. This team won the Eastern championships in thrilling seasonal tourneys for 1930 and 1931.

Gregory was selected for the all-high team for the city of New York in 1927. He was an honor selection on Knute Rockne's All-American College Team for 1930 and on other All-American selections for 1931. Later George became director of the largest youth project for Negroes in America, the Harlem Children's Center of the Children's Aid Society. He still receives the plaudits of all as the former heroic cynosure of the listful eyes of the basketball fans of greater New York.

William King. Another well known basketeer of renown was William "Dolly" King, a star on one of the greatest teams in the East, the Long Island University quint. King attended Alexander Hamilton High School of Brooklyn where he captained the baseball, basketball and football teams. He was equally versatile at Long Island University where he played football, basketball and baseball. His coach, Clair F. Bee, considered him to have reached the pinnacle of his sterling performances in basketball, and he ascended to greatest heights when he played the 1937 game against George Washington University in New York, decisively demonstrating that he was high scorer and the greatest defense player in the game.

Later Basketball. There were many excellent basketeers during subsequent years, and some teams created legendary history. Don Barksdale in February, 1948 was named on the All-Time Pacific Coast Conference Basketball team. All of the players since 1920 were considered, and the play of Barksdale warranted naming him in the estimation of a jury of qualified experts. Not only did Barksdale become a great basketball player but one of the best high jumpers and hop-step-jumpers in the nation. He was selected as a member of the 1948 Olympic basketball squad in recognition of his great play during the Olympic trials. All of the players of the Kentucky University team and the Phillips 66 Oilers qualified by being runner-up and winner respectively. Barksdale's team, the Oakland (California) Bittners lost out to the Oilers. Two players not on the first and second teams to finish were selected. Don was one. He justified his selection by being one of the high ranking scorers in the series of games at the Olympics, and particularly in the game with the Argentine team where America won by two points, Barksdale scored a dozen points in his half time stay in the game as center. In the 1947 season he was high point scorer in the nation, and was sensational as a player in the American League on the Pacific Coast during the 1947–48 season.

Ermer Robinson of Fort Warren, Wyoming, on a soldier's quintet, was reported to be second highest scorer for the 1944 season by Ted Meier of the Associated Press. Robinson flipped in 136 field goals and 52 free throws in 17 games for a grand total of 324 points. The leading point scorer that year was Dick Wilkins of Oregon State playing in 29 games for a total of 345 points. Dick Culberson was the first colored boy to become a member of a "Big Ten" varsity team. He qualified for the Iowa University squad in 1947. Charley Cooper was outstanding at Duquesne University in 1947. Ben Bluitt and Art White were members of Chicago's Loyola College squad in the 1947 season. Norman Skinner at Columbia University was one of the leading point scorers in the Eastern Intercollegiate League.

Always in New York and some other cities north and west colored boys periodically loom up large in the court game. It is noteworthy that in the 1943–44 season there were five colored boys captains of high school and college quints in New York. They were: Tillman Overstreet of Benjamin Franklin High, David Williams of Seward Park High, Irving Sylvester of the High School of Commerce, Norman Skinner of Stuyvesant High and Eddie Younger captain of Long Island University's team.

Since 1938 three colored teams have won the World's professional championship title. The Renaissance won in 1939, the Harlem Globetrotters in 1940, and the Washington Bears in 1943. The Bears defeated the Oshkosh Pros 49–31 before 12,000 spectators in the Chicago Stadium. In the 1947–48 season the Globetrotters won 52 games in a row. They boasted a 21 year total of 2,938 victories against 225 defeats.

During the Second World War many colored aggregations on the basketball court made enviable records in the various theaters of war and in camps here and there over the nation. "Somewhere" in the Pacific, the Hillside's "Little Blues" from the ship Repair Company, won the All-Aleutian cage tournament. They won 22 consecutive games against stiff competition. It would require a chapter to record similar achievements.

The Colored Conference Game. Basketball is played in all of the colored college athletic conferences. It is an expensive sport but an excellent diversion for the students during the long indoor season. The trips are long in most associations. The problem of arriving at a conference championship without the necessity of playing a round-robin series has not been solved.

The Colored Intercollegiate Athletic Association teams, as a group, developed faster than the teams in other conferences. As late as 1922, however, basketball was a weak sister in the C.I.A.A. sports. In the first annual publication of the C.I.A.A. only Hampton and Lincoln had listed lettermen in basketball, and only seven officials, Martin, Lawson, Keys, Gibson, Washington, Reed and Henderson, were approved.

Today in every southern college conference basketball is the pre-eminent indoor season sport. Every year finds a large increase in the number of Negro high schools engaged in the court game. After completion of school days, where most boys learn to play, the love of the contest leads them to continued activity under auspices of private or public recreation agencies or as members of athletic clubs, boys' clubs, or fraternity teams.

College players of first rank, after graduation, find the lure of the game still strong, and easily affiliate with alumni, fraternity, or club aggregations. Soon, however, they lose the brilliance of college days and become our by-gone heroes. The wonder-player of ten or even five years ago lives only in the memory of contemporary worshippers of his brief scintillating days in the limelight. His picture hung on the walls of his Alma Mater, his name on a cup, a book of clippings, and the record of his team connect him with the string of those gone to live only in reminiscences.

Colored College Stars of Recent Years. Basketball in colored college circles during the forties, mainly since the elimination of the center jump, has grown into its greatest popularity in the many conferences. Some of the teams have made legendary history. Ric Roberts, writing in the Pittsburgh Courier, rates the Xavier University team of New Orleans (Bray, Rhodes, Cole, Gant and McQuitter) as the greatest college team of all past time. The Xavier "Ambassadors" of 1935–38 lost only two games in four years, winning 67. They lost in 1935 to LeMoyne, 33–32, and to Clark in 1937 by a 27–26 score. Playing an exhibition game against the famous Renaissance team of 1938, they lost two games by scores of 38–37, and 24–20 in the spacious Xavier gym on the New Orleans campus. These boys played together as a unit at Wendell Phillips High in Chicago and transferred as a team to the southern school.

Clark University's "Panthers" of 1939–41, Roberts declared, was second only to the Xavier outfit. The Panthers won the 1940 Southern Intercollegiate Athletic Conference title, and played every top colored team in the nation for the national title in 1941. Some of these boys are still remembered such as: Abbey Henderson, Sonny Younger, Pop Gates, Hank DeZonie, Joe Johnson and Pemberton.

Virginia Union's "Dream Team" of 1939–40 was, along with those mentioned above, among those to put together at least 20 consecutive wins. The only teams able to halt Coach Hucles' team were Hampton and North Carolina State. This entry into the list of never-to-be-forgotten teams comprised Glover, Frazier, King, Hyde, and Campbell.

Many other teams like Langston's "Homer-Burton-Weldon-Pyles-Webb" combination; North Carolina's "Colbert-Downing-Brown-Ennis-Warmick" quint; the West Virginia Yellow Jackets; the Kentucky State "Thorobreds" and some others ranked high in college conference basketball.

For those who would know the champion basketeers whose names were on the tongues of thousands during their careers at our Negro schools, it will be necessary to secure the bound copies of the splendid annual journals of proceedings of Colored College Conference Athletic Associations. The writer recommends a periodic compilation of the materials of these annuals for every conference. This work and the accompanying statistical study would easily be worth a Master's thesis and would keep college athletic heroes prominently before the aspiring youth now in school.

CHAPTER IX

The National Game

First of the Team Games. Baseball is our oldest team sport. It grew out of cricket and the English game of rounders. It is supposed that baseball, or cricket with a base, was started in New York in 1839 by Abner Doubleday, but this story is sometimes discounted. The game has developed from a two-player, pitcher-catcher team to the present four base, nine-player team.

Prior to and during the Civil War, baseball became a popular sport. It was often played by soldiers. The first college game was between Williams and Amherst in 1859. Big league baseball began in 1876 with the creation of the National League; and its rival association, the American League was formed in 1882. After ten years the American League fell apart to re-form as a stronger league in 1900.

For many years college baseball was the most popular sport even in the North where the seasons for school baseball are short. The usual spring trips of the northern college nines throughout the South were interesting events in the nineties. Especially strong were the Catholic college teams—Holy Cross, Fordham, and Georgetown. Because of the increased popularity of football, track, and other sports, and the cost of baseball, it has lost its earlier glamour and is out of many college athletic programs. Even in the Negro colleges in the South where the seasons are generally longer and more conducive to the game, baseball has met the fate it suffered in many other colleges. But later there followed a trend of revived interest in baseball in college athletics.

Dixie Colored Baseball. It is not known to what extent that Negroes played baseball during slavery, but after freedom the game was copied from the soldiers who frequently played in camp

167

during war days. In the late eighties most country-towns and cross-roads had baseball teams from the Gulf of Mexico to the Mason-Dixon line. The writer remembers with what thrills of emotion he watched or worshipped the colored teams and players in his county of Fairfax in Virginia. Seminary, Bailey's Cross Roads, Fairfax, Falls Church, Vienna, and a host of other towns were represented by teams during the late nineties. Down in Jacksonville, Florida, James Weldon Johnson, the late poet, used to demonstrate the mystery of the pitched curving ball. On the fields of Virginia around Norfolk, Alexandria and Petersburg, from 1885 to 1890, were playing boys who were destined to develop into players like Clarence Matthews of Harvard. Negro players took to baseball with the vim they had shown for boxing for the best part of a century. The legendary accounts of great feats by Negro ball players ought to have been recorded and preserved. In the past ages of hard work and colorful religion, nothing meant so much to the life of an impoverished people after a day or week of toil as the scene and setting of the country-side baseball game.

Negro Professionals Start at Hotel Argyle. The first Negro team composed of paid members is recorded as a playing aggregation that at first was a team of waiters of the Argyle Hotel at Babylon, New York. This club of hotel waiters and bell-hops was organized in 1885 by Frank Thompson, head waiter of the hotel. During that summer the team played nine games with the best of the white semi-pro clubs around New York and Long Island, winning six and losing four. In September, Thompson called them the "Cuban Giants," and started them on a professional career.

Knowing the growing prejudices that had infiltrated into the social structure of the North and East, the management realized that to pass off the boys as Cubans or Spaniards would enable them to play in places where as native Negro boys they would not have been able to make business contacts. On the playing field, a few of the Negro players would put on an act and talk a "gibberish" to each other. Because the New York Giants were a popular team of players, the Cubans added the name "Giants." The name

"Giants" became attached to nearly every prominent colored team for a quarter of a century. One still remembers the Brooklyn Royal Giants, the Bacharach Giants, the Mohawk Giants, the Chicago American Giants, and others.

Leagues Organized. Several efforts were made to form leagues of Negro baseball teams. All the early attempts were doomed to failure. In the spring of 1887, a Negro League was formed on paper, but did not reach the field. In 1889, a league of six white and two Negro clubs was organized in the East but folded up in a few weeks. About 1906 several of the prominent teams in the East, including the Cuban Giants, the Cuban X-Giants, the Washington Giants, the Royal Giants of Newark, endeavored to form the International League, but before midsummer it collapsed.

Leaving the East, one finds that on February 13, 1920, in Kansas City, Missouri, the western circuit of the National Negro Baseball League was organized. Seated in that meeting were Tenny Blount of Detroit, L. S. Cobb of the St. Louis Giants, W. A. Kelley of Washington, John Matthews of the Dayton-Monarchs, Joe Greene of the Chicago Giants, C. I. Taylor of the Indianapolis A.B.C.'s, Elwood Knox of Indianapolis, Andrew "Rube" Foster, J. L. Williamson of Kansas City, Missouri, and Charles Marshall, an Indianapolis newspaperman.

The League upon organizing was chartered in the states of Michigan, Illinois, Ohio, Pennsylvania, New York and Maryland. Those signing the constitution of the newly formed league were Rube Foster, Tenny Blount, J. L. Wilkerson, C. I. Taylor, Joe Greene, and Lorenzo Cobb. Each paid $500 to bind them to the league and constitution. Those who helped with the constitution were Dave Wright of Chicago, Ellwood Knox of Indianapolis, Carey B. Lewis of Chicago, and Elisha Scott of Leavenworth. Rube Foster was named president and secretary. The clubs to represent the League during this first year were the American Giants (Chicago), Chicago Giants, Kansas City Monarchs, St. Louis Giants, Detroit Stars, and the Indianapolis A.B.C's. The next meeting was on December 4, 1920, in Indianapolis. Foster was re-elected president and secretary for the ensuing year. The association now became the National Association of Colored Professional Baseball and the Negro National League. The following teams were added: the Hilldale Club, Columbus Club, the New York Bacharach Giants, and the Cuban Stars.

In 1921–22, the Eastern League came into being. Ed Bolden of the Hilldale Club organized the Eastern League and was president. It consisted of the Harrisburg Giants, the Hilldales, Lincoln Giants, Brooklyn Royal Giants, Bacharach Giants, Baltimore Black Sox, with the Washington Potomacs as an associate club. There was much shifting of teams due to the lack of organized control. Sometime about 1932, the Negro National League and the Eastern League went down. Subsequent to this dissolution "Cum" Posey brought about the East-West organization. This East-West League consisted of Hilldale, Baltimore Black Sox, Detroit Stars, Columbus, Pittsburgh Crawfords, Homestead Grays, Washington Pilots, and Black Yankees. The first world series between Negro teams was held in 1924 and 1925 between the Negro National and Negro Eastern League champion teams. The first teams in 1924 and 1925 were the Hilldale (Eastern), Kansas City (Western). Contenders in 1926 and 1927 were the Chicago American Giants and the Bacharach Giants.

The 1939 Negro American League located in the West started the following teams with franchises in the cities indicated: Kansas City Monarchs in St. Louis, Atlanta Black Crackers in Louisville, Jacksonville Red Caps in Cleveland, Memphis Giants in Memphis, A.B.C.'s in Indianapolis, and the Chicago American Giants in Chicago.

A Negro National League consisted that year of the following: The Elite Giants in Baltimore, Newark Eagles, Toledo, Homestead Grays, the Philadelphia Stars, the New York Black Yankees, and the New York Cuban Stars team managed by Alexander Pompez. This later day Negro National League contrived to function during subsequent years apparently on firmer ground. The clubs carried from fifteen to twenty salaried players and business associates. In the beginning many of the games were staged for exhibition only.

Tom Wilson of the Baltimore Elites was elected president to succeed "Gus" Greenlee, retired.

Another Association existing in the late thirties known as the American Association included the following teams: Baltimore, Hilldale, Greensboro, Winston-Salem, Philadelphia and High Point.

Modernizing Negro Baseball. The colored teams have had many knotty problems to solve. The depression caught many a Negro baseball venture and headed it for the rocks. Greenlee's field, one of the best in the country, bloomed and passed out of existence. Competing leagues and outlaw clubs weakened the holding power of player-contracts, and the disciplinary control of players. Many players would frequently leave a club in mid-season. The feeling of a need to entertain the fun-loving as well as the baseball crowd led to a great deal of clowning by players, and to much un-orthodox baseball behavior, which frequently was distasteful to the real baseball fans. In organized baseball, clowns are engaged to amuse the crowd. Seldom do players entertain with such antics.

Recently, big baseball magnates have been inclined to lease the big baseball parks to Negro teams when the home teams are on the road. In order to serve the baseball public a brand of baseball equal to that furnished by organized baseball clubs of white players, it was voted at the Spring meeting of the Negro National League in 1939 to streamline the game by adopting the following regulations:

Provide for night baseball.

Prohibit players from throwing the ball around between innings.

Permit no delay longer than 20 minutes between games of a double-header.

Pitchers will be allowed only four warm-up pitches between innings.

Owners or secretaries shall be fined if they contact or criticize umpires during or after a league game.

Any club walking off the field shall forfeit the game and its franchise.

No umpire shall be removed except by vote of four of the seven teams. The two leagues have agreed not to "take" players from either league, and dates have been reserved for home-and-home inter-league games during the regular baseball season.

Other leagues of Negro teams of consequence were organized. The Midwestern Baseball League operated from Indianapolis. The Negro International League comprising teams in the Tidewater section took in the teams in Virginia and the Carolinas.

Baseball has become one of the major sport interests of Latin America. Mexico, Cuba, and Venezuela are among the nations to the south of us that take their baseball seriously. So attractive has baseball become that the salaries offered have threatened to take the star players away from the American Negro teams. There is no color line in these non-United States teams. After the regular season in the United States is over, many of the better players go to Cuba, to other islands, or to the mainland countries of South America and play ball during our winter season.

Famous Players. Negro players have been as great and are as highly praised as the stellar lights of the American and the National Leagues. Field performances of mighty men of baseball in Negro leagues equal the feats of the glamorous Cobb, Lajoie, Wagner, Mathewson, Johnson, or Ruth. Many old timers place John Henry Lloyd, a shortstop, in the highest niche in baseball's hall of fame. One radio commentator speaking in St. Louis, in answering a question as to the greatest baseball player in history, commented, "If you ask who, in organized baseball, I would say Babe Ruth, but if you mean in all baseball, the answer would be a colored man named John Henry Lloyd." Another columnist,[1] writing about Negro baseball, said, "It is faster on the bases than major league ball now being played in the American and National circuits; it is almost as swift and spectacular on the field; it lacks the batting form of the white man's big leagues; it has a shortstop, Willie Wells of Newark, who is as good as a dozen men in that position in the majors today; it has pitchers who could fill places on half of the leading teams of the top white leagues." Further, he writes, "In the sixth of the annual All-Star matches which are played at Comiskey Park between two Negro leagues, the American circuit

---

[1] Lloyd Lewis describing East-West game of 1938.

known as the West, and the National called the East, the West won yesterday 5–4. The game was afire with speed. The bases were run with a swiftness and daring absent from the white man's game for twenty years. They stretched singles into doubles, they went down to first so fast that no infield double play succeeded on a ground ball, and one of them, Robinson of the Memphis Red Sox, made a home run inside the park. The aforementioned Wells dragged and beat out as canny a bunt as Comiskey Park ever saw."
"A welcome sight in a big-league park was the willingness of Negro out-fielders to throw out base runners, and of pitchers to whip bunts to second for force plays. Such risks are almost things of the past in the white man's major circuits. Only in batting are the Negro pros inferior. Too many of them preserve the hallmark of the amateur, the 'foot in the bucket;' the shy-away of the front foot as the pitch comes up."

Some of the scribes in Southern cities find themselves amused and at the same time appreciative of the skill shown by Negro players. Jesse A. Linthicum of Baltimore writes, "3,500 fans saw colored teams in action at Oriole Park. Homestead and the Washington Elite Giants played here yesterday. The Giants won the first of a double-header. Fine fielding, unusually good pitching and heavy hitting marked the games. In the first game one of the players hit one over the center-field scoreboard. That feat has been duplicated only twice. The players are giant in size. . . . A long drive was hit toward the centerfield fence. The outfielder was off at the crack of the bat. As he camped under the ball he danced a jig. . . . West, first baseman, is a big fellow who handles himself like a real big leaguer. They say he has not made an error all season, catching the ball one-handed. He bobbled a couple when he put two hands on the ball."

Colonel Edward W. Dale, noted hotel proprietor and sportsman, remembers a game played in Cape May, New Jersey, when the Goroms, a great colored team of that date, played the Cape May Collegians, an all-star aggregation, before President Chester A. Arthur, about 1884. On these teams were players who are remembered as affectionately as the Delehantys, the Cobbs, Wagners,

Lajoies, and others.   Some of these players, who are but legendary heroes to the modern fans, were Booker, Duncan, Ball, and Pete Hill, of the Leland Giants, while Cyclone Joe Williams, Wiley, Santop, Jule Thomas, Langford and Leroy Grant were on the roster of the Lincoln Giants.   Then, there were Danny Despert, Webster, and Hill, of the Royal Giants; Patterson, of Page Fence; Clarence Williams and Stovey, of the Goroms; Ben Taylor, Williams, and Shively, of the A.B.C.'s; Lewis, Hairstone, Hall, Logan, and Harvey Williams, of the Black Sox.   The Bacharach roster bore the names of Leroy Roberts, Marcell Cummings, Henderson, Tread-well, and Dick Lundy.   Most of these old stars lived later on reminis-cences and afforded excellent recitals of past legends to all lovers of baseball with whom they came into contact.   A few of the old clubs still operate, whereas the names of others linger only in the memory of the old timers.   Old timers can recall the exploits of the inde-pendent, or teams of pre-league days, such as the Leland Giants of Chicago, the West Baden Sprindels, the ex-Cuban Giants, Page Fence Giants, Brooklyn Royal Giants, Lincoln Giants, the Indian-apolis A.B.C.'s, Philadelphia Giants, Baltimore Black Sox, Bach-arach Giants, the Goroms, and the New York Giants.

Rube Foster.   The most colorful of Negro ball players, pro-moters and managers was the late Rube Foster, son of a Texas Methodist preacher.   During his active years Foster established a record and a fame that will remain as long as baseball is of interest to Negro players.   He was the founder of organized professional ball along with the lamented C. I. Taylor.   Besides being a pitcher and manager, he holds high rank as a strategist, and measures with Connie Mack and McGraw as a manipulator of inside baseball.   At one time Rube served under McGraw as coach of pitchers for the New York Giants.   He at another time pitched for his club against Rube Waddell and the Philadelphia Athletics.   He was the first of colored managers to match colored teams against big league clubs in post season tilts.

"Cyclone" Williams.   Another immortal in Negro playing ranks was "Cyclone" Joe Williams, who established an all-time record as a mound artist, having to his credit twenty-four years of continuous service from 1910 to 1934. During his career he turned in some marvelous pitching feats. He once pitched a 1–0 night game against the Kansas City Monarchs that went 18 innings. He struck out 24 men, while Brewer, the Monarch pitcher, "whiffed" 19. One of his spectacular feats was his defeat of the Philadelphia Nationals in 1915 after the Phillies had lost the world's championship to the Boston Red Sox. Joe's team, the Lincoln Giants, secured a one run lead in the first inning, and Joe protected this lead going into the ninth inning. He temporarily lost control and filled the bases. The lengthening evening shadows saw this pitcher rise to great heights, striking out the next three batters, Niehoff, Bancroft, and Paskert on nine pitched balls. Hardly could there be a more thrilling baseball climax than this.

Memorable Games. Many observers insisted that such players be signed up by the national leagues. The St. Louis *Globe-Democrat* published a series of articles to give evidence that the magnates, not the players, were responsible for denying to the public better baseball by not using Negro players. The writer began his article with, "Here is the first of a series of reprints of games played between white major leagues and race teams. This will serve to show that the owners and not the players are the ones keeping the color bar in baseball." He then describes a battle between the St. Louis Stars and the Detroit Tigers in which the St. Louis Stars defeated the Detroit Americans 5–4: "The St. Louis Stars," continued he, "outsmarted the Detroit Tigers here today, and the Motor City Club went down to defeat, 5 to 4. In the last of the eighth with the score tied at 4–4, Frank Warfield, of the Stars, singled to left after Russell flied out to Bobby Veach in center field.

"With the dangerous Charleston coming to the bat, the Detroit outfielders moved back near the fences. But Charleston crossed them up with a single just over short, and Warfield streaked for third. With two strikes and one ball on Dan Kennard, the Stars pulled off some daring base running. Charleston beat Woodall's throw to Cutshaw. In the meantime, Warfield dashed for home, sliding across the plate ahead of Cutshaw's return throw to Woodall, to complete a clean double steal and win the game."

Another barnstorming exhibition between the St. Louis team of the National League and the St. Louis Giants in the fall of 1920 showed how well matched were Negro teams and teams of big-league white players.   In the opening game of a series between the Cardinal barnstormers and the St. Louis Negro Giants, the latter team was the victor in ten innings, 5 to 4.   The winning run was scored when Clemons, of the Nationals, dropped a throw to the home plate. Jim Lyons opened the inning for the Giants with a single and took second on a wild pitch.   Hewett bunted safely when A. Lyons, pitcher for the Nationals, fumbled.   Charleston was purposely passed to fill up the bases, Blackwell hit to A. Lyons, and the latter threw home, but Clemons dropped the ball and J. Lyons scored, ending the game.

The Giants got away to a lead of four runs in the first two innings. Charleston drove out a home run in the first session.   In the second, slow fielding errors and hitting mixed in netted the Negroes three runs.   In the fifth, the Cardinals got one of the runs back on some hitting and a couple of force-outs.   In the sixth, the Cards got after Drake, Giant pitcher, and drove him off the slab.   Some well-timed hitting, in which Lavan featured with a double and Clemons with a triple, turned the trick and also netted three runs, tying up the score.

St. Louis Nationals. . . . .   0 0 0 0 1 3 0 0 0 0—4
St. Louis Giants. . . . .   1 3 0 0 0 0 0 0 0 1—5

William Dismukes, describing a game in the Pittsburgh *Courier* (January 26, 1929), said, "One of the long-to-be-remembered games in colored baseball was that played by the Bacharach Giants of Atlantic City, and the American Giants of Chicago, at Chicago, Wednesday, August 16, 1922.   This game, replete with scintillating fielding plays and brilliant pitching, lasted 20 innings, being won by Chicago by a 1 to 0 score.

"This score was made in the last half of the twentieth inning. Torrienti, first batter to face Treadwell in the Chicago half of the last inning, worked Treadwell for a pass. Bobby Williams moved Torrienti up a base by a neat sacrifice. Then Dave Marlarcher, who had entered the game in the ninth inning as a substitute base-runner for Beckwith, singled sharply to right field, Torrienti beating Raminez's throw to the plate.

"Treadwell went the entire route for the Easterners, holding the Chicago gang to nine scattered hits, one a double by Williams, striking out twelve batters, hitting two, and passing seven. For Chicago, Rile started the game, being relieved by Dave Brown, after Duncan, the first batter up in the Bacharach half of the fifth inning, had singled. Brown, during his 14-inning stay on the mound, struck out 10, and issued two bases on balls. He struck out Shively for the third out in the Bacharach half of the twelfth inning and followed it up by striking out Marcell, Lloyd and E. Brown in succession in the sixth inning.

"There were no less than eight two-ply killings during the game. Each side was credited with four. E. Brown's throw to the plate, after catching Lyon's fly, to nip D. Brown, who tried to score after the catch, was the outstanding dual killing of the day. This was a fifth inning play. Each team had nine hits and each committed two errors."

Commenting on a game played between the Hilldales and Monarchs, played at Muelbach's Field, home grounds of the Kansas City Blues, Andrew Rube Foster, founder and president of the Negro National League, after observing the class of play as exhibited by the Kansas City Monarchs and Hilldales in their clash for the world's championship in 1924, characterized the playing of the Hilldale outfielders (Thomas, Briggs and Johnson) as being the best he had ever seen during the series, which went ten games. Not an outfielder threw to the wrong base, not a baserunner advanced an extra base on balls that were hit to the outfield throughout the entire series.

"Biz" Mackey, catcher and manager of the former Washington Elite Giants, in describing a play made by one of the outfielders, Otto Briggs, right fielder, claimed it to be the greatest he had seen. The Kansas City Club put on a rally in the late innings, with Newt

Allen on first and one man out; Dobie Moore hit a long drive to right center, and Briggs ran many feet up an embankment in right center to intercept the ball and throw it back to the infield in an effort to keep the runner from advancing.   Upon climbing up the hill, he turned to look for the ball and, to his amazement, saw it dropping in front of him.   He caught the pellet and threw it to second base, where Frank Warfield grabbed it and touched the bag, for a game-winning double play.   Briggs' throw traveled on a line to the bag. The game was played at Muelbach's Field, home grounds of the Kansas City Blues, Kansas City, Missouri.

Connie Mack's team once played a game against Walter Schlichter's Philadelphia Giants in the Phillies Park at 23rd and Columbia Avenue.   Rube Foster, Nelson, and Clarence Williams were the Giants' battery, while Rube Waddell and Schreckingast were opposing battery forces.   The game went thirteen innings to a 13–13 score with Waddell and Foster each fanning 13 batters, according to Colonel Dale.

Many Negro players have been nominated for baseball's hall of fame by sports writers, but some of the players in professional circles who will go down in history as all-time immortals are the following:

Catchers: Joshua Gibson, "Biz" Mackey, Clarence Williams, Petway.

Pitchers: Joseph Williams, Richard Redding, David Brown, Rube Foster, William Foster and Satchel Paige.

First Base: Ben Taylor, Leonard and Leroy Grant.

Second Base: Samuel Hughes.

Third Base: Jud Wilson and Andrew Jackson.

Shortstop: John Henry Lloyd and Homerun Johnson.

Center Field: Oscar Charleston.

Right Field: Peter Hill.

Left Field: Patterson and Torrienti.

Utility: Richard Lundy and Fred Grant, infield; Dixon and Chester Brooks, outfield.

Manager: Rube Foster.

Others deserving honorable mention are:

Pitchers: Andrew "Stringbean" Williams, Frank Wickware, "Bullet" Rogan, John Donaldson.

Infielders: Frank Warfield, Bingo Demoss, Henry Blackman, William Monroe, Eddie Douglass, John Beckwith, Jim Taylor, Oliver Marcelle.

Outfielders: J. Lyons, Spotswood Poles, Jesse Barbour, Peter Washington, "Clint" Thomas, "Jap" Payne, McNair and Clarence "Fats" Jenkins.

Color Line Bars Best Talent. More and more, year after year, sports writers and baseball managers and magnates bemoaned the fact that tradition and fear prevented them from signing some of the splendid ball players who happen to be identified as Negroes. John McGraw had a Negro ball player named Charlie Grant playing first base on his team twenty years ago. He was represented as an Indian. Things progressed nicely until some of Grant's Negro friends threw a party for him, gave the secret away, and McGraw let him go. Several swarthy boys have managed to pass muster for white during the years.

There have been many instances of colored players on teams with white players. In New England there were a number of colored players on semi-pro team rosters. Colored players have been members of organized leagues of minor brackets. About 1908 there was a mixed league of professionals in Philadelphia just as there were mixed leagues in New England. This Philadelphia League consisted of three colored teams, the Philadelphia Giants, the Cuban X-Giants, the Wilmington Giants, and two teams of white players, the Philadelphia Professionals and the Riverton Palmyra. The last colored catcher on a big league team was Fleet Walker in 1887, of the Toledo American Association, and Toby Higgins was the last colored pitcher in 1888.

Jimmy Powers and Heywood Broun very often belabored the men and conditions that militated against fair play in athletics. On February 25, 1939, Ford Frick, a president of the National League, was reported in an interview to have intimated that the time was not far distant when Negro players would be on major league teams. Obstacles seemed to be many, but prejudice was the father of all. The same amount of intestinal fortitude that makes for a good ball player is required of baseball magnates and high commissioners in order to make baseball a truly democratic sport. Since the need to train and manage a baseball team as a unit in traveling, in hostelries, and in spring training camps presented problems because of racial prejudice of southerners, faint-hearted management refused to test the use of colored ball players in the big leagues. There was no written law against the use of Negroes. There was a fear by club owners that the high commissioners might decline to permit a club to use such a player. It was also felt that violence might result, if or when the southern boys got provoked and used spikes against colored players or the other way around.

There was no doubt but that the colored player is skillful and intelligent enough as a ball player to satisfy the rigid requirements of major league ball. It was even admitted that the Negro player would add color to the game and do for baseball what "Joe" and "Hank" have done for boxing. The achievement of status by Negroes in the exclusive leagues fulfilled this prophecy.

Shirley Povich's Comment. Shirley Povich, writing in the Washington *Post* on Saturday, April 7, 1939, from Orlando, Florida, said, "There's a couple of million dollars' worth of baseball talent on the loose, ready for the big leagues, yet unsigned by any major league clubs. There are pitchers who would win 20 games this season for any big league club that offered them contracts, and there are outfielders who could hit .350, infielders who could win quick recognition as stars, and there is at least one catcher who at this writing is probably superior to Bill Dickey.

"Only one thing is keeping them out of the big leagues—the pigmentation of their skin. They happen to be colored. That's their crime in the eyes of big league club owners." He further states, "Their talents are being wasted in the rickety parks in the Negro sections of Pittsburgh, Philadelphia, New York, Chicago and four other cities that comprise the major league of Negro baseball. They haven't a chance to get into the big leagues of the white folks. It's a tight little boycott that the majors have set up against colored players."

Concerning the rebellion against the forces that conspire to keep the American people from seeing some of the best ball players in the country, Povich writes, "There have been campaigns aimed at smashing the boycott. One New York newspaper openly advocated the signing of Negro players, and Heywood Broun has often berated the baseball magnates for drawing the color line. But despite the presence of thousands of colored customers in the stands, the club owners have blithely hewed to the color line. They are content, seemingly, to leave well enough alone and make no concerted play for Negro patronage."

Povich believed that there are Negro teams that could do very well in big league competition. In his opinion the Homestead Grays that train in Florida each Spring were the best of the colored teams. Members of the Washington American ball team went to see the Homestead Grays play the Newark Eagles at Tinker Field, and Povich said, "They went away with deep respect for colored baseball." He wrote, "Walter Johnson sat in a box at the game, profoundly impressed with the talents of the colored players. 'There,' he said, 'is a catcher that any big league club would like to buy for $200,000. I've heard of him before. His name is Gibson. They call him 'Hoot' Gibson, and he can do everything. He hits the ball a mile. And he catches so easy he might just as well be in a rocking chair. Throws like a rifle. Bill Dickey isn't as good a catcher. Too bad this Gibson is a colored fellow.'

"That was the general impression among the Nats who saw the game. They liked the Homestead catcher, and they liked the big lanky Negro pitcher for the Homesteads, who struck out 12 Newark players in five innings. They liked the centerfielder, who can go a country mile for the ball, and they liked the shortstop, who came up with fancy, one-handed plays all night. They had to like 'em. They were swell ball players.

"Until last season there was a colored pitcher around named 'Satchel' Paige. The colored folks have a penchant for picturesque names for their idols and 'Satchel' Paige was so-called because of the size of his feet. He was six feet three, a righthander and a whale of a pitcher. 'He retired last year at the age of 44,' said Jimmy Wasdell, 'and he was still a great pitcher. I've been on clubs that barnstormed against Negro teams, and in a dozen games against this Paige we never beat him. He beat Paul and Dizzy Dean one night, 1–0, and we got only one hit off him. I was the only minor leaguer on our club.'

"Negro baseball is now a flourishing game, but as long as thirty years ago, the colored folks had their swell ball teams. Walter Johnson, on a barnstorming trip in 1909, went to Harlem to pitch for a colored team against the Lincoln Giants. 'I didn't know it was to be a colored team,' Johnson was saying, 'but they were paying me $600 for the day's work and that was big money. I went up there with my catcher, Gabby Street. Gabby was from Huntsville, Alabama, and he didn't like the idea of playing colored baseball, but the $300 he got was too much to overlook.'

" 'It was the only time in my life that I was ever 2-to-1 to lose. Those were the odds they were offering against me. I'll never forget the first hitter I faced. He was an outfielder they called 'Home Run' Johnson. Up at the plate, he says to me 'Come on, Mr. Johnson, and throw that fast one in here and I'll knock it over the fence.' That's what he did, too. But it was the only run they got off me and I won the game, 2–1.' "

Varsity Men in Baseball. In college baseball of the universities and the colleges of the North and West, colored players have been few. Where they have been found they have occupied a prominent place in the baseball traditions of their schools. About a half decade thereafter, the Gregory name was first heard in athletics. J. Francis was at Amherst and Eugene was at Harvard between 1893 and 1898.

Gregory, lately an educator in Washington, D. C., made a legendary baseball fame at Amherst and Yale. In 1896, against Trinity College, he knocked three home runs in two consecutive innings. Against Harvard in the succeeding afternoon, he accepted ten chances at shortstop without an error, and on the following afternoon against Dartmouth, he scored the winning run with a homer. He went from Amherst to Yale after a successful baseball and track career and baseball captaincy. Coaches Nichols and the Boston pitcher, Hickman, noted Detroit slugger, tried to use him for Yale's baseball team, but the policy that has been Yale's

AMHERST COLLEGE BASEBALL TEAM, 1898

Back row—Foster, Fisher, De Witt, Mitchell, Asst. Mgr., Watson, Rushmore. Middle row—Thompson, Fosdick, J. F. Gregory, Capt., Tinker, Messinger. Front row—Moore, Whitney.

with regard to Negroes in athletics obtained, and he was not permitted to make the Varsity. However, at the Yale Divinity School he was an outstanding player and was elected captain. There is perhaps no single individual of the race who has had so rich an experience in baseball of college and club variety during the halcyon days of the latter nineteenth century, as the late J. F. Gregory, of Miner Teachers College in Washington, D. C. In a letter published by the Washington *Tribune*, Saturday, July 23, 1938, appearing herein in the Appendix, Professor Gregory recounted his baseball days, intermingled with personal reminiscences and philosophy.

Robinson-Matthews-Brown. Other stars appeared in the mid-west at Oberlin College. Merton P. Robinson established quite a reputation. In life he served several Negro colleges efficiently as a coach. Coming from the tidewater fields of Virginia in 1902, there went to Harvard University William Clarence Matthews, who played shortstop or second base and batted in clean-up positions for the Crimson team. Matthews' reputation as a Harvard baseball and football player was noised about throughout the land. He starred at Harvard four years. Like his predecessor, William H. Lewis, he became a successful lawyer, politician, and office-holder during his all-too-short career. In 1894–1897 another Gregory, Eugene, appeared in college baseball. He was a pitcher on the Harvard nine. From the same section of the country from whence hailed Lewis, Jackson and Matthews, there went to Harvard Earl Brown. Earl won his spurs doing spectacular mound duty. His biggest college feat was a no-hit game against Northeastern in 1923. In his senior year he was elected to pitch the annual Harvard-Yale duel, but lost a thrilling game by a score of 2–1.

New England and Negro Players. In New England there have been many boys who sparkled on the diamond as representatives of several colleges. George Crossen of Boston University played shortstop during 1922, '23 and '24, and was voted the most valuable player on the team during his senior year. Charlie Ray was a good outfielder at Bates. William Kindle, later physical director at Talladega, was nominated a valuable player and excellent athlete at Springfield during 1914 and 1915. Harold Martin, athletic commissioner of the C.I.A.A., and physical director of the Miner Teachers College of Washington, D. C., pitched the Norwich

University team to many victories from 1919 to 1921. Harry Thompson was a shortstop on the Dartmouth team in 1919. Up in Vermont during the years 1905 to 1908, Watkins and Williams were playing a great game of ball. G. Lewis Chandler, of Middleburg, and Leslie Simms, of Northeastern University, in the years 1925 and 1926, were Negro representatives. Of course, we all know of Paul Robeson at Rutgers around 1918, and one of his much publicized honors was garnered on the diamond.

The Western College Diamonds. Looking westward, one finds that the Syracuse College nine used Oscar Brown in 1908. After Merton Robinson in 1902, a brother, Howard N. Robinson, carried family recognition on to the Oberlin fields as a catcher from 1908 to 1910. F. M. Sheffield, at second base in 1921 and 1922, and John W. Copeland, a shortstop, who was captain of the team in 1937, were Oberlin highlights in baseball. Sam Taylor, at Northwestern in 1922, was outstanding, and he later became a widely famed professional star.

At Western Reserve in Ohio, Booker T. Spencer was a catcher in 1926. Michigan University once had a colored player named Ash as a member of its nine. In the distant far-west, at the University of Washington, John Prim played left field in 1920.

The Game in the South. One of the handicaps to the registry of more colored players on college nines in the past, and to some extent now, is the southern trip. Because of the colder springs in the North, and the more seasonable baseball weather to the south, many of the prominent teams schedule one or two weeks of baseball with teams from Maryland to South Carolina. The custom obtaining in the south prevented the use of colored players, hence the strength of a team was often below par when it arrived south of the Mason-Dixon line. On an extended trip, hotel accommodations must be considered. A colored athlete in some localities must be housed apart from the team.

Baseball as a major sport has lost much of its popularity since King Football arrived. Baseball is a costly game. The near-

THE LATE JOSHUA GIBSON (DIED, 1947)
(One of the greatest players in modern baseball)

presence of the professionals, and the correspondingly large adver-
tising given the money players in cities and towns overshadows the
college game and limits the gate drawing crowds. For these and
other reasons, college baseball has been minimized or has disap-
peared at many of the larger institutions. Lately, however, there
appear signs of a revival of interest.

Former Greatness of the Game. In the colleges for Negroes,
for many years baseball was the leading sport. When football was
but an infant, college baseball was a lusty and thriving youth.
Especially was this true of the colleges of the far South. There in
the land where the big-leaguers go for Spring training, colored
college ball players developed to great heights several decades ago.

As instances of the earlier status of college baseball in 1913,
Arkansas Baptist College met and defeated most of the colleges in
Mississippi, Tennessee, Arkansas, Texas and Oklahoma, and did
not suffer one defeat in the 1913 season. In the same year, Tuskegee played only four football games, but played a series of sixteen
baseball games, won fourteen, dropping one each to Shaw and
Talladega. In 1912 and 1913, Tuskegee played thirty-six games
and lost three. In those two years, Sloan, a pitcher at Tuskegee,
won seventeen straight games.

An All-Star baseball team for 1913 in the South recorded the
following honor selections: Catcher, Watson, Tuskegee; pitchers,
Sloan of Tuskegee, Barnes of Morris-Brown, and Black of Clark;
first base, Howard, Tuskegee; second base, Sullins, Tuskegee; shortstop, Lewis, Atlanta Baptist College (Morehouse); right field,
G. D. Brock, Atlanta Baptist College (Morehouse), and center field,
Washington, Tuskegee. Livingston College in North Carolina, in
1913, played a series of seventeen games, winning twelve. In a
game with Lutheran College, McCorkle of Livingston pitched a
no-hit game.

Professionals Draft Collegians. Many colored college ball
players continued the display of their wares on the semi-pro and professional diamonds. We were accustomed to reading about "Lar-

HOMESTEAD GRAYS—1946

(One of the fine teams of organized Negro baseball)

Left to Right—"Vic" Harris, Mgr.; Frank Williams, r.f.; Dan Wilson, 3rd b.; Jerry Benjamin, c.f.; Buck Leonard, 1st b.; "Josh." Gibson, c.; Sam Bankhead, s.s.; Wm. "Cool Papa" Bell, l.f.; "Lick" Carlisle, 2nd b.; "Double Duty" Radcliffe, c.

rupin' Columbia Lou," Eddie Collins, Christy Matthewson, Frank Frisch, Sisler, Eddie Plank and "Doc" White, all college bred players. We should also remember "Doc" Sykes, spit-ball artist, and his famous battery mate, who comprised the Howard University battery par excellence when Sykes was studying dentistry. Sykes later was a member of the Baltimore Black Sox, and Wiley was on the roster of the Lincoln Giants during most of his baseball career. "Doc" Wiley became a prosperous dentist in Newark; Sykes, after practicing a while in Baltimore, became a mortician in Decatur, Alabama.

Harold D. Martin, the late coach at several Colored Intercollegiate Athletic Association institutions, C.I.A.A. Commissioner, a four letter man from Norwich University, began his baseball career with the Homestead Grays and finished with the Pittsburgh Keystones, then a member of the Negro National League. Dave Marlarcher and Bobby Williams left the campus of New Orleans University to become a vital cog in the greatest infield of the American Giants. Three Taylor boys were ex-college players. C. I. Taylor was a graduate of Benedict College; John "Steel Arm" Taylor was graduated from Biddle (now Johnson C. Smith); Jim Taylor attended Greeley Institute, and later managed the Chicago American Giants. Owens, Grady Orange, Leroy Taylor and Patterson attended Wiley University in Texas. Tom Williams, "College Boy," referred to by the late "Rube" Foster as the "perfect mound artist," was a student of Morris-Brown College of Atlanta. "Dizzy" Dismukes is an alumnus of Talladega. Leroy "Satchel" Paige was formerly a student at Knoxville College. "Dick" Lundy, of Edward Waters College, Yokeley of Livingstone, and "Bun" Hayes of Johnson C. Smith were a few college players who entered the big game.

CHAPTER X

A New Era in Baseball

Jackie Robinson. Jackie Robinson's entry into organized baseball proved the big event of the decade of the 'forties. For many years colored players have been knocking at the gates of the two big leagues. Several years prior, Judge Landis said there was no "formal or informal or any understanding, unwritten, subterranean or subanything" against the hiring of Negroes. He said, "The possibility of Negroes playing in the major leagues was up to club owners."

On April 14, 1945, Joe Bostic of *Peoples' Voice*, New York, and Wendell Smith of the *Pittsburgh Courier* were able to get Terris McDuffie and Dave Thomas into Brooklyn Dodger uniforms. They were given a tryout and were adjudged a bit too old for major league competition.

On October 23, 1945, after spending $25,000, the Brooklyn system, in search for Negro diamond talent, signed up Jackie Robinson in the presence of Hector Racine and Lieut. Col. Romeo Gauvreau of the Montreal Royals, and Branch Rickey, Jr. who headed the Brooklyn Farm System. The announcement shook the nation with surprise. His failure was predicted by national bigots. But the great body of American sportsmen welcomed the refreshing boldness of Branch Rickey, owner of the Brooklyn baseball syndicate.

Typical of the comment was that of Roger Treat in the Washington *Daily News*, "For now Rickey demands the respect of every American for the courage it took to make the break through the dam of bigotry and hatred. He has done what no other baseball boss has dared to do—throw Jim Crow out of the park to the oblivion where he belongs."

Negro baseball club owners at first were more or less staggered, and foresaw a rush of their talent to the major leagues. Unfortunately, their fears were not justified. Few colored players were

LEO DUROCHER, MANAGER; JACKIE ROBINSON, OF THE BROOKLYN DODGERS—
1948

Robinson, called up from the minor league Montreal team in April, 1947 to play first base for the Brooklyn Dodgers, was named, "Rookie" of the year.   The award was due solely to his ability as a hitter, runner, fielder and team player.   The Dodgers won the National League pennant for 1947. He led the League in stolen bases.   His batting average for his first year was .296.   In mid season, 1949, he was leading the National League players with the highest batting average.

Durocher, known as the Firebrand among managers, later became manager of the New York Giants.

drawn away from the colored leagues. Only three colored boys were placed on the Montreal team in 1946, Jackie Robinson, John Wright and Roy Partlow—the latter two, pitchers.

The advent of a Negro ball player in organized ball games began auspiciously on a Thursday afternoon in Jersey City, N. J. Twenty-five thousand people jammed the Roosevelt Stadium. Jackie was playing second base for Montreal. In that game he batted in four runs, he scored four runs, stole two bases, made one error, getting a home run over the left field fence on his second time at bat. Montreal won 14 to 1. The press around the nation acclaimed the Negro in baseball. Jackie went through the season playing great baseball and wound up on the winning club in the International League, leading the league in batting with a .349 average, and he also led in stolen bases with 40 to his credit.

Robinson was called up from the minor leagues in April of 1947, to become a member of the Brooklyn Dodgers. Although his experience had been at the middle sack or shortstop, overnight he was assigned to first base spot. Throughout the season his play was sensational despite some shortcomings as a first sacker. However, he led the league in stolen bases and ended up with a batting average of .296. All around the circuit the fans turned out in great numbers. Brooklyn played to the greatest crowds in its history. Many were the racial problems the colored boy had to meet and the psychological pressure was great, but he came through with flying colors.

One of the crowning events of his first year's career was the honor of being named by the St. Louis *Sporting News* in the issue of Sept. 17th, 1947, as the ranking "rookie" of the year. The award was made solely on his ability as a hitter, a runner, fielder and team player. He was described as an "Ebony Ty Cobb" for his elusive, daring, base running. He wound up the year a member of the National League champion team and went into the world series. Here again he was one of the marked players of the series and although Brooklyn lost to the New York Yankees after stretching the series to the limit, it was one of the most thrilling of recent years.

Cleveland Indians' fourth game heroes, pitcher Steve Gromek, left, and Larry Doby, congratulate each other following 2–1 triumph over Boston Braves in 1948 World Series. Gromek scattered seven hits, while Doby's homer proved margin of victory. ACME TELEPHOTO . . .

Roy Campanella, Brooklyn Dodger's Great Catcher, 1949

DON NEWCOMB—BROOKLYN DODGERS PITCHER, 1949

Donald Newcomb became the most reliable pitcher on the Brooklyn Dodgers' pitching staff. By September 1949, he had won 14 and lost 6 games, although he joined the Dodgers on May 17th, a month after the League opened. Newcomb is 22 years old, stands 6 ft. 4 in., and weighs 235 pounds. Branch Rickey said his right arm was worth a million dollars. His price tag when with Montreal was $300,000.

Jackie Robinson, a native of Georgia, won recognition in four sports at the University of California at Los Angeles in baseball, basketball, football and track. He entered the Army as a private. He left the services in 1945 with rank of lieutenant. It was in October of the same year Branch Rickey ordained him a member of the Montreal Royals.

Following the entrance of Jackie Robinson into the major leagues in 1945, Johnny Wright and Roy Partlow, Roy Campanella, hard hitting catcher, and Donald Newcomb, a pitcher, were brought up by the Rickey syndicate and assigned to the Nashua team of the New England League. Later Campanella was switched to the Montreal team in the International League when he became the regular backstop for the Royals. He played stellar ball all season. During the 1948 season he became the regular catcher for the Brooklyn Dodgers where he and his team mates Robinson and Newcomb are starring.

More Negroes Crash Gates.   In mid-season of 1947 Dan Bankhead was bought from the Memphis team of the Negro American League by the Brooklyn Dodgers. He pitched briefly in a relief role. His pitching was not so effective but on his first trip at the plate he hit a home run. It was the consensus of many critics that he needed to unlearn some of the pitching habits of a less critical league. He won 17 and lost 5 games for Montreal in 1949.

Larry Doby was purchased by the Cleveland Indians of the American League from the Newark Eagles of the Negro National League in July of the 1947 season.

He was born in Camden, S. C. At six years old he was brought to Paterson, N. J. shortly after the death of his father. Educated in Paterson, he became a four letter man prior to graduation from high school in 1942, when he entered Long Island University. He entered the army in 1943 and was discharged in 1946. He began his sensational career with the Newark Eagles. By June of 1947 he was leading the Negro National League with 14 home runs. Scouted by Bill Killifer for the Cleveland Club, Doby was purchased by President Bill Veeck on July 3, 1947 for $15,000. Doby began immediately with the Cleveland infield and seemed destined

DAN BANKHEAD—BROOKLYN DODGERS PITCHER, 1948

Dan Bankhead, who was returned to Montreal from the Dodgers in 1948, became one of the leading pitchers in 1949. By September he had won 17 games and lost 5. Because the Dodgers were loaded with so many good players both Bankhead and his team mate Sam Jethroe were kept in the minor circuit as a part of the Dodgers organization.

to become a complete flop as the season wore on. However in the 1948 campaign he was shifted to the outfield and became a star player after learning the outfield play, being particularly strong at the bat.

Throughout the season Doby's career was followed with interest. In Washington on the day the Cleveland management was considering sending him back for more seasoning in minor league play, Doby hit a home run in Griffith Stadium approximately 440 feet on July 18, 1948, a feat surpassed only by one hit by Babe Ruth.

He began to improve in his fielding and his batting, winding up the season with an average of 301. The great climax to his 1948 stay in the majors came when Cleveland, after one of the most thrilling league finishes in baseball history, tackled the Boston Braves for the world championship. Doby was the premier hitter in the series and in the crucial third game won with a tie-breaking home run.

John Ritchey, catcher of the Chicago American Giants, signed up with the San Diego Padres of the Pacific Coast Baseball League. Ritchey hails from San Diego, California, and batted .386 for the season with the Chicago Giants.

St. Louis Browns signed two colored players following the trend set by Brooklyn and Cleveland. Willard Brown and Henry Thompson were brought up from the Kansas City Monarchs. The St. Louis team was at low ebb and playing in the cellar of the American League. Many believed that the management signed the two players to lure the cash paying fans to bolster up gate receipts and crowds. Before the season ended both boys were given unconditional releases.

Satchel Paige was signed up with the Cleveland Indians in 1948 and became a strong relief pitcher for the team. In August he also starred and won several games. Paige began pitching semi-pro ball around Birmingham in 1924. In the 1930's he pitched at Bismarck, N. D. and helped win the first semi-pro series in Wichita, Kansas. A fitting climax to his career was his entry into a game of the 1948 world series.

SATCHEL PAIGE, CLEVELAND INDIANS, 1948

The roster of colored players in organized baseball in 1948 included:

Jackie Robinson—Infielder—Dodgers, National League
Roy Campanella—Catcher—Dodgers, National League
Larry Doby—Outfielder—Cleveland, American League
Carlos Santiago—Infielder—Stamford, Colonial League
Carlos Bernier—Outfielder—Stamford, Colonial League
John Ritchey—Infielder—San Diego Padres, Pacific Coast League
Sam Jethroe—Outfielder—Montreal, International League
Pitchers:
Dan Bankhead—Pitcher—on Nashua and St. Paul, American Association
Don Newcombe—Pitcher—Montreal—International League
Satchel Paige—Pitcher—Cleveland—American League
Nate Moreland—Pitcher—Imperials—Sunset League

The Passing of Two Stars.   On January 16, 1947 one of the greatest Negro baseball players, Joshua Gibson, died at 35 years of age. Gibson was a powerful batter and a star catcher playing with the Homestead Grays.   He died in Pittsburgh.   Walter Johnson once said of Gibson, "Had he not been an American colored citizen, he would have been worth $250,000."   In 1927 he joined the Pittsburgh Crawfords, a sand lot team which later grew into Gus Greenlee's famous "Crawfords" of later years.   Three years later, Gibson was signed to play with Cum Posey's Homestead Grays.   After the 1930 and 1931 seasons, Gibson went back to the Crawfords and teamed up with Satchel Paige as the greatest battery in the history of the game.   They played until 1936 when Gibson returned to the Grays. Josh Gibson had his peak batting seasons in 1938 and 1939.   During the 1938 year he hit four home runs in one game in Griffith Stadium in Washington, D. C.   In 1943 he hit three circuit blows in one game in the same park.   It was in 1943 he hit eleven home runs in one of the longest left fields in the league at Griffith Stadium, which mark no white players have ever recorded in that park.   In 1942 he was awarded "the most valuable player" honor while playing in Mexico, and duplicated the feat in Puerto Rico in 1944.

Cumberland Posey, another prominent baseball figure died in March 1946.   He was the co-owner of the Homestead Grays.   Posey was born and lived in Homestead, Pa.   His "Grays" beginning in

THE 1949 CLEVELAND INDIANS—Top Row, Larry Doby; Middle Row, Satchel Paige

1936 won eight out of nine pennants in the Negro National League. Posey devoted his entire life largely to athletics, particularly basketball and baseball.   He started his career in athletics at Duquesne University and Penn State.   He reached the zenith of his career as a member of the famous Leondi Basketball team.   He was responsible for organization of the Grays as a pick-up aggregation of week-end players while he was serving as a Railway Mail Clerk.   Under his leadership the club moved into big time and a paying business.   He was a highly respected member of his community and served for many years as member of the Homestead School Board.

American colored ball players have been accepted as regular players in South American, Mexican and Puerto Rican leagues. Many of them have been managers of these teams.   George Scales and Robert Clark, both of the Baltimore Elite Giants have served as managers in the Puerto Rican League for two seasons.   Among those who have gone to the southern climes in recent years have been Dave Dandridge and Leon Day of the Newark Eagles, and Ray Brown, former Homestead Grays' pitcher, and a host of others.

The advent of the entry of Negroes into major leagues has stimulated baseball in colored collegiate circles.   For example, the Colored Intercollegiate Athletic Association has re-instituted baseball as a major sport.   Some of the far southern colleges have never stopped playing baseball.   A new day in baseball is predicted for Negroes in America.

CHAPTER XI

Pioneers in Tennis

Tennis in the Old World. Tennis is the aristocrat of court games. It has had a long history. Kings and nobility, as well as commoners, have engaged at tennis since the 12th century. Starting as a form of handball, the game added bats and then rackets to give us what we have today. Somewhere in the 13th century a French king constructed an indoor court, and the game took the name "Royal Tennez," which means royal tennis. The British took to tennis; the Irish and Scotch remained true to handball.

After several centuries of great popularity in the British Isles and across the channel as an amateur game, it gradually changed to a professional sport. It became a medieval business, then a racket, with all that term implies in this century. Gamblers bought players, and fixed matches. As with the Greek and Roman games, so fell tennis in the 18th century. The clash of money interests, of gambling, and of amateur sport, then as now, resulted in the decay of the amateur game. Unless wise governors keep the professional and amateur interests in separate fields, a deterioration in the values of sport always results. In A.D. 1600 there were more than 2,000 tennis courts in Paris alone. By the 19th century, after the game had run the gamut of commercialism, there were hardly any public tennis courts in England or France.

Tennis Comes to America. In 1873, a Major Wingfield of the British Army established a game he called Lawn Tennis, and a Miss Mary Outerbridge of Staten Island is supposed to have initiated the first tennis play in America in 1874. It became a game for the athletically inclined elite folk of Lenox, Newport, Lakewood and Tuxedo. Philadelphia and Chicago had courts prior to 1880.

The game had amateur status almost entirely until about 1926, when the late Suzanne Lenglen of France accepted Promoter Pyle's $50,000, and with Mary Brown, Vincent Richards and Howard Kinsey, toured the country. The United States Professional Lawn Tennis Association was formed in 1927.

Negro Tennis Players. In major American sports, it is only in boxing that Negroes antedated American white men. But a little over a decade after tennis was introduced to America, colored players were popularizing the game in various sections of the country. Tuskegee adherents claim the place of the beginning of tennis among Negroes in the South between the years of 1890 and 1895. Among these pioneers were Warren Logan, Emmett J. Scott, S. E. Courtney, and E. T. Attwell.

To the Rev. W. W. Walker the credit seems to belong for pioneering in tennis. As a member of the Chautauqua Tennis Club in 1898, he was the prime mover in sponsoring the first inter-state tournament which was held in Philadelphia. Its first singles champion was Thomas Jefferson of Lincoln University of Pennsylvania, and his award token was a "fine tennis racket." In 1899, another tournament was held in Philadelphia and the Rev. Mr. Walker defeated Henry Freeman of Washington, D. C., for the championship after a closely contested battle. In 1900, the tournament was transferred to Washington, D. C. The Rev. Mr. Walker engaged in the finals with Charles Cook of Howard University, who used the "Lawford" stroke with deadly accuracy, but in the words of the Rev. Mr. Walker, "finally succumbed to my chop and net game."

The Rev. Mr. Walker, in the 1931 program of the American Tennis Association, sets forth three distinct periods in the development of the game. First, "the chop and net game," introduced to Negroes by him, was a style that dominated the play of the period 1899 to 1900. Then from out of the West came forth a less conservative, bolder player and a correspondingly more convincing game of tennis. Edgar G. Brown, colorful, confident, and competent, brought into tennis playing among Negroes the smashing "top-spin and base line game." Brown made a shambles of "pat-ball" tennis and led the group into the modern epoch. The Rev. Mr. Walker credits Brown with doing "more than any other Negro to advance the standard of the game. He introduced and popularized the modern, orthodox game, and younger players for the first time realized that tennis must be studied as a science, and practiced as a most difficult art." The Rev. Mr. Walker said further, "We chop artists, bewildered by Brown's style of play, began to lose our conceit, and then acknowledged the supremacy of the Westerner's technique."

EDGAR G. BROWN

Modern Tennis. The third epoch in tennis presented a progressive group of young players who brought to near perfection the orthodox game of the second epoch. This modern player must be a master in every department of the game. He must be equally at home on the base line or at the net. His back hand and forehand must be equally strong. All present day champions must be versatile, must be adept at court strategy, and must retain physical health and vigor to have a long or successful tennis career.

Out of the irregular sporadic inter-city tennis tournament evolved the idea of a national grouping of tennis interests to broaden and strengthen the motivating, stimulating and controlling factors in the promotion of tennis. These early pioneers, individuals and clubs, have earned a social recompense in the heartfelt appreciation of the thousands of youths who today enjoy the splendid courts, wholesome tournaments, and other outcomes of the work of these enthusiastic beginners.

Pioneers. Among the men and women who blazed the trail in tennis were Charles C. Cook, Ralph V. Cook, Henry Freeman, J. F. N. Wilkinson, E. J. Ridgely and Thomas Johnson, most of whom were members of the Y. M. C. A. Tennis Club of Washington, D. C.; H. Stanton McCard, W. H. Wright, B. M. Rhetta, F. J. Cardozo, J. G. McRae, P. D. Pennington, Lucy D. Slowe, Miss Nicholson, and Ralph Reckling of the Monumental Tennis Club of Baltimore; Jamison, Banton, and Whitten of Wilmington; W. W. Walker, W. H. Jones, J. T. Howard, Boyer, Brock, Adams, Cummings, Nichols, of the Chautauqua Tennis Club of Philadelphia; McLendon and Costa of New Rochelle; Flemming of New Haven, Connecticut; Battle, Austin, Knolls, Hoage of New York City; Gerald Norman, Daisy Reed, Dora Cole Norman, and Kinckle Jones of Flushing Tennis Club in Long Island; Smith of Annapolis, and "Ma" Seames of Chicago.

American Tennis Association Organized. Washington, D. C., was the birthplace of the American Tennis Association. On November 30, 1916, such tennis enthusiasts as H. S. McCard, Wm. H. Wright, B. M. Rhetta, and Ralph V. Cook of Baltimore; Henry Freeman, John F. N. Wilkinson, and Talley Holmes of Washington, founded the organization. The invitation was extended by the "Association Tennis Club," now the James E. Walker Tennis Club. The purposes expressed were fostering and developing the game of tennis among the colored people of the United States, encouraging the formation of clubs and the building of courts, suggesting the formation of local associations, and interesting juniors (16–18 years) as well as boys and girls in the possibilities and advantages of this splendid game.

The first national championships were held in Baltimore, August, 1917, in Druid Hill Park under the auspices of the Monumental Tennis Club of Baltimore. The New York Tennis Association with eleven clubs gave wholehearted support. Twelve other clubs, all in the East, were represented. Two championships were listed, men's singles with thirty-nine entries, and men's doubles with thirteen entries. The first national champions were Talley Holmes and Sylvester Smith.

A.T.A. Officials and Players at Tuskegee, 1931

In a very short while, the national body, pursuing its aims, stimulated the growth of tennis throughout the United States, and new clubs were formed in different sections of the country and joined the American Tennis Association. As far west as California, a federation of tennis clubs organized and applied for membership in the A. T. A.

Tennis Clubs. After its birth in 1916, the American Tennis Association grew to a position of power. In 1949 membership included the following fifteen associations of tennis clubs comprising 134 individual clubs:

Mid-Western Tennis Association................	16 clubs
New York Tennis Association..................	15 clubs
New Jersey Tennis Association................	14 clubs
Southern Intercollegiate Tennis Association.......	13 clubs
North Carolina State Tennis Association..........	12 clubs
Virginia Tennis Association....................	10 clubs
Pennsylvania Tennis Association................	10 clubs
Florida Tennis Association.....................	8 clubs
Georgia Tennis Association....................	8 clubs
South Carolina Tennis Association..............	8 clubs
Western Federation of Tennis Clubs.............	7 clubs
Southern Tennis Association...................	6 clubs
Somers Isle Tennis Association.................	5 clubs
West Virginia Tennis Association...............	5 clubs
New England Tennis Association................	5 clubs

The number of national championships were originally two. In 1917, women's singles were introduced; in 1928, women's doubles and mixed doubles; in 1933, veterans' singles; in 1935, girls' singles, and in 1937, junior doubles and boys' singles.

The great number of entrants occasioned by the increase in title aspirants resulted in the prohibition of any entrant from taking part in more than two events. Juniors under sixteen were also barred from entering any senior events.

FLORA LOMAX (RIGHT) DEFEATS FRANCES GITTENS IN NEW YORK STATE
CHAMPIONSHIP, 1938
Flora Lomax, 1938 Singles Champion of American Tennis Association
National Tournament

Tournament Winners. Space limitations forbid justifiable and suitable comment on all the great and near great men and women tennis stars in the 33 years of organization of the A. T. A. Among the staunch and loyal officers and promoters of Negro tennis stands out a bevy of leaders in professional or civic life. The present prestige of this organization is largely due to the untiring efforts and work of H. Stanton McCard, whose sane leadership and good judgment did much to mold together the American Tennis Association during trying times. He retired from the presidency, leaving a firmly founded organization on durable principles. Gerald Norman of Flushing, New York made a great contribution to the organization as executive secretary of the A. T. A. for more than twenty years.

TALLEY HOLMES

Washington's Influence. Feeling the need for connecting and consolidating the tennis interests in 1910, prior to national organization, J. F. N. Wilkinson, Talley Holmes, J. W. Cromwell, and W. M. Menard, of the Y.M.C.A. Tennis Club of Washington, D. C., and B. Price Hurst of Baltimore toured the cities of Baltimore, Wilmington, Philadelphia, New York, New Rochelle, and New Haven and played games in these cities. These and subsequent visitations led to the call for a larger organization which was effected in 1916. Of these earlier players, none were more versatile than Henry Freeman and J. F. N. Wilkinson of Washington, D. C. Freeman was one of the most graceful of court artists. Wilkinson developed a Tilden-like technique. From this group developed the redoubtable Talley Holmes, who starred for a long time.

Negro College Champions. Of the college boys who have created enviable status in the collegiate field one was Richard

HARMON FITCH (LEFT) CONGRATULATES REGINALD WEIR

Hudlin of the University of Chicago, who was the first colored captain of a varsity sport in the "Big Ten" colleges. Douglass Turner was a letter man in tennis at the University of Illinois and was a runner-up in the "Big Ten" championship in 1929. In the East, Reginald Weir represented the City College of New York. Although our boys have entered many tournaments, local and sectional, in various parts of the country and compete with white players, none had been able to enter the nationals prior to 1947.

In 1928, two remarkable tennis youths, Reginald Weir, then captain elect of the New York City College team, and Gerald Norman, Jr., former captain of the Flushing High School, and New York's Junior Champion, were rejected for the national indoor championships solely because they were Negroes.

The rapid development of tennis in colleges for colored youth is in large measure due to the stimulating and constructive program of the A.T.A. Working with the directors of athletics in the individual colleges, and supplementing their endeavors when the pressure of big team athletics might have erased tennis, Ellwood D. Downing deserves the highest commendation.

College Survey. For more than twenty years the A.T.A. has functioned to strengthen tennis in collegiate circles. In 1926–27 a survey was instituted in 70 colleges. Fifty-six responded or were reached. The information secured showed only a fair amount of interest and little or no encouragement from administrations. Even today too many athletic departments concern themselves too largely with the fates and fortunes of football and basketball, and scanty budgets, or none at all, await the spring sports of track, baseball, tennis, swimming or golf. This showed sad judgment. The survey showed further only 36 institutions had tennis courts, usually of makeshift variety, and poorly maintained. The average number of courts for each college was only two, and only four institutions boasted a tennis coach.

Since the organization of the A.T.A. its efficient General Field Secretary, Ellwood D. Downing, has carried on an intensive campaign for increased tennis interest, more and better courts, and more coaches. He attributes much of the increase and development to the work of Directors Charles Williams at Hampton, and Cleveland Abbott of Tuskegee, in their colleges and in their conferences. Today, practically all of the leading colored colleges have four or more first-class tennis courts, good coaches and other facilities. The game is a major sport.

In the late years the players coming up in the colored collegiate circles have been developing a style of play strong enough to win

DR. E. D. DOWNING PRESENTS 1939 C.I.A.A. TROPHY TO
CHRISTOPHER HUNT

After one of the most colorful and hotly contested Collegiate Tournaments
conducted under the auspices of the Colored Intercollegiate Athletic Association and sponsorship of the American Tennis Association Collegiate
Tennis Committee

THE COLORED INTERCOLLEGIATE TENNIS TOURNAMENT HELD IN WASH-
INGTON, D. C., ON THE COURTS OF THE BANNEKER RECREATION CENTER
UNDER THE AUSPICES OF HOWARD UNIVERSITY, MAY 5-6, 1939

One of the notable developments in school and college athletics has been
the growth of tennis, and other dual and individual activities. Tennis
has a carry-over value of more worth to participants than any of the other
games. The American Tennis Association, in promoting tennis in schools
and colleges, has done a highly commendable job. This picture represents
one of the many culminating engagements of conference tennis.

In the immediate background of the group is visible the Banneker Swimming Pool, one of the largest public pools in Washington. The Banneker
Recreation area represents one of the most costly recreation sites. It cost
far over a million dollars and occupies several city blocks. On it are four
clay tennis courts, four hard-surfaced tennis courts, several fields for base-

ball, softball, football, soccer, and some court games. When completed it
will have a modern track and field and courts for other outdoor games.
On the north is located the Banneker Junior High School which houses
one of the largest gymnasia in the city and many indoor recreation facilities.
In the picture may be seen the tennis teams of most of the C.I.A.A.
colleges and the coaches or athletic directors. Seated in the middle are
President Perrin of the C.I.A.A., President Mordecai Johnson of Howard
University, and Secretary Nabritt of Howard University.

Because of the growth of tennis in the colleges and high schools, the struggle
for top honors in the various sectional and national tournaments is becoming tighter each year. No longer may a seeded or ranking player
coast through the preliminary matches. It will not be long before the bars
against Negro striving in democratically controlled national tennis will be
let down as they now are in large measure in boxing, track, field and many
other American sports.

tournaments and quench the unusual fire of the boys or girls from the North, West, and East. In 1938, at Lincoln University, Franklyn Jackson of Tuskegee, and Nathaniel Jackson of the same school, were winners, singles and doubles. Margaret Peters and Roumania Peters of Washington, D. C., and Tuskegee, respectively, were doubles winners. Cohen of Xavier, Christopher and Douglass Hunt of St. Augustine, have won national honors.

MARGARET AND ROUMANIA PETERS

Women Players. Women have made a splendid contribution to the progress of tennis. Not only have they graced the galleries during play and added enjoyment to the festive entertainment surrounding the club, association, and annual tournaments, but they have increased and improved as participants. They have stimulated programs of tennis among the girls and women throughout the country. Recreation for women owes a debt to these pioneers in their work to extend freedom of activity in sports among women.

Lucy D. Slowe. Naturally some women have made much more brilliant records than others. Also behind the scenes of many a successful tennis growth have been women who will remain unknown to a chronicler. A few of the outstanding performers on the court or promoters of tennis deserve mention. The late Lucy D. Slowe entered the national championships held in Baltimore under the auspices of the Monumental Tennis Club of that city. Miss Slowe won that year, 1917; and, undaunted by three successive annual defeats, she emerged victorious in the national championships again in 1921. Miss Slowe, as principal of the first Junior High School in Washington, D. C., and as Dean of Women at Howard University, carried into education a well rounded personality that influenced, by its example, thousands of girls who idolized her. She was not only a champion of women on the courts, but a leader in education and civic life.

"Mother" Seames. The late Mrs. C. O. Seames of Chicago became a staunch supporter of tennis for Negroes in 1906. There were few colored players about Chicago in those days. Mrs. Seames related that she was past thirty-five when A. L. Turner, father of Douglass Turner, who was a member of the University of Illinois tennis team, taught her to play. Mrs. Seames was a familiar figure at most of the tournaments. She had made it possible for many young players to get to tournaments, and she was a big factor in the development of tennis in and around Chicago.

Miss Laura V. Junior, chairman of the rating committee, performed yeoman service over the years. Her work as an officer in the national, Pennsylvania, and Philadelphia organizations of tennis units deserves high commendation. Another staunch worker for the advancement of girl players was Mrs. Susie Madison.

Association Officers. The list of officers, trustees and various committee members who have provided the machinery for attaining the objectives of the American Tennis Association number a great many leaders in civic and professional activity in many areas of endeavor over the country. A few of the men and women who for a long time were devoted workers in the promotion of tennis are H. Stanton McCard, D. Ivison Hoage, Gerald Norman, Ellwood Downing, J. A. McGriff, Dubissete, Bowden, Furlonge, L. E. Spooner, L. C. Downing, Arthur Chippey, E. K. Jones, J. Mercer Burrell, Cleveland Abbott, Lester B. Granger, Ned Johnson, Mrs. C. O. Seames, Miss Wade, Mrs. Elise Conick, Mrs. S. Madison, Miss Laura V. Junior, Mrs. E. Leonard.

The great progress that the American Tennis Association has made since the presidency of D. Ivison Hoage is reflected partly in the caliber of the play in the nationals, the formation of the effective Tennis Umpires Association headed by C. O. Hilton of New Jersey, and the increased efficiency of all the administrative elements of the organization. Bertram L. Baker, the next executive secretary, succeeding Gerald F. Norman, who for twenty years held the office and contributed his share to the progress of the game, brought youth and vigor to that office.

Bi-Racial Relations in Tennis. In late years, the United States Lawn Tennis Association, while not yet letting down the bars of racial discrimination, has, nevertheless, through some of its very cooperative officers and liberal personalities, rendered fine service to the American Tennis Association. On the occasion of the National Tournament meeting in Washington, D. C., in 1921 the Secretary of War, the Honorable Dwight Davis, donor of the famous Davis Cup and former president of the United States Lawn Tennis Association, served as an umpire during the semi-final matches.

Trophies. Indicative of the love of tennis on the part of many well-wishers are the splendid trophies that are competed for annually. In addition, tennis trophies in profusion adorn the homes of many of the champions. One of the beautiful cups is a sterling silver trophy donated by the Merrick family in 1927 for inter-sectional competition. The section of the country winning the majority of the matches is awarded the trophy for one year. It is known as the "Merrick Trophy" and is valued at $350. The "Williams Trophy" is a sterling silver trophy for inter-collegiate competition donated in 1930 by the employes of the Grand Central Station of New York and named after their "Chief," James Williams. For years players representing the Colored Inter-Collegiate Athletic Association and the Southern Inter-Collegiate Athletic Association met at the "Nationals" and competed for this cup. The college winning held the cup for one year. The "Carrington Trophy" is a sterling silver trophy donated by the Carrington Brothers, of Brooklyn, N. Y., for competition in Long Iaslnd, N. Y. The trophy went for one year to the club whose representative won the event. The "Cockburn Trophy" is a sterling silver trophy donated by

DOWNING AND McGRIFF

Players in Doubles for more than a decade, recently succeeded by McGriff
and McGriff, father and son, as Doubles Entrants in contests of today

Courtesy of "Phila. Tribune"

ORA WASHINGTON, QUEEN OF THE TENNIS COURT

Captain Joshua Cockburn of New York for inter-state competition, in the states of New Jersey, Pennsylvania, and New York. The trophy went to the state winning the majority of matches played. It is valued at $150. The "Hoage Trophy," donated by Dr. D. Ivison Hoage, was for inter-club competition in the Midwest. The following "Three-Leg" trophies are the "Bill Robinson Trophy," donated by Mr. William Robinson of New York for Men's Singles,

THE FREEMAN FAMILY OF WASHINGTON, D. C.

L. to R.—Thomas Freeman, Former Nat'l Boys' Champion; Harold Freeman, 1948 Boys' Champion; Mrs. Lucille Freeman, Mother and Coach; Clyde Freeman, former Nat'l Boys' Champion, and with Thomas, former Boys' Doubles Champion

and the "Bishop Plummer Trophy" for Women's Singles which was won permanently by Miss Ora Washington. Dr. Hoage donated a "Veterans' Singles Trophy" which was entered in competition in 1938.

1939 Tennis Champions. At Hampton in August, 1939, at the "Nationals," the new contenders dethroned all the champions except the singles champion, Mrs. Flora Lomax, and the women's doubles champions, the Peters girls of Washington and Tuskegee. James McDaniels of Xavier won the men's singles; he and his partner Richard Cohen won the men's doubles.

Honorable Mention. Thousands of ambitious tennis players have battled their way through the various tournaments in the different sections about the country. Many hundreds have met annually in the "National." A handful survive and reach the top-most rank of champions. There are those who never become champions, but nevertheless are splendid players. Space permits only the listing of the winners who are mentioned in the Appendix.

CHAPTER XII

Golf

Golf in Scotland. Golf is an old game dating back to the 14th or 15th century, beginning in Holland or Scotland. As far back as 1457, the Scottish Parliament placed a ban on golf because it interfered with the practice of archery; but even though quite severe penalties were attached, few golfers heeded the proscription. One of the first medal-play, 36 holes, tournaments was played in Scotland in 1860.

A Scotchman by the name of John G. Reid who lived in Yonkers is supposed to have been the "Father of American Golf." This was as late as 1888. The St. Andrew's Golf Club of Yonkers was probably the first club. By 1894, there existed a score of golf groups. The first tournament was played at Newport, R. I., September 3, 1894. It is estimated that there are more than 6,000 golf courses in the United States and over 3,500,000 persons play the game each season.

Negro Golfers in Action. Shortly after golf was introduced to America, a few Negroes began to play the game. The use of colored boys as caddies quickened the interest of younger men in golf. Not only did these boys pick up the fine points by apt imitation of the masters of the sport but learned much when many of the exclusive clubs would occasionally hold "caddy" matches. Some of the greatest of golfers today were the "caddy" boys of yester-year.

Negro golfers find their best opportunity today largely on public courses. Golf courses were for many years almost exclusively private. The golf courses and accompanying club houses are expensive to own and maintain. In the last decade there has been a great growth in municipally owned golf courses. Colored golfers in the North and West have taken their turns on the courses with

Opening Drive on Dedication of Langston Golf Course, Washington, D. C.

other Americans. In Baltimore and in Washington there are nine hole courses for colored golfers. The first golf courses for Negroes were probably Mapledale at Stowe in Massachusetts, the Asbury Park course, and the Sunset Hills at Kankakee, Illinois. There are a few country clubs operated or owned by Negroes that have nine hole courses. Among them should be mentioned the Shady Rest Country Club of Westfield, New Jersey, the Sunset Hills Country Club of Kankakee, Illinois; and the Lincoln Country Club of Atlanta, Georgia.

Golf among Negroes is flourishing chiefly in the cities of New York, Philadelphia, Baltimore, Washington, Harrisburg, Atlanta, Jacksonville, Chicago, Cleveland, Detroit, St. Louis, Kansas City, Indianapolis and Los Angeles. Among the prominent clubs should be noted the St. Nicholas of New York City, the New Amsterdam of Palisades, New York; the Wolverine of Detroit; the Fairview of the City of Philadelphia; the Douglas Club of Lancaster; the Yorkshire Club of Pittsburgh; the Monumental of Baltimore; the Royal of Washington, D. C.; the Lincoln of Atlanta; the Trophy Club of Chicago; the Douglas Park of Indianapolis; the Apex Club of Atlantic City; the Keystone Club of Harrisburg; the Shady Rest Club of Westfield, New Jersey; the Cosmopolitan Club of Baltimore; the Forest City Golf Club of Cleveland; the Sunset Hills Club of Chicago; the West Coast Golf Club of Los Angeles. Most of these clubs are affiliated with the United Golfers' Association, the national organization.

United Golfers' Association. The fourteenth annual tournament of the United Golfers' Association was held from August 22–25, 1939, at Griffith Park under the auspices of the West Coast Golf Club. The use of this park was donated by the Los Angeles Board of Park Commissioners in a precedent-smashing action. The West Coast Golfers' Club was offering, as an added attraction, $800 in cash prizes for professional golfers, along with a variety of cups and trophies for the amateurs. About 150 or more Negro golfers entered the National Open and Amateur, and the Southern Open and Amateur each year.

Negro professional golfers have had little opportunity to match their skill with those of other races in the United States. John Shippen, reputed Indian, from Shinnecock, Long Island, entered in 1913 the national championships and finished fourth.

John Shippen.   John Shippen was an instructor on some of the finest courses in the East.   He and his brother, Cyrus Shippen, had been associated with golf as players or instructors since around 1900. Both of these gentlemen had professional privileges at many of the clubs in New Jersey.   John Shippen played rounds of golf with many famous golfers, particularly with the famous Vardon.   For a while, John was credited with the longest American drive record.   He was an instructor on such courses as those of the East Hampton Club in New York, the Merion at Philadelphia, the Spring Lake Golf and Country Club and others.

Professional Golfers.   "Pat" Ball of Chicago, ex-champion among colored golfers, always made a good showing in the open competitions in and around Chicago.   The 1938 professional champion was Howard Wheeler of Atlanta, Georgia.   John Dendy of Asheville, North Carolina, in 1936 and 1937, and Solomon Hughes of Gadsden, Alabama, in 1935, became the earlier day's professional champions.   The first professional to win a national championship was Harry Jackson of Washington, D. C.   Other outstanding "pros" were Porter Washington, of Boston, Massachusetts, "Zeke" Hartsfield and Howard Smith of Atlanta, Georgia; E. Marshall, Green, and Rhu of New Orleans.

The Amateurs Prior to 1939.   Among the amateurs, Frank Gaskins of Philadelphia won three times.   George Roddy of the Agricultural and Mechanical College at Greensboro, was once a captain of the Iowa State College golf team, and twice winner of the Negro amateur championship.   Frank Radcliffe of New York, James McCoy of the same city, Beltran Barker, George Adams, and Albert Harris of Washington, were enthusiastic golfers and did much to promote the game.   In the effort to secure a national organization, several golfers deserve high commendation.   Chief among these was Walther Speedy of the former Windy City Golf Club, which was functioning for golf many years before the United Golfers' Association was formed.

National tournaments were held nearly every year after 1926. Some years they were held on golf courses operated by clubs and at other times on public courses. In 1934, it was voted to hold tournaments on public links where 18 holes were available. Since then the golfers have been afforded a first class test of their abilities and skill. The leading figure in conduct of the first national meeting was Robert Hawkins of the Mapledale Club in Boston. He had operated clubs for colored and white groups, and placed large sums in prize money for the professional contenders. Among the leading golfers of later years were Albert Harris, George Adams, Robert Ball, Edison Marshall, Howard Wheeler, John Dendy, Robert Seymour, Solomon Hughes, Frank Gaskin, George Roddy, Harold Hunter, James McCoy, Lawrence Frierson, Percy Jones, Elmer Brent, Clifford Taylor, John Roux, Hugh Smith, Zeke Hartsfield, E. Jenkins, A. D. V. Crosby, Ben Greene, Clarence Chandler, O. R. Jackson, John Buchanan, and Oscar Clisby. Of the ladies who showed prominence in golf were Marie Thompson Jones, Lucy Williams, Melnee Moyee, Ella Able, Julia Siler, Aileere Davis, Cleo Ball, Sarah Smith, and Ethel Webb Terrell. In Washington, D. C., there has existed a women's golf club, the Wake Robin Club of which about twenty members play regularly.

College Golf. Tuskegee Institute, Alabama, fostered the first inter-collegiate golf championship in 1938. It was played on the Tuskegee Course and was won by Alfred Holmes. Much interest was manifested.

For the first time in the history of the University of Michigan, in 1930, two Negroes entered the All-Campus Golf Tournament. These two Negroes met in the final round and A. D. V. Crosby was the winner; R. G. Robinson was runner-up.

In 1933, the Asheville Country Club of North Carolina had four Negro golfers to play an exhibition match on its course and invited them to stay over and play an exhibition golf match on the Asheville

Municipal Course on Sunday afternoon.   Three of the four Negroes who played were Howard Wheeler, A. D. V. Crosby, and John Dendy.

Golf Championship. The 1939 National Negro Open golf championship was played during the last week in August at Los Angeles, California.   The winner was Clifford Strickland of Riverside, California.   Leading from the start, Strickland added a 75 to a 71, 77, 73 score and finished nine strokes in front of Edison Marshall of Indianapolis; Erroll Strickland of Riverside, a cousin, was third with a score of 305.   Hugh Smith, Atlanta, Georgia, with 306; John Roux, New Orleans, 307; Howard Wheeler, Atlanta, 1938 Open champion, 308; A. D. V. Crosby, Columbus, Ohio, with 309; and William Haze and Pat Ball, Chicago, with 310, were leading contenders.   Par for the Griffith Park municipal course is 71.   In the East, at Atlantic City in the week of August 14, 1939, the Royal Golf Club of Washington, D. C., won the Eastern Golf Association team competition, and won also the Maryland Open championship at Baltimore.

Later Developments. During the Second World War many golf tournaments were passed.   In recent years the most important advance in the golf picture has been the increase in the number of clubs and greater interest in golf all over the nation.   Another notable sign of progress lies in the willingness of some tournaments of national repute to accept the entry of Negro golfers in national and sectional meets.   Some of these have been the Los Angeles Open, the Tam O'Shanter, the Philadelphia Open and the United States Golf Association Open.   Also encouraging has been the fight in many southern cities to insist upon the opening of tax-supported golf links to all citizens.   Much progress has been made in Washington, D. C. and Baltimore.

Colored golfers are able to match strokes with some of the best ranking golfers in America, and have won many friends for the Negro golfer.   One of the regrettable occurrences in 1947 was the refusal of the Richmond, California, Open Tournament to admit Bill Spiller and Ted Rhodes to this tournament although by their showing in the Los Angeles Open they had qualified. They were among the first 60 in this event. Spiller was 25th and Rhodes 23rd. The suit filed by these men because of the humiliation and denial was settled out of court with the promise of the tournament promoters to eliminate racial discrimination in the future.

For the year 1948 the following officers were elected at the midwinter convention of the United Golfers Association: A. D. V. Crosby, president; Sea H. Ferguson of Indianapolis, first vice-president; M. S. Johnson of Pittsburgh, secretary; Ralph H. Chilton of Chicago, treasurer; and Vincent H. Johnson, national tournament director. Indication of the widespread growth of club activity in golf is to be found in the listing of the golfing clubs affiliated with United Golfers Association in the appendix of this volume.

CHAPTER XIII

Negro Girls in Sport

Girls Go In For Track. In 1937, the athletic world was just beginning to become accustomed to the onslaught of male Negro athletes on the records and to Negro champions in sport when up from the deep South came Tuskegee's track and field girls to win the national Amateur Athletic Union women's track and field championship. It is conservative to say that press dispatches created a sensation. Not satisfied with winning the 1937 championships, the Tuskegee team, coached by Christine Petty, won the games in 1938.

Of the eleven events, Tuskegee captured three first places and scored heavily in others to win the team championship. High point winner was Lula Hymes of Tuskegee who scored first place in the 100-meter dash and the running broad jump. The 400-meter relay was also won by Tuskegee.

Negro women had for some time been active in athletic sports. Hampered by tradition and long skirts, only a few games were open to the other sex for many years. A lady might ride side-saddle, play croquet, and bathe in cumbersome dress at the sea-side; she could not don the stream-line attire of the modern girl athlete nor compete in the presence of men. With the modern girl came the nationally heralded tennis, golf and swim champions. Negro girls were not far behind in taking up the sports and playing the games in form.

Why Competition for Girls Is Limited. Other factors that have militated against a wider participation in competitive athletics by school girls have been the various proscriptions or bans on some standard athletic forms because of anatomical or physiological differences between the sexes. Until near puberty, girls and boys

230

PRESIDENT TRUMAN RECEIVES AMERICAN OLYMPIC GIRLS, AND NATIONAL CLASSIC OFFICIALS, OCTOBER 21, 1948

Left to Right—H. H. Riley, E. B. Henderson, Dr. W. N. Rivers, Mrs. Annie Sue Evans, Spurgeon Burke, Mrs. Cleveland Abbott, Alice Coachman of Albany State College, Coach Chris Roulhac of Albany State, Nell Jackson of Tuskegee, Emma Reed of Tennessee, Theresa Manuel of Tuskegee, Audrey Patterson of Tennessee, Mabel Walker of Tuskegee engage in comparable big-muscle games and sports with nearly equal zest, ability and freedom from hazard to health. Later on, and until full maturity, the rapid growth of girls during adolescence, the lowered center of gravity, the attendant emotional changes, combine to render dangerous some of the competitive sports for

many girls. To meet the needs and capabilities of high school girls and college women, physical education leaders have evolved certain changes in the rules and nature of games for girls and have indicated what types of athletic competition are suitable for those of various stages of development. Girls and women today participate for recreation and often in competition with each other in tennis, golf, fencing, swimming, archery, badminton, croquet, table-tennis, hockey, softball, volley ball, basketball, soccer, and forms of track

LULA HYMES, TUSKEGEE

and field. Occasionally other sports are indulged in by women of maturity or of typical man-like build.

Many schools and colleges have sought to prevent the type of exploitation of school girl athletes that has so often beset school boy athletes. Various techniques of competition such as play-days, telegraph meets, and other forms of contests have been used to make sport for sport's sake the major objective of competing groups. Other social and individual outcomes of educational design are sought in the meetings of girl athletes. Recently co-ed college girls in Negro conferences have engaged in some one or the other of the play-day types.

Nevertheless, girl champions in sport are fast becoming popular in America. After school days, and in some places during school days, with adequate physical and mental health safeguards, girls are playing for championship honors in tennis, golf, swimming, basketball, softball and track.

Around the turn of the century there were many excellent tennis players and basketball groups in New York, Washington, Baltimore, St. Louis, Chicago. In New York, under the influence of the Alpha Physical Culture Club, the Smart Set and St. Christopher Clubs, many splendid girl athletes responded on the tennis and basketball courts. Dora Cole Norman and her New York Team of girls were typical of the groups.

Anita Gant. Among the girls who pioneered in athletics for women have been some splendid athletes. In Washington, D. C., Anita Gant,

LOUISE JEFFERSON AND ANITA GANT

a school teacher, still relates herself to tennis after a long career in basketball, swimming, tennis and other sports. Anita Gant was captain of the Y.W.C.A. basketball team for a long period, and this team lost only three inter-city games in nine years. She won the Washington city singles tennis honors for colored women in 1925 and 1926, was national mixed doubles champion of the American Tennis Association with her partner in 1929 and 1930, and was a partner of the national women's doubles championship team in 1933. As a swimmer, Anita was sprint champion and high point scorer for women in the first inter-city meet, 1928 Labor Day meet, at the Francis Pool in Washington. Other Washington girl athletes who have done noteworthily in athletics include Lillian Skinker

Ivy L. Wilson, Mercury Club, N. Y. City

Malone of basketball fame; Isadore Kenny, a good all round athlete; Estelle Wood, Sera Catlett, and Louise Jefferson, noted for swimming.

The Mercury Club.   One of the athletic groups giving particular attention to girl athletes was the New York Mercury Club.   This club reached one pinnacle of success in winning the outdoor championship at Toronto, Canada, in 1938.   The 440 yard medley relay team of the Mercury girls, with a record of 52.7 seconds, and an 880 yard relay team, with a record of 1.49.6, held the unofficial Metropolitan honors in those events.   The girls who achieved the most success for the club were Ivy Wilson, Romona Harris, Gertrude Johnson, Ida Byone, Pearl Edwards, Etta Tate, and Esther Dennis.

Ivy Wilson rocketed to stardom in 1938 and seemed destined to becloud the records set by Pearl Edwards and Gertrude Johnson. Ivy ran the 100 yards in 11.6 seconds.   Gertrude was the first Negro girl to enter five events, the 50, 100, and 220, the baseball throw and the broad jump, and score in each.   Much of the success of the Mercury Club's work for girls was due to the patience, persistence, personality and coaching ability of LeRoy Alston, who brought these girls of track athletic ability together and started them on their honor-winning gait.

National Champion Basketeers.   The 1938–1939 Philadelphia Tribune Girls' team justly claimed national honors.   This quint, piloted by the redoubtable tennis champion, Ora Washington, was organized in 1931.   Each year the team traveled thousands of miles in playing a schedule with the best colored and white teams.   They played the boys' game.   In February and March of 1938, they made a three thousand mile tour of the South covering nearly a dozen states.   In the nine years of activity they made an outstanding record of having lost only six games to colored teams that played boys' rules.   Members of the late aggregation included Captain Ora Washington, Gladys Walker, Virginia Woods, Lavinia Moore, Myrtle Wilson, Rose Wilson, Marie Leach and Florence Campbell.

Chicago Romas. In Chicago there were many good athletes among the fair sex. For a long period after the First World War, there was a team of girls that sparkled on the basketball courts. They were known as the Roma team, coached by Sol Butler, the former Dubuque athletic star. The leader and star player of this quint was Isadore Channels of tennis fame. Some other members of a well rounded quint that never suffered a defeat were Corinne Robinson, Mignon Burns, Lillian Ross, Virginia Willis and Lula Porter, also a tennis star.

Tennis Champions. As tennis players colored girls have for many years earned the plaudits of lovers of athletics. Years before the organization of the American Tennis Association in 1916, however, some girls were engaged in this queen of sports. One of the first to be acclaimed for tennis honors was the late Lucy D. Slowe. Singles champion over the years since 1917 have been: Lucy D. Slowe, 1917, and 1921; M. Rae of Jamaica, B.W.I., 1918, 1919, 1920; Isadore Channels of Chicago, 1922, 1923, 1924, and 1926; Lula Ballard of Philadelphia, 1925, 1927, 1928 and 1936; Ora Washington, of Philadelphia, 1929, 1930, 1931, 1932, 1933, 1934, 1935, and 1937, and Flora Lomax of Detroit, Michigan, in 1938. Recent winners are listed in the Appendix.

Eight girls won women's doubles between 1928 and 1938. They were Lula Ballard, Ora Washington, Blanche Winston, Anita Gant, Bertha Isaacs, Lilyan Spencer, and later two sisters of Washington, D. C., in college at Tuskegee, Margaret Peters and Roumania Peters, who won the doubles championship in 1938. Associated with a man player, or in mixed doubles, Blanche Winston, Anita Gant, Anne Roberts, Martha Davis, Emma Leonard, Flora Lomax, and Lula Ballard won championships in this bracket.

Women in Golf. Golfing women have begun to increase rapidly on the courses. Some of the outstanding ones have appeared in the writing of the story of golf. One of the significant developments is the organization of the only woman's golf club, known as the Wake Robin Golf Club of Washington, D. C. Two of its players had quite a reputation. They were Sara Smith and Ethel Webb Terrell.

Women golfers entered the United Golfers' Association annual tournaments in 1930. Since that time, some excellent players have developed. The first tournament winner was Marie Thompson of Chicago who won also in 1931 and was runner-up in 1932. Lucy Williams of Indianapolis began winning championships in 1921. She was tourney champion in 1936 and 1937, and runner-up in 1930, 1931, 1933, and 1934. Julia Siler broke through to a championship in 1933. In 1934 and 1935 another westerner, Ella C. Able of Indianapolis won the tourney, and in 1936 she was runner-up. Laura Thoroughgood of New York was runner-up in 1935, and Aileen Davis of Chicago was runner-up in 1937. In 1938 Melnee Moyee of Atlanta was winner, and Cleo Ball was runner-up.

Outstanding Girl Athletes. Of the all-round girl athletes appearing here and there many are outstanding for present or past performance. Very few followers of sports for women have not heard of Tydie Pickett of Chicago, Louise Stokes of Malden, Massachusetts, who made the Olympic team, Inez Patterson of Philadelphia, Ivy Wilson and Pearl Edwards of New York, Ora Washington of Philadelphia, and the long list of girl tennis champions over the years of the American Tennis Association.

Inez Patterson. One of the great girl athletes of all time is Inez Patterson, born in Chester, Pennsylvania. This athletic heroine typifies the ability and pluck of champion athletes. Not only has she won honors in competition with her mates, but she has successfully battered down the gates of prejudice and intolerance by her intrepid insistence on the right to meet all comers, by her ladylike sportsmanship, and undeniable athletic prowess.

The story of her athletic accomplishment is a saga. In her junior high school days in Philadelphia, she captained the city champion junior high captain-ball team, won the city junior high round-arm throw, won the 13 miles mileage swim contest, and won individual junior high track honors in 1925. During her career in

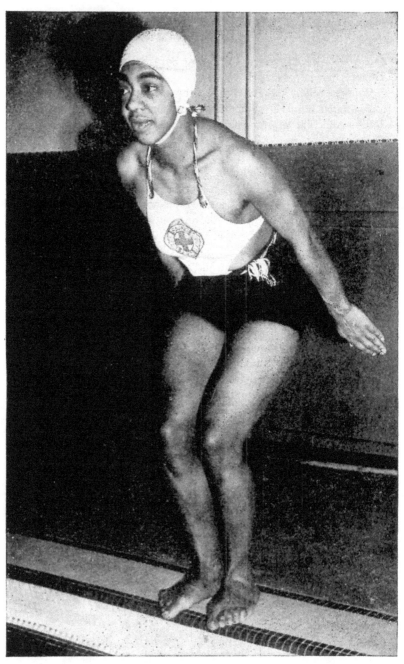

INEZ PATTERSON, PHILADELPHIA'S ALL-ROUND GIRL ATHLETE

West Philadelphia High School for 1925–1928, she was the class manager and only colored girl hockey team player, and set a new record for the round arm basketball throw of 93 feet. During her high school days as a member of the McCoach playground in Philadelphia, Inez made a distance swimming record of 100 lengths of the 90 foot pool in 1927, which record still stands. In the same meet she won the side stroke, double overarm, standing front dive, and swan dive events. She was also captain of the colored city champion girls' basketball team of McCoach Playground. In July 1928, she entered a colored girls' team in the Philadelphia *Inquirer* Newspaper Track Meet held at Franklin Field. Here she won the shot-put event.

Entering Temple University in 1929, Inez made the highest average in athletics of a class of 67 girls, and made the all-Collegiate hockey team for four straight years. During her stay at Temple she made six all-collegiate teams,—in hockey, tennis, basketball, track, volley-ball and dancing. She was the only Negro girl among 500 girls in the "Play Day" at the University of Pennsylvania, swimming on the winning relay team and winning honors in diving. Part of her crowning achievement was the breaking of the barriers that kept colored girls out of the May Day Festival, the American Red Cross examiners' course, and the Women's Athletic Association swimming meet.

Since leaving college she has participated in many local and national championship events. At present, she is devoting her abilities to training girls in recreation and physical education. Her services at the Orange Y.W.C.A., Newark, Montclair, Jersey City and the New York Y.W.C.A. as physical education instructor are memorable. She has organized three general athletic clubs, and a tennis club of the New York State Tennis Association. In 1938 she was appointed National Program Director of the American Tennis Association. She continues at the New York Y.W.C.A.

Another prominent Negro woman athlete is Julia Towns Siler, a graduate of Sumner High School of St. Louis, Missouri. In 1934 she won the National Women's golf championship. She was probably one of the leading Negro women exponents of the game.

She was not only a player of national reputation, but a guiding spirit in organizing women golfers.

Tuskegee Girls. The Tuskegee girls' track and field team has created enviable history in girls' athletics. Since 1936, the record of these girls has been unsurpassed in the story of women's athletics. In 1936, Tuskegee girls won second place in the national meet. In every indoor and outdoor junior championship since 1936, except for the 1943 Lakewood, Ohio meet, the Tuskegee girls have outscored their opponents.   Credit for this remarkable performance is due to the splendid coaching and promotion of the Directors of Physical Education—Mr. Cleveland Abbott and Mrs. Amelia C. Roberts of Tuskegee.

"Buster" Miller, in his Sports Parade column, described the Tuskegee team as the most outstanding team in women's track since their first appearance at Providence, R. I., on July 4, 1936, in the finale of the Olympic tryouts.

"The team tied for second place," wrote Miller, "winning only one event when Miss Mabel Smith leaped 18 feet in the broad jump.

"In 1937, the girls went to Trenton, N. J., and came away with their first national team title. After that, it became a Tuskegee habit. They repeated in 1938 at Naugatuck, Connecticut, and again in 1939 at Waterbury, Connecticut, and again in 1940 at Ocean City, New Jersey. In 1941, the Tuskegee girls really went to town romping off with the indoor and outdoor titles at Atlantic City, New Jersey. They repeated the Ocean City triumph again in 1942. This is getting monotonous, isn't it?

"It was in 1943 that the Tuskegee girls met their first defeat since they started collecting national titles. That year they bowed to the powerful Cleveland Polish Olympic team led by the then incomparable Stella Walsh. In 1944, however, Tuskegee recaptured the national title in the meet at Harrisburg, Pennsylvania, and has kept it ever since, winning both the indoor and outdoor titles in 1945 and now the indoor crown in 1946." Tuskegee girls also won the championships for the years 1947 and 1948.

As mentioned elsewhere, the philosophy underlying some of the

One of Tuskegee's Girl Track Teams

systems prevailing in school and college physical education has prevented participation of girls in athletics on a large scale. Rightly, the health of girls should be and is of first consideration in the programs of most schools. Athletics for girls are primarily for physical development, healthy living and recreation. Yet there is a trend toward a larger share of athletics for girls. There are far more co-ed activities approved by educators than formerly. Greater numbers of girls go in for sports each year.

Despite the narrowed limits prescribed for girls and women, there are girls who ought to display their skill and natural sport ability to a wider extent. These national exponents of women's sports are therefore to be commended for the prominence they have attained. The opportunities and participation ought to increase. The race of man needs the inspiration of strong virile womanhood. Honor is due the pioneers and the present competitors in the field of women's athletics.

CHAPTER XIV

In Various Sports

The great mass of athletes have been directed into the field of their chosen activities largely through the glare and glamour attendant upon some sports. In America the publicity given three major team games serves to guide boys and girls toward them. In England, cricket and soccer receive first call. Boxing has always made a strong appeal to Negro boys. When a few Negro athletes began to score prominently in the dash and broad jump, a large number of imitators followed. It was natural that lacking in the facilities and opportunities for an exploration of neuro-muscular skill in a wide variety of events, Negroes should at first become best known in those sports which did not require expensive outlay, much equipment, or intensive coaching. Hence few Negroes have achieved very much in more expensive and less popular sports of competitive activity.

Here and there may have been one or two good colored contenders in some of the less common varieties of sport but the records show no outstanding Negro champions in archery, auto racing, badminton, billiards, bob-sledding, bowling, canoeing, casting, chess, court tennis, cricket (in America), curling, fencing, gymnastics, handball, hockey, horseshoe pitching,[1] ice-skating, lacrosse, lawn-bowling, motor boating, polo, rackets, rowing, rugby, skeet shooting, trap shooting, skiing, squash rackets, squash tennis, swimming, table tennis, wrestling, and yachting. Yet there have been Negroes who have become famous locally or nationally in some of the less popular or less orthodox sporting activities.

Wrestlers. At least three athletes have arrived at championship caliber in wrestling in collegiate circles. In 1917, Eugene

---

[1] Arthur Wrack, Negro horseshoe pitcher of Brooklyn, won the New York City horseshoe pitching championship, July 15, 1939.

HORSESHOE TOURNAMENT HELD ON THE BANNEKER NIGHT COURTS IN WASHINGTON, D. C., UNDER Y.M.C.A. AUSPICES, WITH PHYSICAL DIRECTOR ARTHUR GREEN IN MIDDLE, JOHN HYSON (LEFT), ALFRED WILSON (RIGHT)

Davidson, of Washington, D. C., won intercollegiate honors as the 125 pound champion for Harvard University in the New England circuit. A little later, Benner C. Turner, 1926, won the New England intercollegiate championship in the same class. Russell Minton wrestled on Penn State's team.

Out on the Pacific Coast that well-known, popular football player and all-round athlete, Walter Gordon of the University of California, starred in boxing and wrestling. He was the heavyweight Pacific Coast Intercollegiate Boxing and Wrestling Champion for 1916, 1917 and 1918. He was honored as All-American football guard on the coast, and served as line coach on the staff of the University of California for the years 1921, 1922, 1923, and 1924. W. Montague Cobb was Amherst's lightweight boxing champion in 1923, and welterweight in 1924. In late years more colored athletes are attempting wrestling.

Crew. The most exacting of all college sports is boat racing. Making the crew is a task for which few are chosen. Rowing requires a powerful body, specially framed, and a stout heart. Only one Negro made a varsity crew before 1940. Joseph Edward Trigg, of Washington, D. C., graduate of M Street High School, gained this distinction by rowing number "7" oar in the Syracuse University varsity shell in 1915. He started as a member of the Freshman crew in 1913 and was a member of the Junior varsity in 1914. He rowed in the Intercollegiate Regatta at Poughkeepsie, N. Y., against Cornell, Columbia, Penn, Wisconsin, Navy, University of California, and University of Washington. In the fall, Trigg played line positions on the varsity football teams of 1913, 1914, 1915 and 1916. In 1915, Trigg was a member of the Syracuse team that on a trip to the coast played the Universities of Montana and Oregon.

Among others who aspired to positions in a racing shell were Joseph Howard Lee of Boston and Haley G. Douglass, a grandson of Frederick Douglass, the great abolitionist. Lee in 1898, and Douglass in 1903, '04 and '05 were members of several Weld Boat crews which were training schools for varsity boats. Although they

SYRACUSE'S VARSITY CREW, 1915, WITH JOSEPH EDWARD TRIGG IN THE CENTER

Trigg was the only Negro yet to make a college varsity oar. He was a freshman crew member at Syracuse in 1913, a junior varsity oar in 1914 and on the varsity crew in 1915. During his career at Syracuse, Trigg was also a varsity football player for four years. Today he is a respected physician in Washington, D. C. Roscoe Giles at Cornell was a third varsity crew member, and had not restrictions existed, he would have advanced to varsity oar. Cecil Bratton attempted crew at Wisconsin and earned a letter, but here again restrictions prevented his participation in regattas. Now that colleges are becoming more liberal it is expected that ambitious Negro athletes will find more opportunity for activity in this sport.

reached high ranking in the Weld Boat races, neither could gain the distinction of rowing a varsity oar. Girls have done better. Harriet Pickens and Hilda Anderson were crew members at Smith College.

Soccer. Negro soccer players have been prominent in schools where soccer is maintained as a college sport. This great sport of the British Isles and elsewhere on the continent has never shared the popularity here that it does there. At the Springfield Young Men's Christian Association Training College, where nearly all sports are a part of the curriculum, soccer held a high place. John H. Burr, once physical director for men at Howard University, was a member of the New England championship team of Springfield in 1921. Robert Gilham also made the college team at Springfield for the 1924, 1925 and 1926 seasons. Probably the greatest soccer player to appear on college teams was Kenneth B. M. Crooks, who starred on the Harvard Varsity teams of 1924, 1925 and 1926.

Weight Lifting. A little known sport in which colored Americans have prominently starred is weight lifting. Of the six members of the weight-lifting team that competed in the World Weight-Lifting championships at Vienna in 1938, two were strong Negro men. John Davis of Brooklyn was winner in the light heavyweight class and John Terry of New York was fourth in the featherweight class and maker of a new world snatch record for his weight. At Woonsocket, R. I., in May, 1938, John Terry was winner of the senior weight-lifting event for the 132-pound class. John Davis was second in the 181-pound class. John Terry was holder of the American record for the two-hands dead lift. Terry won the lightweight title in 1940 and 1941.

In 1941 John Davis hoisted 1005 pounds in three lifts. He has never been beaten since. In September, 1947, in Philadelphia, Davis came within 1½ pounds of his 1941 lift when he raised 1003¼ pounds, 308¾ in the press, 308¾ in the snatch and 285¾ in the jerk. He broke the Olympic record at the 14th Olympiad games by a record breaking hoist of 999½ pounds to become listed as the strongest man in the world.

Although Americans are none too familiar with him, Davis' reputation in foreign countries is comparable to that of Joe Louis and Babe Ruth. In the old world where gymnastics and events of strength are yet appealing, Davis is a famous hero. Here is an event that has great appeal to strong muscular boys and men, yet few Negroes outside of New York and Washington ever qualify or

U. S. Team in the World Weight Lifting Championships at Vienna
Second: John Davis, Winner light heavyweight class. Last, John Terry, maker of a new world's snatch record

practice for the event. It is worthy of stimulation by Y. M. C. A. and recreation institutions.

Fencing. Three decades ago, fencing was quite a sport in many colleges. Today there is a renewal of interest in this medieval activity that flourished when dueling was prevalent. Richard Henry enjoyed the distinction of becoming captain of the varsity fencing team at Springfield in 1926. At Rutgers, in 1938, Ernest Baxter was identified with the Rutgers fencing team, and in 1939 Baxter became also a representative of the school in boxing.

Hockey, Lacrosse, Skiing and Bicycling.   Already there are a few colored hockey players breaking the ice in the professional play. Lowell C. Wormley, a graduate of the Dunbar High of Washington, D. C., now a practicing physician in Phoenix, Ariz., was a varsity member of the Dartmouth College lacrosse team and played a remarkable game during his college career.   At Dartmouth, a score or more years ago, "Buster," now Dr. Wood of New York City, a former M Street High School graduate, was noted for his abilities in ski jumping.   Although no records exist for his feats, his name was on many tongues during his stay at Dartmouth.   Very few Negroes have excelled in the winter sports of the rugged North.   In the early part of the century bicycle racing afforded the fastest man propelled sport of the day.   Racing with the modern bicycle began about 1883 in the New England section of this country.   Around the turn of the century, a dark-skinned riding champion by the name of Major Taylor claimed the spotlight, along with F. L. Kramer, whose name was identified with championships for many years.   The riding duels between Kramer and Major Taylor were classic events.   One, and then the other, would win.   Taylor's name is found in the records as the American professional sprint champion for the year 1900.   Major Taylor's story is given in detail in the Appendix.

Rod and Gun Clubs.   Skeet, otherwise known as "Round the Clock" shooting, came into existence about 1910.   "Skeet" is a Scandinavian word meaning shoot.   Skeet is shooting at clay targets and had a following of over 25,000 shooters in the United States before World War I.   Today, all about the country there exist organized clubs for the purpose of promoting gun marksmanship, and the development of the enjoyment of hunting and fishing. Some of the clubs go in just for hunting and angling as sport.   Others emphasize the competitive side of shooting.   Live bird shooting is legal in only two states, but clay pigeon and skeet target shooting is popular all over.   Throughout the South before and since the Civil War there were colored marksmen who could rival Daniel Boone's legendary skill with the rifle, while "turkey shoots" are

yet popular in many areas.   Military schools and private associations still sponsor tournaments on ranges with guns or pistols.

Some of the most prominent of the clubs are listed and located
as follows:

Twin Sycamore Rod and Gun Club	Red Bank, N. J.
Falcon Rod and Gun Club	Baltimore, Md.
Present Day Rod and Gun Club	St. Louis, Mo.
Deep Sea Anglers Rod and Gun Club	Washington, D. C.
Cornelius Six Point Rod and Gun Club	Coatesville, Pa.
Triangle Rod and Gun Club	Philadelphia, Pa.
Washington Park Rod and Gun Club	Chicago, Ill.

DR. AND MRS. ERNEST B. WETMORE OF MORRISTOWN, N. J.
Both Noted "Skeets" Champions and Sports Followers

Without doubt the most prominent of the individuals connected
with the art of trap and sheet shooting is Dr. E. B. Wetmore of
Morristown, New Jersey.   His exploits and organizing efforts,

more than those of any single person, have been responsible for the extraordinary growth of rod and gun clubs. For many years there was no color line in this sport, but with the glowing record and achievements of Dr. Wetmore, the race curtain began to be drawn until in 1934, the Official Rules of the Amateur Trapshooting Association meeting in Vandalia, Ohio, in stipulating "who may take part in a registered tournament," were amended to read: "Five or more persons, except those of negroid extraction, may take part in Registered Competition, provided they first become members of the American Trapshooting Association. . . ."

This change in ruling followed the participation of Dr. Wetmore in the 12th annual North and South target tournament at the Pinehurst, N. C. gun club, a supposedly "white" event, in 1931. The officials were not aware of Wetmore's racial identity. In the doubles, Dr. Wetmore was paired against W. E. Gladstone, white, of Winston-Salem, N. C. They tied with 89 each, after Wetmore's gun had jammed three times. In the shoot-off the New Jersey marksman broke 22 to 18 targets by Gladstone. His score for the event was 96 out of 100 targets.

On the next day, April 22nd, Dr. Wetmore, then a Class "B" shooter, won the 16-yard championship. He cracked 94 of the first 100 clay birds and 97 of the next 100 for a total of 191. He was one target in front of L. B. Smith of Millbrook, N. Y., who won the class "A" trophy, although having to content himself with second-place honors behind Dr. Wetmore in Class "B."

In the same meet at Pinehurst was Miss Kay C. Hughes, native Washingtonian, of whose African descent the tournament officials were fortunately ignorant. By the time the press heralded the exploits of the pair, Dr. Wetmore and Miss Hughes, now Mrs. Wetmore, were speeding north from the North Carolina resort in post haste. Mrs. Wetmore is a champion in her own right, being top shooter in many matches with women contestants, and holds her own with many of the crack shots among the stronger sex.

Dr. Wetmore holds a room full of trophies and is an ardent angler also. One of his most remarkable victories was his winning of the third leg of the Governor Hoffman trophy which he retired while shooting with his broken arm still in a cast.   On that occasion on July 27, 1936, he was competing against two former state champions and one former world champion.   He won this event by breaking 49 of 50 targets, at 250 yard handicap.   His nearest rival cracked 47.

The redoubtable doctor not only had to meet the competitive skill of his opponents but he fought a losing battle against the prejudice against his race.   One by one the tournaments and some clubs were shut against him.   He tore off the Masonic emblem of his shooting jacket because of the faithlessness of brother trapshooting Masonics.   He saw a club of which he was an accepted life member, disband and reorganize in another county to eliminate his gun. On the other hand, many clubs and shooting friends are still loyal. Before the official national trapshooting fraternity closed its doors against him, he had established an enviable mark.   In 1933, his last year at registered targets, he made 97.6 percent hits out of 4,000 chances—all in class AA competition.   He belongs to the mythical "Century Club," those gun men who have scored 100 out of 100 chances.   His longest straight run without a miss was 487.   Wetmore was permitted to compete twice in live bird competition, before New Jersey banned the sport, and he won both times.   He had captured the Union County tournament eight straight years, before the sport was resumed in 1946.   He won in 1946 and 1947.

Because of his unique contribution to the sport as a competitor and organizer his fellow citizens for fifteen years have held an honor day shoot known as "Wetmore Day" in which some of the best shooters from a wide area compete.   This event annually is followed by a famous banquet sponsored by the Twin Sycamore Rod and Gun Club, composed of many of the prominent citizens of Northern Jersey.   The saga of the Wetmores is a record of devotion to a hobby that has paid dividends in the extension of good fellowship among thousands of devotees of the art of fine living through sports.   Dr. Wetmore, besides being a devotee to the art of shooting and a fisherman of repute, is a successful dental practitioner, a Past Master of Alpha Lodge #116 F & A M of Newark, N. J., a member of Chi Delta Mu and Chi Lambda Kappa Fraternities. He is a native of Jacksonville, Fla., and a graduate of Howard University Dental School.

In the Midwest there are quite a few active clubs that carry on Trap and Skeet shooting as well as general hunting. Dr. A. J. Offord, president of the Washington Park Gun Club and School of Marksmanship, is active in the promotion of the sport in his section of the country. His wife, Mrs. Bobbie L. Offord is quite an expert, having won the Western National Women's Championship in August, 1946, as one of her triumphs. The Washington Gun Club owns a forty acre tract of land, and modern buildings are being erected.

Jockeys. The jockey, or race horse pilot, has always been listed as an athlete. The ability to ride a horse to victory requires neuro-muscular coordinations of the finest sort. Negro jockeys were familiar figures to followers of the sport of kings some years ago. Racing records hidden away in the faded yellow tomes of Richard Fox's sporting gazettes are replete with mention of the diminutive colored riders who clung to the backs of their speeding mounts during earlier American life. There are many who hope that the fairer-minded, bold horse owners and stewards will make it possible for colored jockeys to sit again astride racing steeds on the tracks of democratic America. Although colored riders and trainers are yet to be found about the racing stables of the country, few colored jockeys break by the bars set against them because of race.

Colored jockeys have ridden "Derby" winners. In 1875, Oliver Lewis, astride H. P. McGrattis' colt, Aristides, came home in front in the Kentucky Derby. Isaac Murphy held the record for Derby winnings. Murphy won three Kentucky Derby races. Only recently was his record surpassed and then only by the noted Eddie Arcaro. Some of the other colored boys who have led their careening horses down the home stretch to gain the prize money and fame are Billy Walker, G. Lewis, "Babe" Hurd, E. Henderson, Lonnie Clayton, "Soup" Perkins, Jimmy Winkfield and Willie Simms.

As late as 1911, Jesse Conley rode Coltson, named after the famous colored trainer, Raleigh Coltson, to a third place in the

Clarence Reed," a Most Successful Jockey

Derby. Jimmy Winkfield, up on Alan-a-Dale, in the twenty-eighth Derby, raced his mount to win in the fast time of 2 minutes, 8¾ seconds. Another Negro jockey, "Monk" Overton, rode six winners in one day's racing at Washington Park, Chicago, July 10, 1891.

One of the Derby races that will long be remembered by the followers of the fortunes of the riders and horses was the twenty-eighth Derby, run on May 4, 1902. Alan-a-Dale was the colt, owned by Major T. C. McDowell. A stablemate, Rival, a famous and loudly heralded colt Abe Frank, and a less renowned pony, Inventor, were leading contenders. Each horse carried 117 pounds and the cash prize was $4,850, large for that time, but little today. On a fast track they were off. Rival broke in front. But he was soon back in last place as Alan-a-Dale, ridden by the celebrated jockey, Jimmy Winkfield, was leading the field by four lengths, with Abe Frank coming up. Winkfield sent his mount along as though it were a three-quarter mile dash instead of a Derby race. He raced the half in 48, and had his field struggling behind. On the home stretch, Abe Frank dropped out, and Inventor, benefited by the killing pace, was closing like a house afire. However, Winkfield was master of the situation, riding hands and heels to win by a scant neck. The time was 2 minutes, 8¾ seconds, and was a glorious finish. The winning colt was dead lame after the race.

The story of colored jockeys has been such a thrilling one and because this saga has never been fully told, we have had Mr. Buster Miller, Sports Editor of the *New York Age*, compile the record performances of Negroes of the saddle and have presented this history in the appendix of this book.

Bowling. Hundreds of thousands of Americans are to be found in bowling alleys each year. Bowling is one of the best of activities that contribute to health, sociability and recreation. Yet in only a few cities is bowling possible for Negroes. The Chicago *Defender* bowling tournament attracts hundreds of bowlers who make good scores. The 1938 *Defender* tournament men's singles was won by

F. S. Usher. His winning score was 161–169–202, for a total of
532. The public does not yet realize that every city ought to have
bowling alleys and afford bowling to the men and women of all
races. It would mean much for the morale of the citizenry during
the winter months.

In late years bowling has been taken up by colored men and
women in many cities all about the country. The National Bowling
Association was organized on August 20, 1939 in Cleveland, Ohio.
The cities represented were: Cleveland, Cincinnati, Columbus,
Toledo, Indianapolis, Chicago, Racine, and Detroit.

The first officers were: Wynston T. Brown, president; L. Huntley,
vice-president; Richard Benton, secretary; Brownie Cain, treasurer;
and Henry Harden, organizer. The officers for 1948 were: Martin
C. Kelley, president; Sydney V. Celestine, vice-president; Miss
Geraldine Wells, secretary; Mrs. Mary L. Wilkes, treasurer; and
Elmer Reed of Cleveland, historian.

Because of their contribution to organized bowling the following
have been made Life Members: Wynston Brown, Jack Robinson,
J. Elmer Reed, Oscar McDonald, Viola Crosswhite, Ferley Carr,
Joseph Blue, Brownie Cain, Isaac Rivers, Leroy Brown, Richard
Benton, Henry Harden, George Porter, J. Roden, June Watts,
James Watts, Geraldine Wells, Clarence King, Lucius Huntley,
and Dwight Guy. Joe Louis also has been named Honorary member.

In the Appendix we have listed the winners of national bowling
tournaments. It has been estimated that Negroes have invested
nearly a million dollars in bowling alleys, employ over 400, and
the National Bowling Association boasts over 5,000 members.

Swimming. Negro swimmers have been developing slowly but
surely. There are as yet not many standard pools where Negroes
may swim all the year round. Yearly practice is necessary to learn
and perfect the strokes, dives and techniques of competition. Outdoor, publicly owned and supported pools have developed in some
of the cities where Negroes had no supervised swimming. Some
Negro colleges have good pools, and in one or more of them standard
pools are being constructed. To motivate learning and develop

perfection in swimming, some sort of meetings are necessary. If the swim meet is too costly, the techniques of the increasingly popular telephone or telegraph meets are possible where the results and times of each race are telephoned or telegraphed and announced at the other meeting.

The swimming meets under Amateur Athletic Union auspices which have been held in Washington, D. C., for colored swimmers, otherwise denied A. A. U. competition in this city, have served to increase the interest and ability of swimmers annually. In the matter of records, Negro swimmers have hardly approached the marks set by Weissmuller, Flanagan, Medica, Eleanor Holm, Helene Madison, Katherine Rawls and others, but this, as in so many sports, is simply due to the lack of equal facilities and coaching.

Only a few Negroes have gone far in competition with the swimmers of other racial elements. Here as elsewhere, the bar sinister has blocked entry in many places. In high school swimming in some of the northern cities colored boys have had the chance to compete. As an instance of the progress made, Mitchell Lewis, of the Northwestern High School, of Detroit, reached the finals in the Metropolitan Detroit swim meet. He was the first swimmer of his race to compete in this event since 1925, when Clarence Gatliff was captain of the Cass Technical High swim team.

Maurice Jackson of Howard University of Washington, D. C., formerly of the Armstrong High School, of that city, entered several years ago a national A. A. U. swimming contest and scored second in the 100 yard free style race in which the winner established a new record. Williams of New York and Colburn of Philadelphia, have won A. A. U. honors. John Strothers of Pittsburgh was second in the 50 meters Junior Outdoor A. A. U. championships in Pittsburgh, Aug. 13, 1938. Inez Patterson, the excellent girl athlete of Philadelphia and New York, was a splendid swimmer. Charles Pinderhughes at Dartmouth and John Pinderhughes at Springfield were collegiate swimmers in 1939.

The inter-city meets and inter-school meets between units in Philadelphia, New York, Baltimore, Pittsburgh, and Washington have brought out some good talent. Notable among the swimmers that have come forward are Frederick Douglass, Maurice Jackson, Ernest Marshall, Sterling Thomas, Granville Hill, Charles Pinderhughes and Raymond Carroll, of Washington, D. C.; Leroy Williams, of New York; John Strothers, of Pittsburgh; and Ernest Colburn, of Philadelphia. Among the girls who have done highly creditable work are Edith Jetter, of New York; Audrey Stacks, of Washington; and Henrietta Brown, of Baltimore.

Negroes in the Olympic Games. Colored athletes were not in the first of the modern Olympics, but they entered the second set of modern games. The original Olympic games began 776 B.C. The winners of the early games were more than athletic heroes. They were the idols of the nation. Often after death they were worshipped as minor gods, and the town in which they lived was considered to be favored by the gods. Every prominent athlete aspired to such unusual honors. The Olympic games were revived at Athens in Greece in 1896.

The Negro athlete first appeared in these international contests in the 1904 games held at St. Louis. A colored boy by the name of George Poage, of the Milwaukee Athletic Club, raced Harry Hillman to a new record in the 400 meter race, which Hillman won in the new time of 49⅕ seconds. Hillman and Poage met for another race in the 400 meter hurdles. Here again Poage was Hillman's nearest competitor at the finish. Again Hillman made a new record of 53 seconds, but it was disallowed, because he knocked over the last hurdle.

At London in 1908, the late John B. Taylor of Pennsylvania, intercollegiate champion for the 440, was America's Negro contender. The 400 meter race in these Olympics occasioned a great deal of bickering. Carpenter of Cornell, Robbins of Harvard, and Halswelle of England, finished in that order but because an official ran on the track and interfered the race was ordered to be re-run. In this new race, the Americans would not compete and Halswelle won. Taylor had begun to weaken from the ravages of the dread disease from which he succumbed shortly after these games.

MAL WHITFIELD, of Ohio State, American Olympic Winner of 800 Meter
Race, 1948 Olympics.

Howard Drew was a contender in the sprints and broad jump for America in the 1912 games at Stockholm, but an injured leg kept Drew from competing in the finals of the 100, to which event he had advanced through the trials.

At Antwerp in 1920, Sol Butler was the Negro hope. But his fate was no better than that of his predecessors. He pulled a tendon the first qualifying jump and the chances of America in the broad jump went glimmering. Earl Johnson was one of the Yankee team members but could not measure up with the Scandinavians. Harry Edwards, a Negro from the British West Indies, scored third in the sprint race that Paddock won.

At Paris in 1924, DeHart Hubbard started American Negroes on to winning ways when he annexed the broad jump on July 8, 1924, by leaping 24 feet, 5½ inches. Ned Gourdin, of Harvard, finished second.

Jack London, Negro runner from British Guiana, was second to Percy Williams, of Canada, in the 1929 sprint event at Amsterdam. Phillip Edwards, once house surgeon at the Barbados General Hospital, began his three-time Olympic quest by running fourth in the 800 meter race. Earl Johnson again succumbed along with the rest of the Americans to the superb Finns.

Eddie Tolan, Metcalfe and Gordon were the stars of the 1932 Olympics. Tolan won the 100 meters in the record time of 10.3 seconds, and the 200 meters in 21.2 seconds. Metcalfe was runner-up in the 100 and third in the 200 meters race. Competing against two noted world record holders, Edward Gordon won the broad jump with a leap of 25 feet, ¾ inch. Chuhei Nambu, of Japan, held the world's record at 26 feet, 2½ inches, and Gordon's other competitor, Sylvio Cator, of Haiti, had been a world record holder with a jump of more than 25 feet. A high school boy, Cornelius Johnson, destined to create a world record, tied with four jumpers at 6 feet, 5⅝ inches for second place in the 1932 Olympics, but was fourth in the jump-off.

From the 1904 Olympics down to the 1948 games, the Negro athletes have been giving signs of greater and greater advancement. In 1936 in Berlin they came near making a sweep of the leading

1938 Decathlon Entrants, Including Scisco of Tuskegee
and Ed. Gordon of the Grand Street Boys' Club

Va. State Track Team, 1938

U. S. Team to England, France, Belgium, Switzerland, and Italy
Including Ben Johnson and Cornelius Johnson

track and field events.   These events are too fresh in the minds of the present generation to require more than to name the winners and the place winners.   The peerless Jesse Owens won the 100 meters in 10.3 seconds, the 200 meters in 20.7 seconds, the running broad jump by 26 feet, 5$\frac{5}{16}$ inches, and was a member of the sprint relay team.   Archie Williams won the 400 meter race in 46.5 seconds; in the same race, Jimmy Luvalle was third.   John Woodruff won the 800 meters in one minute and 52.9 seconds.   Phil Edwards was third.   Ralph Metcalfe was second in the 100 meters and was a member of the record-breaking sprint relay team.   Mack Robinson was second in the 200 meter race.   Cornelius Johnson won the high jump with 6 feet 7$\frac{15}{16}$ inches, and David Albritton was second with a jump of 6 feet, 6$\frac{3}{4}$ inches.   Fritz Pollard, Jr., was second in the high hurdle race.

It is no exaggeration to say that America was astounded as the succession of names of the colored winners came across the Atlantic over radio.   Americans were proud of their dark-skinned heroes, especially when competing in a country ruled by a superior race philosophy.

The 1948 Olympiad.   Because of the Second World War, the 1940 and 1944 Olympics were not held.   London was the site of the Olympics in 1948.   Two hundred, sixty athletes in 13 different sports made up the American team.   Fifty-eight were colored athletes. They sailed with the American team on the *S. S. America* early in July, 1948.

The track team comprised Barney Ewell of Lancaster, Pa., Harrison Dillard of Baldwin-Wallace College, Edward Conwell of Jersey City, Mal Whitfield of Ohio State University, Dave Bolen of the University of Colorado, Willie Steele of San Diego State College, Herbert Douglass of the University of Pittsburgh, and Lorenzo Wright of Wayne University.

The 1948 Olympics were somewhat short of the 1936 Olympics in glamourous performances by colored athletes from America, but in some respects Negro athletes were more prominent in the later games than in Hitler's day.   There was no Jesse Owens to steal

N. C. A. A. CHAMPIONS FOR 1939

1. Mack Robinson, Univ. of Oregon; 2. Mozelle Ellerbee, Tuskegee Institute; 3. Fred Wolcott, Rice Institute. Robinson, a place winner in the 1936 Olympics at Berlin, is one of the fastest 200 meter runners in the world. Ellerbee, the 1938 Amateur Athletic 100-Meter Champion, lost to Jeffrey in 1939; Wolcott lost his high hurdle crown to Schoolboy Batiste for 1939.

the show as he did in Fascist Berlin, nevertheless, up to the 800, except for one victory won by Mel Patton of America, the colored boys did as well as in the 1936 games. What was most significant was the extension of colored athletes from America into athletics beyond the men's track games.

For the first time a colored player was a star on the American basketball team. Had it not been for the all-round greatness on

Left—DAVE BOLEN, 1948 A.A.U. 600 Yard Champion, and Member 1948
Olympic Winning Relay Team
Right—PHIL THIGPEN, Seton Hall's Great Middle Distance Runner

ALICE COACHMAN, Jumping for Olympic World Crown in 1948, London, Olympics

the court of Don Barksdale of the Oakland Bittners, it is conceivable that this nation might not have emerged triumphant. For the first time a colored weight lifter won the title of the strongest human when John Davis set two Olympic records in the heavyweight class. Davis exceeded the "jerk" lift by 28 pounds. His lift of 391¼ pounds topped the old standard of 363¼ by Yohanna Suhaar of Estonia in Berlin. His "snatch" record of 314 pounds was 8¼ pounds better than his own world record in this phase. Davis was top man in the American weight lifting which scored 63 points, 33 more than the second place Egypt aggregation.

Another first was recorded when the American Olympic team had for its women members six colored girls from America, Cynthia Thompson of Jamaica, and others from the foreign nations. Four of these girls, Theresa Manuel, Nell Jackson, Mabel Walker and Alice Coachman were from Tuskegee and Emma Reed and Audrey Patterson were from Tennessee State. All put up a great battle in their events. Audrey Patterson won a third place medal for world honors in the 200 meter dash. It was left to Alice Coachman, who originally was a student at Tuskegee, currently at Albany State Teachers College in Georgia, to win the coveted crown of an Olympiad champion. Alice won the running high jump in the wind and rain and became the only American woman to win a track event. Her jump of 5 feet, 6⅛ inches, eclipsed the Olympic record of 5 feet 5¼ inches set by Jean Shirley and Babe Didrikson of the U. S. A. in 1932. A colored girl, Victor R. Beckett of Jamaica, with a leap of 5 feet, 2½ inches was fourth in the event. Miss Coachman, although specialist for the Olympics, holds two victories over that sterling Polish runner, Stella Walsh, in the 100 meters, winning in 1945 and 1946. She has equalled the world's record of 6.4 seconds for the 50 meter event.

Americans have scored with only two boxing champions in the last four Olympiads. Of the eight weight class champions in the American team, four were colored boys. They were: James Mitchell, of Redmond, California, bantam; Edward Johnson of Kansas City, featherweight; Wallace Smith of Cincinnati, lightweight; Horace Herring of St. Petersburg, Florida, welterweight;

and Washington Jones of Lovejoy, Illinois, middleweight. Norvell Lee, heavyweight, a Howard University student from Covington, Virginia; and Frank Daniels a middleweight from Bakersfield, California, were two of the eight alternates to go to London. Although these boys put up a splendid fight, only Horace "Hank" Herring reached the finals where he lost on a split decision.

ARTHUR WINT (JAMAICA) Wnning Olympic 400 Meter Run, London, 1948   EDWARD CONWELL, N. Y. UNIVERSITY SPRINTER; Indoor A.A.U. 60 Yard Sprint Champion

Track and field colored men athletes were easily the stars of the games. Some represented the British Kingdom, others, South America and Africa. American track and field men dominated. Harrison Dillard, a world champion hurdler was the surprise winner of the premier sport event, the 100 meters. Dillard, who from the war years in Italy and who, back in the States, had won 82 consecutive races, a score more than any other track athlete had ever done, tried to qualify for both the 100 and the high hurdles in Milwaukee tryouts. Because of the closeness of the trials and finals of these two events, Dillard did not qualify in the final heat of the hurdles, but did in the 100.

In the finals of the Olympic 100 meters, Dillard defeated Barney Ewell in a photo-finish, in 10.30 seconds, equalling the Olympic record. Only one white winner had captured a sprint since 1928 when Percy Williams of Canada won both sprint races. In 1932 Tolan won both and Jesse Owens duplicated in 1936. Mel Patton of California took the 200 meter race in a close race with Barney Ewell. Both runners were so close, they were timed in 21.2 seconds by the electric timer.

Lloyd La Beach of Panama, who had previously equalled the world record in the 100 yards and 100 meters event scored third place in both the 100 and 200 meters sprint. Herbert McKenley was fourth in the 200 meters.

The 400 meter relay team caused more excitement than any other event. The American team led off with Barney Ewell, followed by Lorenzo Wright and Harrison Dillard with Mel Patton (white) anchor man. A British judge ruled America had lost the race because in his judgment, Ewell and Wright had passed the baton beyond the zone mark. Ewell protested vigorously and insisted that coach Dean Cromwell protest. A showing of the pictures convinced the Olympic jury of appeals that Barney was right, and the English team relinquished the medals to the Americans.

One of the great winners of the year loomed up in Mal Whitfield, who was a veteran enrollee at Ohio State. At the tryouts, Whitfield won both the 400 and 800 meters races. In London he won the 800 meters race in one minute, 49.4 seconds, a new Olympic record, but could not stave off the drive of Jamaica's great runner, Arthur Wint in the 400 meters, which Wint took in 46.2 seconds to equal the Olympic record. Herbert McKenley was second and Whitfield third, with Dave Bolen fourth. Whitfield also anchored the American winning 1600 meter relay team.

Willie Steele of San Diego College in California had only to jump twice to win the running broad jump which several colored

boys have done in the last half dozen Olympics. His distance was
25 feet 9 inches. Herbert Douglas of Pittsburgh was third in this
event and Lorenzo Wright of Detroit took fourth place.

Point Distribution Among Olympic Games Winners

Name and Country	Event	Place	Time, Dist., Hgt.	Pts.
Harrison Dillard, USA	100 Meters	First	**10.3 seconds	10
Mal Whitfield, USA	800 Meters	First	*1:49.2 secs.	10
Willie Steele, USA	Brd. Jump	First	25 ft., 9 in.	10
Alice Coachman, USA	High Jump	(w) First	*5 ft., 6⅛ in.	10
Arthur Wint, Jamaica	400 Meters	First	**46.2 seconds	10
Barney Ewell, USA	100 Meters	Second	10.4 seconds	5
Barney Ewell, USA	200 Meters	Second	21.2 seconds	5
Arthur Wint, Jamaica	800 Meters	Second	1:49.4 secs.	5
Herb McKenley, Jam.	400 Meters	Second	46.4 seconds	5
Mal Whitfield, USA	400 Meters	Third	46.6 seconds	4
Herb Douglas, USA	Brd. Jump	Third	24 ft., 10 in.	4
Audrey Patters'n USA	200 Meters (w)	Third	No Time	4
Lloyd LaBeach, Pan.	100 Meters	Third	10.5 seconds	4
Lloyd LaBeach, Pan.	200 Meters	Third	21.4 seconds	4
Dave Bolen, USA	400 Meters	Fourth	46.8 seconds	3
Lorenzo Wright, USA	Brd. Jump	Fourth	24 ft., 8 in.	3
Herb McKenley, Jam.	200 Meters	Fourth	21.6 seconds	3
MacDonald Bailey, GB	100 Meters	Sixth	10.8 seconds	1
				100

Symbols: * New Olympic record; ** Equals Olympic record; (w) Women's events.

Recapitulation: 5 first, 4 seconds, 5 thirds, 3 fourths, 1 sixth. Total 100.

Negro Team Captains. One of the highly significant evidences
of the tolerance and idealism of athletic sport at its best is shown by
the tribute rendered deserving Negro athletes on college teams by
whites who elect them to team captaincy. This honor has been
frequently awarded in track and field. Seldom does that honor
come to the colored athlete in the major team games. Too often
the politics involved in the selection of team captain for football
prevent honoring the best player on the team even though he may
be the most capable leader. No All-American star has ever been
selected captain of his college football team.

Admitting that there may have been other players who have

LORENZO WRIGHT, WAYNE UNIVERSITY
SPRINTER AND BROAD JUMPER. Member
1948 Olympic Team

WILLIE STEELE, NATIONAL
BROAD JUMP CHAMPION, and
Olympic Broad Jump Winner
—From San Diego College

been elected captains, one finds from the available sources that
the following Negroes received this tribute by their fellow athletes in
the mixed-colleges of the country before 1940.

TRACK AND FIELD

Year	*Name*	*College*
1921	Clifton Wharton	Boston University
1923	John Burr	Springfield College
1924	Charles West	Washington and Jefferson
1926	Charles Drew	Amherst College
1929	Edward Utterback	University of Pittsburgh
1930	James Barnes	Oberlin College
1930	Gaines and Loving	Western Teachers' College
1933	John W. Brooks	University of Chicago
1934	Ralph Metcalfe	Marquette University
1937	James T. Smith (Co.-Capt.)	University of Indiana
1937	Calvin Beckett (Co.-Capt.)	Marquette University
1938	Ben Franklin	Boston University
1938	Ben Johnson	Columbia University
1938	James Peacock	Temple University
1939	William Watson	University of Michigan
1939	John Woodruff	University of Pittsburgh
1939	Edward Burke	Marquette University

CROSS COUNTRY

1930	John Enoch	Colgate University

FOOTBALL

1891	William H. Lewis	Amherst College
1905	W. H. Craighead	Massachusetts State
1907	Fenwick H. Watkins	University of Vermont
1926	Charles Ray	Bates College
1938	Homer Harris	Iowa University

BASEBALL

1898	J. Francis Gregory	Amherst College
1937	John W. Copeland	Oberlin College

BASKETBALL

1908	Fenwick H. Watkins	University of Vermont
1931	George Gregory	Columbia University
1937	Larry Bleach	University of Detroit

TENNIS

1927	Richard Hudlin	University of Chicago
1931	Reginald Weir	New York City College

FENCING

1926	Richard Henry	Northeastern University

Boy Athletes. Dipping way down into schoolboy athletics, one finds many thrilling feats on the part of boys of elementary school ages. Under the public school athletic leagues in various cities, a quarter of a century ago, elementary schoolboys competed in modified track and field programs and in some team sports. Much could be written of the exploits of these boys who gave their all for dear old public school number 9 or 10. Even today the youngsters of elementary and junior high schools engage in competitive sport which provides all of the sensations, records, and thrills of the events of the older boys.

In every city where by reason of locality we find Negro boys in preponderance, championship honors in athletics accrue with little exception to these schools in undue proportions. The names of Douglass or Lincoln or Dunbar in the larger cities usually identify the schools that win a high percentage of track and field honors.

A very full story of the achievement of schoolboy athletes may be written about these lads, many of whom found promising athletic careers limited to school days.

Marble Champion. One of the outstanding juvenile winners in sport of the year 1938 was the 13-year-old marble champion of the United States, Leonard Tynes, of Chicago. Credit for his remarkable victory belongs to his aunt, Mrs. Jessica Gaines, who took charge of Leonard, an orphan. The champion attended the Burke School, Fifty-fourth and South Parkway, and his proficiency in marble shooting was largely a result of the help and coaching of John M. Turner, who was athletic director of Washington Park playground.

In becoming champion of the United States, Tynes, at 13 years of age, had to run the gauntlet of intolerance and race prejudice. In order to spare the feelings of the contestant from Alabama, who in the regular "drawing" was to meet Tynes, in a preliminary, a secret "drawing" was had, and Andrew Tanana, of Throop, Pennsylvania, who it was thought would be the next champion, was matched with Tynes.

Battle for Fair Play. So incensed were the representatives of the Scranton, Pennsylvania, *Times*, that they withdrew both of their contestants rather than subscribe to the un-American, unsportsmanlike management. Said the Scranton *Times* in an editorial, "It is with no desire to indulge in any mock heroics that the *Times* stands forthright on the issue raised. There is behind the action of the *Times* a principle and ideas and ideals for honest and square sportsmanship, and it means too much to the future in the way of liberation from a fettered past to fail to protest the action of the tournament managers.

"The boys of America, blacks or whites, Jews or Gentiles, Protestants or Catholics, are the dependency of the country's future. It is in the early stages of their lives that they imbibe the spirit of love of country, love of humanity, fairness in sports, honesty in business and a decent regard and tolerance for the rights and the beliefs of others.   Marble tournaments should not be permitted to spoil these decent virtues.

"The marble tournament, when it draws the color line, is un-American and no American city, no American newspaper and no American standing for the square deal can take pride in what happened and be

DR. CLILAN B. POWELL, SENIOR MEMBER, NEW YORK STATE ATHLETIC COMMISSION

a party to the rotten deal put upon the sportsmanship of the youth of the country by the 'gentlemen' responsible for the disgusting episode at Ocean City, New Jersey.

"The *Times* wants no further truck with any kind of a game in which it is 'fixed' to deprive any boy, no matter what his race, creed or color, of any equal opportunity to win a sporting event in which it requires skill acquired after painstaking effort and real stoutness of heart to compete against the country's best."

FORMER COMMISSIONER MORTON AND PITCHER "BILL" HOLLAND

Norman Gables in 1947 won the Philadelphia *Inquirer* marble tournament. He won eighteen games and lost six. A white lad was runner-up with seventeen wins and seven losses, and Leroy Wiles, a colored lad, had sixteen wins and eight losses. If this contest had been held in Richmond, Va., or Washington, D. C., a white boy would have won and the local dailies would have printed stories that this white lad was the marble "champion" of the city.

Checkers. Checkers is a sport. It is not a game of brawn, but requires brains. Leslie E. Green of Omaha, Nebraska, has been checker champion of his State for four consecutive years and in 1948 was a contender in national competitions. In unofficial match play he has defeated the best checkerists in Iowa, Missouri and Kansas. In 1935, he entered and won the Nebraska State Checker Championship, and won four years consecutively in 1935, 1936, 1937 and 1938. He set two State checker records. Charged with being a professional, he was barred from further competition since 1939. In August, 1946, he entered the Tournament of Champions, a national competition in checkers, held in Newark, N. J., sponsored by the American Checkerist Magazine. He won throughout the preliminaries, but lost in the major events to Willie Ryan of New York City, world champion straight checker player and editor of the *American Checkerist Magazine.*

Commissioners of Athletics. In sport, in most matters of judgment, the arbiter has absolute authority. Referees, umpires, and judges in certain realms are monarchs. Democracy has its limits in sport. Dictatorial powers are necessary at times. There is a trend toward the vesting of powers of control in the hands of a small commission or in a single head. Major league baseball, small leagues and many collegiate conferences trust important disputes and decisions to commissioners. Negro professional baseball submitted to a limited dictatorship for a few years. Commissioners Ferdinand Morton and William C. Hueston labored efficiently for a few seasons.

One of the best examples of commission government is that of the Pennsylvania boxing commission, on which several Negro members have served. Commissioners White, Robert Nelson and Judge Rainey have set high standards for proficiency in athletic control, and at the same time for improvement and safeguards of the rights and privileges of all athletes regardless of race or creed.

CHAPTER XV

Conference Athletics in Negro Colleges

The Inter-Scholastic Athletic Association. Until 1906, there were no organized Negro school or college associations for the promotion or control of athletics. Very few educational institutions sponsored athletics other than baseball and football. Here and there were the rudiments of track and field, and occasionally basketball. With the advent of track and field meetings came the opportunity for the first organization of schools to foster athletics. In 1906, there met in Washington, D. C., several educators who planned an association of colored schools for athletic purposes. It was called the Inter-Scholastic Athletic Association of the Middle Atlantic States, and among its first members were Howard University, the M Street High School and Armstrong Manual Training School of Washington, D. C., the Douglass High School of Baltimore, and the Howard High School of Wilmington, Delaware. The first activity sponsored was a track and field meeting, May 30, 1906, at Howard University. Competition was afforded in open and closed events. Later this organization developed basketball and football leagues and conducted two mammoth indoor track meets in Washington, D. C. Although the main basketball and track competition was between high schools, events were staged for college competition. The Inter-Scholastic Athletic Association fostered athletics in the Middle Atlantic region for many years, being succeeded by various conference groups, the latest being the South Atlantic High School Athletic Association which includes many of the original schools of the I.S.A.A., and others in Maryland, Delaware and Virginia. The charter representatives of the Inter-Scholastic Athletic Association were Garnet C. Wilkinson, William A. Joiner, W. J. Decatur, Robert N. Mattingly, Ralph V. Cook and Edwin B. Henderson.

277

SEVENTH ANNUAL INTERPRETATION MEETING OF THE COLORED INTERCOL-
LEGIATE ATHLETIC ASSOCIATION HELD AT HOWARD UNIVERSITY, SEPTEM-
BER, 1938

At these annual meetings of the coaches, officials, athletic directors and
newspaper correspondents, the rules of football and basketball, and the
problems of officiating are discussed.   At this season many of the men are
fresh from the coaching schools and summer schools of the North and

NUAL C.I.A.A. INTERPRETATION
HOWARD UNIVERSITY, SEPT. 17 36

West and bring the latest points of view for demonstration or discussion. The meetings are rotated from college to college in the jurisdiction of the various conferences. Frequently some outstanding authority in the field of athletics or education appears. The interpretation meetings as well as many annual meetings of the various conferences become valuable in-service training institutes which serve to establish higher ideals in sport. Groups like this one can be duplicated in most of the conference areas of the South.

College Athletic Conferences.   Two college athletic associations began about 1912.   The first was the Colored Inter-Collegiate Athletic Association, the other being the North Carolina Inter-Collegiate Athletic Association.   Some of the membership of the North Carolina Conference merged with the Colored Inter-Collegiate Athletic Association in later years.   The first C.I.A.A. constitution was published in the Inter-Scholastic Athletic Association handbook [1] of 1913.   Since these pioneer organizations, other colleges in regional proximity have banded together for the purpose of developing and controlling athletic growth and competition.   Today there are many scholastic conferences and at least seven college associations in the southern section of the country, where there has been little bi-racial cooperation for the development of athletic sport.

The well known organizations include these seven: Colored Inter-Collegiate Athletic Association, operating chiefly among the states of Pennsylvania, Maryland, Virginia, West Virginia, North Carolina, and the District of Columbia; the Southern Inter-Collegiate Athletic Conference of Colleges in Alabama, Georgia, Florida, South Carolina, Tennessee, Louisiana; the Midwestern Athletic Association of Colleges in Ohio, West Virginia, and Kentucky; the Southwestern Athletic Conference of Colleges in Texas, and Arkansas; the South-Central Athletic Conference of Colleges in Mississippi; the South-Atlantic Athletic Conference of Colleges in North and South Carolina and Georgia; and the Middle Atlantic Athletic Association of Junior Colleges and Normal Schools in West Virginia, Maryland, New Jersey, Delaware, and Pennsylvania.

Evils of Non-Conference Athletics.   Conference athletic growth has paralleled other demonstrations of the Negroes' ability to organize and cooperate for worthy social ends.   In the early days games between colleges were on an individual contractual basis.   There

---

[1] This handbook was edited by the writer and two associates, W. A. Joiner and G. C. Wilkinson, for 1910, 1911, 1912, 1913, and was the only book dealing with general athletics for Negroes at that time.

were often no eligibility requirements for players who represented a college on a team. Sportsmanship was an in-and-out virtue. Officials of ability and worth were rare. Few opportunities were afforded for meetings of competing units for discussion of problems. Naturally, contracts to play were often worthless or easily broken; since the only objective of a contest was victory, players were often not even members of the college; and all of the evils of uncontrolled or unregulated athletics were present. To bring these institutions into organized groups for mutual advantage and to enforce rules and regulations proved the ability of Negroes to sacrifice selfish practices for the greater good and the development of better athletics. To arrive at the high level of accomplishment that most of these athletic conferences have reached, required attributes of character and social aims of the highest order.

Outcomes of Organization. Only through conference groupings has athletics been raised to standards compatible with those of educational institutions. The conference method of promotion and control has resulted in more nearly securing desirable outcomes. Some of the achievements accredited to these organizations, and their far-seeing leadership should be noted in detail. The arrangement of schedules in football, basketball, baseball, track and tennis has been accomplished in annual meetings. These are published in the press and bulletins months in advance. Premium is placed on sportsmanship. Coaches, rules, regulations and practices have worked to make sportsmanly conduct a prominent outcome. In the past, some players have represented institutions through the preparatory department, the college, and the professional school as long as they were enrolled in the institution. Often players were failing in all scholastic work, paid no tuition, and were connected with the institution only to engage in athletics. Although many athletes today in some schools are still "hired" for athletic purposes, the great mass of athletes are eligible as bona fide students of amateur standing. Conference activity has facilitated the growth of many forms of athletics that were new or not popularly supported. Tennis, track, golf, swimming, boxing, wrestling, and cross-country are some

of the competitions that have been sponsored through the endeavor
of the conference organization.

Development of Coaching Staff. The greatest single contribution of the conference college machinery has been the development
of a corps of coaches as physical educators whose worth has often
been considered the most valuable college influence in the education
of youth. Coaches of early teams often were mere teachers of the
skills and strategy of the game. Victory was the only aim of the
game. Any trick or unfair advantage to win was, to many coaches,
justifiable means. Often the coach was a white man because of his
former connection with big-time athletics. With the coming of
conference athletics, the coach found longer tenure assured him at
many colleges. The seasonal coach has been largely supplanted by
the physical educator, a member of the college faculty. The constant association with the coaches at annual meetings, and at the
various tournaments and contests have forced the coach of low
ideals to grow to the stature of the more socially advanced director
of athletics. Today there are no better teachers on many faculties
than the coaches. Many institutions are better known to the rank
and file by their coaches than by their presidents, and in some
instances, the coaches are more influential for good citizenship and
character training than any other educator on the faculty.

Referees and Game Officials. One other result of conference
techniques and organization has been the improvement of officiating
in the various games. The degree with which a group accepts the
dictum of an arbiter in athletic contests is often a good indication of
the social development of that group. In the beginning of school
and college athletics, one of the first considerations for an acceptable
official was that he be a white official. Somehow for years it was
not thought possible for a Negro official to be capable of officiating
in a game where all of the contestants and spectators were colored.
Some of the leading educators and institutions would not risk the
use of a colored umpire or referee. Eventually they were used, and
even then, it was contended their compensation should not be that
of white men.

Since the conference activity, however, there has been a development of a number of competent efficient officials of sterling character. One of the earliest organizations of officials was the Eastern Board of Officials located in Washington, D. C. Among the pioneers in this field were Garnet C. Wilkinson, Benjamin Washington, A. Kiger Savoy, Edwin B. Henderson, Haley G. Douglass, Merton P. Robinson, W. H. J. Beckett, and John F. Wilkinson. Garnet Wilkinson, as a football referee, established a high standard, and exerted more influence on the game than any one individual connected with it. In the vicinity of the C.I.A.A., the several boards of officials have joined to form the Affiliated Boards of Officials. In the locale of the various conferences, competent boards of officials have been organized. Frequently the coaches and officials have combined for mutual growth and development. Each year the names and addresses of the various football officials' groups are published in the Football Guide. The conferences exercise certification powers, arrange for interpretation meetings and adopt measures to promote and facilitate good officiating.

Altogether the conferences have eliminated many of the glaring evils of the old games. Recruiting, subsidizing, proselyting, overnight transferring, professionalism, forfeiture of games, leaving the field, over-long athletic careers in college, no physical examination, weak scholastic requirement, and poor sportsmanship are some of the weaknesses that have been abolished or moderated in college athletics as a result of the conference organization and leadership.

Without good leadership the accomplishments recognized would not have been attained. A brief summary of the organized efforts and account of these conferences and their leaders will indicate the progress and power of many. Much valuable material has not been included for many circles, chiefly because no efficient record keeping has been maintained. Some of the older conferences are now engaged in salvaging misplaced records but were too late for publication here. Hence, some interesting data are not published. In the future, now that the weakness has been glaring, greater evaluation or continuous preservation of athletic happenings will ensue.

THE EASTERN BOARD OF OFFICIALS

Seated—(left to right) Harris, Washington, Martin, Rivers, Henderson, Savoy, Pinderhughes, Burr, Jackson, Douglass, Contee, Westmoreland. Standing—Trigg, Cupid, Drew, Patterson, Williams, Young, Lacy, Greene. The Eastern Board is the oldest organized officials group in Negro conferences. It originated about 1905 with small discussion groups that met prior to football games with G. C. Wilkinson, now First Assistant Superintendent of Schools in Washington. At first it took in the officials of several states. It is now a local board. From this group was initiated the organization of the Affiliated Board of Officials which comprises the Middle Atlantic, the Baltimore, the Piedmont, the West Virginia, the

Eastern and the Virginia boards. The Affiliated Board is recognized as
spokesman for the group of local boards by the Colored Intercollegiate
Athletic Association. Over two-thirds of the present membership of the
Eastern Board, which numbers more than thirty members, are directors
or teachers of physical education, athletics or recreation. Not only is football an interest of the group, but various sections of the Board specialize
in study and officiate in baseball, softball, basketball, boxing, handball,
swimming, track and field, tennis, and other sports. In some conferences
the coaches and officials have combined to form groups for the study of
the rules and problems of officiating. Many football players after graduation turn to these boards for continuation of an active participation in
the several phases of sports.

GIDEON SMITH, HAMPTON

HARRY R. JEFFERSON, HAMPTON

HENRY A. KEAN, TENNESSEE STATE

CHARLES H. WILLIAMS, HAMPTON

Hampton's Football Squad, 1931, C.I.A.A. Champions

The Colored Intercollegiate Athletic Association. The better known of Negro college conferences for athletic purposes is the Colored Intercollegiate Athletic Association. It is now thirty-seven years old. This conference was organized in February, 1912, by representatives of Hampton Institute, Howard University, Lincoln University, Shaw University, and Virginia Union University who met at Hampton in response to a call sent out by Ernest J. Marshall, formerly of Howard University. The representatives of the founders of the C.I.A.A. were Allen Washington and Charles H. Williams of Hampton, George Johnson of Lincoln, W. E. Atkins, Charles R. Frazier and H. P. Hargrave of Shaw, J. W. Barco and J. W. Pierce of Virginia Union.

Charles H. Williams. The most influential personality in the C.I.A.A. during its turbulent growing days was Charles H. Williams, physical director at Hampton Institute. Through his far-seeing leadership, educational and civic grasp of objectives of college athletics over three decades ago, and his persistent effort, he, with each recurring set of officials brought about a powerful organization in the development of Negro youth. Almost as effective an officer over the years was the secretary-treasurer, J. L. Whitehead. Presidents who have headed the C.I.A.A. during the first 37 years have been Ernest J. Marshall, Charles R. Frazier, E. P. Davis, M. P. Robinson, W. A. Rogers, W. G. Alexander, T. L. Puryear, J. W. Barco, J. T. Taylor, Frank Coleman, Charles H. Williams, H. C. Perrin, George G. Singleton, John H. Burr and Paul Moore.

There has been a steady athletic progress since the inception of the C.I.A.A. In the early years, the football schedules were meager. There was no regular scheduled basketball series. Baseball was the strongest sport. In 1912 Lincoln played only three games of football, two of which were with Howard and Hampton; one basketball game, but the baseball team won four and lost two baseball games on a southern trip. In the same year, Union University had a football, baseball, basketball and tennis team. Hampton had these four teams and in addition had a track team and a boat club. Further progress in the C.I.A.A. is shown in the development of

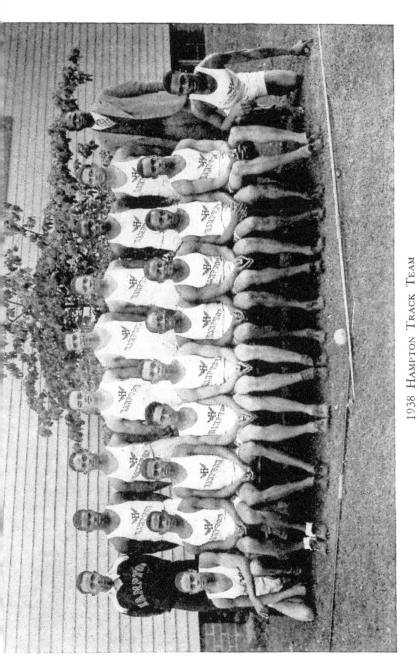

1938 Hampton Track Team

Front row—Furcron, Martin, Hart, Wilson, Watson—Captain, Washington, Griffin, Jeffries, Smith, Brownley.
Back row—Amos—trainer, Minnis, Antoine, Joyner, Sharpe, Stiles, Childs, Byrd, Coach Gideon E. Smith.

other sports.   In recent years boxing and wrestling have become popular.   Most of the schools have developed boxers and many, wrestlers.   Soccer at Hampton, Lincoln and Howard has been a competitive activity in various seasons.   At one or two colleges rudimentary golf has appeared.   Hampton was also a pioneer in physical education for its students.   Now nearly all of the C.I.A.A. schools offer courses in physical education.

First All Star Selections.   In 1912 Hampton won two and lost one basketball game, this to Howard University.   In football Hampton defeated the Lancaster Club, Union, Lincoln, Shaw and lost to Howard.   Howard University in that year was victor in basketball, football and track.   The first all-American Negro team for this conference was selected by the writer in 1911 and appeared in the Washington *Star*.   It consisted of the following players:

Player	School	Position
Oliver	Howard	l. e.
Aiken	Hampton	l. t.
Johns	Shaw	l. g.
Warner	Hampton	c.
Clelland	Howard	r. g.
Goss	Lincoln	r. t.
Slaughter	Howard	r. e.
Pollard	Lincoln	l. h.
Gray	Howard	r. h.
Collins	Lincoln	q. b.
Brown	Shaw	f. b.

Since the beginning days of this conference, full schedules in football and basketball have been the rule.   Track meets are looming larger every season.   The athletes are showing better form and performing creditably in the hurdles, pole vault and other field events.   Some of the athletes are making good in big-time games where the best of the current crop of college athletes perform.   George Williams of Hampton for two years was the javelin winner at the Penn Relays, where he established a record throw.   His best distance had exceeded 215 feet.   The relay teams of Union, Hampton, Lincoln, Howard, Virginia State and Morgan have led many white relay contenders to the tape.   Johnny Borican had startled the

Morgan State "Bears," 1947

SINGLETARY OF ST. AUGUSTINE

athletic world with his sterling running during the 1938 and 1939 seasons. Singletary was a great dash man for several seasons. He held the C.I.A.A. 100 and 220 yards record. Spalding and Ross of Morgan were in the spotlight at several Penn Relay Games.

The C.I.A.A. is an associate member of the National Collegiate Athletic Association and a member of the American Olympic Association. The record of the Colored Intercollegiate Athletic Association is a tribute to the good sense, social enterprise, initiative and resourcefulness of the athletic representatives and school officials of these growing Negro colleges.

The South-Central Athletic Conference. The South-Central Athletic Conference was organized in 1923 at Haven Teachers College, Meridian, Mississippi, in a meeting called by E. M. Walker, an instructor at Haven. The following institutions were represented in this meeting and became charter members of the Conference: Alcorn Agricultural and Mechanical College, Campbell College, Haven Teachers College, Jackson College, Mississippi Industrial College, Mount Beulah College, Okolona Industrial School, Rust College, and Tougaloo College. The Conference lost Haven Teachers College when that institution was discontinued in 1930. During the course of the years Lane College, Natchez College, Prentiss Institute and Utica Institute have held temporary membership in the Conference. For a two-year period, also, the organization experimented with high schools; and Oak Park Vocational School, Wechsler High School, Bolivar County Training School, and Magnolia Street High School enjoyed partial affiliation. Piney Woods School was admitted to membership in 1925. Because Walker exhibited such unusual initiative and foresight in organizing the Conference, he was made its first president, and served from 1923 to 1926.

When the South-Central Athletic Conference was organized the deplorable and unethical practices carried on in the territory it served were legion. The playing of ineligible athletes, especially men who were not bona fide students, the repudiation of financial obligations, fostering and encouraging the intimidation of visiting

COACHES EDWARD P. HURT AND TALMADGE L. HILL OF
MORGAN COLLEGE, BALTIMORE, MARYLAND

Coaches Hurt and Hill have enjoyed an enviable reputation for successful tutoring of Morgan College's wonder-
full football teams which played 54 games, winning 47
and tying 7. Morgan's teams during this period scored
1,179 points as against 110 points scored by all of her
opponents from 1932 until November 24, 1938. The
advent of high powered football at Morgan resulted in
a commodious football stadium and a progressive athletic and physical education department. Morgan's two
coaches have also succeeded in coaching track and basketball teams that have won many C.I.A.A. championships.

teams by spectators—these and many other instances of poor sportsmanship were practiced deliberately by those supervising athletics. However, since its inception, the Conference has grown in strength and usefulness, and its great leavening influence has been felt to such an extent within its service area that any violations of recognized codes are now extremely rare.

As far as conditions in this section of the country would permit, the South-Central Athletic Conference has attempted to pattern itself along the lines of that great pioneer in the field of Negro athletic associations, the Colored Intercollegiate Athletic Association; and those whose responsibility it has been to guide the South-Central Athletic Conference to its present sphere of usefulness are deeply indebted to the officials of the C.I.A.A. who have, from time to time, offered the benefit of their experience and advice. Too much credit cannot be given the men who have served the Conference as presidents down through the years, as it has been largely through their efforts that the organization has attained the heights, and commanded the respect and commendation of all who have upon their hearts and minds the absorbing problem of training properly the Negro youth of this section.

For years baseball was the great and only game of southern colleges. With the coming of football and basketball, baseball interest declined. Later, a plea was made for revival of the game in the southland which yet furnishes the greatest number of major league ball players. Every effort ought to be made to encourage baseball. It will be worth the expense added to the budget. The South-Central Athletic Conference is one of the conferences about the nation that has maintained annual baseball schedules although most conferences had abolished baseball.

The South-Central Athletic Conference formal championship awards began in 1927. The officers of this area began making these very stimulating awards for baseball in 1927, football in 1930, and basketball in 1934.

The Middle Atlantic Athletic Association. The Middle Atlantic Athletic Association was organized in 1931 at Cheyney Teachers

College. The first president was J. C. Williamson of Cheyney. Present schools and colleges in the Conference were the Bordentown Industrial School, Maryland State Normal, Cheyney Teachers College, Coppin Teachers College, Delaware State College for Negroes, Downingtown Industrial School, Princess Anne Academy, and Storer College. Some of the best competition took place in the events sponsored by the schools of the Middle Atlantic Athletic Association. None of these industrial schools and teachers colleges have a large enrolment, hence they cannot furnish full time competition for the larger schools in the area.

The Mid-Western Athletic Association. The Mid-Western Athletic Association was organized in March, 1932, in response to the call of R. B. Atwood, president of Kentucky State College. Its original members were the Kentucky State College, West Virginia State College, Wilberforce University, and Louisville Municipal College. The membership reported for 1939 comprised Wilberforce, Kentucky State, Lincoln University of Missouri, Tennessee State, West Virginia State, and Louisville Municipal College.

Among the many influential men who have labored to promote the progress of this conference are R. E. Clement, J. A. Lane, R. B. Atwood, G. F. Robinson, and the late G. D. Brock. Game officials who have been responsible for the smooth running of annual contests are R. E. Clement, Melville Whedbee, Jesse Lawrence, Moreland Forte, Frank Stanley, James E. Cook, Fay Young, and P. W. L. Jones. Many of the men named have a reputation of athletic prominence far beyond the confines of the jurisdiction of the M.W.A.A.

The South Atlantic Athletic Conference. The South Atlantic Athletic Conference consisted of the following colleges and schools of Georgia, North and South Carolina and Tennessee: Benedict College and Allen University of Columbia, Claflin College of Orangeburg, Harbison College of Irmo, Voorhees Institute of Denmark, Friendship College of Rock Hill, Morris College of Sumter, South Carolina; Paine College and Haines Junior College

KENTUCKY STATE COLLEGE FOOTBALL CHAMPIONS, '37–'38

of Augusta, Georgia; Georgia State College of Savannah; Livingstone College of Salisbury, North Carolina; Swift Memorial Junior College and Morristown College of Tennessee.

The Southern Intercollegiate Athletic Association. Next to the C.I.A.A., probably the most widely known conference is the Southern Intercollegiate Athletic Association. This conference,

FRANKLIN FORBES, MOREHOUSE

formerly known as the Southeastern Conference, grew out of a meeting at Morehouse College, Atlanta, Georgia, on December 30, 1913, for the purpose of considering the regulation of intercollegiate athletics. At this first meeting the institutions were represented by the following: W. B. Metcalf, Fisk University; C. L. Allen, State Normal School; H. T. Heard and I. C. Arnold, Clark University; J. M. P. Metcalf, Talladega College; J. D. Stevenson, Tuskegee Institute; J. D. Avent, Florida Agricultural and Mechanical College; John Hope and S. H. Archer, Morehouse College; D. H. Sims and E. C. Mitchell, Morris Brown University; J. B. Watson, Jackson College; E. T. Ware and G. A. Towns, Atlanta University. W. B. Metcalf of Talladega was chosen temporary president, and G. A. Towns of Atlanta University, temporary secretary. Permanent officers elected were E. C. Silsby, Talladega, president; J. D. Avent, Florida Agricultural and Mechanical College, first vice-president; J. W. Work, Fisk University, second vice-president; and G. A. Towns, Atlanta University, secretary-treasurer.

Fourteen colleges comprise the membership. Alabama was represented by Alabama State Teachers College, Tuskegee Institute and Talladega; Louisiana by Xavier University; Tennessee by LeMoyne, Knoxville, Lane College and Fisk University. South Carolina was represented by South Carolina State and Benedict College. Georgia was represented by Morris Brown, Morehouse College and Clark University. Florida had one institution as a member, the Florida Agricultural and Mechanical College. The work done by the conference is of the highest order. It is difficult to single out for special comment the individuals who have contributed most to the development of the high standard the Southern Conference has set. However, the influence of B. T. Harvey of Morehouse, of Physical Director Cleveland Abbott of Tuskegee and of W. H. Kindle of Fisk has been of inestimable value. This praise in no way detracts from the officers, past and present, and the great body of coaches and officials who have rendered sterling services to the youth of the South.

The Southwestern Athletic Conference. In December, 1920, five Texas colleges met to organize an athletic association of colleges. They were Prairie View, Wiley, Bishop, Sam Houston, and Paul Quinn. The group took the name, the Southern Athletic Conference and adopted a constitution. In January, 1922, Texas College joined. Later the name was changed to the Southwestern Athletic Conference. The story of the causes that emphasized a need for organization parallels that of most conferences. Players were lost through proselyting, some were hired to play, scheduled games might or might not take place, teams walked off the field, and other evils were present. Under conference rules some of such actions take place, but they are few. A vast change has come about. There is more interest in the games, the games are played better, and the crowds are larger. Texas College football team in 1935 was adjudged worthy of national honors among Negro teams. Texas College gridironers defeated the 1937 National Champions, Kentucky State, by a score of 33 to 6; and in 1937, the Florida Agricultural and Mechanical College of the Southern Conference was defeated by the Prairie View College team when this eleven

XAVIER UNIVERSITY TRACK TEAM, 1939

occupied third place in the Southwestern Conference rating for the season.

For the past few years, the membership of this conference has consisted of Wiley, Bishop, Prairie View, Texas, Colored Normal and Industrial University at Langston, Arkansas State College and Southern University.   Paul Quinn and Samuel Houston are not now members.   The oldest representative, from point of service, was D. C. Fowler, who missed but one meeting after Texas College was admitted in 1922.   He was Director of Athletics at Texas College, official historian for the conference, and a past president.   Another large contributor to the effectiveness of the Association is the efficient secretary-treasurer, E. B. Evans of Prairie View College, who has held this position for many years.   Much praise is due the efforts of President M. W. Dogan of Wiley College, for it was he who saw the need for an organization, and for years urged that it be consummated.   Of course, officiating is not a perfect function in the games of the conference, but over the span of thirty years, a great improvement is seen.   As in other sections, the early officials were white, but today a very capable organization of colored coaches and officials exists.

Annual Meetings as Educational Institutes. A feature of conference athletics is the annual gathering.   Some of the older associations have made their greatest strides through the media of annual meetings.   Here practically all of the coaches, athletic faculty advisors, many athletes, the press, officials and often the institutional heads meet in what often might be described as an institute or an in-service training conference.   Here it is that the ideals of athletic endeavor, as well as the learning of new techniques, are caught or taught.   The discussions abound with the materials and methods of education for citizenship and racial uplift through athletics.   After the dust, mud, mire and embroiled spirit of the field of competition have gone, the rival groups lose the emotional excitement or depression of victories and defeats, and a new season is in contemplation.   Then the ideals of sport flavor the meetings. Resolves move to higher planes.

Failure to Publish Records.   Another group of values accruing from conference organization is the increased importance given to record keeping, and to the need for fostering a wider range of bi-racial contacts in sport.   Part of the delay for this book was the inability to secure recorded data from some of the college associations.   Many individual colleges and schools have been too satisfied to pass down by memory the traditions and records of games and contests.   The mere record of lists of victories and defeats, the names of officers and schools help to make the tradition that binds members of a group together.   Only by 1939 did the oldest conferences attempt to gather and publish the unbroken history of games played, won and lost.

Bi-racial Activity.   In the early athletic history after the Civil War, many white and colored teams and individuals met on the field of sport.   Then came a period of cessation of contacts until seldom did Negro and white teams play together.   Especially in baseball is this true.   Later, however, with Negro boys almost in demand in liberal parts of the country, and with the line of bi-racial contests being advanced into a growing tolerant South, Negro conferences are commencing to give and should give increasing attention to fostering and sponsoring bi-racial activity in sport.   In Virginia, in Texas, and elsewhere, there are signs pointing to a recognition on the part of social leaders that sports can lead to strengthened democracy.   Southern white teams are increasingly withdrawing the "gentleman's agreement" when their players go north.   Negro college conferences need to affiliate with national bodies governing sport.   What the C.I.A.A. and some others have done in joining the National Collegiate Athletic Association and the Olympic Committee needs to be followed by more associations.

Carry Over Sports Not Stressed.   There is yet much opportunity for improvement in the ways and means for better athletics. The program of college and school sports is unduly limited.   Football, basketball, and in some places baseball, overbalance the sports curriculum.   The student body and the paying spectator have an

Virginia State 1938 Football Squad That Broke Morgan's Winning Streak

appetite whetted for these team games. Track and field, the oldest form of sport, is too much neglected in most schools. The individual nature of track makes it a valuable educational asset. Its strength as a racially valuable sport is too little regarded. There are many developments in this field but not nearly enough. Student interest needs to be diverted from football and basketball and redirected towards many other forms of athletic games to meet modern life. Especially are cross-country and distance running worthy of being emphasized.

Increased Teaching Personnel Needed. There is need for more personnel in the coaching field. Colleges should modify their requirements in order to get some of the nationally famous athletes

BRUCE OF HOWARD UNIVERSITY WINS 1500 METER RACE IN FIRST OUT-DOOR A.A.U. MEET ADMITTING COLORED ATHLETES AT COLLEGE PARK MARYLAND, JUNE, 1948

on their faculty pay rolls while they are in their athletic prime. They should not be required to have the Master's degree or higher awards for first employment. Many of these young men would be of greatest service while yet in the heyday of their competing ability. Boys need to be shown by competent demonstrators how to jump, vault, and hurdle. Opportunity for higher degrees for certification may come to these great athletes through extension courses, semester leaves, and attendance at summer schools. As assistants to the older coaches, these younger athletes should be able to adjust themselves to the new situations involved in working in some of our institutions for colored youth.

Of course, many Negro schools and colleges have great need for better facilities. The larger institutions have fairly good gymnasia and athletic fields. A few have swimming pools. None has a modern field house where for indoor games a large spectator following is possible. Few tracks are standard. Seating is ample only here and there. However, newer and better gymnasia and athletic fields are in the making.

Courts for handball, squash, lacrosse, and golf courses are absent or rudimentary. Fencing, wrestling and boxing are beginning. Swimming is possible in a few schools. Archery, badminton, ping pong, bowling, and tennis interests are growing. Crew is unknown. These and many more activities are necessary in the young life of boys and girls; even in that of men and women for the larger leisure they will inherit.

Character Education Through Athletics. So rapidly have the materials of sports been increased that many concepts of the ideals and social values of athletics to the individual as a member of a race and as a citizen have been crowded out. On the secondary level athletics have been but miniature phases of the college sport. Educators, products of college athletics as participants or spectators, have neglected to realize the educational implications of schoolboy athletics. The coaches in high schools, as faculty members, seldom need to win to hold a job. Facilities, equipment and supplies are usually a part of the general budget. All of the program for the boys and girls can be truly educational in helping them toward objectives of health and character.   To prostitute these aims for the less important objectives of championships is almost criminal.

On the college level, it is extremely doubtful if Negro colleges must or ought to follow the commercially motivated athletic systems of some of the colleges in the land.   Too many boys in our schools are being taught in the academic curriculum that honesty and good character are the greatest needs of a college education, but through the athletic policy and practices of the institution, they are learning that dishonesty, muckerism, and beating the game also pay.   That school, college or conference that teaches through the physical, as well as the mental, the ideals of law and order, honesty, and good sportsmanship will in the long run mean more to America and to the Negro race.

CHAPTER XVI

Our High School Athletes

Facilities Lacking. Famous college athletes usually, but not always, become known for athletic achievement in high schools. In some cities their careers become public when they are still in junior high school. Jesse Owens and Barney Ewell were interscholastic record breakers before they matriculated at Ohio State and Penn State respectively. Yet noted runners like Dismond and Woodruff created no noticeable flare of greatness when in high school. There have been many phenomenal athletes whose sun rose and set with their high school careers. Some of the boys who set scholastic circles afire failed to be heard of in college areas. This was truer of the past than of our day. Let a boy stir the secondary school world as did a De Correvant, an Owens, a Ewell, a Gregory or a Sidat Singh, and his opportunities for a college life are numerous. He will be as sought for as is the valuable painting of a master. All he has to be sure of is that he has sufficient entrance credits, and in some of the more commercially minded institutions the requirements for entrance have been waived.

Negro athletes who are fortunate enough to display their talent in the high schools of the truly democratic cities of the North, East or West have an advantage over many equally good or better schoolboy athletes who have to attend some of the good and not so good high schools of the South. One of the reasons Negro boys have been so successful lately in the hurdles, the pole vault, the high jumps, and many special track or field events is because from junior high schools on through high schools these youths have had the advantage of well made tracks, pits, good equipment, and expert teaching. Even in football, many high school lads have better coaching than is possible in some of our best colleges. Coach Ted Wright, a Baker University ex-player, who did so much to exalt Xavier football teams, believes high school coaching must be of a higher standard in order to give Negro college coaches better material to work with. He says, "The reason we can't use the Notre Dame system in many of our colleges is because the boys from our own high schools haven't sufficient knowledge of fundamentals and of 'inside' football to fit into an intricate system. Thus we must adopt a less intricate system to conform to the players. The advantage the coach in major Northern universities has is that the scholastic stars come to him well versed in gridiron intricacies and he can pick the men he wants to fit into his system." Wright believes that some progress is being made, but that it will be even more rapid when high school coaches as well as varsity tutors take the summer school coaching courses which are being offered in many of the big Northern colleges.

In a survey made by the writer for a national health fact finding committee in 1934, it was revealed that only a handful of Negro high schools in the South had prescribed physical education courses. It is in these courses that the elements of athletics and game experiences are learned. The more modern health and physical education programs for boys and girls in junior and senior high schools have for content the skills of practically all the team games Americans play, and the modern trend is to teach also skills in from one to two dozen sport and recreational activities that are individual or dual in nature like golf, tennis, handball, and archery.

More Favored High Schools. For a number of years border state schools in Wilmington, Baltimore, and Washington; in Kentucky, West Virginia, Kansas, and Missouri, where dual systems prevail, have enjoyed a slightly advanced physical education curriculum, but in no school system of these mentioned do the facilities for colored boys and girls equal or even approach those for the white children. In the earlier days, the schools of Washington, D. C., had probably the most favorable conditions of all the dual systems for the promotion and development of athletics. Today Baltimore has outstripped Washington in many ways. In Wilmington athletics are picking up. The high schools of West Virginia are making great improvement. In North Carolina, Virginia, Kentucky, Alabama, Kansas, Missouri and one or two other states the separate schools are taking on organized athletics and physical education.

Prior to the time of conference athletics in secondary schools, Baltimore and Washington were engaging in inter-city scholastic competition. Football and baseball were played by teams representing the M Street High School in Washington before 1900. Track was developed about 1901. Basketball was played before 1906. Athletes graduating from the M Street High School were starring in the New England and some western colleges as early as 1904. Some of the athletes whose feats are engraved upon the records of these colleges are Edward Gray, John Pinkett, Hugh Shippley, Joseph Trigg, William Hastie, Eugene Clark, Montague Cobb, Charley Drew, Buster Wood, Cedric Francis, John Rector, Maynard Garner, Maurice Curtis, and a number of other equally good participants.

From Armstrong High School of Washington, D. C., which boasts the first gymnasium erected for colored secondary schools, went to the colleges more than a score of excellent athletes in those early days. Whittington Bruce, Ernest Hardy, Melanchthon Wiseman, Jimmy Burwell, Graham Burwell are quickly recalled. More recently, the Cardozo High School of Washington has sent many good athletes to the colleges.

Among the men who have made a life's profession in the field of health and physical education and who are or have been employed in the colored junior and senior high schools of Washington should be mentioned Charley Pinderhughes, former Howard University athlete; Perry Jacobs, formerly of Lincoln University; Harry Graves, formerly of Michigan State; Duvall Evans of Lincoln University; Jerry Adams of Harvard; Isaac Newton Miller, John E. Young, Raymond Contee, Joseph Drew, Welford Jackson, Vantile Harris, Kermit Trigg, Isaac Cupid, Louis Williams of Howard; and Donald Porter of Indiana. Prominent among the faculty coaches who were identified with earlier athletic teams of Armstrong, Dunbar and Cardozo High Schools were Edgar P. Westmoreland, Walter L. Smith, Garnet C. Wilkinson, J. D. Aiken, Haley G.

Douglass, Cato W. Adams, Benjamin Washington, Maurice Clifford, Samuel Compton, R. N. Mattingly, G. H. Murray, Frank Perkins, Francis Gregory, and Cyrus Shippen.

Forty miles away from the Nation's Capital, athletics in the city of Baltimore started almost contemporaneously with the movement in Washington.   In 1901, Ralph V. Cook organized the first football team of Douglass High School.   The opponents for that season were the Morgan College Preparatory and the M Street High School (Dunbar) of Washington, D. C.   The opponents in baseball were the M Street High School, the Annapolis High School, and the Morgan Preparatory School.   In 1904, Howard M. Smith, a teacher, organized the first track team for Douglass.   In 1906 this team entered the first Inter-Scholastic Track Meet at Howard University on May 30.   In 1906, William H. J. Beckett added basketball to the competitive sports at Douglass.   Football, basketball, baseball and track comprised the list of interscholastic sports until 1921, when L. U. Gibson, a graduate of Springfield College, added swimming and tennis to the lists.   Many of the good athletes that have matriculated in colleges of the North were graduated from Douglass High School; but, as with the Washington schools, in recent years the bulk of better Baltimore athletes have entered colored colleges.   Among the early coaches who molded athletes in Baltimore were Leonard U. Gibson, Ernest H. Brown, W. A. Giles, J. A. B. Callis, Reuben Jones, Daniel Clark, Sylvester W. Ginn, Elmer A. Burgess, Howard Wright, William Wright, Walter Webb and the late Ralph V. Cook.

Howard High School of Wilmington, Delaware, was one of the pioneers in high school athletics.   As early as 1906, Howard High was competing in the track and field events of the Inter-Scholastic Athletic Association in Washington, D. C.   Many excellent athletes have passed through the Delaware institution.   Arthur Wheeler, Neville Reed, George T. Whitten, and Millard Naylor developed sterling teams in that school.

Since these beginning days, the Wiley Bates High School of Annapolis, the Dunbar, Booker T. Washington, and the Vocational School of Baltimore; the Manassas and Parker-Gray High Schools of Virginia have joined these schools to form the South Atlantic High School Athletic Association which has done much to make high school athletics successful in this section of the country.

Over Emphasis of High School Athletics. In many cities athletic life centered around high school teams. Around the turn of this century the high school team was to the population in the larger cities what the much advertised big college or professional team is to the city today. The annual high school games were the rallying focus of sporting interests. Even today the bane of educational athletics is the attempt of many old line educators to make varsity athletics in high school or in junior high school a replica of collegiate varsity sport, with all the evils that have been associated with high-powered commercial athletics. In small towns of one high school it is difficult not to pervert high school athletics and thus make less easy the pursuit of educational aims through athletics.

As an instance of the place high school sport held in the life of the urban population a number of years ago, and of the general trend toward a more comprehensive recreational life for larger cities we cite the following review of the period in St. Louis in 1912, and the athletic life in that city in 1937 when the quarter-century celebration of the St. Louis *Argus* was held.

1912

"In 1912 physical recreation for colored St. Louisans was practically centered in three places, Sumner High School, the two colored playgrounds and the Future City Athletic Club. In that day there was no Y.M.C.A. or Y.W.C.A. with a gym; there was no other race high school in the vicinity with a gymnasium but Sumner; there was no place for amateur boxing; basketball was still in its infancy, especially among colored high schools, and it was merely a class period game at Sumner; only about two games of football were played a season here, the Thanksgiving classic between Sumner and Lincoln University (in that day the high school students were much older and larger than today), and the pre-Thanksgiving classic between Sumner and Lincoln of East St. Louis; Field Day was in vogue but was only an inter-class meet of Sumner trackmen; mixed boxing bouts were against the law; tennis was quite limited, with only one court available to colored citizens, and there was no place for them to play golf.

1937

"Shifting scene from these lean days of bodily exercise over the span of one quarter of a century to '37, one finds a more encouraging situation. The colored St. Louisan is now enjoying his share of activity in many forms of sports and athletics. Now there are eight high schools in the vicinity for high school sports and athletics: There is not only a Y.M.C.A. with a splendid swimming pool and gymnasium, but there are two community houses complete (Adams and Compton) and two others underway; there are colored baseball parks in St. Louis, East St. Louis, Kinloch, Webster Groves and Kirkwood; there are mixed bouts and good colored amateur and professional boxers can fight in the best rings in the city and are very much in demand; there are many tennis courts available; there is a golf course open to all players; colored and white basketball games are not at all unusual." [1]

Growth of High School Conferences.   One has but to read of the state tournaments in basketball and the increasing number of high school conference football games, and the growing number of track meets to realize the improved liberalization of high school education in the South.   Just a few years ago many southern high schools were clinging to the moss laden subjects of outmoded curricula, while neglecting health, recreation, worthy use of leisure, citizenship, vocations, and character, which are the objectives to be sought through living the educational content of the school. Later, education for life made progress as evidenced by what was going on in southern schools.   Not the least of these more modern trends is the use of play and recreation.   In the season 1938–1939 a National High School Tournament was sponsored at the State

---

[1] From the Anniversary edition of the St. Louis *Argus*, 1937.

Normal at Fayetteville, North Carolina. Another basketball tourney of national proportions took place at Tuskegee. At this meeting were expected representatives from the Garnet High of West Virginia, Roosevelt High of Gary, Indiana, and the finalists in state championships from Tennessee, South Carolina, Mississippi,

SOUTH ATLANTIC HIGH SCHOOL ATHLETIC ASSOCIATION IN ANNUAL CONFERENCE (1947)

L. to R. Front Row— R. B. Thompson, Sec.; L. R. Evans, Pres.; L. W. Gibson, C. L. Pinderhughes, M. N. Naylor, E. H. Brown.

Second Row—P. S. Hardesty, J. Saunders, J. Burr, J. Q. Adams, D. Porter, P. Harris, F. Holland

Third Row—W. F. Cain, P. L. Jacobs, J. Marchand, D. Brown, E. Burgess, Mrs. M. Brown, J. Parker, L. White

Back Row—C. R. Stewart, R. Gaddis, C. Lawson, E. L. Brown, D. Henry, W. Payne, W. E. Brown, T. W. McIntyre, S. R. Hall, F. A. Gregory, E. B. Henderson

Florida, Georgia, Alabama, Kentucky, and other states. In Greensboro, North Carolina, on February 25, ten of the tournament winning teams from Virginia and North Carolina met to liquidate the championship of the neighboring states. Over one hundred high schools in North Carolina engaged in preliminary matches and out of the various sectional contests there emerged twenty-seven "A" and "B" teams for the gathering at Fayetteville. From the basketball melee, handled flawlessly, the E. E. Smith High School of North Carolina, coached by H. A. Black, won the championship in the final match over Smithfield, coached by Brutus Wilson, the former noted Morgan College basketeer. One could repeat this story for the high schools in Texas, Arkansas, Louisiana, and other states. These experiences doubled during the past ten years.

Soon athletic heroes in the high schools of the North, East and West became myriad. Shortly after the First World War and the great exodus of peon labor from the South to the industrial centers of the North, Negro athletes gradually began to compete on favorable terms with boys of all races in the junior and senior high schools. But before this, there were many glorious exploits being performed by the schoolboys of New York, Philadelphia, Boston, Cleveland, Chicago and Detroit.

Negro High School Track Stars. In New York City in 1909, Lloyd Gilbert and Eugene Williams were both members of the High School of Commerce. A. H. Hunter was a fast track star at Stuyvesant High School. Peter Green of the Commercial High School of Brooklyn was picked by the critics of this early period as the best high school pitcher in Greater New York and received the special prize offered by the Brooklyn *Eagle* for being the most popular and effective pitcher of that season. Benjamin Wright was a high school shot-putter, discus thrower, broad jumper and quarter-miler with a fine reputation at football on the Townsend Harris High School team. James Ravanelle was the 100 yard champion for Greater New York high schools. He ran the distance in the fast time of 10.2 seconds at the Thirteenth Regiment Armory and was heralded by the celebrated sprinter Bernard J. Wefers as the find of the country. Ravanelle was entered in meets all around the East as an attractive competitor.

Others elsewhere were making themselves known. In Boston, Irving Howe of the English High School created a sensation as a sprinter. In Philadelphia there was a host of sterling schoolboy athletes. Roland Elsey was a consistent point winner at Southern High. W. Warrick was a member of the relay team of that school. A. Young was a good half-miler on the Central High Team, and M. R. Nelson was a steady place winner for Lower Merion High School team. Later on Joe Rainey, now Judge Rainey, was a sensation on the tracks as a member of the Central High team.

Since the beginning of the century colored boys have appeared nearly everywhere on high school teams. On June 4, 1927, the Associated Press reported to the country, "CHICAGO, June 4 (AP).—Four athletes carried Northeast High School of Detroit into the interscholastic track championship of America today. This quartet, matching speed and brawn with 1,000 other boys from 182 high schools in thirty-three States, won the twenty-third national interscholastic meet, held under the auspices of the University of Chicago on Soldiers' Field, by scoring 23 points.

"The squad from Fort Collins, Col., winners of the 1925 and 1926 titles, finished second with 18¾ points. Cass Tech High of Detroit, a three-man team, was third with 12 points. Kokomo, Ind., tied with Masonic Home High of Fort Worth, Texas, for fourth with ten points each.

"Three world's records for interscholastic competition were smashed and another was tied. . . .

"The third prep record to fall was in the 220-yard low hurdles when Eugene Beatty, one of the negro members of the winning Detroit team, leaped the barriers in 0:24 2-10, beating the previous record of 0:24 8-10, hung up by C. Cory of University High, Chicago, in 1913.

"Eddie Tolan, negro sprinter from Cass High, Detroit, tied the world's record for the 100-yard dash when he broke the tape in 0:09 4-5."

Eight meet records in the academy division were bettered.

Team Game Aces. Not only in track but in basketball, did Negro high school athletes star in the cities. The Wendell Phillips High School in Chicago, the Roosevelt High School in Gary, Indiana, were among the schools having enviable basketball history. In New York City when Sidat Singh was a high school student, three of the five all-star basketeers of the city were colored boys. George Gregory earned the captaincy of his squad at DeWitt Clinton, and on his team were three Negro lads. Dolly King was a star on his Brooklyn High Team. In New Jersey during the 1939 season Hoax Brown was nominated All-State in basketball. Julius Irwin, Jr., known throughout the Chicago South Side as the "Jeep," was without a doubt Englewood High School's most valuable football player during the 1938 season. His ability to play all four of the backfield and two line positions helped the Purple and White team time after time. "Jeep" was taught by Joe Lilliard to kick.

Irwin played practically 60 minutes of each game, seldom being substituted despite his injuries. "Jeep" was always called upon when yardage was needed most. By his brilliant defensive, practically alone he kept Du Sable scoreless during the last half of playing. His plunging against Du Sable and broken field running against Harrison Tech kept both teams worried. Irwin's superb blocking helped to make it possible for "Dangerous" Dan Dumas to score against Tilden and Kelly.

"Jeep's" running, kicking, passing, blocking and tackling were missed the following season by the Purple and White gridders. His work in wrestling was also outstanding. He won the interclass championship in the 155-pound class. In the first year of competition against other high schools, he won eight straight bouts, four by falls, and four by time advantage. In the city high school meet held at the University of Chicago fieldhouse in 1938, he won the championship in the 155-pound class. In the A. A. U. meet in 1938 in the open division he got as far as the semi-finals, finally losing after competing against wrestlers from Big Ten colleges, and "old veterans."

Irwin became instructor of the Englewood High mat team. He was the leading contender for the Englewood High School middleweight boxing championship. He played on two championship soft-ball teams; one of them won the Chicago *Defender* tournament in 1936. He played baseball, football, wrestled, ran on the track, and boxed for Aces A. C.

In all large cities and on many small town high school football teams, colored boys played important parts. From California to Boston these teams were spotted with colored faces. Because of the hundreds of cases occurring each season but a few instances can be given of this trend. On Saturday, November 19, 1938 as reported in full in the daily papers, the country's greatest high school football game was played when Washington High, better known as Massilon High, and the Canton, Ohio, McKinley High battled for the Ohio championship, at Massilon. These two schools had been feuding since 1894, and a crowd of 20,000 watched the high school classic. Both high schools numbered many colored boys on their squads. On the Massilon squad were the following: Fred Moody, end; H. Gillom, end; John Russell, guard; R. Clendening, guard; W. Clendening, quarter-back, and Fred Toles, end; on the McKinley team there were three first string colored stars.

At Pittsburgh, Pennsylvania, three colored boys were selected on the All-High Pittsburgh team by the players and coaches of the City Conference. These included Earl Childs, sensational end of Westinghouse; Gabel Patterson, Schenley High's great ball carrier; and "Val" Sterling, end of Langley High.

Another example of the growth of racial participation in the athletic life of the secondary school is the all-star selection of the Akron, Ohio, schools. The Cleveland *Plain Dealer* of Saturday, November 19, 1938, records thus: "Macon Williams, South's Negro halfback and most dependable runner, and Fritz Graf, St. Vincent's punting ace, complete the first string backfield. Eddie Sherfield, South's six-foot-three Negro pass-grabber, and Bohla were honored with first team end positions. Kenny Proctor and Bill Strickland—colored—were given the edge for the guards position."

At Proviso High, of Maywood, Illinois, Leicester Farmer was attracting the attention of college coaches. He completed his first year of scholastic competition brilliantly. Farmer won the 100-yard dash and broad jump in the State meet, and he was a potential champion in both events—having made 10 seconds in the century and leaped over 24 feet in the broad jump.

Joe Batiste. In 1939 one of the later sensational flashes to attract nationwide attention was Joe Batiste. This athlete was a senior at Tucson High School in Arizona. Joe was 18 years old. He skimmed the 120 high hurdles, 3 feet 3 inches in 14 seconds flat. He had a high school world mark of 14.5 seconds for the 42-inch hurdles. Over the low hurdles he had registered 23.8 seconds. He broad jumped over 23 feet, high jumped 6 feet 6⅞ inches, ran the 100 yards in 10 seconds flat, pole vaulted 11 feet, and hurled the 12-pound shot 48 feet.

Entering the A. A. U. meet in Nebraska, Batiste performed better than most of the Negro athletes of whom much was expected. A press account describes his hurdle race in the junior games thus: "One of the classic performances of the entire show was the race between the high school boy, Batiste, who had lowered the record in a trial heat from 14.5 to 14.4 over the high hurdles, and Marsh Farmer, the one-armed athlete from Texas. Farmer won the event but had to go at a terrific pace to head off this new sensation, Batiste, and had to beat the record a second time by making the jumps in 14.2 seconds." Batiste placed second in the junior American Athletic Union high jump. The most remarkable event of the boy's career was his victory over Wolcott in the senior A. A. U. 120 high hurdles on the next day, July 4, 1939. In this event, Wolcott, unbeaten for two years in any kind of competition, stumbled at the ninth hurdle. Before he had recovered his stride, Batiste went on to win in the fast time of 14.1 seconds. Wolcott finished second and Tolmich third.

Cardozo High School. Among the remarkable high school performances of later years was the record of the Cardozo High School of Washington, D. C., and its coach Sylvester "Sally" Hall. Of course, in many southern cities there had been steady and almost phenomenal growth of interest in athletics for school boys on the secondary level.

Many cities could boast of a coach who has been highly successful both in producing excellent athletes and as a trainer of character. We tell the story of Cardozo High School's coach and athletes as an

CARDOZO HIGH SCHOOL (WASH., D. C.) 1947–48 TRACK SQUAD
(Middle Atlantic A.A.U. Class B Champions; Bridgeton, N. J., H. S. Relay Carnival Group III Champions; South Atlantic H. S. Athletic Conference Champions; Wash. D. C. Colored High School Champions)
Bottom Row, L. to R.—S. R. "Sal" Hall, Coach; George Carter, Vernon Cooper, Marcellus Boston, Captain; Dewey Wiseman, William Sturdevant, Henry Johnson
Second Row—Arthur Smith, Manager; James Byrd, Alphonso Jones, Framous Edwards, Alwishes Jones, Frazier Edwards, Clarence Rivers
Third Row—Thomas Kendricks, George Sibert, Willis Holmes, Rudolph McGoines, Herbert Brewer
Fourth Row—Wesley King, Russell Williams, Joseph Walker, Edward Woodland, Lorenzo Moon
Fifth Row—William Drummond, Edward Allen, Samuel Tyner

indication of what can be done even under adverse circumstances if the coach is trained, keeps abreast of the most modern techniques and takes advantages of even meagre facilities.

Cardozo High School is a crowded old building turned over to Negroes located on a triangle between highly travelled arteries in the congested area of Washington, D. C. There is only one gymnasium which is not standard approximately 45 by 60 feet. There is not a foot of play space available out of doors. Coach Hall has trained national high school champions in a hallway part of which is of tiling and part wooden flooring. For football, baseball and outdoor track it is necessary to travel to a field at least a half mile away. He has had approximately from 300 to 400 boys to work with in a school where there are about 1000 girls. Yet with these handicaps his output, as set forth in the Appendix, has excited the admiration of sportsmen everywhere.

Many stories of schoolboy athletes could be written here but space and time limit the recording of the achievement of the hundreds of colored boys who are striving to excel in the many athletic games North and South. Each year brings forth a new crop of strivers, many of whom find in athletics the interest that makes school life endurable or happy. From here many go upward to fame, to further fields of usefulness and enlarged life.

CHAPTER XVII

Athletics in World War II

Sports in Our Armed Forces. As a part of the training program to teach physical skills, to increase strength and endurance and to build and maintain morale, the armed forces launched a stupendous campaign among our soldiers, sailors and marines at home and abroad. Commanders of all echelons of the armed services realized the importance of a well organized athletic program. A policy of mass participation by the greatest number of service personnel possible was established.

To those who were not skillful performers in a sport, competent instructors were assigned to teach and to develop the required techniques and skills. Those who already possessed a high degree of skill were placed on "All-Star" teams and provided the spectator interest which in turn greatly aided in developing pride in one's outfit. Most notable of this type of assignment was the job performed by the World's heavyweight boxing champion known to the world as "Joe Louis," but to the GI as "Sergeant Joe Louis." The extent to which this fine character's influence reached can easily be ascertained by noting the great numbers of Negro boxers who constituted the roster of almost any service boxing squad. This was especially true in the army. Similarly, other outstanding Negro stars in track and field, football, basketball, swimming, and boxing through outstanding performances contributed immeasurably to the maintenance of a high state of morale among the allied troops. Athletic and recreation officers served wherever there were men gathered behind the front lines or at camps in the United States. Most of the officers were trained personnel. In civilian life many had been professional directors of physical education or recreation. Some were handed commissions at the start. Outstanding college athletic coaches were used as civilian consultants and as aides in sports clinics all over the world.

Millions of dollars were spent on athletics. Top athletes like Joe Louis were billed on most of the war fronts to give routine exhibitions for many who had seen them only in the movies. The appearance of these star athletes was a treat to the millions who saw them in action.

GENERAL BENJAMIN O. DAVIS MEETS S/SGT. JOE LOUIS in London where Joe was giving Exhibitions for GIs during War

In practically every camp there was a continuing series of tournaments and games for the GIs moving in and out. Right out of gun shot range great championship meets and games were held. At Fort Huachuca as at most training centers, boys learned sports, and were coached for many teams. Some of them had never seen a basketball, volley ball or soccer ball and in some instances, a football. From the dark South came thousands to whom organized sport was brand new. On the other hand, our champions, coming

Top—Girl WAACS at Ft. Huachuca, 1945

Rosana Lewis, Kansas City; Lorese Jackson, of Wynnewood, Oklahoma;
Mildred Gilmore, Chicago; Fleter Richardson of Livingston, Alabama;
Margaret Barnes of Kalamazoo, Michigan

Bottom—Aleutian Islands Boxing Champions, 1945

L. to R.—Ben Skelton, Navy, Lt. Hwt. Champion; Art. Donovan, Referee;
Willie Brown, Hwt. Champion

and going, were given a chance to use their specialties. For example, Columbia's track captain, Ben Johnson, coached the U. S. Army and Navy personnel stationed at Bremen for the Communication Zone championship held July 26th, 1945 in the United Kingdom. Ben was attached to the so-called "Red Ball Express" unit.

Corporal John "Big Train" Moody of the 5th Army, formerly all-colored American football star from Morris Brown, competed in Italy's Spaghetti Bowl's football game at Florence, Italy on New Year's Day, January, 1945. His Fifth Army team, with Moody as fullback, toppled the 12th Air Force "Bridgebusters" by a score of 20–0 before a crowd of 15,000. On the same team were Sgt. Dwight Reed, former star at Minnesota, and Willie Steele, San Diego's athlete and Olympic broad jump champion.

John Brown, former All-Colored Inter-Collegiate Athletic Association center at North Carolina College, in Durham, and now a member of the Los Angeles Dons, pro team in the All-America Conference, also competed in the Spaghetti Bowl game. He served the Army in Italy.

Nathaniel Boyd, former South Carolina State star, and the only colored boy on the squad, personally led his team, the Chanor Base "Maroon Raiders," to victory over the Seine Section "Clowns" in the Theater Service Forces Football League opener at the Buffalo Stadium in Paris. Boyd scored both touchdowns.

Chief Cook Jim Stallings, holder of 11 decorations for heroic feats during six years of service in a United States submarine, was the only colored player on the Submarine Base football team in 1944.

Negro tracksters were prominent wherever meets were held. The Mediterranean Theater of Operation cinder path team headed by Pfc. Harrison Dillard, Olympic star, engaged in seven track meets in four months, losing only to the E.T.O. outfit 69–54. On this team among others were: Sgt. Don Evans of Woodbury, N. J.; Pvt. Harry Waters of Wildwood, N. J.; Sgt. Pete White, trainer, of New York City; Pfc. Russel Jones of Lawnside, N. J.; Cpl. Roscoe Brown, also of Lawnside; Pfc. Mitchell Williams of Philadelphia; George Foster of Newark; Sgt. Thenlo Knowles of Santa Monica;

Cpl. John Miles of Macon, Georgia; Pvt. Frank Stevens of Birmingham; Sgt. Lloyd Crable of Cleveland; Mel Ellerbee of Tuskegee; Sgt. Lee Farmer of Maywood, Illinois; Pvt. Robert Smith of Ocean Springs, Mississippi; Pvt. Richard Ford of Detroit and Pvt. James Tucker of Houston, Texas.

Colored athletes stole the spotlight in the first Allied track and field games in the Mediterranean Theater in July, 1944. Before 25,000 military and civilian spectators the colored boys won four of the twelve events and the relay title. Pvt. Willie Steele was a double winner. Ford of Detroit and Smith of Ocean Springs, Mississippi were also first place winners.

Negro boxers were greatly in evidence as winners in practically all the notable tournaments. In December, 1944, of the eight champions of the Fifth Army championships, Sgt. Andrew Roy of Wheeling, W. Va., and Cpl. Melvin Pullen of Dayton, Ohio, members of the 92nd Division and Ezzard Charles of the Q. M. Department were winners.

The All-India Inter-Allied boxing show drew over 30,000 spectators. The colored GIs stationed on the Ledo Road stole the show. Of the nine winners, four were American Negroes, one white American, one Britisher, one American Indian and two Anglo-Indians. The colored boys winning were: Cpl. Ernie Copeland, welterweight of the Bronx; Pvt. George Evans of Oakland, California, senior middleweight; Harold Augusta of St. Louis, light heavyweight and Cpl. Morris Stafford of Philadelphia, heavyweight.

Cpl. Jethro Jeffers of Chicago won the heavyweight championship in the 1943 South Pacific championships. He was awarded the Alice Fay medal emblematic of supremacy in the heavyweight ranks.

Colored basketball and baseball teams shared in many areas and colored players were on many of the honor teams. One of the outstanding teams in baseball was the Army Post Battalion team that won the Caledonia championship in the summer of 1944. This team was named the All-Island team. The summer diamond series ran for four months with forty teams engaged and included top college, pro and semi-pro stars.

The above mentioned sports events are but a very few of the noteworthy occasions where the colored boys were the cynosure of thousands. Some day a full story will be told of the part these GI athletes played to win the plaudits and good will of people all over the world.

THE WARRIORS—CHAMPION BASKETBALL TEAM, CAMP PICKETT, VIRGINIA, 1945. (One of the many fine basketball teams in Army camps)

Standing, L. to R.—R. Matthews, F. Crozier, Lt. Basil B. Oliver, Coach; Charles Young, W. Barton

Kneeling, L. to R.—J. Lloyd, J. McMillian, J. Tyler, W. Chandler, J. Campbell, L. Harrod, W. Spence

We name in another chapter some of the casualties among our great pre-war athletes. Some of our former athletes have returned unable, because of injuries, ever to compete again. One of the sad stories, that could be duplicated many times is the fate of

Cpl. Travers A. P. Henry of Bryn Mawr, Pa., known to thousands as "Kid Chocolate." He is now a legless veteran. The former great lightweight champion had a hectic Army career. He was wounded landing in North Africa in November 1942 by a fragment from a French 75 mm. shell. Then in the Tunisian campaign he was hit in the body by machine gun bullets and spent several months in the hospital. As a member of the "Fighting Quarter-masters," Cpl. Henry had several trucks shot from under him. It was during the bleak days of Salerno that an anti-personnel mine went off and shrapnel ripped his legs and body. Now with the same courage and heroism that made him one of the greatest of modern day ring fighters in the lightweight division he is carrying on philosophically after serving his country so valiantly.

Negro GIs as athletes engaging in many camps in America and all over the world not only helped to keep up the morale of their comrades fighting in a world that democracy might survive, but by participation in sports helped to melt away the prejudices that an Army of segregated racial units tends to perpetuate. They too helped to win the war.

On Sunday, Sept. 23, 1945, T/Sgt. Joe Louis was presented with the "Legion of Merit" medal by Major General Clarence H. Kells, Commander General, New York Port of Embarkation at Fort Hamilton, for "exceptional meritorious conduct in the performance of outstanding services" during his tour of Army Camps and hospitals in the United States, England, Africa and Italy. He put on 96 exhibitions before 2,000,000 soldiers in the various theaters of war and entertained at hospitals in the period, August 30, 1943, to October 10, 1944. Boxing shows staged by fighter Joe Louis added many thousand dollars to the Army's relief funds.

CHAPTER XVIII

Gains Despite Some Losses

Many individuals and institutions have been responsible for the widening opportunities for Negroes to extend their participation in athletics. The gentlemanly conduct of Negro athletes themselves has been the most effective lever in opening wide the door. Organization of individuals into associations for the promotion of many sports activities has been a factor in stimulating the growth of sports and in breaking down the barriers. The press and the influence of Negroes on athletic boards have effectively increased participation.

In this chapter we have cited a few of the many promotions and programs of action whereby progress has been made. Some of the great figures who have done their job but passed on have been mentioned. The Second World War, besides decreasing the spirit of racial Fascism, offered opportunity for thousands of our youth to engage in programs of sports fostered by the armed forces. Interracial contests stimulated tolerance. Sadly, but inevitably, many of our most promising athletes died in action or while in service. We wish the listing of all these heroes could be recorded in this volume, along with those we have published, but space is limited.

Amateur Boxing. One of the great opportunities for colored boxers has been the amateur boxing contests sponsored by a newspaper chain and the American Athletic Union. The record of these colored boys in the various contests is impressive. Of the thirty-two finalists, in the final of the Diamond Belt Tournament held in Detroit in January, 1939, twenty were colored. Of the eight weight classes, Negro boxers won seven championships. These finalists competed in the National A.A.U. meet in the city of San Francisco.

In the Chicago Mid-western championships, in amateur glove circles, the colored boxers have won many honors. In 1929, Roosevelt Haines and Edward Wills were finalists; in 1930 Chauncy

CHAMPION ATHLETES OF 1948
Top, L. to R.—Satchel Paige, Joe Louis, Alice Coachman
Bottom—Buddy Young, Harrison Dillard.
(Courtesy—*Color* Magazine, Charleston, W. Va.)

Crain was lightweight champion; in 1932 Edward Ward won the lightweight title; in 1933, Edward Ward was lightweight winner; in 1934, Joe Louis won the light heavyweight and Otis Thomas won the heavyweight titles; in 1935, Dave Clark was welterweight and Lorenzo Pack heavyweight champion; in 1936, Jesse Lends, Jackie Wilson, and Milton Shivers made the team; in 1937, William Joyce, a featherweight; Vernon Patterson and Al Wardlow were welterweight team winners; and in 1938 Dan Merritt won honors.

In New York, the eastern championships found many Negroes invading the tournaments. These boys have done splendidly and have created a most favorable reaction among lovers of the sport. From the tournaments being held in Virginia and other States, there is hope that soon some sterling Negro boxers will be coming up from the South to enter the lists with the amateurs from all about America. Ex-college athletes, recreation leaders, college physical directors, and Negro sports writers have here a challenge to give to less privileged boys in southern states a chance to emulate Joe, John and Henry.

Further Development. Amateur boxing has attracted thousands of lads all about the nation. This sport, and track and field, have presented fewer obstacles to race athletes than other sports. Although boxing is one of the most emotional of sports, white boys have not been loath to mix it up with colored boys. Since so many of the professionals are colored boys, and to aim for championships they must be met, mixed bouts on the amateur level have not been difficult to arrange in most places in the nation.

The Amateur Athletic Union has sponsored boxing since the year 1888 but colored boys did not begin to make wholesale assaults on the records until the early part of the 'thirties. As an indication of the strength of Negro boxers, of the eight different weight classes in the year 1943 six of the championships went to colored boys.

Golden Gloves tournaments also have been open to colored boys above the Mason and Dixon line, and in some instances in the early years colored boys could come through an elimination of local colored contenders and meet all competitors in the North. Many of the champions in pro circles today were the Amateur Athletic Union or Golden Gloves champions of former years. Joe Louis was a 175 pound champion in the Amateur Athletic Union tournament of 1934 and Ray Robinson was a Golden Gloves winner in the lightweight division in 1940.   There has been no indication of the racial identity in the listings, and some Negro boxers may have been overlooked.   It has also been impossible to get a complete record of Golden Gloves winners.   Some of the Amateur Athletic Union national champions over the years have been as follows:

112 pound class, 1944, Cecil Schoonmaker of New York; 1936, Jackie Wilson of Cleveland and 1947, Robert Holliday.

118 pound class, 1936, William Joyce of Gary, Ind.; 1941, Raymond Brown of Chicago; 1942, Bernard Docussen of New Orleans; 1944, Nick Saunders of St. Louis.

126 pound class, 1932, Richard Carter of New York; 1940, Frank Robinson of Pittsburgh; 1943, Jackie Floyd of Philadelphia; 1944, Major Jones of Philadelphia; 1945, Virgil Franklin of Oklahoma.

135 pound class, 1943, Charles Hunter of Cleveland.

147 pound class, 1940, Henry Brimm of Buffalo; 1943, Charles Cooper of Washington, D. C.

160 pound class, 1939, Ezzard Charles of Cincinnati; 1942, Samson Powell of Cleveland; 1943, Samson Powell of Cleveland.

175 pound class, 1934, Joe Louis of Detroit; 1939, James Reeves of Cleveland; 1941, Shelton Bell of Wilberforce; 1942, Robert Foxworth of St. Louis; 1943, Robert Foxworth of St. Louis; 1944, Ray Standifer of Cleveland; 1946, Robert Foxworth of St. Louis.

Unlimited weight class, 1937, James Robinson of Philadelphia; 1940, Wallace Cross of East Orange; 1943, Walter Moore of Chicago; 1945, Charles Lester of Cleveland; 1946, Charles Lester of Cleveland.

Among the Golden Glovers we can identify:

112 pound class, 1941, Diogenes Leon; 1942, R. Neil of Utica; 1945, Francisco Garcia of New York.

118 pound class, 1940, Jimmy Joyce of Gary; 1943, Leroy Jackson; 1945, Adolph Calderon; 1948, Juan Venegas, N. Y.

126 pound class, 1945, Wray Carter of Chicago; 1948, Johnny Thompson of Buffalo.

135 pound class, 1935, Sedgwick Harvey; 1940, Ray Robinson of New York; 1941, Jerry Moore; 1948, John Saxton of Brooklyn.

147 pound class, 1943, Johnny Wilson.

160 pound class, 1942, Charles Conway; 1948, Johnny Carr.

175 pound class, 1940, James Richie of Chicago; 1941, Danny Cox; 1942, Joe Carter; 1948, Ken Johnson.

Heavyweight class, 1939, Buddy Moore; 1945, Luke Baylock of Chicago; 1948, Coley Wallace.

Recreation. Unemployment and larger leisure are among the social problems that have suggested recreation as a partial solution. Educators have felt the need for education that integrates all forces for happier living. Coordination of the many activities and agencies now serving communities to afford more meaning to living under the complexity of modern civilization, is being provided for throughout the country. Unless provision is made for wholesome expression through games, athletics, crafts, drama, music, and other cultural forms, people will resort in larger numbers for longer times to the passive and vicarious entertainment of the night clubs, taverns, and music halls.

An important field of services employing many athletes and students of education and social work is opening up in recreation. The late E. T. Attwell, field director of colored work of the National Recreation Association, did yeoman service in the field. On the same staff, Clarence Cameron White was a director of music. Among the former athletes who served in this field at some time were: Former Professor T. J. Anderson of Howard University, then assistant to Mr. Lewis R. Barrett, recreation director for Washington, D. C.; De Hart Hubbard, recreation leader in Cincinnati, Ohio; George Gregory, director of a large recreation project in New York; and Harry Parker, director of recreation for colored people in Greensboro, North Carolina. In many cities as part time or full time employees, our athletes continue fit while serving as playground workers, life guards, or community recreation directors. Holland at Ithaca and Sidat-Singh in Washington at one time found such use for their athletic talent and prestige. Many women are leaders in the field of recreation. Here in Washington, a pioneer worker was the late Mrs. Gabrielle Pelham.

Other cities in southern states are developing social centers, community houses, playgrounds and recreation systems. These institutions are fostering the discovery and training of future Negro athletes. Many are sponsoring a wide range of programs. During the year 1938 boxing was promoted in many sections of the South where theretofore no agency could be found that would undertake such an activity. This boxing expansion will provide hundreds of aspirants for the general round-up of boxing material to secure American champions for future Olympics.

Many Negro teams are as well uniformed as the best squads in the country. Stadia and fields are approaching in facilities the football fields of the average American college. Since the depression and the increase of appealing Saturday contests, no one locale has a monopoly on large attendance. A Thanksgiving Day game is still the rule among Negro college teams, and the largest crowds are recorded at that time. One reason for the falling off in some of the Saturday crowds in border states is due to the presence of colored players of national stature on white teams, and to the prominence of some of the teams that play in Mid-west and East. The effective colorful broadcasts keep many fans lined up at the radio. One hope for revived attendance lies in the prospect of some well matched games between good white teams and our colored college elevens. For social and athletic growth this is a development much to be desired.

A few decades ago, the press of the country carried little athletic or sports material in its columns. By leaps and bounds space for sports has grown to the extent of pages and entire sections. The staff of city papers, dealing with accounts and comment concerning sports, has grown to large proportions. Many of the sports reporters of former years are our most widely read columnists in other fields today. Heywood Broun and Pegler were once reporters of athletic and sporting events. There are many prominent writers of syndicated sports material. Most of these commentators can be classified as liberals. Some seem to have no race prejudice. Among the fairest and the best were Damon Runyon, John Kieran, Jimmy Powers, Dan Parker, Joe Williams, Albert Ward, Bob Considine, John Lardner, Hugh Bradley, Shirley Povich and Grantland Rice.

The Negro Press. The Negro press, like the Negro educator, author, and publisher, was slow to evaluate the selling qualities of well told athletic stories and gossipy comment. For years, newspapers written for racial consumption printed little more than sorrow and crime stories, social and political news. Then came a young

brand of reporters who went out after the happenings that appealed to the young generation, and to those for whom baseball, football, boxing, track and field, and basketball had active or reminiscent meaning. Among these writers should be listed "Fay" Young and Al Monroe of the *Chicago Defender*, Romeo Dougherty of the New York *News*, Bill Gibson, "Art" Carter, and Sam Lacy of the *Afro;* Randy Dixon and Chester Washington of the *Courier;* P. B. Young, Jr., and E. B. Rea of the *Journal and Guide;* St. Clair Bourne of the New York *Amsterdam News;* Russ Cowan of the *Detroit Tribune;* Alvin Moses of the Associated Negro press, and a former great writer, Rollo Wilson. During recent years sports writing as a profession has grown to great proportions. Many of the sports reporters have been promoted to positions as managers and editors of the prominent weekly journals. *The Pittsburgh Courier* has probably the greatest number of full and part time sports writers. Among the more prominent of these men who later wrote so vividly and entertaining were Eddie Burbidge and J. T. Gibson on the Pacific Coast;   ·
Johnson of *The Kansas City Call;* Fred Leigh, Franklin Bourne and Al Sweeney of *The Afro-American;* Lin Holloway of *The Norfolk Journal and Guide;* Russ Cowan of *The Michigan Chronicle;* A. S. Young of *The Cleveland Call and Post;* George Lisle of the Negro Newspaper Publishers Association; Joe Bostic of *The New York Amsterdam News;* Marion Jackon of *The Atlanta Daily World;* and Wendell Smith, Al Dunmore, Herman Hill, Jack Saunders, Rick Roberts, J. Don Davis, and Rollo Wilson of the *Courier.* Sam Lacy of *The Afro-American* was the first of the writers elected to the Baseball Writers' Association. There are many other good men on local sheets all around the nation.

The publicity afforded institutional athletes has been invaluable. It has helped to account for the realization of the educational content of athletics and physical education. Much of the building of stadia, of increased facilities and personnel has resulted from the sports pages. Coaches, athletic officers, and athletes owe most of their stature in the public eye to the boys who write of their feats. In return the news organization has grown. Many readers turn to the sports section immediately after a cursory examination of the news-headlines. Frequently, beginning with the reading of the sports page, many youthful readers find interest in other parts of the paper and become frequent readers.

Until a few years ago there was no binding of any of the weekly Negro Newspapers in the Library of Congress. Of the myriads of bound volumes from cities and counties about the nation, this Library in Washington had less than a half dozen bound volumes of Negro papers. These included the New York *Age*, the Chicago *Defender* and the 1938 binding of the *Afro-American*. This fact has made extremely difficult the matter of securing authentic accounts of many athletic or sporting events. With the exception of the *Crisis*, *Opportunity*, and a few extant and current magazines, there are no periodicals that recount a continuous story of Negro athletes and their deeds.

Publicity. The Negro press has developed a technique for reporting football news, comment, build-up and contests that adds greatly to the appeal of the game. Players respond to codes of sportsmanship and good citizenship requirements to a larger degree as a result of the educational and civic values of sports pages. The selection of star players and all-star aggregations has helped. The writer was probably one of the first news correspondents who essayed the selection of all-star teams for the early teams prior to 1910. With the tremendous growth in college football since Walter Camp began selecting football all-star elevens, there have been numerous selections of these mythical or dream teams. For the colored conferences, the various leading newspapers have given many pages to pictures and feature write-ups of all-colored-players.

The matter of selecting a championship aggregation for the year varies by virtue of the location and leanings of those who select the team for national honors. Since the coming of the post season "bowl" games, a better estimate of the worth of teams and excellence of players of the various conferences and sections is possible.

The Work of Paul W. L. Jones. The contribution to football by Paul W. L. Jones, superintendent of the Colored Industrial School of Cincinnati, is valuable. For a number of years Jones has arrived at a champion aggregation of all the conferences, and designated teams as national Negro Football Champions. As with the other national selections this decision is naturally subjective, even with the aid and advice of many other selectors. Since 1922 Jones has acclaimed the following teams as national champions:

NATIONAL NEGRO FOOTBALL CHAMPIONS

1922—West Virginia State
1923—Howard
1924—Lincoln, East; Tuskegee, South; Paul Quinn, Southwest
1925—Howard
1926—Howard
1927—Tuskegee, South; Bluefield, Midwest and East; Oklahoma, Southwest
1928—Bluefield, Midwest and East; Wiley, South and Southwest
1929—Tuskegee
1930—Tuskegee
1931—Wilberforce
1932—Wiley, South and Southwest; Morgan, East; Kentucky State and Wilberforce, Midwest
1933—Wilberforce
1934—Kentucky State
1935—Kentucky State, Texas, Morgan
1936—West Virginia State
1937—Kentucky State
1938—Florida Agricultural and Mechanical
1939—Langston University
1940—Morris Brown College
1941—Langston University
1942—Florida Agricultural and Mechanical College
1943—Morgan State College
1944—Johnson C. Smith University
1945—Wiley College
1946—Tennessee State College
1947—Tennessee State College (Midwest, South and Southwest)
　　　　Shaw University
　　　　(East and Southeast)

Morgan College Record. One of the most remarkable records in football, resulting from excellent coaching, was climaxed in 1938 in the overthrow of the Morgan College team of Baltimore. This juggernaut, the Morgan football team, went from 1932 to Thanksgiving Day, 1938, without losing a game. The feat brought Associated Press comment throughout 1937 and 1938. Until Morgan met Virginia State in the last game of the 1938 season, Morgan played 54 games, winning 47 and tying 7. Since 1930, Morgan had won six C.I.A.A. championships in football.

This remarkable record left Morgan tied with California University in the number of games before a defeat. The American Sports Publishing Company lists Washington University team, an unbeaten team, 1907–1917, with 59 games won and 4 tied; Michigan University, 1901–1905, with 56 games won and 1 tied; and California University, 1920–1925, with 50 games won and 4 tied.

Morgan's success lies in the largest measure to the football brains and coaching ability of Edward P. Hurt and Talmadge L. Hill. These two former star football players could take a few good players and much mediocre material and in game by game steadily round out a team that always reached a peak in form for the crucial game period. Only on November 24, 1938, in Petersburg was it seen for once a Morgan team was not able to live up to its reputation. The Virginia State team knew its lessons on that day and refused to allow the tradition and terror of a Morgan team to defeat it.

Here is what the Morgan team did between 1932 and 1938:

Year	Morgan	Opponents	
1932	38	Cheyney	0
	33	A. & T.	0
	24	Union	0
	29	Lincoln	0
	6	Hampton	6
	13	Howard	6
	33	N. C. State	0
	10	Va. State	7
1933	25	Cheyney	0
	37	A. & T.	0
	25	Union	0
	45	Lincoln	0
	60	Bluefield	0
	27	Howard	0
	47	N. C. State	0

Year	Morgan	Opponents	
1933	13	Hampton	6
	40	Va. State	0
1934	7	A. & T.	0
	34	Cheyney	0
	0	Union	0
	19	Lincoln	0
	0	Bluefield	0
	0	Howard	0
	28	Hampton	0
	8	Va. State	0
1935	32	Cheyney	0
	19	A. & T.	7
	13	Union	0
	26	Lincoln	0
	12	Bluefield	9
	38	Howard	0
	13	Hampton	0
	32	Va. State	7
1936	47	Miner	0
	6	Union	0
	13	Lincoln	0
	6	Bluefield	6
	40	Howard	0
	20	A. & T.	3
	7	Hampton	6
	6	Va. State	6
1937	39	A. & T.	0
	31	Bluefield	0
	19	Lincoln	6
	20	Miner	0
	12	Union	7
	26	Hampton	0
	21	Va. State	6
1938	22	Howard	0
	0	Union	0
	21	Lincoln	0
	6	Bluefield	0
	12	A. & T.	0
	19	Hampton	7
	0	Va. State	16
Totals..Morgan..	1,179	Opponents	110

More Recent Achievement. Since 1939 colored Americans have made great progress in many promotional activities related to athletics and sports in general. Behind the racial wall and against the barriers through participation in sports and in the advancement thereof they have increased respect for the race of colored people everywhere, and advanced the status of citizenship in America. We have listed some of the highlights in this field during these years.

Washington, D. C.–A. A. U. Fight. In Washington, D. C. the Branch of the National Association for the Advancement of Colored People made much progress against bigotry in sport. The local Amateur Athletic Union in contrast with the national policy prohibited colored athletes from participating in open Amateur Athletic Union events. The device used was to interpret the sanctioning power granted local autonomous units to safeguard amateurism so as to bar colored boys from competing in open amateur tournaments. Whenever the would-be sponsor of an athletic event applied for a sanction to hold such games, a condition was written on the back of the permit as follows: "The Registration Committee of the District of Columbia Association of the Amateur Athletic Union does not sanction mixed racial competition or exhibitions under its jurisdiction. Accordingly any infraction of this regulation will result in the suspension of the athletes competing and the refusal of further sanction to the sponsoring organization."

This rule prevented many Washington athletes from qualifying for sectional or national contests which required local elimination trials. Only one set of champions was recognized from a jurisdiction. The rule was condemned by many of the leaders in amateur athletics throughout the nation but the national body did not or could not restrain the local branch of the Amateur Athletic Union.

In 1945 the District of Columbia Branch of the National Association for the Advancement of Colored People instituted suit on behalf of the amateur boxers of the 12th Street Branch Young Men's Christian Association to secure abrogation of this practice. In the court of first instance the trial did not come off until after the Amateur Athletic Union championships in Boston were held, and the court ruled the case moot.   However on appeal the Federal Court of Appeals in the District of Columbia unanimously remanded the case back to the lower court for trial on its merits.   Before the case came on the docket for trial, the Washington Amateur Athletic Union by a vote of 12–4 voted to sanction mixed boxing and track. This partial victory was in large part due to the influence of the publishers of local newspapers.   Mr. Eugene Meyer, owner of *The Washington Post,* withdrew sponsorship of the local tournament so long as the racial ban was imposed.   Mrs. Eleanor Patterson of *The Times-Herald* withdrew from sponsorship of the Golden Gloves tournament for similar reason.   *The Washington Star,* anxious to make a success of a big amateur indoor meet in the new National Guard Armory, brought pressure on the local Amateur Athletic Union.   But the greatest credit for change of attitude belongs to the many citizens of Washington and many organizations for protesting, picketing, and boycotting Amateur Athletic Union boxing events.

The Color Bar in British Boxing Falls.   For many years the British Boxing Board of Control had a rule denying to colored Empire fighters the right to participate in championship matches. Charles Dommall, secretary of the BBB C, felt "a departure from the rule was neither desirable nor necessary."   He was quoted as saying, "It is only right that a small country such as ours should have championships restricted to boxers of white parents,—otherwise we might be faced with a situation where all our British titles are held by colored empire boxers."   On the other hand, *The London Daily Express* in an editorial, "Why the Color Bar," said, "No more ridiculous reason could be given for the perpetuation of a deplorable condition than the alleged explanation given by the secretary, for the continuation of the color bar to British Empire champions."

The color bar was finally lifted by vote of the British Boxing Board of Control.   On June 4, 1946, a London paper carried the headlines, "Black Night for British Boxing."   The night before five colored boxers knocked out their opponents.   The three Turpin brothers, Kid Tanner, and Cliff Anderson all hailed from British Guiana, famous for colored boxers.

Fair Play in Bowling. The National Committee for Fair Play in Bowling met in June 1948 in the Hotel Piccadilly in New York City and mapped out extensive plans to acquaint the American public with the policy of discrimination and segregation practiced by the American Bowling Congress. This committee headed by Mayor Humphrey of Milwaukee, and co-chaired by Miss Betty Hicks, formerly a U. S. women's tennis champion, included Philip Murray, former Senator James Mead, Walter Reuther, and many other prominent Americans. Dr. J. B. Nash, Director of Physical Education, New York University, in a stirring speech, called the National Committee for Fair Play in Bowling the "torch bearer of a great ideal." The committee plans to solicit the cooperation and support of several national organizations.

In December, 1947, the Missouri Valley Conference voted to end all racial discrimination in athletics in its member schools, to become effective in September 1950. The deadline was set in order to give members time to adjust their local conditions. The Conference includes: St. Louis University, Drake, Creighton, Wichita, Oklahoma A. and M. College, and Tulsa.

Through the efforts of *The Michigan Chronicle* and the liberal elements in Michigan the coaching department of Michigan State College was forced to eliminate that phase of racial discrimination which prevented a colored player from engaging with his team in play with a southern college team. On October 25, 1947, Half-back Horace Smith played against Kentucky at East Lansing. This was the first time in the history of Michigan State College that one of its colored players had been allowed to compete against a southern school.

Athletic Board Members. More and more representative colored citizens are being placed on state and local athletic boards. The interest in boxing with corresponding increase in gate returns has been due in large part to the popular acceptance of mixed boxing. In the state of New York the senior member of the New

York State Athletic Commission is Dr. Clilan B. Powell. Dr. Powell has been a power in athletic circles in New York and has quietly but effectively safeguarded the interests of all citizens. In Michigan, Russ J. Cowan, managing editor of *The Michigan Chronicle* was appointed to the State Boxing Commission in January, 1948. Cowan was formerly a member from 1944 to 1946. Because of popular support he was re-appointed and will serve until June, 1951. J. Harry Battis, prominent Republican in Philadelphia, was named secretary to the State Athletic Commission in 1945. Norman O. Houston was appointed by Governor Earl Warren in 1944 to membership on the five-man California Boxing Commission. David Howard of Philadelphia, a long time judge of amateur boxing, was appointed a Judge of boxing events in Philadelphia. Prior to this appointment J. Arthur Brown had been named to a position on the State Athletic Commission, formerly held by the late Robert J. Nelson, second Negro to serve as chairman of the State Athletic Commission. Ralph Metcalfe is now serving on the Illinois State Athletic Commission.

Prominent Men in Athletic Organization. During recent years many promising individuals grew important as national figures in the realm of sporting events. With the coming of radio and sports commentators on the air, quite a number of colored men have been so engaged. One of the pioneers is Jocko Maxwell of Newark, who has completed sixteen years as sports commentator. He started with the now defunct station WNJ and joined WWRI in New York City in 1939, and was named station sports director in 1942. During the war he handled sports and recreation for the 375th Engineers in England, Belgium and Germany. He was heard three times weekly with his "Sportscope," is the author of several sports books and writes sport stories for several magazines.

Walter Gordon, first Negro in the history of football at the University of California to win its "C" left his coaching position at the school in 1948 because of the increased duties of his law practice and his membership on the California Board of Prison Terms and Paroles. Gordon was the oldest coach in the school's history from point of continuous service. In 1918 he was awarded the Percy Hall Trophy as most valuable player, and became coach and scout for 24 years. His son became the third Negro in the University of California to win the big "C" which happened in 1941. A fourth colored player won his letter in 1942.

Coach Major Cleveland Abbott, director of athletics and head football coach at Tuskegee Institute has served there over 26 years. He joined the faculty in 1923. His success has been phenomenal. Beginning with meagre facilities, Major Abbott now has a modern gymnasium, swimming pool, athletic field and teaching staff that compares favorably with the better colored colleges in the nation. His most notable success has been the development of track athletics for girls. With the assistance of Mrs. Amelia Roberts, he has yearly produced a girls' track team that has been the envy of all. One of his former pupils was the only American woman to win an Olympic track event. The Major is the only colored member of the Olympic Committee of the Amateur Athletic Union. Following the death of D. Ivison Hoage, former president of the American Tennis Association, Major Abbott was elected president and he is leading the association to greater heights.

J. L. Whitehead retired in 1946 from the executive-secretary position in the Colored Inter-Collegiate Athletic Association after serving 22 consecutive years. Mr. Whitehead ably succeeded Charles H. Williams of Hampton Institute, one of the founders of the Colored Inter-Collegiate Athletic Association. He resigned because of increased duties as business manager of the St. Paul Polytechnic Institute at Lawrenceville, Va.

Negro baseball has entered a crucial period as the better players are getting offers from the older leagues. Until this era Negro baseball had made much progress but needed a "czar." The leaders of organized Negro baseball elected a former athlete of note, reputable citizen and prominent clergyman, Rev. John H. Johnson to the post of President of the Negro National League with large powers. He is doing a good job.

For the first time, a colored coach was mentioned as "Coach of the Year" in the national selections of 1945. Thirty-eight coaches around the nation were named. Coach Edward P. Hurt of Morgan was one named. Coach Hurt with his able assistant, Talmadge L. Hill, from 1930 to 1945 brought Morgan College into the championship column 11 times in football, 3 in basketball, and 8 times in track. Morgan's long winning streak of 54 consecutive victories in football over six years (1932–1938) created a new national pigskin record.

Michael (Mike) S. Jacobs, President of the Twentieth Century Sporting Club, a czar of the nation's boxing industry, made millions for himself, his club and colored boxers, and made possible the addition of hundreds of thousands to the Army and Navy Relief. Because he helped maintain a truly American ideal in management and promotion of boxing with the aid of the sterling character of Joe Louis, Mike Jacobs deserves plaudits from the sporting fraternity.

Chester Ray Stackhouse, white, because of strong beliefs in tolerance and true Americanism attempted for five years to secure a berth as coach at a Negro college. In 1947, Mr. Stackhouse gave up a good paying job as assistant coach at the University of Michigan to become assistant coach of football and coach of basketball at Lincoln University in Pennsylvania. Stackhouse was all-conference center of the Michigan Collegiate Conference in 1927–28. In accepting the position at Lincoln, he gave up active participation in his lucrative business in the Stackhouse Real Estate and Construction business at Ann Arbor. His philosophy for this departure is summed up in his statement of a "strong belief I have that one's social contribution to society is more important than one's material success in life." Stackhouse resigned as Lincoln's coach in 1948, and Irving "Moon" Mondschein, one of the nations top white athletes, was appointed to this position in 1949. Perhaps we are nearing the era when race will not be a factor in the careers of athletic coaches.

Dave Gunn, one of the immortals in the football life of Hampton Institute, is the physical director at the exclusive school for boys in Lenox, Massachusetts. Although the student body and faculty, with the exception of one of Dave's sons, are composed of white citizens, this colored man was made coach.

Dr. Reginald Weir of New York City in 1948 became the first colored tennis player to play in the United States Lawn Tennis Association's national indoor tournament. He defeated his first opponent, Tommy Lewyn, but lost to Bill Talbert, No. 1 seeded player who was the fourth best amateur in the country and member

DAVID GUNN, FORMER STAR ATHLETE AT HAMPTON INSTITUTE. SINCE 1939, DIRECTOR OF PHYSICAL EDUCATION AND COACH AT THE LENOX SCHOOL FOR BOYS, LENOX, MASS.
Sitting, L. to R.—C. Bowen; R. Kemble; S. Chalufour, Capt.; S. Lazarus; R. Watson.
Standing, L. to R.—S. Mitchell, Mgr.; S. Choate; E. Serafine; Mr. Gunn; J. Buckner; B. Gibson; A. Clegg.

of the 1946 Davis Cup team. Dr. Weir was one of the best colored tennis players back in 1931, and was captain of the City College Tennis team of New York. Weir qualified for the nationals by reaching the semi-finals in the tournament of the Eastern Indoor Association.

Joe Yancey, coach of the New York Pioneer Club was named head coach of the Jamaica Olympic Team by the British Government. It was he who directed the fortunes of the island's track team which included Arthur West, Herbert McKenley and others. Yancey has been one of the most successful managers of club athletics. Because of his success he was awarded the New York Track Writers' annual award in 1947 as the man who had done most to further track activities in the Metropolitan area in that year.

John R. Tunis of Rowayton, Connecticut, has been a crusader for American sportsmanship which knows no color line. As a writer he has contributed many sports books in which he has dramatized the fight for tolerance. One of his books for boys, "All-American," has forced its way into the supplementary English libraries of many school systems.

Necrology.   Over the years it was inevitable that many men prominent in the annals of sport should pass off the scene of the living. The normal peace time obituaries have been accentuated by the death of so many young men who gave up their lives for democracy in the Second World War.   We mention but a few of the men who have gone but whose efforts in the field of sports will not be soon forgotten.

Ira Lewis, one of the pioneers in sport-reporting in the Negro press, died in August 1948.   From the position of sports editor of the *Pittsburgh Courier* he rose to the presidency of the Courier company. During his career in charge of the sports section he fought many battles to win democracy through sports for our colored citizenry, and lived to see some of his objectives gloriously attained.

Romeo Dougherty died in December 1944.   He also rose from the sports pages to the role of editorship of *The Amsterdam News* and other papers.   It was Dougherty with Ira Lewis and Fay Young who sought to bring peace between the old Eastern League in Negro baseball and Rube Foster's Negro National League.   Dougherty was in the thick of the fight to prevent Dempsey from giving

Harry Wills the run-around. He was the official historian for such forgotten teams as the Incorporators, the Alpha Physical Culture Club, the Spartan Field Club, the Loendi of Pittsburgh, the Forty Club of Chicago, the Vandals of Atlantic City, the Smart Set of Brooklyn, the St. Cyprian Club of New York, the 12th Street Young Men's Christian Association of Washington and many others.

"Cum" Posey died in March 1946. Cumberland Posey was a great competitor. He was a native of Homestead, Pennsylvania, and after a luminous career in his home town high school engaged in sports at Duquesne and later at Penn State. His greatest fame as an athlete was in basketball and baseball. He became a great promoter and organizer. He, with Charley Walker and later with Rufus Jackson, built the Homestead Grays up to the point where this team became one of the foremost baseball teams in the nation.

James "Candy Jim" Taylor at 64, one of the famous figures in Negro baseball, died in 1948. Taylor, a long time manager of the Chicago American Giants, had assumed the pilot's role with the Baltimore Elite Giants for 1948. He had been identified with the game for nearly a half-century.

Dr. D. Ivison Hoage, president and one of the founders of the American Tennis Association, died on January 23, 1945. Dr. Hoage headed the Ideal Tennis Club of New York until it joined with the Walker Memorial Club of Washington, D. C. and others to form the American Tennis Association. Until 1930, he served as chief referee at the annual tournaments of the American Tennis Association.

Southwestern athletic circles in December 1945 lost one of their noted coaches and trainers when Harry J. Long, brother of Fred T. Long, toppled from the bench and died on the eve of attaining a long hope, that of winning a national title among colored college teams. On Saturday, December 15, 1945 just as the Wiley College team was winning the Orange Blossom classic on Phillip's field in Tampa, for the 10th win of the season against no losses or ties, Coach Long suffered the attack from which the end came. He was a professor of biology at Wiley, and completed work in science for the doctorate at the University of Michigan.

Two notable characters in the athletic world lost their lives in the service of their country before reaching the combat zones.   The colorful Lt. Sidat Singh, whose exploits have been vividly recounted in the pages of our earlier edition, lost his life while in routine training over Lake Michigan in 1943.   Major Harold D. Martin, on a routine flight from Tuskegee to Washington, D. C., crashed with a companion near Reedsville, N. C. on Friday, March 23, 1944. Major Martin was formerly a coach at Virginia Union, Shaw University, Virginia State and lately at Miner Teachers College in Washington, D. C.   He was the first Negro to be graduated from Norwich University in Connecticut and was captain of the football team at the military academy.   He was the first commissioner of athletics in the Colored Inter-Collegiate Athletic Association.

In combat zones, one of the first casualties of the war was the death in action of Alva Johnson, director of athletics and physical education at Storer College at Harpers Ferry, West Virginia. Johnson was the first death in action from among the 9,000 members of the American Association for Health, Physical Education and Recreation.   A box space on the cover of the Journal honored him.

Lieutenant Sam Bruce, one of the noted athletes at the Agricultural and Technical College in Greensboro, North Carolina, met his death in action while fighting as a member of the 99th Fighter Squadron in western Italy in early 1944.   Bruce became famous in collegiate athletics along with Homer Harris.   Both came from the West.   Bruce's home was in Seattle, Washington.

Many budding athletic careers were cut short by the war.   Among them were: T.-Sgt. James H. Stewart, former Evanstown Township high school star who was killed in Calcutta.   Sergeant Robert A. Johnson, one of the stellar athletes in football and basketball at St. Augustine College from 1931 to 1935, was killed in action in Belgium in 1945.   Calvin Searles, one of the outstanding golfers who played in the 1943 Tam O'Shanter open was killed in action in the European theater.

CHAPTER XIX

The Meaning of Athletics

Play in Antiquity. All through recorded history athletics have meant much to mankind. With savage or civilized peoples, games and sports have been a way to culture or to the development or maintenance of physical vigor. Peoples and governments have used athletics for festival occasion or to train men for war.

Primitive man learned early that fleetness of foot, or strength of limb and body were means by which to escape from danger, or to live in health. As civilized man found substitutes for labor in slaves—human, chemical or physical—he found in games a method to insure growth and normal physiological functioning of the body. More recently organized play serves to combat the individual and social deteriorating forces of urban life.

Play is almost instinctive. Many animals participate in racing, climbing, and forms of playful combat. Among men, foot racing, boxing, wrestling, throwing, swimming, and climbing have been common to all races. Soccer-like games were played by Asiatic people three thousand years ago. The Indians developed a ball and racket game. Ancient Romans indulged in throw and catch play. Fencing or combative sword, spear or stick exercises have been the sport of many peoples in many lands. Of all athletic forms, however, dancing has been most universal.

Among the ancient nations, neither India nor China produced records of any outstanding organized athletic sports. Repression, isolation, religion and their peculiar spiritual philosophy were opposed to the development of a system of athletics. On the other hand, the lands of Egypt, Assyria, Babylon, and Palestine give abundant evidence of the spirit of progress and national growth, and here we find records to show that wrestling, swimming, hunting, acrobatics, ball-playing and dancing were significant parts of their

349

national culture. Persia, under Cyrus the Great, developed athletics as a means of preparation for war.

Greek Games. It remained for Greece, however, to set before the world the most striking example of athletic sport and its influence on the culture of a whole world. Throughout the Homeric age, roughly between 1000 B.C. and 500 B.C., athletic sports were prominent. Chariot and foot races, boxing, and wrestling were the important events. These events usually marked the entertainment features of great funerals or sacrificial ceremonies before the gods. The exploits of Odysseus in his wandering from Troy to Ithaca are full of legendary accounts of athletic contests.

The most noted of organized games recorded in history are the Greek contests known as the Olympian games. From these games the Greeks dated their time and history, and established 776 B.C. as the date of the earliest Pan-Hellenic festival. Each series of these games was held once every four years. During the golden age, the glory of Greece was reflected in the festival occasions marked by athletic competition. But, as in many instances in the civilization of our day, the games eventually took on commercial aspects. Athletes trained for years and did little else in order to prepare for the contests on the plains of Olympus. Men who formerly practiced during leisure time found it impossible to compete with the athletes who developed their bodies rigorously and spent all of their time perfecting skills. The amateur sportsmen dropped out, and the professional athletes engaged in the gladiatorial spectacles for the glory that later brought dividends in lands or money, and frequently state pensions.

Beginning with the fifth century B.C., the Greeks gave a demonstration of national participation in athletics that has never been equalled in the world's history. Sparta became famed for the vigor of its training of the body in order to make its citizens strong and healthy. Boys and girls were exercised publicly in running, jumping, wrestling, throwing weights, and hurling the javelin. The young boys were inured to physical hardships by the most severe training. Their food was coarse and scanty. Their beds were hard; and one garment was all they were allowed in all seasons. Thieving for food was not immoral. Getting caught was a crime. The story of the boy who concealed a fox and, to avoid detection, allowed it to gnaw into his entrails until he fell dead, is typical of the legends that indicate the rigorous nature of Spartan training of youth. That Sparta had the best army in the world attests their philosophy of youthful education and physical training.

The other Grecian state, Athens, planned the education of its youth to fit the boy for social, political, military, and religious life. Emphasis was placed upon discipline of the mind, on morals, as well as that of the body. Three main studies of the curriculum were gymnastics, grammar, music. Physical education was given the largest and most prominent part in the training of youth. The men of Athens had recourse to physical training in the state supported gymnasia known as the Academy, the Lyceum, and the Cynasargus.

It is worth recounting at this point some of the trends and phases of the decay of Grecian athletics, because there may be social planners or educators with vision and courage to avoid for our civilization, the pre-disposing causes that marked the decay of athletics and older civilizations. The ancient Greeks with this great culture were not wise enough to foresee that they were on the brink of destruction. Shall we be able to mark our steps toward progress or retrogression?

The Decline of Greek and Roman Games. The decline of the Grecian games accompanied the deterioration of the Greek nation. The advent of professionalism in which athletes carried over-eating, over-training, and over-development to such extremes that they developed ponderous brutish bodies was the beginning of the end. Contests of the earlier days set forth the physical types we find preserved in the sculpture of the Greeks of the cultural age, and this art is the marvel of all civilizations.

The decay of athletics was also marked, strangely enough, by a great increase in the construction and improvement of gymnasia and stadia which developed rapidly all through the Greek and Roman periods of seemingly sustained national growth. But this provision for many athletic facilities was not a sign of improvement of athletics. The people became more and more interested in games as spectacles. The stadia were erected to insure comfort to the hordes of spectators who attended to watch the hired or professional athletes entertain them. Here and there were real attempts to rebuild athletics, to strengthen the youth, and to keep the bodies of men fit for health and citizenship. But, in the main, their efforts failed to salvage the wreck of the spirit of the earlier Greek games. Alexander the Great, although powerful and athletic in stature himself, would not enter the games or favor them.

On being asked if he intended to enter the foot-race at Olympia, he replied, "Yes, if I had kings for my antagonists." He could gain no honor by entering the lists with professionals. Realizing as many modern rulers do, the social and political necessity for giving the people entertainment and spectacles, although disdaining athletic contests, he nevertheless promoted great carnivals and exhibitions. He instituted "brilliant Olympic games at Aegae and at Dium, at which he offered prizes for tragic poets, musicians, and rhapsodists, and entertained the people not with athletic competitions but with hunting of wild beasts, and with fencing or fighting with the staff."

The palestra and gymnasia lost their significance as places where gymnastics and athletics shared with music, art, learning and philosophy. They became the meeting places of intellectuals. Plato delivered his discourses in the Academy; Aristotle took his walks in the Lyceum. Rich men financed the building of new gymnasia. They became the modern rich man's clubs. Intellectuals and wealthy men engaged in but little strenuous physical exercise. Slaves did the work. Most of the athletes at the national games were not free citizens, but professionals from conquered lands.

As early as 228 B.C. the Romans, who posed as champions and kinsmen of the Greeks, took an active part in the promotion of Greek games. The weakening Greeks finally fell prey to their more virile Roman neighbors, who in turn fell heir to some of the traditions and spirit of the Greek games. The Romans conquered the Greeks in war, but the Greeks conquered the Romans in mind.

BEN JOHNSON WINNING "100" AT PENN RELAYS, 1938

Ideal of Greek Games Foreign to Romans. The Roman people, like all vigorous nations, were fond of physical exercises. They were not keen on competitions for fun's sake or for recreation. All their games had as objectives the hardening and training of the youth for war, just as today many militarists would do with the boys of the R.O.T.C. and institutional camp activities. To Roman and Spartan, athletics were only a means to the end of military efficiency, quite unlike the early Athenian ideal of a sound harmoniously developed mind and body for a citizenship of peace or war. The Roman, brutalized by constant fighting, wanted more exciting entertainment than athletic competitions of running, jumping, throwing, and playing with the ball. He preferred the gladiatorial combat, and brought into his games the exciting, often bloody exhibitions, copied mainly from some of the festivals of conquered nations. In the century before Christ, the Romans showed such a little consideration for the effete nature of the declining Greek nation that, on one occasion, they transferred all of the Greek contests from Olympia to Rome, leaving only the boys' footrace to be decided at Olympia.

After a while the Romans, no longer occupied incessantly with war, fell under the influence of inordinate desire for amusement and entertainment. Festival after festival was added to their calendar, and ambitious politicians and rulers provided lavishly for spectacles to win the favor of the Roman populace. The Grecian and Roman games drew to a close. The last Olympic records of Africanus occurred about 217 A.D. The Romans finally began to engage in desperate struggles with the hordes of invading tribes. Although for a century or more games were held intermittently, eventually in 393 A.D. the Christian emperor Theodosius, in order to wipe out all traces of paganism, adopted Christianity as the state religion, and abolished the Grecian games which were still festivals in honor of Zeus and the other gods.

Parallelism in Modern and Ancient Sport Trends. Is there not much parallelism in the social and political events of our civilization and those of the days of ancient Greece and Rome? How can we keep existent the amateur spirit in games for the maintenance of healthy citizens, and for the training of youth in acceptable personal and civic character? Will our stadia and gymnasia become merely assembly places for the exhibition of professional athletes? Will this tendency to more spectatorship lessen the interest of youth and adults in self-participation in health giving sport? Will the morals of our people break down under the urge of more and bigger athletics for the few? Will there be less opportunity or motivation, by educators and social planners for the masses? In the answer to these and similar social questions may lie the solution of problems of great import bearing on the progress or decline of our civilization.

Health and Games. Supervised athletics can be made to contribute greatly to individual and national health. At present, the emphasis in health work is largely upon the removal of causes, and effecting the cure of disease. Important as this health service is, too many health workers are neglecting some most effective agencies to keep youth and older people functioning normally and healthfully. Physical play is nature's way of building strong healthy animal bodies. But civilization, with its restrictive urban environment and its confining social limitations, interferes with the methods that nature and society have used to insure healthy generations.

Health engineers know that through muscular exercise the vital organs of the physical machine generate energy and effect structural and metabolic changes that are essential to wholesome functioning of the human being. But very few individuals will play or recreate solely for the purpose of keeping healthy. Fewer people understand or appreciate the possibility of the creation of mental or physical power, or of the possible promotion of health and happiness from a wise and judicious engagement in physical activity of recreational nature. Not until they become sick, or too unsightly thin or obese, will the average run of people look to exercise and sport as a means of the attainment of physical vigor, attractive appearance, or functioning motility.

Wise educators, social planners, and governments in all ages have sought to promote athletics for the purpose of motivating physical play, physical training, and activity leading to healthy bodies and healthy minds. Pernicious, selfish and blind leaders often are quick to view athletics simply as a means of self-glorification or a way to build their institutions for profit to themselves. Too many educators and administrators are today mindful only of winning athletes and winning teams as build-ups for larger schools, more salaries, and a greater personal or institutional prestige.

Character and Athletic Sport. This prostitution of athletes and of athletics leads eventually to the generation of faulty or unsocial or even criminal characters, and frequently leads to ruined bodies of athletes and to a life long existence of poor health, or to early graves. Of eight members of a basketball team on which the writer played, four were dead before they were forty years old, three of tuberculosis. For a succession of years many prominent athletes, especially in basketball, died in early manhood, largely because of exploitation by unscrupulous or ignorant directors of athletics, coaches or school heads who considered only the victories and their results and gave too little thought to the boy or the game for socially approved ends. The ideal school or college athletic set-up will utilize athletic activity not as an end in itself. There are many educational outcomes that may follow wise curricular use of games and sports. Social hygiene will find a strong ally in sanely conducted athletics. Temperance advocates may benefit where real and not pseudo-educators are in charge of educational institutions. Too frequently the athlete becomes the gambler, disinclined to honest toil or too inflated in ego to accept modest compensation for work. Often sex-promiscuity, physical and social disaster follow unbalanced attitudes toward self and the world because of weak or dishonest athletic policies during the boy athlete's day in school.

Today we read of delinquency and crime and the immoral trends during youth. In our crowded city dwellings, urges to destroy property, or to be regardless of the rights and privileges of others, lead youth rapidly to the juvenile courts, reformatories and to social banishment. The youth in prison outnumber the old offenders.

Yet our schools are crowded. Attempts to organize for play and recreation increase through the media of clubs, Y. M. C. A.'s, playgrounds, schools, and recreation associations. The objectives too often become only those of championships. If play and recreation have preventive influence upon crime and delinquency, wherein do we fail to make greater headway in the solution of the problems involved? Too much do we take for granted that in themselves without well trained leadership, play and athletic games furnish the crucible in which good character is molded. This is simply wishful thinking.

Play an Offset to Nervous Deterioration. Hospital beds for confinement, or for curative treatment of the mentally ill are increasing. Nervous breakdowns, neural irritability, sexual abnormalities are multiplying throughout the land. Despite efforts to train the human mind and body, in order that they may make satisfactory adjustment to an exceedingly taxing, changing, destructive industrialization of society, we are failing. Suitable recreation, a healthy environment, some satisfactions, and feelings of security are claimed to be some of the means for prevention of deterioration of nerve mechanisms of the human body. Can athletics help? When and how do they fail?

Education of youth should include opportunity for play, games and athletics. Education through the physical should be offered in every institution wherein youth lives. The objectives should include development of a stout, well-formed, nicely poised body; a rugged endurable nervous mechanism; emotional balance; ethical qualities embraced in the category summarized as sportsmanship; some skill in and a desire to engage in forms of physical activity during most of life. Athletics for all should be a leading aim in education.

Good Sportsmanship Taught. Far down in the beginnings of child life, in organized play or athletic contests, every effort should be made to teach the boy or girl competing, that success in the physical activity itself is not the end result. The concomitant values ought to be made evident in accord with the possibilities of appreciation by the boy or girl at various stages of development. This cannot be begun too early. The boy must be made to realize that in striving to win he must also keep the good will of his fellows, and exhibit the traits that the masses of society admire. Every effort must be made to discourage dishonesty, poor sportsmanship, and the feeling of depression in losing. He must be taught to do his best, to avoid excuses for losing, and to congratulate his opponents. If the social group in which the athletes perform is properly led to show appreciation of victorious striving and good sportsmanship, good athletics and character-building inevitably result.

Emotional Control; Law and Order. All people, for most of their lives, will be spectators in the arena of life. Even the star athlete will be more frequently an onlooker than a performer during his career. How to behave and conduct oneself as a spectator, as a part of a gathering, large or small, requires training in emotional control and expression, and in other personal qualities. The individuals who drop dead, become nervous sweating wrecks, or seek narcotics for relief when they listen to a radio description of a prize-fight in which a Joe Louis or Henry Armstrong engages, are typical of those to whom education for life has failed to bring about a proper sense of values or ability to control one's emotions under stress. Here again, if early in school, games can be used to train for spectatorship, for appreciation of the exhibition, or for learning to govern one's own reaction and responses, the next generation will be able to solve better some of the social problems involved in group reactions under the stimulus of emotional excitement, whether the occasion be a football game, a prizefight, or an attempt at lynching. The writer has freshly in mind several recent playground meets of boys and girls where the children might be said to have had a good time, but where most of the lessons of law and order, discipline, and ethical character went with the winds. Yet, more careful planning, more understanding of the possibilities of achieving greater worth-while social contributions on the part of workers and officials, might have made these annual playground meets a means of development of appreciation of civic virtues second to no one other educational project. It is also true with schools, especially with secondary schools, that many administrators are either too weak or too careless, or too ignorant of the opportunity afforded for development of spectatorship and self-control in their contests and sponsored exhibitions.

Sacrifice of Character Training for Institutional Prestige. Many of the administrators inherit the traditions and understandings of college athletics, and bring these into public school education. Coming from a college environment in which athletics are often conducted after the pattern of the old Greek and Roman games in their decay and at their worst, many of these leaders cannot adjust their administration of schoolboy athletics to the philosophies of education, or to the intelligent applications of the principles of health or personality development. Hence in so many institutions the athletes who might go forth well-balanced, vigorous, socially-minded citizens, leave the school with a series of triumphs and trophies, with bodies unfit for a long life of service, and with attitudes towards society and living that make them socially unfit, and often gangsters and racketeers. Those who come out unscathed do so despite the school athletic programs. The use of games for contributions to the physical, moral, and social education of youth cannot be overlooked by the directors or agencies that sponsor recreation and athletics. It is high time that real educators, not political savants in the education field, oppose all forms of play and game activities that do not have positive molding influences for the good of the individual and society.

Christian Brotherhood Compatible with Athletic Contest. One other aspect of the social implications of athletics is the large opportunity an athlete or an athletic setting has to develop a real Christian brotherhood among men of the minority and majority groups in our cosmopolitan American life, and in the greater field of international relationships. At one time a great Pope was decrying extreme racism, when anti-Semitism was raging as a political philosophy in Italy and Germany, and when in the United States many vexing social and economic problems were so involved with racial factors.   Athletics can and do in many instances contribute much to the friendliness, good-will and helpful contacts for Christian brotherhood.   When athletes are allowed to compete with each other, representing different racial or social groups, and when they observe rules of sportsmanlike play in the contests, the reaction upon them and those who witness the competitions almost invariably results in more toleration, greater respect, and appreciation of the oneness of the human race.

As a rule, the greatest offenders against this social force are our older citizens in many high places, who for selfish purposes turn thumbs down on bi-racial sports, when such play might bring about mutual good will and respect among minorities or different races. Although our Negro athletes do compete and receive honors and accommodations in even the dictator-ridden lands, these same athletes cannot yet compete with athletes of colleges of sovereign states like the University of Maryland.

Negro Athletes Defeat Nazism.   Can anyone doubt that the appearance of Jesse Owens in Berlin did not reduce adherence to some of Hitler's super-man Aryan philosophy to a mere figment in the minds of thousands of Germans?   Is it not possible that the oppressed races in Germany and elsewhere revived hope of a coming promised land of racial brotherhood and opportunity since their rulers have passed on, when they witnessed the long string of victories of Ben and Cornelius Johnson, Ellerbee, Owens, Williams, Luvalle, Metcalfe, Woodruff, Watson, Albritton, Walker, Robinson, and Borican?   The rise and fall of human emotions spurred by the conquering fists of Joe Louis, Armstrong, and John Henry Lewis brought to men everywhere something of the feelings of respect and reverence that were felt by the masses when David slew Goliath, and Sampson the Philistines.   Likewise this feeling exists on the occasions of athletic contests all along the pathway of man from the cave days down to the destruction of the idealism of Aryan superiority by Joe Louis, when he laid low the Schmeling myth.

Opinion on Colored Athletes.   Into the minds of columnists and commentators came wonder or consternation because of these

U. S. TRACK TEAM WHICH TOURED JAPAN
Including Dave Albritton, Kermit King and John Woodruff

U. S. TEAM TOURING SCANDINAVIAN COUNTRIES, 1938
Front row: Melvin Walker, Ohio State University

NITED STATES TEAM THAT DEFEATED GERMANY, 122–92, AT BERLIN AUG. 13–14,
1938
Colored athletes included B. Johnson, Herbert, M. Walker, Cruter, Ellerbee,

feats. Why was it that these few boys of a handicapped minority group succeeded so remarkably, when thousands of lads, favored with fine training, good nutriment, healthy living environment, and an equally burning wish to succeed, fought just as hard with all their might to triumph in these contests?   Every conceivable hypothesis was advanced to account for the bewildering supremacy of Negro sprinters.   Scientific experiment and much "logic" were used to substantiate the guesses.   Some reasons suggested were sincerely adduced; others were typical of propaganda used for the purpose of discrediting the achievements of the Negro.   Among the guesses made or hypotheses advanced were the following: The Negro was a better sprinter because he had a long thin shank, a long heel, a peculiar patella, a shorter thigh, a stronger tendon of Achilles or larger adrenalin glands.   Some said that the colored boy was limited in a choice of activity; running was natural, required no special equipment, and possibly he had a greater conditioned fear complex, —hence the ability to flee faster.   Many years ago, one commentator accounted for the greater running ability of the late John B. Taylor, of the University of Pennsylvania, by ascribing to him, a bronze-colored Negro, the calf-form of a white man.   All typical Negroes were supposed to have long spindle-shaped legs.

About that time two students at the University of Louisiana meas-ured the time of the knee-jerk of nearly one hundred white and one hundred colored boys in Louisiana.   The time of the reflex of the colored boys was perceptibly faster than that of the white boys.   Inferentially perhaps, since the nerve reaction was a reflex or spinal cord synapse affair, and the higher brain centers did not need to function, and since many lower animal movements are largely reflex-acts, the faster reflex might suggest that the Negro was simply closer to the beast kingdom.

Dr. Cobb's Research.   The work of Dr. W. Montague Cobb, head Professor of Anatomy at Howard University Medical College, done at Western Reserve University with Jesse Owens as a subject, scientifically disposed of many of the hypotheses advanced by some of the most prominent followers and writers in the field of physical education or sport. In an article, published in the *Journal of Health and Physical Education* in January, 1936, Dr. Cobb showed that Negro athletes, although categorically designated as American Negroes, do not even look alike. "Genetically we know that they are not constituted alike. There is not one single physical feature, including skin color, which all of our Negro champions have in common which would identify them as Negroes. Not one of them could be considered a pure Negro according to Herskovits' recent definition." Extending his view, he said, "the anthropologist fails to find racial homogeneity even among white sprinters."

After an extended examination and comparison of the skeletal and muscular systems and neuro-muscular coordinations of Jesse Owens and similar elements or scale measurements of white men, Professor Cobb concludes, "The split-second differences in the performances of the great Negro and white sprinters of past and present are insignificant from an anthropological standpoint. So are the differences in the achievements of the two races in the broad jump. The physiques of champion Negro and white sprinters in general, and of Jesse Owens in particular, reveal nothing to indicate that Negroid physical characters are anatomically concerned with the present dominance of Negro athletes in national competition in the short dashes and the broad jump."

Dr. Cobb further states, "Jesse Owens, who has run faster and leaped farther than any human being has ever done before does not have what is considered the Negroid type of calf, of foot, or heel bone. Although the world mark for the broad jump has remained the property of Negro athletes for a surprisingly long period, it would seem that the technique of the jump is the only feature involved in the matter of supremacy, for Negro and white sprinters have demonstrated equal speed for the preliminary run." Dr. Cobb pointed out that Chuhei Nambu, the retiring world's champion broad jumper, belongs to a people with anatomical build the opposite of the Negroid in pertinent features. The Japanese are short of stature, short of limb, long thighed, and short-legged. If the view that racial anatomy was important in the Negro's success were correct, these are just the specifications a jumper should not have. Dr. Cobb concludes, "Hence we see no reason why the first man to jump twenty-seven feet should not be a white athlete or the first man to run the mile in four minutes a Negro."

We need in America only to get a new deal in statesmanship. As long as local politicians who thrive on a vote and electorate fed on racial prejudice are allowed to stave off opportunities for the youth of the race to meet on the fields of friendly rivalry in sports, just so long will we have many of the costly segregated social systems and institutions which have for their outcomes the antithesis of Christian brotherhood.

Recreational Activity a Means to Health.   Negro participation in athletics has increased rapidly in the past few years.   Some of this progress has been due to the greater attention paid to the physical abilities of boys and girls in the school curriculum.   Of course, even today there are many educators who have failed to realize the potential power for education of youth for citizenship in a school program of physical education.   Yet more and more throughout the South physical education and recreation are receiving much attention.

There are many services designed to protect community health and incidentally save the lives of more Negroes.   Communities dislike the stigma of high disease or mortality rates.   Hence many social and civic projects are launched to prevent disease, especially contagious disease.   Some educators and school systems value health measures but do not favor expenditures for physical education and play.   In one large Tidewater Virginia city, the principal of a large Negro school devoid of gymnasium or play space was asked why it was that with such a plant no provision was made for a gymnasium or a play program.   He replied, "The Director of Health and Physical Education of the city schools opposed the erection of a gymnasium on the theory that 'Negroes are largely tubercular, and what they need is rest and not further activity.' " Even our sectional or national educational organizations for Negroes find little or no place in their programs for recreation, physical education, mental or emotional hygiene.

Through the medium of athletics, through the contributions of our athletic ambassadors of good will, there are signs that indicate our coming to a higher plane of racial tolerance. Men in many places are beginning to believe that moral rearmament is a surer way to save civilization than by economic or warfare rearmament. There is hope that racial and national dislikes will give way to a more significant realization of brotherhood. In good sportsmanship we have the essence of the golden rule. Athletes of all races can, if they will, make a contribution to the maintenance of civilization, second to no other force or institution of society. Will they? Negro athletes have done much already to break down, for themselves and less privileged races, barriers to a fuller freedom. Such athletes must keep following in the course set by those whose story we have herein but briefly told.

APPENDIX

This book is not a reference work. Because of the interest of some readers in facts, dates and records, we list some of the statistical data concerning Negro athletes, and have compiled some of the records of athletic and sporting performances. Necessarily only the highlights and brief summaries are possible. Had space permitted, the mere records of the combats of colored boxers would have furnished romantic charm and thrilling memories to the lovers of the manly art. In this day of the trend toward a physically effete civilization and the emasculation of rugged human life, recall to the battles of the heroes of the prize ring of old ought to stir vicarious experiences. For no good reason we have not listed the fights of a few of the champions who were not consistent or long time holders of the crowns they won.

Track and field data have been culled from the official publications of the Amateur Athletic Union of America, the National Collegiate Athletic Association, and the Intercollegiate Association of Amateur Athletes of America. These performances are of known Negroes who have competed in the events authorized by or held under the direct auspices of the organizations sponsoring amateur or collegiate athletics.

A story of the experiences of Professor J. Francis Gregory in baseball told in a letter to the *Washington Tribune* is reprinted and also a story of Major Taylor, brilliant bicyclist of the nineties.

In this appendix will be found a complete record of Negro jockeys in important racing stakes. We are indebted to Frank Menke for use of his compilation of leading racing stakes and jockeys, and particularly to Buster Miller, Sports Editor of the New York Age for his article and comments anent Negro jockeys.

From Major Cleve Abbott and his department at Tuskegee we publish here the sterling performances of the girls of Tuskegee and of the nation in track and field.

Here also are the winners of past years in golf, tennis, and bowling of the "National" associations. College championships in vari-

ous major sports as records of the colored conferences have been
listed in this section of the book.

Major Taylor—The Fastest Bicycle Rider in the World

A half century ago, the athletic career of one of the greatest
Negro athletes in America began. Born in 1878 in Indianapolis,
Marshall W. "Major" Taylor was destined to win the plaudits of
millions of people all over the world, as one of the most remarkable
champions of all time. He won three undisputed American sprint
championships in 1898, 1899 and 1900. For three seasons he
invaded Europe and defeated all of the cycling champions before
huge throngs in the great racing stadia of the continent. Australia
bid him a royal welcome and on three melodramatic trips there, he
established enviable records and good comradeship.

The role of the Negro athlete to-day in the eyes of the American
public is accepted. In Major Taylor's time, although many of his
racing competitors were fair, the leading professionals sought by
every knavery within and without the racing rules to keep him from
winning. No stouter heart ever prevailed in the annals of sportsmen than beat in the body of the ebony Apollo of the racing
fraternity.

Major Taylor won some of his most noted victories before he was
18 years old. He began as a trick rider. Philanthropic white
friends helped him establish an early reputation as a racer. Later
his prowess earned him the support of the leading sports' management of his day. The appearance of Major Taylor at a racing
meeting at home or abroad, assured the financial success of great
sport managers of a few decades ago.

When 10 years old, Walter Sanger made a mark of 2:18 for the
mile at the Capital City track in Indianapolis. Taylor could not
race him because "color" barred all competition between them.
Some of Taylor's friends secured him entry to the track before
the crowd had gone. After a few warming-up heats, Taylor tore

off a 2:11 mile, seven seconds under the much touted Sanger. On the same afternoon behind pace, he established a record of 23⅗ seconds for the ⅕ mile oval, a mark that lasted as long as the Indianapolis track stood.

So bitter was the prejudice, he could not enter any races where white men rode. On one occasion, a 75 mile road race between Indianapolis and Matthews, Indiana was scheduled. White friends secreted Major Taylor in the woods behind scratch. After the start, he rode from his hiding place and followed the pack for half the distance. Then he went to the front and rode the last 25 miles in a blinding rainstorm and won the race one hour before the nearest competitor.

Taylor Moves to Massachusetts. Because of the race feeling in Indianapolis, Major Taylor and his manager "Birdie" Munger, a staunch friend, went to live in Worcester, Massachusetts. Munger advised Taylor that if he would train faithfully, refrain from tobacco and intoxicants, he would become the fastest bicycle rider in the world. To following this advice, the Major ascribes his successful career.

In 1898, Major Taylor determined to go after the American Sprint Championship. Although the big racing syndicates, the League of American Wheelmen and the National Racing Association would not admit colored riders to membership, Taylor's drawing powers and the backing of white friends and a liberal press, forced managements in all of the cities except Baltimore and points south, to admit him to the racing events. Sanctions were refused to St. Louis and other cities to hold championship events if Taylor was barred. In the 1898 season, he defeated all the champions among whom were Eddie Bald, Arthur Gardiner, Tom Butler and Owen Kimble.

Major Taylor continued as champion in 1899 and 1900. During his first championship year, he was first in 21 races; second, 13 times, and third, 11 times. He secured in the racing point system, 121 points for the year against 113 by Arthur Gardiner. In 1899, he was first in 23 starts; second in three, and lost only two races. In

1900, under a new point system, he scored 40 points with his next competitor Frank Kramer, scoring 20.

Taylor Invades Europe and Australia. In the early season of 1901, Major Taylor invaded Europe and in two months competed in 57 races, almost a race a day while on the continent. He rode in France, Belgium, Italy, Switzerland, Denmark and Germany. He defeated time and again, the great national champions; Jacquelin, Quivy, Dutriew, Founeau of France; Ellegarde of Denmark; Arend and Muringer of Germany; Grognia of Belgium; Ferrari and Boxio of Italy and scores of others who ranked in popular acclaim on par with the Louises, Owenses, Dempseys, Schmelings, Carpentiers and Carneras of our day. Three times Major Taylor was honored and welcomed in Europe. On his return to America he could have engaged in enough races to have won the American championships in 1901 and 1902, but the conniving of the riders and gamblers linked with shady practices, made it impossible for him to compete and score points enough to be counted the national champion.

Major Taylor entered into a contract to race in Australia. Full of misgivings because of the reputation Australia had toward Orientals, he found on entering the harbor of Sydney, streamers of welcome, the sounding of sirens and horns and throngs of Australians waiting for the arrival of this black son from America. His racing career in Australia rivalled his successes on the continent. He was bitterly fought in "pockets" and with personal abuse by the Americans who came over to compete for the prize money. He defeated them all despite some of the most despicable life endangering tricks. Many were suspended from Australian tracks. In consideration of the excellent sportsmanship of Australians, he named his only daughter born on one of his Australian trips, Rita Sydney. This little girl could not be a rider but proved her interest in sports by graduating from the Sargent's School of Physical Education.

In 1903, Taylor suffered a collapse, but returned to the track in 1908 and was a champion contestant until he hung up his wheel in 1910. He wrote fair poetry. He was an ardent race man, a believer in clean living, high ethical standards and Americanism.

Evaluation. Despite all the wiles of his adversaries, Taylor met them at their own game and was able to defeat them more times than they could outwit him.   In all racing, it is possible for two or more racers working in collusion to "box" a competitor and thus enable another man to win.   In prize money contests, the winnings are split between the collaborators and the conspirators.   The rules of racing coupled with the weakness of officials made "boxing" a common thing when the Major was riding.   It was the skill of his trick riding days coupled with his powerful "jump" that usually put to no avail the coterie of racers who fought him at every meeting. With a rider in front on the pole, another outside, and another in the rear, the Major would follow pace until about in the middle of the last turn, he would "jump" his wheel on the pole in a flash and lead a merry chase to the tape.   Frequently when up against his foul racing opponents, he would lightly slap the front rider's rear wheel, causing him to veer slightly and the Major would "jump" through on the pole and defy the bunch.

Major Taylor promised his mother he would never race on Sunday.   He kept this promise, turning down thousands of dollars by entering no contracts for Sunday races.   He did not drink or smoke and trained with the fervor of a religionist.   His career was an honor to America.   President Theodore Roosevelt personally saluted him with a great tribute.   Millions of Americans and foreigners were thrilled by his performances.   The influence of this great American sportsman of color was felt over the entire world. He made thousands of dollars and was one of America's most honored sons.   His autobiography is a most thrilling story and his life long battle against race prejudice was as valiant a struggle as that of Nat Turner, Denmark Vesey or Frederick Douglass.   His career was as brilliant around the turn of the century as was the meteoric glory of Jesse Owens or Joe Louis in the annals of sport two generations later.

BILL RICHMOND

Born at Richmond, Staten Island, N. Y., August 5, 1763.   Died December 28, 1829, in London, England.   (Height 5 ft. 9 in.; weight 175 lbs.)

1805—May 21—Won from Youssep in 6 rounds.   July 8—Won from Jack Holmes in 26 rounds.   October 8—Lost to Tom Cribb in 1 hour 30 minutes.

1809—April 11—Won from Isaac Wood in 23 rounds. April 14—Won from Jack Carter in 25 minutes. August 9—Won from George Maddox in 52 minutes.

1810—May 1—Won from Young Powers in 15 minutes.

1814—April 7—Won from Jack Davis in 13 rounds.

1815—August 11—Won from Tom Shelton in 23 rounds.

THOMAS MOLINEAUX

Born in Georgetown, D. C., 1784. Reared in Virginia. Died in Galway, Ireland, August 4, 1818. (Height 5 ft. 8½ in.; weight 185 lbs.)

1810—July 14—Won from Tom Blake in 8 rounds. December 10—Lost to Tom Cribb in 33 rounds.

1811—May 21—Won from Jim Rimmer in 21 rounds. September 28—Lost to Tom Cribb in 11 rounds.

1813—April 2—Won from Jack Carter in 25 rounds.

1814—May 27—Won from Bill Fuller in 2 rounds.

1815—March 10—Lost to George Cooper in 14 rounds.

PETER JACKSON

Born: St. Croix, West Indies, July 3, 1861. Died in Australia, July 13, 1901. (Height 6 ft., 1½ in.; weight, 192 lbs.)

1883—Won, four; draw, one.

1884—Won, one.

1886—Won from Tom Lees in 30 rounds—Australian championship.

1888—Won fights as follows: George Godfrey, 19 rounds; Jack McAuliffe, 24.

1889—Won: Patsy Cardiff, 10; Shorty Kincaid, 12; Mike Lynch, 2; Paddy Brennan, 1; Jack Fallon, 2; Alf. Mitchell, 3; Jack Partridge, 5; Jim Young, 3; Jack Watts, 3; Coddy Meddlings, 3; Alf. Ball, 3; Jack Watson, 2; Jem Smith, 2; Sailor Brown, 4.

1890—Won: Jack Fallon, 2; Gus Lambert, 4; Dick Keating, 1; Ed. Smith, 5; Tom Johnson, 1; Joe Goddard, 8. No-decision: Jack Ashton.

1891—May 21, Draw, Jim Corbett, 61 rounds.

1892—Won: Al. Fish, 2; Jack Dalton, 3; Frank Slavin, 10.

1898—March 22, Lost, Jim Jeffries, 3 rounds.

1899—Draw, 1; lost, 1.

GEORGE DIXON

Born at Halifax, Nova Scotia, July 29, 1870. Died in Boston in 1909. (Height 5 ft. 3½ in.; weight 115 to 122 lbs.)

1886—Won from Young Johnson in 2 rounds.

1887—Won from Elias Hamilton in 8 rounds, and from Young Mack in 3 rounds.

1888—Won, ten fights; draw, one.
1889—Won, ten; draw, one; lost, one.
1890—Won, twelve; draw, one.
1891—Won, nine; draw, two.
1892—Won, seven; draw, two.
1893—Won, nine; draw, two; lost, two.
1894—Won, seven.
1895—Won, seven; draw, three.
1896—Won, one; draw, three; lost, one.
1897—Won, three; draw, two; lost, one.
1898—Won, three; draw, one; lost, one; no-decision, two.
1899—Won, seven; draw, one; no-decision, one.
1900—Lost, three; no-decision, one.
1901—Lost, four; draw, three; no-decision, two.
1902—Won, one; draw, four; lost, three; no-decision, two.
1903—Won, three; draw, three; lost, five.
1904—Won, two; draw, one; lost, one.
1905—Lost, one.
1906—Won, one; lost, one.
Summary: Fought 148 battles; knockouts, 19; won, 60; lost, 23; draw, 38; no-decision, 7; knocked-out by, 1.

JOE GANS

Born: November 25, 1874. Died, 1910, in Baltimore, Md. (Height, 5 ft., 6¼ in.; weight, 133 lbs.)
1891-1894—Won, 12.
1895—Won, 9; draw, 2.
1896—Won, 11; draw, 1; lost, 2.
1897—Won, 3; draw, 1.
1898—Won, 12; draw, 1.
1899—Won, 12; draw, 2; lost, 1.
1900—Won, 11; draw, 2; lost, 2.
1901—Won, 9; draw, 2 (won lightweight title).
1902—Won, 10; draw, 2.
1903—Won, 7; draw, 5; lost, 1.
1904—Won, 11; draw, 2.
1905—Draw, 2.
1906—Won, 4; draw, 3. (Sept. 3, won on a foul from Nelson—42 rounds.)
1907—Won, 3.
1908—Won, 3. Knocked-out by Battling Nelson, July 4th and September 9.
1909—Draw, 1.
Summary—Fought 152 battles; knockouts, 54; won, 63; lost, 4; draw, 10; no-decision, 17; knocked-out by, 4.

JACK JOHNSON

Born: March 31, 1878, at Galveston, Texas. Died June 10, 1946. (Height, 6 ft. ½ in.; weight, 220 lbs.)

1899—Lost, 1.
1901—Won, 6; draw, 1; k. o. by Joe Choynski.
1902—Won, 12; draw, 4.
1903—Won, 6; no-decision, 1.
1904—Won, 3; no-decision, 1.
1905—Won, 6; no-decision, 2; lost, 5.
1906—Won, 5; draw, 1; no-decision, 2.
1907—Won, 6.   Defeated Bob Fitzsimmons.
1908—Won, 3; no-decision, 3.
1909—Won, 2.   Knocked-out Stanley Ketchell, July 4.
1910—Won, 1.   Knocked-out Jim Jeffries, July 4.
1912—Won, 1.
1913—Won, 2.   Fights in Paris.
1915—Won, 2.   In Madrid.   Knocked-out by Jess Willard in Havana.
1918—Won, 1.   In Madrid.
1919—Won, 5.   In Madrid and in Mexico.
1920—Won, 2.
1923—Won, 1.
1924—Won from Homer Smith in Montreal.
Summary—Fought in 89 ring battles; knockouts, 29; won, 33; lost, 4; draw, 5; no-decision, 14; knocked-out by, 2.

HENRY ARMSTRONG

Born: St. Louis, Mo., December 12, 1912.   (Height, 5 ft. 5 ¼ in.; weight 134 lb.)

1932

Knockouts—Bobby Calmes, 3; Bud Taylor, 2; Vincente Torres, 3; Johnny De Foe, 4; Vince Trujillo, 2.
Won—Gene Espinoza, 4; Max Tarley, 4; Mickey Ryan, 6; George Dundee, 6; Perfecto Lopez, 6; Steve Harky, 6; Perfecto Lopez, 8; Young Corpus, 6.
Draw—Perfecto Lopez, 4; Perfecto Lopez, 4; Perfecto Lopez, 6.
Lost—Eddie Trujillo, 4; Al Greenfield, 4; Baby Manuel, 6.
No Decision—Hoyt Jones, 4.

1933

Knockouts—John Granone, 5; Gene Espinoza, 7; Max Tarley, 3; Joe Conde, 7; Ventura Arana, 5.
Won—Kid Moro, 10; Baby Manuel, 10; Davey Abad, 10.
Draw—Kid Moro, 10.
Lost—Baby Arizmendi, 10.

1934

Knockouts—Sal Hernandez, 2; Baby Casanova, 3; Lester Marston, 7; Leo Lomelli, 5.

Won—Varras Milling, 10; Mark Diaz, 8; Midget Wolgast, 10.

Draw—Perfecto Lopez, 8.

Lost—Baby Arizmendi, 12.

1935

Knockouts—Tully Corvo, 7; Alton Black, 7.

Won—Davey Abad, 10; Frankie Covelli, 8.

Lost—Davey Abad, 10.

1936

Knockouts—Alton Black, 8 rounds; Pancho Leyvas, 4; Juan Zurita, 4; Tommy Ganzon, 1; Gene Espinoza, 1; Joey Alcanter, 6.

Won—Ritchie Fontaine, 10; John Defoe, 10; Baby Arizmendi, 10; Buzz Brown, 10; Mike Belloise, 10.

Lost—Joe Conde, 10; Ritchie Fontaine, 10; Tony Chavez, foul, 8.

1937

Knockouts—Baby Cazanova, 3; Tony Chavez, 10; Moon Mullins, 2; Varias Millings, 4; Joe Rivers, 4; Mike Belloise, 4; Pete DeGrasse, 10; Frankie Klick, 4; Wally Hally, 4; Mark Dias, 4; Jackie Carter, 4; Alf Blatch, 3; Lew Massey, 4; Benny Bass, 4; Eddie Brink, 3; Johnny Cabello, 2: Orville Drouillard, 5; Charlie Burns, 4; John DeFoe, 4; Bobby Dean, 1; Joe Marciente, 3; Peter Sarron, 6 (earned feather-weight title); Billy Beauhuld, 5; Joey Brown, 2; Tony Chavez, 1; Johnny Jones, 2.

Won—Aldo Spoldi, 10.

1938

Knockouts—Enrico Venturi, 6; Fran Castillo, 3; Tommy Brown, 2; Chalky Wright, 3; Al Citrino, 4; Everett Rightmier, 3; Charley Burns, 2; Eddie Zivic, 4; Lew Feldman, 5.

Won—Baby Arizmendi, 10; Barney Ross, 15 (won welter-weight title), May, 26; Lou Ambers, 15 (won light-weight title, August 17, 1938)

JOHN HENRY LEWIS

Born: May 6, 1914, Los Angeles, California

1931

Knockouts—Tommy Cadena, 1; Pietro Georgi, 1; Sammy Bass, 1; Roy Gunn, 3; Kid Valdone, 3.

Won (decision)—Jake Henderson, 4; Roy Imm, 4; Tiger Flowers, 6; Lloyd Phelps, 8.

1932

Knockouts—Fred Lenhart, 4; Jimmy Hanna, 6.
Won—James J. Braddock, 10; Yale Okum, 10; Lou Scozza, 10.

1933

Knockouts—Terris Hill, 3; Tuffy Dial, 3; Emmet Rocco, 7.
Won—Maxie Rosenbloom, 10; Frank Rowsey, 10; Tom Patrick, 10.

1934

Knockouts—Sandy Casanova, 3; Bobby Brown, 3; Pietro Georgi, 2; Earl Wise, 3;
Tony Palori, 2; Yale Okum, 3.
Won—Norman Conrad, 10; Tony Shucco, 10.

1935

Knockouts—Don Petrin, 7; Frank Wotanski, 3; Terry Mitchell, 6; Tom
Patrick, 1: Izzy Singer, 1; Lou Poster, 5; George Simpson, 2; Cole-
mans Johns, 2.
Won—Emilio Martinez, 10; Bob Olin, 10; Frank Rowsey, 10; Bob Olin, 15
(won world light heavyweight title); Dutch Weimer, 10.

1936

Knockouts—Tiger Jack Fox, 3; Al Stillman, 5; Cyclone Lynch, 2; Don God-
win, 1; Dutch Weimer, 5; Tony Shucco, 8; Jim Merriott, 3; Tiger
Hairston, 1; Clarence Burman, 2.
Won—Eddie Simms, 10; Jock McAvoy, 15 (title defense); Izzy Singer, 10;
Charles Massera, 10; John Anderson, 10; Max Marek, 10; Al Gainer,
12; Len Harvey, 15 (title defense).

1937

Knockouts—Art Sykes, 6; Chester Palutis, 7; Donald Barry, 5; Babe Davis, 3;
Harold Murphy, 4; Pret Farrar, 6; Jack Kranz, 3; Bob Olin, 3; Sal-
vadore Ruggierello, 4; Isadoro Gastanaga, 9.
Won—Al Ettore, 15; Hans Birkie, 10; Emilio Martinez, 10; Patsy Peroni, 10;
Al Ettore, 10; Willie Reddish, 10; Italo Colonello, 12; Johnny Risko, 10.

1938

Knockouts—Leonard Neblitt, 8; Fred Lenhart, 3; Emilio Martinez, 4 (title
defense); Elmer Ray, 12; Dominic Ceccarelli, 3.
Won—Emil Scholz, 10; Bud Mignault, 10; Bob Tow, 10; Dominic Ceccarelli,
10; Jimmy Adamick, 10; Al Gainer (title defense), 15.

1939

Knockout by—Joe Louis, January 25, 1939.
Draw Decisions: 1933—Fred Lenhart, 10.
1934—Young Firpo, 10; Donald Barry, 10.
1936—George Nichols, 10.
1937—Al Ettore, 10.
Lost Decisions: 1932—Maxie Rosenbloom, 10.
1934—James J. Braddock, 10.
1935—Maxie Rosenbloom, 10; Abe Feldman, 10; Maxie Rosenbloom, 10.
1936—Emilio Martinez, 10.
1937—Isadore Gastanaga, 10.

JOSEPH LOUIS
Born: Lexington, Alabama, May 13, 1914.

1934

July 4	Jack Kracken	Chicago	k.o.	1 round
July 11	Willie Davies	Chicago	k.o.	3 rounds
July 29	Larry Udell	Chicago	k.o.	2 rounds
Aug. 13	Jack Kranz	Chicago	won	3 rounds
Aug. 27	Buck Everett	Chicago	k.o.	2 rounds
Sept. 11	Otto Borchuk	Detroit	k.o.	4 rounds
Sept. 25	Adolph Wiater	Chicago	won	10 rounds
Oct. 24	Art Sykes	Chicago	k.o.	3 rounds
Nov. 30	Charles Massera	Chicago	k.o.	3 rounds
Dec. 14	Lee Ramage	Chicago	k.o.	8 rounds

1935

Jan. 4	Patsy Perroni	Detroit	won	10 rounds
Jan. 11	Hans Birkie	Pittsburgh	k.o.	10 rounds
Feb. 21	Lee Ramage	Los Angeles	k.o.	2 rounds
Mar. 8	Donal Merry	San Francisco	k.o.	3 rounds
Mar. 29	Natie Brown	Detroit	won	10 rounds
Apr. 12	Roy Lazer	Chicago	k.o.	3 rounds
Apr. 22	Biff Bennett	Dayton	k.o.	1 round
Apr. 25	Roscoe Toles	Flint, Michigan	k.o.	6 rounds
May 3	Willie Davis	Peoria, Ill.	k.o.	2 rounds
May 7	Gene Staunton	Kalamazoo	k.o.	3 rounds
June 25	Primo Carnera	New York	k.o.	6 rounds
Aug. 7	King Levinsky	Chicago	k.o.	1 round
Sept. 24	Max Baer	New York	k.o.	4 rounds
Dec. 13	Paolino Uzcudun	New York	k.o.	4 rounds

1936

Jan. 17	Charley Retzlaff	Chicago	k.o.	1 round
June 19	Max Schmeling	New York	k.o. by	12 rounds
Aug. 17	Jack Sharkey	New York	k.o.	3 rounds
Sept. 22	Al Ettore	Philadelphia	k.o.	5 rounds
Oct. 9	Jorge Brescia	New York	k.o.	3 rounds
Dec. 14	Eddie Simms	Cleveland	k.o.	1 round

1937

Jan. 11	Stanley Ketchell	Buffalo	k.o.	2 rounds
Jan. 29	Bob Pastor	New York	won	10 rounds
Feb. 17	Natie Brown	Detroit	k.o.	4 rounds
June 22	James H. Braddock	Chicago	k.o.	8 rounds
	(won heavyweight championship).			
Aug. 30	Tommy Farr	New York	won	15 rounds

1938

Feb. 23	Nathan Mann	New York	k.o.	3 rounds
Apr. 1	Harry Thomas	Chicago	k.o.	5 rounds
June 22	Max Schmeling	New York	k.o.	1 round

1939

Jan. 25	John H. Lewis	New York	k.o.	1 round
Apr. 17	Jack Roper	California	k.o.	1 round
June 28	Tony Galento	New York	k.o.	4 rounds
Sept. 30	Bob Pastor	Detroit	k.o.	11 rounds

1940

Feb. 9	Arturo Godoy	New York	won	15 rounds
Mar. 29	Johnny Paycheck	New York	k.o.	2 rounds
June 20	Arturo Godoy	New York	k.o.	8 rounds
Dec. 16	Al McCoy	Boston	k.o.	6 rounds

1941

Jan. 31	Red Burman	New York	k.o.	5 rounds
Feb. 17	Gus Dorazio	Philadelphia	k.o.	2 rounds
Mar. 21	Abe Simon	Detroit	k.o.	13 rounds
Apr. 8	Tony Musto	St. Louis	k.o.	9 rounds
May 23	Buddy Baer	Wash., D. C.	k.o.	7 rounds
June 18	Billy Conn	New York	k.o.	13 rounds
Sept. 29	Lou Nova	New York	k.o.	6 rounds

1942

Jan. 9	Buddy Baer	New York	k.o.	1 round
Mar. 27	Abe Simon	New York	k.o.	6 rounds

1946

June 19	Billy Conn	New York	k.o.	8 rounds
Sept. 18	Tami Mauriello	New York	k.o.	1 round

1947

Dec. 5	Joe Walcott	New York	won	15 rounds

1948

June 25	Joe Walcott	New York	k.o.	11 rounds

BEAU JACK (Sidney Walker)—Lightweight Champion—1943

1940

May 20	Frankie Allen	Holyoke	draw	4 rounds
May 27	Wm. Bannick	Holyoke	k.o.	3 rounds
June 17	Jackie Parker	Holyoke	lost	4 rounds
July 14	Joe Polowitzer	New Haven	lost	6 rounds
July 21	Joe Polowitzer	New Haven	won	6 rounds
Aug. 19	Jackie Parker	Holyoke	lost	4 rounds
Aug. 26	Carlos Daponde	Holyoke	won	4 rounds
Sept. 2	Jack Small	Holyoke	k.o.	4 rounds
Sept. 16	Ollie Barbour	Holyoke	k.o.	3 rounds
Sept. 23	Tony Dupre	Holyoke	k.o.	2 rounds
Oct. 14	Abie Cohen	Holyoke	k.o.	3 rounds
Oct. 21	Ritchie Jones	Holyoke	k.o.	3 rounds
Nov. 4	Joe Stack	Holyoke	won	6 rounds
Dec. 2	Jim Fox	Holyoke	won	6 rounds
Dec. 16	John Buff	Holyoke	k.o.	1 round
Dec. 30	Mel Neary	Holyoke	k.o.	3 rounds

1941

Jan. 27	Mexican Joe Silva	Holyoke	lost	6 rounds
Feb. 10	Mexican Joe Rivers	Holyoke	k.o.	4 rounds
Feb. 24	Lefty Isrow	Holyoke	k.o.	3 rounds
Mar. 10	Mickey Jerome	Holyoke	k.o.	3 rounds
Mar. 24	Mexican Joe Silva	Holyoke	won	6 rounds
Apr. 7	Tony Iacovacci	Holyoke	k.o.	6 rounds
Apr. 21	Bob Reilly	Holyoke	k.o.	7 rounds
Apr. 28	Harry Gentile	Holyoke	k.o.	1 round
May 5	Chester Rico	Holyoke	draw	8 rounds
May 19	George Salamonde	Holyoke	k.o.	8 rounds

June 2	Tommy Spiegel	Holyoke	won	8 rounds
June 16	George Zengaras	Holyoke	won	8 rounds
Aug. 5	Minnie DeMore	Brooklyn	k.o.	3 rounds
Aug. 14	Al Roth	Brooklyn	k.o.	5 rounds
Aug. 26	Guillermo Puentes	New York	won	6 rounds
Sept. 19	Al Reid	New York	k.o.	7 rounds
Oct. 14	Tom Spiegel	Brooklyn	won	8 rounds
Oct. 31	Guillermo Puentes	New York	won	8 rounds
Dec. 1	Sam Rivers	Brooklyn	k.o.	3 rounds
Dec. 8	Fred Archer	New York	lost	8 rounds
Dec. 29	Fred Archer	New York	lost	8 rounds

1942

Jan. 5	Carmelo Fenoy	Holyoke	won	10 rounds
May 22	Bobby Ivy	New York	won	8 rounds
June 23	Guillermo Puentes	New York	k.o.	1 round
July 3	Bob McIntyre	Ft. Hamilton	k.o.	6 rounds
July 7	Cosby Linson	New York	k.o.	8 rounds
Aug. 1	Ruby Garcia	Elizabeth	k.o.	6 rounds
Aug. 18	Carmine Fatta	New York	k.o.	1 round
Aug. 28	Billy Murray	New York	won	10 rounds
Sept. 22	Joe Torres	Wash., D. C.	k.o.	4 rounds
Oct. 2	Chester Rico	New York	won	8 rounds
Oct. 12	Terry Young	New York	won	10 rounds
Nov. 13	Allie Stolz	New York	k.o.	7 rounds
Dec. 18	Tippie Larkin	New York	k.o.	3 rounds

1943

Feb. 5	Fritzie Zivic	New York	won	10 rounds
Mar. 5	Fritzie Zivic	New York	won	12 rounds
Apr. 2	Henry Armstrong	New York	won	10 rounds
May 21	Bob Montgomery (Title)	New York	lost	15 rounds
June 21	Maxie Starr	Wash., D. C.	k.o.	6 rounds
July 19	John Hutchinson	Philadelphia	k.o.	6 rounds
Oct. 4	Bob Ruffin	New York	lost	10 rounds
Nov. 19	Bob Montgomery (Title)	New York	won	15 rounds

1944

Jan. 7	Lulu Costantino	New York	won	10 rounds
Jan. 28	Sammy Angott	New York	draw	10 rounds
Feb. 15	Maxie Berger	Cleveland	won	10 rounds
Mar. 3	Bob Montgomery (Title)	New York	won	15 rounds
Mar. 17	Al Davis	New York	won	10 rounds
Mar. 31	Juan Zurita	New York	won	10 rounds
Aug. 4	Bob Montgomery	New York	won	10 rounds

1945

Dec. 14	Willie Joyce	New York	won	10 rounds

1946

Jan. 4	Morris Reif	New York	k.o.	4 rounds
Feb. 8	Johnny Greco	New York	draw	10 rounds
May 31	Johnny Greco	New York	won	10 rounds
July 8	Sammy Angott	Wash., D. C.	k.o.	7 rounds
Aug. 19	Danny Kapilow	Wash., D. C.	won	10 rounds
Oct. 2	Buster Tyler	Elizabeth	lost	10 rounds

1947

Feb. 21	Tony Janiro	New York	k.o. by	4 rounds
Nov. 3	Humberto Zavalo	St. Louis	k.o.	4 rounds
Dec. 16	Frankie Vigeant	Hartford	won	10 rounds
Dec. 29	Billy Kearns	Providence	won	10 rounds

RING RECORD OF BOB MONTGOMERY
Born, February 10, 1919, Sumpter, S. C.

1937
Amateur bouts, 24—won 22; lost, 2

1938

Oct. 23	Johnny Buff	Atlantic City	k.o.	2 rounds
Oct. 27	Pat Patucci	Atlantic City	k.o.	2 rounds
Nov. 4	Eddie Stewart	Philadelphia	k.o.	2 rounds
Nov. 10	Joe Beltrante	Atlantic City	k.o.	3 rounds
Nov. 17	Red Rossi	Atlantic City	k.o.	2 rounds
Dec. 8	Jackie Sheppard	Atlantic City	won	8 rounds

1939

Jan. 19	Harvey Jacobs	Atlantic City	k.o.	1 round
Feb. 2	Charley Burns	Atlantic City	won	8 rounds
Feb. 23	Jay Macedon	Atlantic City	won	8 rounds
Mar. 9	Billy Miller	Atlantic City	k.o.	2 rounds
Mar. 16	Frank Saia	Philadelphia	k.o.	4 rounds
Mar. 30	Benny Berman	Atlantic City	won	8 rounds
Apr. 13	Young Raspi	Atlantic City	k.o.	6 rounds
Apr. 20	Eddie Guerra	Atlantic City	won	8 rounds
May 1	George Zengares	Philadelphia	draw	10 rounds
May 23	Norment Quarles	Philadelphia	k.o.	4 rounds
June 15	Charley Burns	Atlantic City	k.o.	2 rounds
June 21	Tommy Rawson	Philadelphia	k.o.	1 round

July 3	Frankie Wallace	Philadelphia	won	10 rounds
Aug. 14	Jimmy Murray	Philadelphia	k.o.	3 rounds
Aug. 24	Ray Ingram	Atlantic City	won	10 rounds
Oct. 5	Charley Gilley	Atlantic City	k.o.	6 rounds
Oct. 23	Mike Evans	Philadelphia	won	10 rounds
Nov. 10	Tommy Speigel	Philadelphia	lost	10 rounds
Nov. 27	Mike Evans	Philadelphia	k.o.	1 round

1940

Jan. 29	Al Nettlow	Philadelphia	draw	10 rounds
Mar. 11	Al Nettlow	Philadelphia	won	10 rounds
June 3	Al Nettlow	Philadelphia	won	12 rounds
July 5	Jimmy Vaughn	Atlantic City	k.o.	2 rounds
Sept. 16	Norment Quarles	Atlantic City	draw	10 rounds
Nov. 25	Sammy Angott	Philadelphia	lost	10 rounds

1941

Jan. 28	Julie Kogan	Brooklyn	won	8 rounds
Feb. 7	Al Nettlow	New York	won	8 rounds
Mar. 3	George Zengaras	Philadelphia	k.o.	3 rounds
Apr. 28	Nick Peters	Philadelphia	k.o.	3 rounds
May 16	Lew Jenkins	New York	won	10 rounds
June 16	Manuel Villa	Baltimore	k.o.	1 round
June 30	Wishy Jones	Washington, D. C.	k.o.	4 rounds
July 3	Frankie Wallace	Atlantic City	k.o.	3 rounds
July 14	Slugger White	Baltimore	won	10 rounds
Sept. 8	Mike Kaplan	Philadelphia	won	10 rounds
Oct. 10	Davey Day	Chicago	k.o.	1 round
Oct. 24	Julie Kogan	Chicago	won	10 rounds
Oct. 30	Frankie Wallace	Williamsport, Pa.	k.o.	5 rounds
Dec. 8	Jimmy Garrison	Philadelphia	k.o.	4 rounds

1942

Jan. 5	Mayon Padlo	Philadelphia	k.o.	8 rounds
Mar. 6	Sammy Angott	New York	lost	12 rounds
Apr. 20	Joey Peralta	Philadelphia	won	10 rounds
May 8	Carmen Notch	Toledo	won	10 rounds
July 7	Sammy Angott	Philadelphia	lost	12 rounds
Aug. 13	Bobby Ruffin	New York	won	10 rounds
Oct. 6	Maxie Shapiro	Philadelphia	lost	10 rounds
Dec. 1	Maxie Shapiro	Philadelphia	won	10 rounds

1943

Jan. 8	Chester Rico	New York	k.o.	7 rounds
Feb. 22	Lulu Constantino	Philadelphia	won	10 rounds
Apr. 5	Roman Alvarez	Philadelphia	k.o.	4 rounds
Apr. 30	Gene Johnson	Scranton	won	10 rounds
May 3	Henry Vasquez	Holyoke	won	8 rounds
May 21	Beau Jack (Title)	New York	won	15 rounds
July 4	Al Reasoner	New Orleans	k.o.	6 rounds
July 20	Frankie Willis	Washington, D. C.	won	10 rounds
Aug. 23	Fritzie Zivic	Philadelphia	won	10 rounds
Oct. 25	Pete Scalzo	Philadelphia	k.o.	6 rounds
Nov. 19	Beau Jack (Title)	New York	lost	15 rounds

1944

Jan. 7	Joey Peralta	Detroit	won	10 rounds
Jan. 25	Ike Williams	Philadelphia	k.o.	12 rounds
Feb. 18	Al Davis	New York	k.o. by	1 round
Mar. 3	Beau Jack (Title)	New York	won	15 rounds
Apr. 28	Joey Peralta	Chicago	won	10 rounds
Aug. 4	Beau Jack (Non-Title)	New York	lost	10 rounds

1945

Feb. 13	Cecil Hudson	Los Angeles	won	10 rounds
Mar. 20	Genaro Rojo	Los Angeles	k.o.	8 rounds
May 8	Nick Moran	Los Angeles	lost	10 rounds
July 9	Nick Moran	Philadelphia	won	10 rounds

1946

(Honorably discharged from U. S. Army.)

Feb. 3	Bill Parsons	New Orleans	won	10 rounds
Feb. 15	Leo Rodak	Chicago	won	10 rounds
Mar. 8	Tony Pellone	New York	won	10 rounds
Mar. 21	Ernie Petrone	New Haven	k.o.	4 rounds
June 28	Aillie Stolz	New York	k.o.	13 rounds
July 29	George Larover	Springfield, Mass.	won	10 rounds
Aug. 19	Wesley Mouzon (Non-Title)	Philadelphia	k.o. by	2 rounds
Nov. 26	Wesley Mouzon (Title)	Philadelphia	k.o.	8 rounds

1947

Jan. 20	Eddie Giosa	Philadelphia	k.o.	5 rounds
Feb. 7	Tony Pellone	Detroit	lost	10 rounds
Feb. 25	Joe Barnum	Los Angeles	k.o.	7 rounds

Mar. 31	Jesse Flores	San Francisco	k.o.	3 rounds
May 12	George LaRover	Philadelphia	won	10 rounds
June 2	Julie Kogan	New Haven	won	10 rounds
June 9	Frankie Cordino	Springfield, Mass.	won	10 rounds
Aug. 4	Ike Williams (Title)	Philadelphia	k.o. by	6 rounds
Nov. 24	Livio Minelli	Philadelphia	lost	10 rounds
Dec. 22	Joe Angelo	Boston	lost	10 rounds

RING RECORD OF IKE WILLIAMS

Born August 2, 1923, Brunswick, Ga.

1940

Apr. 1	Patsy Gall	Hazelton, Pa.	draw	6 rounds
June 14	Billy Hildebrand	Mt. Freedom, N. J.	k.o.	6 rounds
July 19	Joe Romero	Mt. Freedom, N. J.	k.o.	2 rounds
Nov. 11	Tony Maglione	Trenton	lost	8 rounds

1941

Jan. 6	Tommy Fontana	Trenton	won	8 rounds
Feb. 19	Cary Zullo	Perth Amboy, N. J.	k.o.	2 rounds
Mar. 5	Joey Zodda	Perth Amboy, N. J.	lost	6 rounds
Mar. 19	Joe Genores	Perth Amboy, N. J.	won	5 rounds
Apr. 9	Johnny Rudolph	Perth Amboy, N. J.	won	6 rounds
Apr. 14	Hughie Civatte	Trenton	k.o.	3 rounds
Oct. 1	Freddy Archer	Perth Amboy, N. J.	lost	6 rounds
Oct. 27	Benny Williams	Newark	draw	6 rounds
Nov. 3	Vince DeLia	Newark	won	6 rounds
Dec. 16	Eddie Dowl	Perth Amboy, N. J.	won	6 rounds

1942

Mar. 26	Pedro Firpo	Atlantic City	won	8 rounds
Apr. 10	Angelo Panatellas	Atlantic City	k.o.	5 rounds
Apr. 24	Billy Roache	Perth Amboy, N. J.	won	8 rounds
May 7	Abie Kaufman	Atlantic City	won	8 rounds
June 29	Ivan Christie	Newark	k.o.	5 rounds
July 29	Angelo Maglione	Trenton	k.o.	3 rounds
Sept. 10	Charley Davis	Elizabeth, N. J.	won	8 rounds
Oct. 20	Eugene Burton	White Plains, N. Y.	k.o.	4 rounds
Dec. 7	Bob Gunther	Trenton	won	8 rounds
Dec. 21	Sammy Daniels	Baltimore	won	6 rounds
Dec. 31	Ruby Garcia	Atlantic City	won	6 rounds

1943

Jan. 29	Jerry Moore	New York	won	6 rounds
Feb. 22	Sammy Daniels	Philadelphia	k.o.	2 rounds
Feb. 23	Bob McQuillen	Cleveland	k.o.	3 rounds
Mar. 8	Billy Speary	Philadelphia	k.o.	2 rounds
Apr. 2	Rudy Griscombe	New York	k.o.	3 rounds
Apr. 5	Ruby Garcia	Philadelphia	won	8 rounds
Apr. 21	Joey Genovese	Cleveland	k.o.	4 rounds
May 7	Lefty LaChance	Boston	won	8 rounds
May 14	Ray Brown	Philadelphia	won	10 rounds
July 19	Jimmy Hatcher	Philadelphia	k.o.	6 rounds
Aug. 24	Tommy Jessup	Hartford	k.o.	5 rounds
Aug. 31	Johnnie Bellus	Hartford	won	10 rounds
Sept. 13	Jerry Moore	Springfield, Mass.	won	10 rounds
Oct. 1	Lefty LaChance	Boston	k.o.	4 rounds
Oct. 22	Sgt. Ed Perry	New Orleans	k.o.	2 rounds
Oct. 29	Gene Johnson	New Orleans	won	10 rounds
Nov. 8	Johnny Hutchinson	Philadelphia	k.o.	3 rounds
Nov. 29	Willie Cheatham	New Britain, Conn.	won	8 rounds
Dec. 13	Mayo Padlo	Philadelphia	won	10 rounds

1944

Jan. 25	Bob Montgomery	Philadelphia	k.o.	12 rounds
Feb. 28	Ellis Phillips	Philadelphia	k.o.	1 round
Mar. 13	Leo Francis	Trenton	won	8 rounds
Mar. 27	Joey Peralta	Philadelphia	k.o.	9 rounds
Apr. 10	LeRoy Saunders	Holyoke, Mass.	k.o.	5 rounds
Apr. 18	Mike Delia	Philadelphia	k.o.	1 round
May 16	Luther (Slugger) White	Philadelphia	won	10 rounds
June 7	Sammy Angott	Philadelphia	won	10 rounds
June 23	Cleo Shans	New York	k.o.	10 rounds
July 10	Joey Peralta	Philadelphia	k.o.	1 round
July 20	Julie Kogan	New York	won	10 rounds
Aug. 29	Jimmy Hatcher	Washington, D. C.	won	10 rounds
Sept. 6	Sammy Angott	Philadelphia	won	10 rounds
Sept. 19	Freddy Dawson	Philadelphia	k.o.	7 rounds
Oct. 18	Johnny Green	Buffalo	k.o.	2 rounds
Nov. 2	Ruby Garcia	Baltimore	k.o.	7 rounds
Nov. 13	Willie Joyce	Philadelphia	lost	10 rounds
Dec. 5	Lulu Constantino	Cleveland	won	10 rounds
Dec. 11	Dave Castilloux	Buffalo	k.o.	5 rounds

1945

Jan. 8	Willie Joyce	Philadelphia	won	12 rounds
Jan. 22	Maxie Berber	Philadelphia	k.o.	4 rounds
Mar. 2	Willie Joyce	New York	lost	12 rounds
Mar. 26	Dorsey Lay	Philadelphia	k.o.	3 rounds
Apr. 18	Juan Zurita	Mexico City	k.o.	2 rounds
	(NBA Title)			
June 8	Willie Joyce	New York	lost	10 rounds
Aug. 14	Charley Smith	Union City, N. J.	won	10 rounds
Aug. 28	Gene Burton	Philadelphia	won	10 rounds
Sept. 7	Nick Moran	New York	won	10 rounds
Sept. 19	Sammy Angott	Pittsburgh	k.o.	6 rounds
Nov. 26	Wesley Mouzon	Philadelphia	draw	10 rounds

1946

Jan. 8	Charley Smith	Trenton	won	10 rounds
Jan. 20	Johnny Bratton	New Orleans	won	10 rounds
Jan. 28	Freddy Dawson	Philadelphia	draw	10 rounds
Feb. 14	Cleo Shans	Orange, N. J.	won	10 rounds
Feb. 22	Ace Miller	Detroit	won	10 rounds
Mar. 8	Eddie Giosa	Philadelphia	k.o.	14 rounds
Mar. 11	Eddie Giosa	Philadelphia	k.o.	1 round
Apr. 30	Enrique Bolanos (Title)	Los Angeles	k.o.	8 rounds
June 12	Bobby Ruffin	Brooklyn	k.o.	5 rounds
Aug. 6	Ivan Christie	Norwalk, Conn.	k.o.	2 rounds
Sept. 14	Ronnie James (Title)	Cardiff, Wales	k.o.	9 rounds

1947

Jan. 27	Gene Burton	Chicago	lost	10 rounds
Apr. 14	Frankie Conti	Allentown	k.o.	7 rounds
Apr. 25	Willie Russell	Columbus, O.	won	10 rounds
May 9	Ralph Zannelli	Boston	won	10 rounds
May 26	Juste Fontaine	Philadelphia	k.o.	4 rounds
June 22	Tippy Larkin	New York	k.o.	4 rounds
Aug. 4	Bob Montgomery (Title)	Philadelphia	k.o.	6 rounds
Sept. 29	Doll Rafferty	Philadelphia	k.o.	4 rounds
Oct. 10	Talmadge Bussey	Detroit	k.o.	9 rounds
Dec. 12	Tony Pellone	New York	won	10 rounds

RAY ROBINSON—WELTERWEIGHT CHAMPION—1948

1940

Oct. 4	Joe Echeverria	New York City	k.o.	2 rounds
Oct. 8	Silent Stafford	Savannah	k.o.	2 rounds

Oct. 22	Mitsos Grispos	New York	won	6 rounds
Nov. 11	Bobby Woods	Philadelphia	k.o.	1 round
Dec. 9	Norment Quarles	Philadelphia	k.o.	4 rounds
Dec. 12	Oliver White	New York	k.o.	3 rounds
		1941		
Jan. 4	Henry LaBarba	Brooklyn	k.o.	1 round
Jan. 13	Frank Wallace	Philadelphia	k.o.	1 round
Jan. 31	George Zangaras	New York	won	6 rounds
Feb. 8	Ben Cartegena	Brooklyn	k.o.	1 round
Feb. 21	Bobby McIntyre	New York	won	6 rounds
Feb. 27	Gene Spencer	Detroit	k.o.	5 rounds
Mar. 3	Jimmy Tygh	Philadelphia	k.o.	8 rounds
Apr. 14	Jimmy Tygh	Philadelphia	k.o.	1 round
Apr. 24	Charley Burns	Atlantic City	k.o.	1 round
Apr. 30	Joe Ghnouly	Washington, D. C.	k.o.	3 rounds
May 10	Vic Troise	Brooklyn	k.o.	1 round
May 19	Nick Castiglione	Philadelphia	k.o.	1 round
June 16	Mike Evans	Philadelphia	k.o.	2 rounds
July 2	Pete Lello	New York	k.o.	4 rounds
July 21	Sammy Angott	Philadelphia	won	10 rounds
Aug. 27	Carl Guggino	Long Island City	k.o.	3 rounds
Aug. 29	Maurice Arnault	Atlantic City	k.o.	1 round
Sept. 19	Maxie Shapiro	New York	k.o.	3 rounds
Sept. 25	Marty Servo	Philadelphia	won	10 rounds
Oct. 31	Fritzie Zivic	New York	won	10 rounds
		1942		
Jan. 16	Fritzie Zivic	New York	k.o.	10 rounds
Feb. 20	Maxie Berger	New York	k.o.	2 rounds
Mar. 20	Norman Rubio	New York	k.o.	7 rounds
Apr. 17	Harvey Dubs	Detroit	k.o.	6 rounds
Apr. 30	Dick Banner	Minnesota	k.o.	2 rounds
May 28	Marty Servo	New York	won	10 rounds
July 31	Sammy Angott	New York	won	10 rounds
Aug. 21	Ruben Shank	New York	k.o.	2 rounds
Aug. 27	Tony Motisi	Chicago	k.o.	1 round
Oct. 2	Jacob LaMotta	New York	won	10 rounds
Oct. 10	Izzy Jannazzo	Philadelphia	won	10 rounds
Nov. 6	Vic Dellicurti	New York	won	10 rounds
Dec. 1	Izzy Jannazzo	Cleveland	k.o.	8 rounds
Dec. 14	Al Nettlow	Philadelphia	k.o.	3 rounds

1943

Feb. 5	Jacob LaMotta	Detroit	lost	10 rounds
Feb. 19	Jackie Wilson	New York	won	10 rounds
Feb. 26	Jacob LaMotta	Detroit	won	10 rounds
Apr. 30	Freddie Cabral	Boston	k.o.	1 round
July 1	Ralph Zannelli	Boston	won	10 rounds
Aug. 27	Henry Armstrong	New York	won	10 rounds

1944

Oct. 13	Izzy Jannazzo	Boston	k.o.	2 rounds
Oct. 27	Lou Woods	Chicago	k.o.	9 rounds
Nov. 17	Vic Dellicurti	Detroit	won	10 rounds
Dec. 12	Sheik Rangel	Philadelphia	won	10 rounds
Dec. 22	George Martin	Boston	k.o.	7 rounds

1945

Jan. 10	Billy Furrone	Washington, D. C.	k.o.	2 rounds
Jan. 16	Tommy Bell	Cleveland	won	10 rounds
Feb. 14	George Costner	Chicago	k.o.	1 round
Feb. 23	Jake LaMotta	New York	won	10 rounds
May 14	Jose Basora	Philadelphia	draw	10 rounds
June 15	Jimmy McDaniel	New York	k.o.	2 rounds
Sept. 18	Jimmy Mandell	Buffalo	k.o.	5 rounds
Sept. 26	Jacob LaMotta	Chicago	won	12 rounds
Dec. 4	Vic Dellicurti	Boston	won	10 rounds

1946

Jan. 14	Dave Clark	Pittsburgh	k.o.	2 rounds
Feb. 5	Tony Riccio	Elizabeth	k.o.	4 rounds
Feb. 15	O'Neill Bell	Detroit	k.o.	2 rounds
Feb. 26	Cliff Beckett	St. Louis	k.o.	4 rounds
Mar. 4	Sammy Angott	Pittsburgh	won	10 rounds
Mar. 14	Izzy Jannazzo	Baltimore	won	10 rounds
Mar. 21	Fred Flores	New York	k.o.	5 rounds
June 12	Freddy Wilson	Worcester.	k.o	2 rounds
June 25	Norman Rubio	Union City	won	10 rounds
July 12	Joe Curcio	New York	k.o.	2 rounds
Aug. 15	Vinnie Vines	Albany	k.o.	6 rounds
Sept. 25	Sidney Miller	Elizabeth	k.o.	3 rounds
Oct. 7	Ossie Harris	Pittsburgh	won	10 rounds

Nov. 1	Cecil Hudson	Detroit	k.o.	6 rounds
Nov. 6	Artie Devine	Cleveland	k.o.	10 rounds
Dec. 20	Tommy Bell (Title)	New York	won	15 rounds

1947

Mar. 27	Bernie Miller	Miami	k.o.	3 rounds
Apr. 3	Fred Wilson	Akron	k.o.	3 rounds
Apr. 8	Eddie Finazzo	Kansas City	k.o.	4 rounds
May 16	George Abrams	New York	won	10 rounds
June 24	Jimmy Doyle (Title)	Cleveland	k.o.	8 rounds
Aug. 21	Sammy Secreet	Akron	k.o.	1 round
Aug. 29	Flash Sebastian	New York	k.o.	1 round
Oct. 28	Jackie Wilson	Los Angeles	k.o.	7 rounds
Dec. 10	Billy Nixon	Elizabeth	k.o.	6 rounds
Dec. 19	Chuck Taylor (Title)	Detroit	k.o.	6 rounds

JACKIE WILSON—Featherweight Champion—1941
(Jack Benjamin Wilson)
Born, 1909, Arkansas

1940

Feb. 12	Frankie Covelli	Chicago	won	10 rounds
Mar. 31	Harris Blake	New Orleans	lost	10 rounds
Apr. 25	Bobby Green	Lancaster, Pa.	won	10 rounds
June 3	Leo Rodak	Chicago	lost	10 rounds
Aug. 20	Harry Jeffro	Youngstown, O.	lost	10 rounds
Dec. 12	Frank Terranova	Baltimore	won	8 rounds

1941

Jan. 23	Maxie Shapiro	Baltimore, Md.	won	10 rounds
Feb. 11	Joe Marinelli	Youngstown, O.	won	10 rounds
Mar. 31	Matt Perfetti	Baltimore, Md.	won	10 rounds
Apr. 21	Leo Rodak	Baltimore, Md.	lost	10 rounds
July 17	Chalky Wright	Baltimore, Md.	lost	10 rounds
Oct. 27	Leo Rodak	Toledo, O.	lost	10 rounds
Nov. 18	Richie Lemos	Los Angeles	won	12 rounds
	(N. B. A. Featherweight Championship)			
Dec. 16	Richie Lemos	Los Angeles	won	12 rounds

1942

Feb. 20	Abe Denner	Boston	lost	10 rounds
Mar. 2	Terry Young	New York	lost	8 rounds

1943

Jan. 18	Jackie Callura (N. B. A. Title)	Providence	lost	15 rounds
Mar. 18	Jackie Callura (N. B. A. Title)	Boston	lost	15 rounds
Apr. 26	Willie Pep	Pittsburgh	lost	12 rounds
May 17	Danny Petro	Washington	k.o.	10 rounds
June 7	Jimmy Phillips	Washington	won	10 rounds
June 28	Lew Hanbury	Washington	k.o.	7 rounds
July 26	Tony Costa	Providence	won	10 rounds
Aug. 30	Lulu Constantino	Washington	won	10 rounds
Oct. 4	Larry Bolvin	Providence	lost	10 rounds
Oct. 22	Freddie Pope	Cleveland	lost	10 rounds
Dec. 6	Tony Costa	Providence	lost	8 rounds

1944

Sept. 19	Cleo Shans	Washington, D. C.	won	10 rounds
Oct. 17	Pedro Hernandez	Washington, D. C.	lost	10 rounds

1945

Jan. 8	Harry Jeffra	Baltimore	won	10 rounds
Jan. 22	Pedro Hernandez	Washington	won	10 rounds
Mar. 12	Cleo Shans	Baltimore	won	10 rounds
Apr. 7	Chalky Wright	Baltimore	n.c.	7 rounds
June 25	Freddie Russo	Baltimore	lost	10 rounds

1946

Mar. 11	Willie Joyce	Washington	k.o. by	5 rounds
Mar. 26	Willie Pep	Kansas City	lost	10 rounds
May 3	Jackie Graves	Minnesota	lost	8 rounds
June 18	Enrique Bolanos	Los Angeles	k.o. by	7 rounds
Sept. 11	Star Misamis	Oakland	lost	10 rounds
Sept. 24	Star Misamis	Oakland	lost	10 rounds
Oct. 22	Luis Castillo	San Jose	won	10 rounds
Nov. 18	Luis Castillo	San Jose	lost	10 rounds
Dec. 17	Mario Trigo	San Jose	lost	10 rounds

1947

Jan. 8	Speedy Cabanella	Sacramento	lost	10 rounds
Jan. 20	Buddy Jacklich	San Francisco	lost	10 rounds
Apr. 7	Freddie Steele	Vancouver	k.o.	7 rounds
Apr. 25	Manny Ortega	El Paso	k.o. by	10 rounds
May 12	Jackie Turner	Vancouver	lost	10 rounds
May 30	Jackie Turner	Vancouver	lost	10 rounds
Sept. 1	Joey Dolan	Spokane	lost	10 rounds
Sept. 22	Simon Vegara	Ocean Park	k.o. by	9 rounds

CHALKY WRIGHT—Featherweight Champion—1942

(Albert Wright)

Born, February 10, 1912, Durango, Mexico.

1940

Jan. 16	Sammy Julian	Brooklyn	won	8 rounds
Jan. 29	Paul Junior	Portland, Me.	lost	10 rounds
Feb. 19	Frankie Gilmore	Baltimore	won	10 rounds
Feb. 22	Mike Martinez	Baltimore	k.o.	3 rounds
Mar. 11	Charley Gomer	Baltimore	k.o.	4 rounds
Apr. 1	Tommy Speigel	Baltimore	won	10 rounds
Apr. 29	Cocoa Kid	Baltimore	lost	10 rounds
June 24	Saverio Turiello	Baltimore	won	10 rounds
July 15	Joey Silva	Baltimore	k.o.	7 rounds
Aug. 12	Paul Junior	Philadelphia	k.o.	5 rounds
Sept. 9	Joey Fernando	Baltimore	k.o.	4 rounds
Oct. 7	Teddy Baldwin	Philadelphia	k.o.	4 rounds
Dec. 9	Jimmy Leto	Baltimore	lost	10 rounds

1941

Jan. 6	Johnny Williams	New York	k.o.	5 rounds
Jan. 14	Norment Quarles	Jersey City	won	8 rounds
Feb. 4	Norman Rahn	Jersey City	k.o.	2 rounds
Feb. 19	Frank Terranova	Allentown	k.o.	6 rounds
Feb. 24	Maurice Arnault	Baltimore	k.o.	2 rounds
Mar. 6	Texas Lee Harper	Washington	k.o.	3 rounds
Mar. 17	Chas. Schnaupoff	Wilkes-Barre	k.o.	5 rounds
May 1	Charley Varre	New York	won	8 rounds
May 22	Sal Bartolo	New York	won	8 rounds
May 29	Norment Quarles	Atlantic City	won	8 rounds
June 3	Guillermo Puentes	Long Island City	won	8 rounds
June 17	Lloyd Pine	Wilkes-Barre	k.o.	2 rounds
June 24	Bobby McIntire	Long Island City	k.o.	5 rounds
July 17	Jackie Wilson	Baltimore	won	10 rounds
Aug. 5	Pancho Villa	Long Island City	k.o.	6 rounds
Sept. 11	Joey Archibald	Washington	k.o.	11 rounds
Oct. 2	Joey Peralta	Wilkes-Barre	lost	10 rounds
Oct. 14	Leo Rodak	Washington	won	10 rounds
Oct. 31	Ray Lunny	San Francisco	won	10 rounds
Nov. 28	Jess Morales	San Diego	k.o.	6 rounds

1942

Jan. 13	Bobby Ruffin	New York	lost	10 rounds
Feb. 3	Richie Lemos	Los Angeles	k.o.	6 rounds
Feb. 19	Ritchie Fontaine	Oakland	won	10 rounds
Mar. 24	Jorge Morelia	Los Angeles	k.o.	6 rounds
Apr. 6	Vern Bybee	San Francisco	lost	10 rounds
May 7	Lulu Constantino	New York	won	8 rounds
June 19	Harry Jeffra	Baltimore	k.o.	10 rounds

(Title Bout—World Featherweight Championship)

July 13	Lou Transparenti	Baltimore	k.o.	4 rounds
Aug. 6	Allie Stolz	New York	lost	10 rounds
Aug. 15	Curley St. Angelo	Springfield	k.o.	2 rounds
Aug. 27	Joey Marinelli	Detroit	k.o.	2 rounds
Sept. 25	Lulu Constantino	New York	won	15 rounds

(Title Bout—World Featherweight Championship)

Oct. 13	No No Cuebas	Hartford	k.o.	4 rounds
Oct. 20	Henry Vasquez	New Haven	k.o.	8 rounds
Nov. 20	Willie Pep	New York	lost	15 rounds

(Lost the World Featherweight Championship)

1943

Jan. 15	Joe Peralta	New York	won	10 rounds
Feb. 15	Morris Parker	Newark, N. J.	k.o.	4 rounds
Feb. 23	Joe Peralta	St. Louis	won	10 rounds
Mar. 10	Joey Pirrone	Cleveland	k.o.	3 rounds
May 17	Frankie Carto	Baltimore	k.o.	8 rounds
May 25	Billy Pinti	Brooklyn, N. Y.	k.o.	4 rounds
June 4	Phil Terranova	New York	k.o.	5 rounds
July 3	Kid National	Havana, Cuba	k.o.	8 rounds
July 21	Lulu Constantino	Cleveland	lost	10 rounds
Aug. 9	Angel Avila	Washington, D. C.	k.o.	7 rounds
Oct. 26	Patsy Spataro	Brooklyn	k.o.	2 rounds
Nov. 8	Billy Banks	Philadelphia, Pa.	k.o.	5 rounds
Nov. 19	Al Reasoner	New Orleans	k.o.	2 rounds

1944

Jan. 25	Al Brown	Panama	k.o.	5 rounds
Feb. 10	Al Carlos	Panama	k.o.	6 rounds
Mar. 5	Young Finnegan	Panama	draw	10 rounds
May 1	Clyde English	Scranton	k.o	7 rounds
May 22	Sammy Daniels	Baltimore	k.o.	8 rounds
June 5	Vince Del Orto	Washington	k.o.	3 rounds
July 10	Ruby Garcia	Houston	k.o.	8 rounds

July 17	Johnny Cockfield	Norfolk	k.o.	5 rounds
Sept. 29	Willie Pep	New York	lost	15 rounds
	(For Featherweight Title)			
Dec. 5	Willie Pep	Cleveland	lost	10 rounds

1945

Feb. 5	Willie Joyce	Philadelphia	lost	10 rounds
Apr. 9	Jackie Wilson	Baltimore	n.c.	7 rounds
Apr. 17	Willie Joyce	Los Angeles	won	10 rounds
July 31	Henry Jordan	Brooklyn	k.o.	6 rounds
Aug. 28	Enrique Bolanos	Los Angeles	won	10 rounds
Sept. 21	Humberto Zavala	New York	won	10 rounds
Oct. 5	Bobby Ruffin	Detroit	won	10 rounds
Nov. 2	Leroy Willis	Detroit	won	10 rounds
Dec. 14	Johnny Bratton	New Orleans	won	10 rounds

1946

Jan. 25	Pedro Firpo	New York	won	10 rounds
Feb. 19	Enrique Bolanos	Los Angeles	lost	10 rounds
Mar. 5	George Hansford	Milwaukee	k.o.	4 rounds
Mar. 27	Frankie Moore	Oakland	k.o. by	1 round
Apr. 17	Frankie Moore	Oakland	lost	10 rounds
Aug. 27	Johnny Dell	New York	lost	10 rounds
Oct. 15	Enrique Bolanos	Los Angeles	lost	10 rounds
Nov. 27	Willie Pep	Milwaukee	k.o. by	3 rounds

1947

May 25	Frankie Saucedo	Juarez	draw	10 rounds
June 24	Larry Cisneros	Albuquerque	lost	10 rounds

JOE (Sandy) SADDLER—Featherweight Champion—1948

1944

Mar. 7	Earl Roys	Hartford	won	8 rounds
Mar. 21	Jock Leslie	Hartford	k.o. by	3 rounds
Mar. 27	Al King	Holyoke	k.o.	2 rounds
Apr. 17	Joe Landry	Holyoke	k.o.	1 round
May 8	Joe Torres	Trenton	won	6 rounds
May 15	Joe Torres	Holyoke	won	6 rounds
May 23	Domingo Diaz	Jersey City	won	6 rounds
June 13	Joe Torres	Union City	won	8 rounds
June 15	Lou Alter	Ft. Hamilton	lost	6 rounds
June 23	Lou Alter	New York	draw	4 rounds
July 11	Clyde English	Dexter	won	6 rounds

July 18	Ben Saladino	Brooklyn	k.o.	3 rounds
July 25	Al Pennino	Brooklyn	won	6 rounds
Aug. 8	George Know	Brooklyn	k.o.	3 rounds
Aug. 18	Clifford Smith	New York	won	6 rounds
Nov. 11	Manuel Torres	New York	k.o.	6 rounds
Nov. 13	Ken Tomkins	Newark	k.o.	1 round
Nov. 24	Manuel Torres	New York	k.o.	5 rounds
Nov. 28	Percy Lewis	Jersey City	k.o.	1 round
Dec. 12	Young Tony	Jersey City	k.o.	2 rounds
Dec. 16	Earl Mintz	Brooklyn	k.o.	2 rounds
Dec. 26	Midget Mayo	Newark	k.o.	3 rounds

1945

Jan. 13	Tony Oshiro	Brooklyn	won	6 rounds
Jan. 15	Lucky Johnson	Newark	k.o.	1 round
Jan. 22	Joey Puig	New York	k.o.	1 round
Jan. 26	Benny May	New Brunswick	won	6 rounds
Feb. 19	Joe Gatto	New York	k.o.	1 round
Mar. 10	Harold Gibson	Brooklyn	won	6 rounds
Mar. 19	Joe Montiero	New York	k.o.	4 rounds
Mar. 22	George Knox	Camden	k.o.	4 rounds
Apr. 2	Jimmy Allen	Newark	k.o.	1 round
Apr. 19	William Anderson	Detroit	k.o.	5 rounds
Apr. 30	Chillendrina Valencia	Detroit	k.o.	9 rounds
June 18	Caswell Harris	Baltimore	k.o.	3 rounds
June 25	Bobby Washington	Allentown	k.o.	2 rounds
June 29	Leo Methot	New York	k.o.	1 round
July 23	Herbert Jones	Baltimore	k.o.	3 rounds
July 24	Joe Monterro	Brooklyn	k.o.	5 rounds
July 30	Lou Rivers	New York	k.o.	4 rounds
Aug. 16	Louis Langley	Brooklyn	k.o.	1 round
Aug. 20	Bobby English	Providence	k.o.	3 rounds
Aug. 27	Earl Mintz	Providence	k.o.	3 rounds
Sept. 21	Ritchie Myashiro	New York	won	6 rounds
Dec. 2	Benny Daniels	Holyoke	won	6 rounds
Dec. 14	Joe Monterio	Boston	won	8 rounds
Dec. 21	Filberto Osario	New York	won	6 rounds

1946

Jan. 17	Sam Zelman	Orange	k.o.	1 round
Feb. 18	Bob McQuillen	Detroit	lost	10 rounds
Apr. 8	Ralph LaSalle	New York	k.o.	1 round
Apr. 11	John Wolgast	Atlantic City	won	8 rounds

Apr. 25	Pedro Firpo	Atlantic City	won	8 rounds
June 13	Cedric Flournoy	Detroit	k.o.	4 rounds
July 10	George Cooper	Brooklyn	k.o.	7 rounds
July 23	Phil Terranova	Detroit	lost	10 rounds
Aug. 5	Dom Amoroso	Providence	k.o.	2 rounds
Aug. 22	Pedro Firpo	Brooklyn	won	10 rounds
Oct. 10	Jose Rodriguez	Atlantic City	k.o.	3 rounds
Nov. 12	Art Price	Detroit	won	10 rounds
Dec. 9	Clyde English	Holyoke	k.o.	3 rounds
Dec. 26	Lou Marquez	Jamaica	k.o.	2 rounds
Dec. 30	Leonard Caesar	Newark	k.o.	2 rounds

1947

Jan. 20	Dusty Brown	Holyoke	k.o.	4 rounds
Jan. 27	Humberto Zavala	New York	k.o.	7 rounds
Feb. 7	Larry Thomas	Asbury Park	k.o.	2 rounds
Mar. 8	Leonardo Lopez	Mexico City	k.o.	2 rounds
Mar. 29	Carlos Malacara	Mexico City	won	10 rounds
Apr. 14	Charles Lewis	New York	won	10 rounds
May 2	Joe Brown	New Orleans	k.o.	3 rounds
May 9	Melvin Bartholomew	New Orleans	won	10 rounds
June 3	Jimmy Carter	Washington, D. C.	draw	10 rounds
Aug. 14	Leslie Harris	Atlantic City	k.o.	5 rounds
Aug. 29	Miguel Acevedo	New York	k.o.	8 rounds
Sept. 17	Angelo Ambrosano	Jamaica	k.o.	2 rounds
Oct. 3	Humberto Sierra	Minneapolis	lost	10 rounds
Oct. 13	Al Pennino	New York	k.o.	4 rounds
Oct. 26	Lino Garcia	Caracas	k.o.	5 rounds
Nov. 9	El Barquerito	Caracas	k.o.	5 rounds
Dec. 5	Lino Garcia	Havana	k.o.	3 rounds
Dec. 13	Orlando Zuluta	Havana	won	10 rounds

1948

Feb. 2	Charlie Noel	Holyoke	won	10 rounds
Feb. 9	Joey Angelo	New York	won	10 rounds
Mar. 5	Archie Wilmer	New York	won	8 rounds
Mar. 8	Thompson Harmon	Holyoke	k.o.	8 rounds
Mar. 23	Bobby Timpson	Hartford	won	10 rounds
Apr. 10	Luis Monagas	Caracas	k.o.	3 rounds
Apr. 17	Joe Diaz	Caracas	k.o.	8 rounds
Apr. 26	Young Tanner	Aruba	k.o.	5 rounds
May 24	Harry Lassain	Holyoke	won	10 rounds

June 29	Chico Rosa	Honolulu	lost	10 rounds
Aug. 18	Kid Zefine	Panama	k.o.	2 rounds
Aug. 23	Aquilla Allen	Panama	k.o.	2 rounds
Oct. 11	Willie Roache	New Haven	k.o.	3 rounds
Oct. 29	Willie Pep (Title)	New York	k.o.	4 rounds
Nov. 19	Thomas Beato	Bridgeport	k.o.	2 rounds
Nov. 29	Dennis Brady	Boston	won	10 rounds
Dec. 7	Eddie Giosa	Cleveland	k.o.	2 rounds
Dec. 17	Terry Young	New York	k.o.	10 rounds

WINNERS OF "THE RING'S" MERIT AWARD FOR
1928 to 1944

1928—Gene Tunney
1929—Tommy Loughran
1930—Max Schmeling
1931—Tommy Loughran
1932—Jack Sharkey
1933—No Award
1934—Barney Ross and Tony Canzoneri
1935—Barney Ross

1936—Joe Louis
1937—Henry Armstrong
1938—Joe Louis
1939—Joe Louis .
1940—Billy Conn
1941—Joe Louis
1942—Ray Robinson
1943—Fred Apostole
1944—Beau Jack

WORLD TRACK AND FIELD RECORDS

Recognized by the International Amateur Athletic Federation, 1948. (These are records made by colored athletes.)

EVENT	RECORD	HOLDER	WHERE MADE	DATE
100 yds.	9.4 s.	Jesse Owens*	Ann Arbor	May 25, 1935
220 yds.	20.3 s.	Jesse Owens	Ann Arbor	May 25, 1935
		Jesse Owens	Chicago	June 20, 1936
		Lloyd LaBeach	California	
100 mtrs.	10.2 s.	Jesse Owens	Chicago	June 20, 1936
200 mtrs.	20.3 s.	Jesse Owens	Ann Arbor	May 25, 1935
440 yds.	46.3 s.	H. McKenley	Berkeley	June 28, 1948
120 high hurdle	13.6 s.	Harrison Dillard		
220 low hurdle	22.5 s.	Harrison Dillard*		
400 mtrs.	39.8 s.	U. S. Team at Berlin, Aug. 9, 1936 (*Owens, Metcalfe*, Draper, Wykoff)		
16 lbs. shot put	58 ft. ⅛ in.	Charles Fonville	Michigan	April 1948**
Run. br. jump	26 ft. 8¼ in.	Jesse Owens	Ann Arbor	May 25, 1935

*Co-holder of record.
**Applied for.

OLYMPIC RECORDS

EVENT	RECORD	HOLDER	WHERE MADE	DATE
100 mtrs.	10.3 s.	{ Eddie Tolan	Los Angeles	1932
		{ Harrison Dillard	London	1948
200 mtrs.	20.7 s.	Jesse Owens	Berlin	1936
400 mtrs.	46.2 s.	Arthur Wint	London	1948
800 mtrs.	1:49.2 s.	Mal Whitfield	London	1948
High jump	6 ft. $7^{15}/_{16}$ in.	Cornelius Johnson	Berlin	1936
Run. br. jump	26 ft. $5^{5}/_{16}$ in.	Jesse Owens	Berlin	1936
400 m. relay	39.8 s.	(*Owens, Metcalfe,*		
		Draper, Wykoff)	Berlin	1936
High jump	5 ft. $6^{1}/_{8}$ in.	Alice Coachman	London (Women)	1948

OLYMPIC TRACK AND FIELD CHAMPIONS

EVENT	RECORD	WINNER	DATE
100 mtrs.	10.3 s.	Eddie Tolan	1932
	10.3 s.	Jesse Owens	1936
	10.3 s.	Harrison Dillard	1948
200 mtrs.	21.2 s.	Eddie Tolan	1932
	20.7 s.	Jesse Owens	1936
400 mtrs.	46.5 s.	Archie Williams	1936
	46.2 s.	Arthur Wint (Jamaica)	1948
800 mtrs.	1 m. 52.9 s.	John Woodruff	1936
	1 m. 49.2 s.	Mal Whitfield	1948
Run. high jump	6 ft. $7^{15}/_{16}$ in.	Cornelius Johnson	1936
Run. broad jump	24 ft. $5^{1}/_{8}$ in.	DeHart Hubbard	1924
	25 ft. $3/_{4}$ in.	Edward Gordon	1932
	26 ft. $5^{5}/_{16}$ in.	Jesse Owens	1936
	25 ft. 8 in.	Willie Steele	1948
Run. high jump	5 ft. $6^{1}/_{8}$ in. (women)	Alice Coachman	1948

AMERICAN TRACK RECORDS

DISTANCE	TIME	HOLDER	WHERE MADE	DATE
60 yds.	6.1 s. (dirt track)	Ralph Metcalfe	Notre Dame, Ind.	Mar. 11, 1933
		Jesse Owens	Chicago, Ill.	Mar. 9, 1935
		Bill Carter	Indianapolis, Ind.	Mar. 15, 1941
		Ben Johnson	New York City	{ Feb. 5, 1938 { Mar. 12, 1938
		Herbert Thompson	New York City	Feb. 4, 1939

AMERICAN TRACK RECORDS—*Continued*

DISTANCE	TIME	HOLDER	WHERE MADE	DATE
60 yds.	6.1 s.*	Barney Ewell	New York City	Feb. 7, 1942
		Herbert Thompson	New York City	Mar. 14, 1942
		Herbert Thompson	New York City	Mar. 27, 1943
		Edward Conwell	New York City	Feb. 26, 1944
		Edward Conwell	New York City	Mar. 9, 1946
100 yds.	9.4 s.	Jesse Owens	Ann Arbor, Mich.	May 25, 1935
220 yds.	20.3 s.	Jesse Owens	Ann Arbor, Mich.	May 25, 1935
220 yds.	21.2 s. (2)	Ralph Metcalfe	Milwaukee, Wis.	June 2, 1933
300 yds.	29.8 s.	Herbert McKenley	Randall's Island, N. Y.	July 2, 1946
440 yds.	48.1 s.* (dirt track)	Herbert McKenley	Chicago, Ill.	Mar. 9, 1946
600 yds.	1 m. 10.2 s.*	John Borican	New York City	Mar. 8, 1941
880 yds.	1 m. 50.5 s.*	John Borican	New York City	Mar. 25, 1942
880 yds.	1 m. 47.7 s.*(5)	John Woodruff	Hanover, N. H.	Mar. 14, 1940
1000 yds.	2 m. 8.8 s.*	John Borican	New York City	Mar. 11, 1939
1320 yds.	3 m. 2.6 s.*	John Borican	New York City	Feb. 4, 1940
1320 yds.	3 m. 1.2 s.*(5)	John Borican	Hanover, N. H.	Mar. 14, 1940

RUNNING—METRIC DISTANCES

60 mtrs.	6.6 s.*	Jesse Owens	New York City	Feb. 23, 1935
		Ben Johnson	New York City	Feb. 23, 1935 / Feb. 26, 1938
		Herbert Thompson	New York City	Feb. 25, 1939
100 mtrs.	10.2 s.	Jesse Owens	Chicago, Ill.	June 20, 1936
200 mtrs.	20.3 s. (straightaway)	Jesse Owens	Ann Arbor, Mich.	May 25, 1935
400 mtrs.	48.4 s.*(5)	James B. Herbert	Hanover, N. H.	Mar. 14, 1940
600 mtrs.	1 m. 20.3 s.*	James B. Herbert	New York City	Feb. 26, 1938
800 mtrs.	1 m. 48.6 s.	John Woodruff	Compton, Cal.	June 7, 1940
800 mtrs.	1 m. 50 s.*	John Borican	New York City	Mar. 25, 1942
800 mtrs.	1 m. 47.7 s.*(5)	John Woodruff	Hanover, N. H.	Mar. 14, 1940

RELAY RACING

1600 meters (4 × 400)—3 m. 15 s. (long track) New York Univ. (Stanford Braun, Harold Bogrow, James McPoland, *James B. Herbert*) Hanover, N. H., Mar. 14, 1940.

*Indoor records.

1 mile (4 × 440)—3 m. 15 s. (long track) New York Univ. (Stanford Braun, Harold Bogrow, James McPoland, *James B. Herbert*) Hanover, N. H. Mar. 14, 1940.

4 miles (4 × 1 m.)—17 m. 16.1 s. Indiana Univ. (M. Truitt, *J. Smith*, T. Deckard, D. Lash) Philadelphia, April 23, 1937.

HURDLE RACING

220 yds: Ten 2 ft. 6 in. hurdles—22.5 s., Harrison Dillard, Berea, Ohio, June 8, 1946. (Tied record.)

23 s., Around a turn—Harrison Dillard, Minneapolis, Minn., June 22, 1946.

Jumping—Without Weights

Running high jump—Board take-off—*6 ft. 9¼ in., Ed Burke, New York City, Feb. 27, 1937.

Dirt take-off—6 ft. 9¾ in., Melvin Walker, Indianapolis, Ind., Mar. 20, 1937.

Running broad jump—26 ft. 8¼ in., Jesse Owens, Ann Arbor, Mich., May 25, 1935.

*25 ft. 9 in., Jesse Owens, New York City, Feb. 23, 1935.

NOTEWORTHY TRACK PERFORMANCES

The reference numbers define the track formation where events were held. Records made on tracks around a turn prior to March, 1915, were measured 18 inches outward from the inner edge of the border, and since that time have been measured 12 inches from the border.

*Indicates indoor record.   (c) indicates best record by an American citizen.

RUNNING

DISTANCE	TIME	HOLDER	WHERE MADE	DATE
50 yds.	5.1 s.*	Barney Ewell	Philadelphia, Pa.	Feb. 10, 1939
70 yds.	7 s.*	Ralph Metcalfe	Morgantown, W. Va.	Feb. 11, 1933
150 yds.	14.1 s.	Herbert Thompson	Randalls Island, N. Y.	July 17, 1938
200 yds.	18.9 s.	Barney Ewell	Rochester, N. Y.	June 6, 1942
2–3 mile	2 m. 39 s.*	John Borican	New York City	Feb. 1, 1931

RELAY RACING

400 yds. (4 × 100)—37.5 s., United States Team (Russell Sweet, Cy Leland, George Simpson, *Eddie Tolan*), Chicago, Ill., Aug. 27, 1930.

2400 yds. (4 × 600)—4 m. 50.7 s., New York Univ. (George Hagans, Stanford Braun, Leslie MacMitchell, *James B. Herbert*), New York City, May 24, 1940.

WOMEN'S AMERICAN RECORDS

DISTANCE	TIME	HOLDER	WHERE MADE	DATE
50 yd. run	5⅘ s.*	Elizabeth Robinson	Chicago, Ill.	July 27, 1929
50 yd. run (c)	6.1 s.*	Jeannette Jones	Philadelphia, Pa.	Apr. 6, 1940
50 yd. (dirt track)	6 s.*	Elizabeth Robinson	Chicago, Ill.	Mar. 19, 1931
50 mtr. run	6.4 s.	Alice Coachman	Harrisburg, Pa.	July 14, 1944
100 yds. run (c)	10.9 s.	Jean Lane	Cincinnati, Ohio	May 29, 1940
220 yds. run (c)	25.1 s.	Elizabeth Robinson	Milwaukee, Wis.	June 20, 1931
Run. broad jump	(c)18 ft. 1½ in.	Lulu Mae Hymes	Waterbury, Conn.	Sept. 3, 1939

RELAY RACING

440 yds. medley relay (50, 60, 110, 220)—*52.4 s., Mercury A. C. (Pearl V. Edwards, Ila I. Bynce, Gertrude Johnson, Esther P. Dennis), New York, June 26, 1939.

800 mtrs. (4 × 200)—1 m. 49.6 s., Mercury A. C., (Gertrude Johnson, Esther Dennis, Ila I. Bynce, Ivy Wilson), Jersey City, N. J., Oct. 16, 1938.

880 yds. (4 × 220)—1 m. 49.6 s., Mercury A. C., (Gertrude Johnson, Esther Dennis, Ila I. Bynce, Ivy Wilson), Jersey City, N. J., Oct. 16, 1938.

WOMEN'S NOTEWORTHY PERFORMANCES

DISTANCE	TIME	HOLDER	WHERE MADE	DATE
60 yds. (dirt track)	6.9 s.*	Elizabeth Robinson	Oak Park, Ill.	Mar. 27, 1931
70 yds. (dirt track)	7.9 s.*	Elizabeth Robinson	Chicago, Ill.	Mar. 19, 1931

A.A.U. NATIONAL CHAMPIONSHIP RECORD

SENIOR OUTDOOR—MEN

220 yds. (slight curve)	.21 s.	Eddie Tolan, Unat., Detroit, Mich.	1931
Broad jump	26 ft. 3 in.	{ Eulace Peacock, Shore A. C., Belmar, N. J.	1935
		{ Jesse Owens, Ohio State Univ.	1936
Pentathlon	3304 pts.	John Borican, Shore A. C.	1938

RECORDS AT METRIC DISTANCES

100 mtrs. run.	10.3 s.	Barney Ewell, Penn. State College	1941–45
800 mtrs. run.	1 m. 50 s.	John Woodruff, Univ. of Pittsburgh	1937
200 mtrs. hurdles (around turn)	23.3 s.	W. H. Dillard, Baldwin-Wallace College	1946

Appendix 401

SENIOR INDOOR—MEN

60 yds. run.	6.1 s.	Herbert Thompson, Jersey City, Bd. of Rec.	1943
		Edward Conwell, N. Y. U.	1944
75 yds. run.	7⅗ s.	H. P. Drew, Springfield, H. S.	1913
1000 yds. run.	2 m. 10.5 s.	John Borican, Asbury Park A. C.	1942
Medley relay (440, 100, 220, 300)	1 m. 54.4 s.	New York Univ., (*J. Herbert*, J. Fanboner, S. Braun, G. Hagans)	1940
Run. high jump	6 ft. 9¼ in.	Edward T. Burke, Marquette Univ.	1937
Run. broad jump	25 ft. 9 in.	Jesse Owens, Ohio State Univ.	1935

RECORDS AT METRIC DISTANCES

60 mtrs. run.	6.6 s.	Herbert Thompson, Unat., Jersey City	1939
		Jesse Owens, Ohio State Univ.	1935
		Ben Johnson, Columbia Univ.	1935, 1938
600 mtrs. run.	1 m. 20.3 s.	James Herbert, New York Univ.	1938
Medley relay (400, 100, 200, 300)	1 m. 59.7 s. (heat)	New York Curb Exchange A. A. (*J. Herbert*, H. Hoffman, E. O'Sullivan, G. Dee)	1937
100 mtrs. run.	10.4 s.	James Johnson, Illinois State Nor,	1933
		Eddie Morris, So. Cal. A. A.	1940

SENIOR OUTDOOR—WOMEN

50 yds. run.	5⅘ s.	Betty Robinson, Illinois W.A.C.	July 27, 1929
50 mtrs. run.	6.4 s.	Alice Coachman, Tuskegee Inst.	July 8, 1944
200 mtrs. run.	26 s.	Gertrude Johnson, Mercury A. C.	Sept. 25,1937

A.A.U. NATIONAL TRACK CHAMPIONS
SENIOR OUTDOOR MEN
100 Yards Run—100 Meters

1912	H. P. Drew	Springfield (Mass.) High School		10 s.
1913	H. P. Drew	Springfield (Mass.) High School		10⅖ s.
1916	A. E. Ward	Chicago A. A.		10 s.
1917	A. E. Ward	Chicago A. A.		10⅕ s.
1929	Eddie Tolan	University of Michigan		10 s.
1930	Eddie Tolan	Univeristy of Michigan		9.7 s.
1932	Ralph Metcalfe	Marquette University	(100 mtrs.)	10.6 s.

100 Yard Run—100 Meters—Continued

1933	Ralph Metcalfe	Marquette University	(100 mtrs.)	10.5 s.
1934	Ralph Metcalfe	Marquette University	(100 mtrs.)	10.4 s.
1935	Eulace Peacock	Shore A. C. Belmar, N. J.	(100 mtrs.)*	10.2 s.
1936	Jesse Owens	Ohio State University	(100 mtrs.)	10.4 s.
1938	Ben Johnson	N. Y. Curb Exchange A. A.	(100 mtrs.)	10.7 s.
1941	Barney Ewell	Penn. State College	(100 mtrs.)	10.3 s.
1944	Claude Young	University of Illinois	(100 mtrs.)	10.5 s.
1945	Barney Ewell	Camp Kilmer, N. J.	(100 mtrs.)	10.3 s.
1946	Bill Mathis	University of Illinois	(100 mtrs.)	10.7 s.
1947	Bill Mathis	University of Illinois	(100 mtrs.)	10.5 s.
1948	Barney Ewell	Unattached	(100 mtrs.)	10.6 s.

*With wind

220 Yards Run—200 Meters

1913	H. P. Drew	Springfield (Mass.) High School		22⅘ s.
1914	I. T. Howe	Unattached, Boston		22⅕ s.
1916	A. E. Ward	Chicago A. A.		21⅗ s.
1917	A. E. Ward	Chicago A. A.		22⅕ s.
1929	Eddie Tolan	University of Michigan		21.9 s.
1931	Eddie Tolan	Unattached, Detroit		21. s.
1932	Ralph Metcalfe	Marquette University	(200 mtrs.)	21.5 s.
1933	Ralph Metcalfe	Marquette University	(200 mtrs.)	21.1 s.
1934	Ralph Metcalfe	Marquette University	(200 mtrs.)*	21.3 s.
1935	Ralph Metcalfe	Marquette Univ. Club	(200 mtrs.)*	21. s.
1936	Ralph Metcalfe	Marquette Univ. Club	(200 mtrs.)	21.2 s.
1938	Mack Robinson	University of Oregon	(200 mtrs.)	21.3 s.
1939	Barney Ewell	Penn. State Col.	(200 mtrs.)	21. s.
1945	Elmore Harris	Shore A. C., N. J.	(200 mtrs.)	21.9 s.
1946	Barney Ewell	Shanahan Catholic Club, Phil.	(200 mtrs.)	21.2 s.
1947	Barney Ewell	Shanahan Catholic Club, Phil.	(200 mtrs.)	21. s.
1948	Lloyd LaBeach	California	(200 mtrs.)	21. s.

440 Yards Run—400 Meters

1925	Cecil G. Cooke	Salem-Crescent A. C., New York		49.2 s.
1944	Elmore Harris	Shore A. C., Long Branch	(400 mtrs.)	48. s.
1945	Herbert McKenley	Unattached, Boston	(400 mtrs.)	48.4 s.
1946	Elmore Harris	Shore A. C., N. J.	(400 mtrs.)	46.3 s.
1947	Herbert McKenley	Unattached, Boston	(400 mtrs.)	47.1 s.
1948	Herbert McKenley	Unattached, Boston	(400 mtrs.)	46.3 s.

880 Yards Run—800 Meters

1929	Phil Edwards	New York Univ.		1 m. 55.7 s.
1937	John Woodruff	Univ. of Pittsburgh	(800 mtrs.)	1 m. 50 s.
1942	John Borican	Asbury Park A. C.	(800 mtrs.)	1 m. 51.2 s.

1944	Robert Kelly	Univ. of Illinois	(800 mtrs.) 1 m. 51.8 s.
1945	Robert Kelly	Univ. of Illinois	(800 mtrs.) 1 m. 54.1 s.
1947	Reginald Pearman	New York University	(800 mtrs.) 1 m. 50.9 s.

Five Mile Run

1921	R. E. Johnson	E. Thompson S.W.A.A., Pittsburgh	25 m. 53 3/5 s.
1922	R. E. Johnson	E. Thompson S.W.A.A., Pittsburgh	25 m. 33 s.
1923	R. E. Johnson	E. Thompson S.W.A.A., Pittsburgh	26 m. 52 s.

Ten Mile Run—15 Kilometers

1921	R. E. Johnson	E. Thomson S.W.A.A., Pittsburgh	53 m. 20 4/5 s.
1924	R. E. Johnson	E. Thomson S.W.A.A., Pittsburgh	54 m. 29 3/5 s.
1930	Gus Moore	Brooklyn Harriers A.A.	55 m. 21 s.

Senior Cross-Country—Individual

1928	Gus Moore	Brooklyn Harriers A. A.	31 m. 18 s.
1929	Gus Moore	University of Pittsburgh	31 m. 10 s.
1942	Frank Dixon	New York Univ.	31 m. 52 s.

120 Yards High Hurdles—110 Meters

1946	Harrison Dillard	Baldwin-Wallace College	(110 mtrs.) 14.2 s.
1947	Harrison Dillard	Baldwin-Wallace College	(110 mtrs.) 14 s.

220 Yards Low Hurdles—200 Meters

1944	Elmore Harris	Shore A. C., L. Branch, N. J.	(200 mtrs.) 24.1 s.
1946	Harrison Dillard	Baldwin-Wallace College	(200 mtrs.) 23.3 s.
1947	Harrison Dillard	Baldwin-Wallace College	(200 mtrs.) 23.3 s.

Running High Jump

1932	Cornelius Johnson	Los Angeles H. S.	6 ft. 6 5/8 in.
1933	Cornelius Johnson	Los Angeles H. S.	6 ft. 7 in.
1934	Cornelius Johnson	Compton (Cal.) Junior Col.	6 ft. 8 5/8 in.
1935	Cornelius Johnson	Compton (Cal.) Junior Col.	6 ft. 7 in.
1936	* Cornelius Johnson	Compton (Cal.) Junior Col.	
	Melvin Walker	Ohio State Univ.	6 ft. 8 in.
	David Albritton	Ohio State Univ.	
1937	David Albritton	Ohio State Univ.	6 ft. 8 5/8 in.
1938*	Melvin Walker	Unattached, Toledo, Ohio	6 ft. 7 in.
	David Albritton	Ohio State Univ.	
1942	Adam Berry	Southern Univ.	6 ft. 7 in.
1945	David Albritton	Unattached, Dayton, Ohio	6 ft. 5 3/4 in.
	Joshua Williamson	Camp Plauche, La.	6 ft. 5 3/4 in.
1946	David Albritton	Dayton A. C., Ohio	6 ft. 6 7/8 in.
1947	David Albritton	Unattached	6 ft. 6 in.

*Won on either, jump-off or fewer misses.

Running Broad Jump

1920	Sol Butler	Dubuque (Iowa) College	24 ft. 8 in.
1921	E. O. Gourdin	Harvard University	23 ft. 7¾ in.
1922	DeHart Hubbard	Unattached, Cincinnati	24 ft. 5⅛ in.
1923	DeHart Hubbard	Univ. of Michigan	24 ft. 7¾ in.
1924	DeHart Hubbard	Univ. of Michigan	24 ft.
1925	DeHart Hubbard	Unattached	*25 ft. 4⅜ in.
1926	DeHart Hubbard	Century A. C., N. Y.	25 ft. 2½ in.
1927	DeHart Hubbard	Unattached	25 ft. 8¾ in.
1929	Edward I. Gordon, Jr.	Univ. of Iowa	24 ft. 4¼ in.
1932	Edward Gordon	Univ. of Iowa	25 ft. 3⅜ in.
1933	Jesse Owens	East Tech. H. S., Cleveland	24 ft. 6⅜ in.
1934	Jesse Owens	Ohio State Univ.	25 ft. ⅞ in.
1935	Eulace Peacock	Shore A. C., Belmar, N. J.	26 ft. 3 in.
1936	Jesse Owens	Ohio State Univ.	26 ft. 3 in.
1937	Kermit King	Pittsburg (Kan.) Teachers Col.	25 ft. 1½ in.
1938	William Lacefield	Univ. of Cal. at Los Angeles	25 ft. 3⁄10 in.
1939	William Lacefield	Unattached, Los Angeles	25 ft. 5½ in.
1945	Herbert Douglas	Unattached, Pittsburgh, Pa.	24 ft. ⅛ in.
1946	William Steele	San Diego State College	24 ft.
1947	William Steele	San Diego State College	24 ft. 9¼ in.
1948	Fred Johnson	Michigan State College	25 ft. 4½ in.

*With Wind.

Running Hop, Step and Jump

1922	DeHart Hubbard	Unattached, Cincinnati	48 ft. 1½ in.
1923	DeHart Hubbard	Univ. of Michigan	47 ft. ½ in.
1944	Don Barksdale	Camp Lee, Va.	47 ft. 2⅞ in.

Throwing the Discus

1941	Archie Harris	Unattached, New Jersey	167 ft. 9½ in.

Putting 16-Lb. Shot

1939	Lilburn Williams	Xavier Univ., New Orleans	53 ft. 7 in.

A.A.U. ALL–ROUND CHAMPIONS

1942	Joshua Williamson	Asbury Park (N. J.) A. C.	6031 points

DECATHLON CHAMPIONS

1941	John Borican	Asbury Park A. C.	5666 points
1943	William Watson	Detroit Police A. A.	5994 points

PENTATHLON CHAMPIONS

1921	Edw. Gourdin	Harvard Univ.	12 points
1922	Edw. Gourdin	Unattached, Boston	10 points
1933	Eulace Peacock	Shore A. C. (N. J.)	3221.85 points
1934	Eulace Peacock	Shore A. C. (N. J.)	3258.46 points
1937	Eulace Peacock	Temple Univ.	3030 points
1938	John Borican	Shore A. C., Elberon, N. J.	3304 points
1939	John Borican	Shore A. C., Elberon, N. J.	2947 points
1941	John Borican	Asbury Park A. C.	3244 points
1943	Eulace Peacock	U.S.C.G., Manhattan Beach	3225 points
1944	Eulace Peacock	U.S.C.G., New York	2852 points
1945	Eulace Peacock	U.S.C.G., New York	3148 points

SENIOR CHAMPIONS—INDOOR—MEN

1933	Ralph Metcalfe	Marquette University	(60 mtrs.) 6.7 s.
1934	Ralph Metcalfe	Marquette University	(60 mtrs.) 6.7 s.
1935	Ben Johnson	Columbia University	(60 mtrs.) 6.6 s.
1936	Ralph Metcalfe	Marquette Univ. Club	(60 mtrs.) 6.7 s.
1937	Ben Johnson	Columbia University	(60 mtrs.) 6.8 s.
1938	Ben Johnson	Columbia University	(60 mtrs.) 6.6 s.
1939	Herbert Thompson	Unattached	(60 mtrs.) 6.6 s.
1940	Mozelle Ellerbe	Tuskegee Institute	(60 yds.) 6.2 s.
1941	Herbert Thompson	Unattached	(60 yds.) 6.2 s.
1942	Barney Ewell	Penn. State	(60 yds.) 6.2 s.
1943	Herbert Thompson	Jersey City Dpt. of Rec.	(60 yds.) 6.1 s.
1944	Ed Conwell	New York University	(60 yds.) 6.1 s.
1945	Corp. Barney Ewell	Camp Kilmer, N. J.	(60 yds.) 6.2 s.
1946	Thos. A. Carey	N. Y. Pioneer Club	(60 yds.) 6.3 s.
1947	Ed Conwell	Unattached, N. Y.	(60 yds.) 6.1 s.
1948	William Mathis	Unattached, N. Y.	(60 yds.) 6.1 s.

75 YARDS RUN

1913	H. P. Drew	Springfield H. S.	7.6 s.

600 YARDS RUN—600 METERS

1928	Phil Edwards	New York University	1 m. 14.2 s.
1929	Phil Edwards	New York University	1 m. 12 s.
1930	Phil Edwards	Hamilton Olympic Club	1 m. 13.6 s.
1931	Phil Edwards	Hamilton Olympic Club	1 m. 12.6 s.
1938	James Herbert	New York University (600 mtrs.)	1 m. 20.3 s.
1941	James Herbert	Grand Street Boys' Assn.	1 m. 12 s.
1943	Lewis Smith	Prairie View (Tex.) College	1 m. 13 s.

600 *Yards Run—600 Meters—Continued*

1945	Elmore T. Harris	Shore A. C., N. J.	1 m. 13.2 s.
1946	Elmore T. Harris	Shore A. C., N. J.	1 m. 12.9 s.
1948	David Bolen	Unattached, N. Y.	1 m. 11.8 s.

1000 YARDS RUN—1000 METERS

1939	John Borican	Shore A. C.	(1000 mtrs.) 2 m. 28.6 s.
1940	John Borican	Shore A. C.	2 m. 13 s.
1941	John Borican	Shore A. C.	2 m. 11.5 s.
1942	John Borican	Asbury Park A. C.	2 m. 10.5 s.
1948	Phil Thigpen	Seton Hall	2 m. 16.4 s.

1 MILE RUN—1500 METERS

1943	Frank Dixon	New York University	4 m. 09.6 s.

60 YARDS HIGH HURDLES

1944	Edward Dugger	Unattached, Dayton, Ohio	7.5 s.
1945	Edward Dugger	Unattached, Dayton, Ohio	7.5 s.
1946	Edward Dugger	Unattached, Dayton, Ohio	7.6 s.
1947	Harrison Dillard	Baldwin-Wallace College	7.4 s.
1948	Harrison Dillard	Baldwin-Wallace College	7.2 s.

60 YARDS LOW HURDLES

1944	Edward Dugger	Unattached, Dayton, Ohio	7.2 s.
1946	Edward Dugger	Unattached, Dayton, Ohio	7 s.
1947	Harrison Dillard	Baldwin-Wallace College	6.9 s.

RUNNING HIGH JUMP

1927	C. W. Major	St. Bonaventure College	6 ft. 4⅛ in.
1935	Cornelius Johnson	Compton Jr. College	6 ft. 7 in.
1936	Ed Burke / Cornelius Johnson	Marquette University / Compton J. C.	} 6 ft. 8¹⁵⁄₁₆ in.
1937	Ed Burke	Marquette University	6 ft. 9¼ in.
1938	Lloyd Thompson / Cornelius Johnson / Mel Walker	Xavier University / Compton J. C. / Grand Street Boys	} 6 ft. 6 in.
1939	Mel Walker	Unattached, Toledo, Ohio	6 ft. 8 in.
1941	Mel Walker	Tennessee State A. A.	6 ft. 6½ in.
1942	Joshua Williamson	Asbury Park A. C.	6 ft. 6½ in.
	Adam Berry	Southern University	6 ft. 6½ in.
1943	Pvt. Joshua Williamson	Camp Pickett, Va.	6 ft. 6 in.
1944	David Albritton	Unattached, Dayton, Ohio	6 ft. 6 in.
1945	Sgt. Joshua Williamson	Camp Plauche, La.	6 ft. 6 in.

RUNNING BROAD JUMP

1932	Everett Utterback	Pittsburgh University	23 ft. 8 in.
1934	Jesse Owens	Unattached, Columbus, Ohio	25 ft. 3¼ in.
1935	Jesse Owens	Ohio State University	25 ft. 9 in.
1936	Sammy Richardson	Achilles Club, Toronto	24 ft. 3 in.
1937	Sammy Richardson	Achilles Club, Totonto	24 ft. 7⅜ in.
1938	Edward Gordon, Jr.	Grand Street Boys	23 ft. 4 in.
1939	Edward Gordon, Jr.	Grand Street Boys	23 ft. 10⅛ in.
1943	Pvt. Barney Ewell	Camp Lee, Va.	23 ft. 8 in.
1944	Barney Ewell	Camp Lee, Va.	26 ft. 6 in.
1945	Corp. Barney Ewell	Camp Kilmer, N. J.	23 ft. 11 in.
1946	Samuel Richardson	N. Y. Pioneer Club	24 ft. 3⅜ in.
1947	Herbert Douglas	University of Pittsburgh	24 ft. 5⅛ in.

OUTDOOR—WOMEN CHAMPIONS

50 METERS

1933	Louise Stokes	Onteora Club, Malden, Mass.	6.6 s.
1935	Louise Stokes	Onteora Club	6.7 s.
1936	Ivy Wilson	Mercury A. C., New York	6.7 s.
1939	Gertrude Johnson	Mercury A. C.	6.7 s.
1940	Jean Lane	Wilberforce University	6.6 s.
1941	Lucy Newell	Tuskegee Institute	6.6 s.
1942	Jeanette Jones	Harrisburg A. A.	6.7 s.
1943	Alice Coachman	Tuskegee Institute	6.5 s.
1944	Alice Coachman	Tuskegee Institute	6.4 s.
1945	Alice Coachman	Tuskegee Institute	6.5 s.
1946	Alice Coachman	Tuskegee Institute	6.5 s.
1947	Alice Coachman	Albany State College	6.8 s.
1948	Juanita Watson	Tuskegee	6.5 s.

100 METERS

1938	Lula Hymes	Tuskegee Institute	12.4 s.
1940	Jean Lane	Wilberforce University	12 s.
1941	Jean Lane	Wilberforce University	12.4 s.
1942	Alice Coachman	Tuskegee Institute	12.1 s.
1945	Alice Coachman	Tuskegee Institute	12 s.
1946	Alice Coachman	Tuskegee Institute	12.3 s.
1947	Juanita Watson	Tuskegee Institute	13.1 s.

200 METERS

1937	Gertrude Johnson	Mercury A. C.	26 s.
1941	Jean Lane	Wilberforce University	25.2 s.
1948	Audrey Patterson	Tennessee State College	26.4 s.

80 METER HURDLES

1937	Cora Gaines	Tuskegee Institute	12.8 s.
1941	Leila Perry	Tuskegee Institute	13.2 s.
1942	Lillie Purifoy	Tuskegee Institute	12.6 s.
1944	Lillie Purifoy	Tuskegee Institute	12.8 s.
1945	Lillie Purifoy	Tuskegee Institute	12.5 s.

RUNNING HIGH JUMP

1939	Alice Coachman	Tuskegee Institute	5 ft. 2 in.
1940	Alice Coachman	Tuskegee Institute	4 ft. 11 in.
1941	Alice Coachman	Tuskegee Institute	5 ft. 2¾ in.
1942	Alice Coachman	Tuskegee Institute	4 ft. 8 in.
1943	Alice Coachman	Tuskegee Institute	5 ft.
1944	Alice Coachman	Tuskegee Institute	5 ft. 1⅝ in.
1945	Alice Coachman	Tuskegee Institute	5 ft.
1946	Alice Coachman	Tuskegee Institute	5 ft.
1947	Alice Coachman	Albany State College	5 ft. 1 in.
1948	Emma Reed	Tennessee State College	4 ft. 11⅜ in.

RUNNING BROAD JUMP

1936	Mable Smith	Tuskegee Institute	18 ft.
1937	Lula Hymes	Tuskegee Institute	17 ft. 8½ in.
1938	Lula Hymes	Tuskegee Institute	17 ft. 2 in.
1947	Lillie Purifoy	Tuskegee Institute	17 ft. 6 in.

DISCUS THROW

1944	Hattie Turner	Tuskegee Institute	101 ft. 7¾ in.

BASEBALL THROW

1944	Hattie Turner	Tuskegee Institute	214 ft. 6 in.

INDOOR SENIOR—WOMEN CHAMPIONS

50 METERS RUN

1941	Jean Lane	Wilberforce University	6.8 s.
1945	Alice Coachman	Tuskegee Institute	6.1 s.
1946	Alice Coachman	Tuskegee Institute	6.4 s.
1948	Juanita Watson	Tuskegee Institute	6.5 s.

200 METERS RUN

1941	Jean Lane	Wilberforce University	25.1 s.
1948	Audrey Patterson	Tennessee State College	26.4 s.

50 Yard Hurdles

1946	Lillie Purifoy	Tuskegee Institute	7.8 s.

50 Meters Hurdles

1941	Lillie Purifoy	Tuskegee Institute	8.1 s.

440 Yards Relay

1945	TUSKEGEE INSTITUTE	(Nell Jackson, Lillie Purifoy, Rowena Harrison, Alice Coachman)	53.6 s.
1946	TUSKEGEE INSTITUTE	(Mabel Walker, Jewel Johnson, Nancy Carter, Juanita Watson)	1 m. 1 s.

400 Meters Relay

1941	TUSKEGEE INSTITUTE	(Lucy Newell, Leila Perry, Hester Brown, Rowena Harrison)	50.1 s.
1948	TUSKEGEE INSTITUTE	(Hayes, Taylor, Watson, Jackson)	51.8 s.

Running High Jump

1941	Alice Coachman	Tuskegee Institute	5 ft. 1 in.
1945	Alice Coachman	Tuskegee Institute	4 ft. 8 in.
1946	Alice Coachman	Tuskegee Institute	4 ft. 6⅞ in.
1948	Emma Reed	Tennessee State College	4 ft. 11⅜ in.

Standing Broad Jump

1941	Lucy Newell	Tuskegee Institute	8 ft. 1⅞ in.

NATIONAL COLLEGIATE TRACK CHAMPIONS (COLORED)
1921–1946
100 Yards

YEAR	TIME	NAME	SCHOOL
1925	9.8 s.	Hubbard	Michigan
1932	9.5 s.	Metcalfe	Marquette
1933	9.4 s.	Metcalfe	Marquette
1934	9.7 s.	Metcalfe	Marquette
1935	9.8 s.	Owens	Ohio State
1936	9.4 s.	Owens	Ohio State
1938	9.7 s.	Ellerbe	Tuskegee
1939	9.8 s.	Ellerbe	Tuskegee
1940	9.6 s.	Ewell	Penn. State
1941	9.6 s.	Ewell	Penn. State
1944	9.7 s.	Young	Illinois
1946	9.6 s.	Mathis	Illinois

220 YARDS

YEAR	TIME	NAME	SCHOOL
1931	21.5 s.	Tolan	Michigan
1932	20.5 s.	Metcalfe	Marquette
1933	20.4 s.	Metcalfe	Marquette
1934	20.9 s.	Metcalfe	Marquette
1935	21.5 s.	Owens	Ohio State
1936*	21.3 s.	Owens	Ohio State
1937	21.3 s.	Johnson	Columbia
1938	21.3 s.	Robinson	Oregon
1940	21.1 s.	Ewell	Penn. State
1941	21.1 s.	Ewell	Penn. State
1944	21.6 s.	Young	Illinois
1946	21.3 s.	McKenley	Illinois
1947	20.7 s.	McKenley	Illinois
1948	21.1 s.	La Beach	California

440 YARDS

1931	48.3 s.	Williams	So. Calif.
1935	47.7 s.	Luvalle	UCLA.
1936*	47 s.	Williams	California
1944	47.9 s.	Harris	Morgan State
1946	47.5 s.	McKenley	Illinois
1947	46.2 s.	McKenley	Illinois

880 YARDS

1937	1 m. 50.3 s.	Woodruff	Pittsburgh
1938	1 m. 51.3 s.	Woodruff	Pittsburgh
1939	1 m. 51.3 s.	Woodruff	Pittsburgh
1944	1 m. 55.1 s.	Kelley	Illinois
1946	1 m. 52.6 s.	Smith	Va. Union
1948	1 m. 51.1 s.	Whitfield	Ohio State

120 YARDS HIGH HURDLES

1940	13.9 s.	Dugger	Tufts
1941	14 s.	Wright	Ohio State
1942	14.2 s.	Wright	Ohio State
1945	14.9 s.	Walker	Illinois
1946	14.1 s.	Dillard	Baldwin Wal.
1947	14.1 s.	Dillard	Baldwin Wal.

*Around turn—new record.

220 Yards Low Hurdles

YEAR	TIME	NAME	SCHOOL
1935	23.4 s.	Owens	Ohio State
1936	23.1 s.	Owens	Ohio State
1941	23.4 s.	Wright	Ohio State
1942	23.7 s.	Wright	Ohio State
1944	23.9 s.	Harris	Morgan State
1945	24 s.	Walker	Illinois
1946	23 s.	Dillard	Baldwin-Wal.
1947	22.3 s.	Dillard	Baldwin-Wal.

400 Meters Hurdles

1948	52.4 s.	Walker	Illinois

High Jump

1928	6 ft. 6⅝ in.	King	Stanford
1936	6 ft. 6⅛ in.	Albritton	Ohio State
1936	6 ft. 6⅛ in.	Walker	Ohio State
1937	6 ft. 6¼ in.	Albritton	Ohio State
1937	6 ft. 6¼ in.	Cruter	Colorado
1938	6 ft. 8⅜ in.	Albritton	Ohio State
1938	6 ft. 8⅜ in.	Cruter	Colorado
1942	6 ft. 7¾ in.	Berry	Southern

Broad Jump

1923	25 ft. 2 in.	Hubbard	Michigan
1925	25 ft. 10⅞ in.	Hubbard	Michigan
1929	24 ft. 8½ in.	Gordon	Iowa
1930	25 ft.	Gordon	Iowa
1931	24 ft. 11⅜ in.	Gordon	Iowa
1933	24 ft. 4¾ in.	Brooks	Chicago
1935	26 ft. 1⅜ in.	Owens	Ohio State
1936	25 ft. 10⅞ in.	Owens	Ohio State
1937	25 ft. 3¼ in.	King	Kansas S.
1938	25 ft. 1⅛ in.	Lacefield	UCLA.
1940	24 ft. 10¼ in.	Robinson	UCLA.
1947	26 ft. 6 in.	Steele	San Diego State
1948	24 ft. 11⅛ in.	Steele	San Diego State

Shot Put

1948	54 ft. 10⅞ in.	Fonville	Michigan
1948	54 ft. 7 in.	Fonville	Michigan

Javelin

1932	215 ft.	Williams	Hampton

The Negro in Sports

INTERCOLLEGIATE ASSOCIATION OF AMATEUR ATHLETES
OF AMERICA CHAMPIONS (COLORED) (*IC–4A*)
1876–1947 OUTDOORS

100 YARDS

YEAR	TIME	NAME	SCHOOL
1937	9.8 s.	Johnson	Columbia
1940	9.7 s.	Ewell	Penn. State
1941	9.6 s.	Ewell	Penn. State
1942	9.5 s. *	Ewell	Penn. State
1944	9.8 s.	Conwell	N. Y. U.
1946	9.7 s.	Douglas	Pittsburgh

220 YARDS

1937	21.2 s.	Johnson	Columbia
1940	20.9 s.	Ewell	Penn. State
1941	20.7 s.	Ewell	Penn. State
1942	20.5 s. *	Ewell	Penn. State

440 YARDS

1904	49.2 s.	Taylor	Pennsylvania
1907	48.8 s.	Taylor	Pennsylvania
1908	52.2 s.	Taylor	Pennsylvania
1926	48.8 s.	Cooke	Syracuse
1933	46.9 s.	Luvalle	UCLA.
1935	47 s.	Luvalle	UCLA.
1937	47 s.	Woodruff	Pittsburgh
1938	47 s.	Woodruff	Pittsburgh
1939	47 s.	Woodruff	Pittsburgh
1940	48.1 s.	Herbert	N. Y. U.

880 YARDS

1928	1 m. 56.8 s.	Edwards	N. Y. U.
1929	1 m. 52.2 s.	Edwards	N. Y. U.
1937	1 m. 52.1 s.	Woodruff	Pittsburgh
1938	1 m. 53.5 s.	Woodruff	Pittsburgh
1939	1 m. 51.5 s.	Woodruff	Pittsburgh
1947	1 m. 51.5 s.	Pearman	N. Y. U.

ONE MILE RUN

1945	4 m. 29.4 s.	Simms	N. Y. U.

* Record not allowed because of wind.

120 YARD HIGH HURDLES

YEAR	TIME	NAME	SCHOOL
1940	14.3 s.	Dugger	Tufts
1941	14.1 s.	Dugger	Tufts

220 YARD LOW HURDLES

1940	23.2 s.	Dugger	Tufts
1943	24.1 s.	Halliburton	N. Y. U.
1947	23.7 s.	Johnson	Mich. State

HIGH JUMP

| 1937 | 6 ft. 5⅛ in. | Burke | Marquette |

BROAD JUMP

1921	23 ft. 10¾ in.	Gourdin	Harvard
1937	23 ft. 6½ in.	Johnson	Columbia
1940	23 ft. 8¼ in.	Ewell	Penn. State
1941	24 ft. 2¾ in.	Ewell	Penn. State
1942	24 ft. 6¼ in.	Ewell	Penn. State
1946	23 ft. 11 in.	Douglas	Pittsburgh
1947	24 ft. 7⅜ in.	Johnson	Mich. State

16 POUND SHOTPUT

| 1912 | 162 ft. 4½ in. | Cable | Harvard |
| 1913 | 156 ft. | Cable | Harvard |

IC–4A INDOOR TRACK AND FIELD CHAMPIONS 1922–1947
(COLORED)

60-YARD DASH

1937	6.3 s.	Johnson	Columbia
1938	6.3 s.	Johnson	Columbia
1940	6.3 s.	Ewell	Penn. State
1942	6.2 s.	Carter	Pittsburgh
1943	6.3 s.	Conwell	N. Y. U.
1944	6.3 s.	Conwell	N. Y. U.

50-METER DASH

| 1935 | 5.9 s. | Johnson | Columbia |
| 1936 | 6 s. | Thomas | Pittsburgh |

60 YARD HIGH HURDLES

1940	7.3 s.	Dugger	Tufts
1941	7.4 s.	Dugger	Tufts
1947	7.5 s.	Haliburton	N. Y. U.

600 YARD RUN

YEAR	TIME	NAME	SCHOOL
1940	1 m. 11.2 s.	Herbert	N. Y. U.

1000 YARD RUN

1940	2 m. 17.2 s.	Callender (S.)	N. Y. U.

IC–4A CROSS COUNTRY CHAMPIONS

1942	27 m. 8.4 s.	Dixon	N. Y. U.

HIGH JUMP

YEAR	HT. OR DIST.	NAME	SCHOOL
1945	6 ft. 3 in.	Robeson	Cornell
1946	6 ft. 4 in.	Robeson	Cornell

BROAD JUMP

1930	23 ft. 5¼ in.	Utterback	Pittsburgh
1931	23 ft. 9⅜ in.	Utterback	Pittsburgh
1935	23 ft. 11¹⁄₁₆ in.	Johnson	Columbia
1937	24 ft. ⅛ in.	Johnson	Columbia
1940	24 ft. 8⅛ in.	Ewell	Penn. State
1942	25 ft. 2½ in.	Ewell	Penn. State
1946	24 ft. 2 in.	Douglas	Pittsburgh
1947	24 ft. 2⅞ in.	Douglas	Pittsburgh

1C–4A OUTDOOR CHAMPIONSHIP RECORDS
(By Colored Athletes)

EVENT	RECORD	HOLDER	WHERE MADE	DATE
100 yd. dash	9.6 s.	Barney Ewell	Penn. State	May 31, 1941
			(co-holder)	May 29, 1942
100 mtr. dash	10.5 s.	Benjamin W. Johnson	Columbia	May 31, 1935
			(co-holder)	
220 yd. dash	20.7 s.	Barney Ewell	Penn. State	May 31, 1941
220 mtr. dash	20.7 s.	Barney Ewell	Penn. State	May 31, 1941
400 yd. run	47 s.	John Woodruff	Pittsburgh	May 29, 1937
				June 4, 1938
				May 27, 1939
400 mtr. run	46.9 s.	James E. Luvalle	UCLA	May 27, 1933
400 mtr. run	46.1 s.	Archie Williams	UCLA	June 19, 1936
880 yd. run	1 m. 51.2 s.	John Y. Woodruff	Pittsburgh	May 27, 1939
120 yd. hurdles	14.1 s.	Edward Dugger	Tufts	May 31, 1941
110 mtr. hurdles	14.2 s.	Edward Dugger	Tufts	June 29, 1940
Run. br. jump	25 ft. 10⅞ in.	DeHart Hubbard		June 13, 1925

1C–4A   INDOOR CHAMPIONSHIP RECORDS

(By Colored Athletes)

EVENT	RECORD	HOLDER	WHERE MADE	DATE
50 mtr. dash	5.9 s.	Benjamin W. Johnson	Columbia	Mar. 2, 1935
60 yd. dash	6.1 s.	Benjamin W. Johnson	Columbia	Feb. 5, Mar. 12,1938
		Barney H. Ewell	Penn. State	Feb. 7, 1942
		Edward Conwell	N. Y. U.	Feb. 26, 1944
60 mtr. dash	6.6 s.	Benjamin Johnson	Columbia	Feb. 23, 1935 Feb. 26, 1938
60 yd. hurdles	7.3 s.	Edward Dugger	Tufts	Mar. 2, 1940
Run. br. jump	25 ft. 2½ in.	Barney Ewell	Penn State	Mar. 7, 1942

As partial evidence of the potency of colored track and field athletes in view of the comparatively few colleges and clubs to which these athletes are attached, are listed the events won by them at the national A.A.U. track meets since 1938:

OUTDOOR

YEAR	EVENT	WINNER	HOME OR AFFILIATION
1939	200 mtrs.	Barney Ewell	Penn. State
	110 mtr. hurdles	Joe Batiste	Tucson, Arizona
	Shot put	Lilburn Williams	Xavier University
1940	Decathlon	Bill Watson	Detroit, Mich.
1941	100 mtrs.	Barney Ewell	Penn. State
	Discus	Archie Harris	Indiana
	Pentathlon	John Borican	Columbia
	Decathlon	John Borican	Columbia
1942	800 mtrs.	John Borican	Columbia
	High jump	Adam Berry	Southern University
1943	400 mtrs. relay	Pioneer Club	New York
	1000 mtrs. relay	Grand Street Boys' Club	New York
	3000 mtrs. walk	James Wilson	New York
	High jump	Pete Watkins	Fort Sam Houston, Texas
	Decathlon	Bill Watson	Detroit, Mich.
	Pentathlon	Eulace Peacock	Coast Guard
1944	100 mtrs.	Claude Young	Illinois University
	400 mtrs.	Elmore Harris	Shore A. C.
	800 mtrs.	Bob Kelley	Illinois University
	200 mtr. hurdles	Elmore Harris	Shore A. C.
	1600 mtr. relay	Pioneer Club	New York

YEAR	EVENT	WINNER	HOME OR AFFILIATION
	10 kilometer walk	James Wilson	New York
	Running hop, step, jump	Don Barksdale	Camp Lee, Virginia
1945	100 mtr.	Barney Ewell	Penn. State
	200 mtrs.	Elmore Harris	Shore A. C.
	400 mtrs.	Herbert McKenley	Boston College
	800 mtrs.	Robert Kelley	Illinois University
	High jump	Albritton and Williamson	
	Broad jump	Herbert Douglas	Pittsburgh University
	1000 kilometer walk	James Wilson	New York
	400 mtr. relay	Pioneer Club	New York
	Pentathlon	Eulace Peacock	Coast Guard
1946	100 mtrs.	Billy Mathis	Illinois University
	200 mtrs.	Barney Ewell	Shanahan A. C.
	400 mtrs.	Elmore Harris	Shore A. C.
	110 mtr. high hurdle	Harrison Dillard	Baldwin Wallace College
	200 mtr. low hurdle	Harrison Dillard	Baldwin Wallace College
	High jump	David Albritton	
	Broad jump	William Steele	San Diego, Cal.
	400 mtr. relay	Pioneer Club	New York
	1600 mtr. relay	Pioneer Club	New York
1947	100 mtrs.	Wm. Mathis	University of Illinois
	200 mtrs.	Barney Elwell	Unattached
	400 mtrs.	Herbert McKenley	Illinois
	800 mtrs.	Reginald Pearman	N. Y. U.
	110 mtr. hurdles	Harrison Dillard	Baldwin Wallace College
	200 mtr. hurdle	Harrison Dillard	Baldwin Wallace College
	Running high jump	Dave Albritton	Unattached
	Running broad jump	William Steele	San Diego
1948	100 mtrs.	Barney Ewell	Unattached
	200 mtrs.	Lloyd LaBeach	Panama
	400 mtrs.	Herbert McKenley	Unattached
	Running broad jump	Fred Johnson	Michigan State

INDOOR

YEAR	EVENT	WINNER	HOME OR AFFILIATION
1941	60 yds.	Herbert Thompson	Jersey City
	600 yds.	Jimmy Herbert	Grand Street Club
	1000 yds.	John Borican	Shore A. C.
	High jump	Mel. Walker	Tenn. State A. C.
1943	60 yds.	Herbert Thompson	Jersey City
	600 yds.	Lewis Smith	Prairie View

YEAR	EVENT	WINNER	HOME OR AFFILIATION
	One mile	Frank Dixon	New York University
	High jump	Josh Williamson (tied)	Unattached
	Broad jump	Barney Ewell	Unattached
1944	60 yds.	Edward Conwell	New York University
	60 yd. high hurdle	Ed Dugger	Tufts
	60 yd. low hurdle	Ed Dugger	Tufts
	High jump	Dave Albritton (tied)	Unattached
	Broad jump	Barney Ewell	Unattached
1945	60 yds.	Barney Ewell	
	60 yd. high hurdle	Ed Dugger	Dayton A. C.
	600 yds.	Elmore Harris	Shore A. C.
	High jump	Josh Williamson	Unattached
	Broad jump	Barney Ewell	Unattached
1946	60 yds.	Tom Carey	Pioneer Club
	60 yd. high hurdle	Ed Dugger	Dayton A. C.
	60 yd. low hurdle	Ed Dugger	Dayton A. C.
	600 yds.	Elmore Harris	New York
	Broad jump	Samuel Richardson	Pioneer Club
1947	60 yds.	Ed. Conwell	New York
	60 yd. high hurdle	Harrison Dillard	Baldwin Wallace College
	60 yd. low hurdle	Harrison Dillard	Baldwin Wallace College
	Running broad jump	Herbert Douglas	University of Pittsburgh
1948	60 yds.	Bill Mathis	Unattached
	600 yds.	Dave Bolen	Unattached
	1000 yd. run	Philip Thigpen	Seton Hall
	60 yd. high hurdle	Harrison Dillard	Baldwin Wallace College
	Sprint Medley relay	N. Y. Pioneer Club	(McCants, Carey, Tucker, Carty)
	Running broad jump	Lorenzo Wright	Wayne University

TRACK RECORD OF JESSE OWENS

May 20, 1933—Columbus, Ohio—Broke interscholastic broad jump mark with a leap of 24 feet, 3¾ inches.

June 17, 1933—Soldiers' Field—Equalled world's record for 100 yards in 9.4 seconds; 220 yards in 20.7 seconds; running broad jump by 24 feet, 9⅝ inches. Each performance smashed existing school boy record and the 9.4 seconds tied the best world record.

Feb. 24, 1934—Madison Square—New indoor broad jump record, National Senior A.A.U. Track and Field Championship, 25 feet, 3¼ inches.

March 23, 1935—Madison Square—Equalled world indoor record for 60 yards in 6.1 seconds—jointly held by Owens and Metcalfe.

Feb. 23, 1935—Madison Square—Set new National A.A.U. Senior broad jump mark of 25 feet, 9 inches.

Lowered world record in 60 meters to 6.5 seconds in semi-finals but was beaten in finals by Ben Johnson—record equalled.

April 5, 1935—St. Louis Relays—Equalled world indoor mark for 50 yards of 5.2 seconds.

April 26, 1935—Drake Relays—New American broad jump record, 26 feet, ¾ inch. First American to jump over 26 feet.

May 25, 1935—Ann Arbor, Michigan World Record Broad jump—26 feet 8¼ inches.

June 22, 1935—N.C.A.A. Games, Berkeley, Cal.—Won five events; scoring 40 of the 40⅕ points scored by Ohio State's team. None broke records.

June 27, 1935—San Diego, Cal.—Scored only double victory in far western championships.

July 4, 1935—Lincoln, Nebraska—Lost to Eulace Peacock twice in National A.A.U. championships. Finished third to Peacock and Metcalfe in 100 meters, in which Peacock ran to equal world record of 10.2 seconds. Jesse Owens jumped 26 feet, 2¼ inches, but was beaten by Peacock at 26 feet, 3 inches.

July 4, 1936—Princeton, N. J.—Equalled National A.A.U. meet record in 100 meters—10.4 seconds and equalled meet record in broad jump at 26 feet, 3 inches.

July 11, 1936—Randall's Island—Qualified for Olympic competition by winning 100 meters in 10.4 seconds. Qualified in broad jump at 26 feet, 3 inches.

July 12, 1936—Randall's Island, N. Y.—Qualified for Olympic competition, running 200 meters in 21 seconds, world's mark for distance around one curve.

August 3, 1936—Berlin, Germany—Won Olympic 100 meters in 10.3, equalling the world and Olympic record, winning by one yard from Ralph Metcalfe, U. S.

August 4, 1936—Berlin, Germany—Won Olympic broad jump championship, 8.06 meters, or 26 feet, 5²¹⁄₆₄ inches, establishing a new Olympic record.

August 5, 1936—Berlin, Germany—Won Olympic 200 meters 21.2, breaking Olympic and world mark around one curve, defeating Mack Robinson, of U. S., by 5 meters.

August 9, 1936—Berlin, Germany—Teamed with Metcalfe, Foy Draper, and Frank Wykoff to win 400 meter championship in 40 seconds flat, equalling world record.

RECORDS OF TODAY AND YESTERDAY

One of the earliest attempts to keep records of Negro athletes was the annual publication of the standard performances made in the Inter-Scholastic Athletic Association games held in Washington, D. C. These records were published in the 1911 Handbook of the American Sports Publishing Library.

I. S. A. A. RECORD HOLDERS

TRACK AND FIELD—SCHOLASTIC

100 yards dash—1906, F. M. Steele, H.A., 10⅕ s.; 1911, J. Burwell, A.T.H.S., 10⅕ s.

220 yards dash—1906, F. M. Steele, H.A., 23⅘ s.; 1908, W. Bacon, M Street H.S., 23⅘ s.; 1908, Vickers, H.A., 23⅗ s.; 1911, P. Dines, A.T.H.S., 23⅖ s.

440 yards dash—1907, C. Young, H.A., 54⅗ s.; 1908, H. B. Dismond, H.A., 52⅖ s.

880 yards run—1907, W. Wilson, Baltimore H.S., 2 m. 15⅗ s.; 1911, O. Walker, A.T.H.S., 2 m. 14⅖ s.

1-mile run—1906, I. Milton, H.A., 5 m. 28 s.; 1907, Turner, H.A., 5 m. 5⅗ s.; 1908, Bristol, H.A., 5 m. 3 s.; 1909, H. Penn, M Street H.S., 4 m. 57⅕ s.

120 yards hurdle race—1907, W. F. Williams, M Street H.S., 18⅗ s.

220 yards hurdle race—1906, E. Gray, M Street H.S., 27 s.

12-pound shot-put—1906, G. Kyle, H.A., 36 ft.; 1907, Barber, M Street H.S., 37 ft.; 1908, E. Gray, M Street H.S., 37 ft. 6 in.; 1909, W. Nalls, M Street H.S., 37 ft. 9½ in.; 1910, R. Beckwith, A.T.H.S., 40 ft. 3½ in.

12-pound hammer—1906, E. Gray, M Street H.S., 96 ft.; 1907, E. Gray, M Street H.S., 111 ft. 5 in.

Running high jump—1906, W. F. Williams, M Street H.S., 5 ft. 7 in.

Running broad jump—1909, W. Haynes, M Street H.S., 17 ft. 8 in.; 1910, H. Wallace, H.A., 18 ft. 4½ in.

OPEN EVENTS

100 yards dash—1906, D. Boston, Baltimore H.S., 11⅕ s.; 1907, McMechen, H.U., 10⅕ s.; 1908, W. English, unattached, 10⅕ s.

220 yards dash—1908, W. English, unattached, 24⅘ s.

440 yards dash—1907, D. Munroe, unattached, 54⅕ s.

880 yards run—1908, O. Walker, Garrison School, 2 m. 19 s.; 1909, M. Curtis, A.A.C., 2 m. 14⅕ s.; 1910, W. Wilson, D.A.A., 2 m. 12⅕ s.

1-mile run—1907, D. Munroe, unattached, 5 m. 15 s.; 1909, J. Clifford, unattached, 5 m. 8 s.

120 yards hurdle race—1908, G. Kyle, H.U., 18⅘ s.

12-pound shot-put—1907, W. English, unattached, 38 ft. 9¼ in.

12-pound hammer throw—1907, H. Thurman, H.U., 121 ft.

Running high jump—1907, T. Watkins, H.U., 5 ft. 3 in.; 1908, D. Munroe, unattached, 5 ft. 3 in.; 1911, C. George, H.A., 5 ft. 8 in.

Running broad jump—1907, W. English, 21 ft. 1 in.; 1908, W. English, unattached, 21 ft. 7 in.

Pole vault—1907, T. Warrick, H.U., 9 ft. 3 in.; 1908, J. B. Brown, H.U., 9 ft. 6 in.

Discus throw—1908, G. Kyle, H.U., 81 ft. 3 in.

2-mile run—1909, A. Toomey, M Street H.S., 11 m. 47 s.

RECORD OF CARDOZO (Washington) HIGH SCHOOL TRACK TEAM

YEAR	EVENT	RECORD	WINNER	MEET AND PLACE
1943	Running br. jump	21 ft. 9 in.	Eugene Wright	Schenectady Inter-scholastic Sport Carnival
1944	100 yards	9.8 s.	Wm. Mathis	Schenectady Inter-scholastic Sport Carnival
1944	220 yards	22.1 s.	Wm. Mathis	Memorial Day Eastern Championships—Providence
1944	100 yards	9.9 s.	Wm. Mathis	Memorial Day Eastern Championships—Providence
1945	880 relay	1:32.4 s.	(Baucom, McCaskell, Turner, Mathis)	Providence
1945	60 yards	6.3 s.	Wm. Mathis	Nat'l H. S. Indoor Meet
1945	50 yards (B)	5.5 s.	Wm. Mathis	Middle Atlantic A. A. U.
1946	440 relay	45. s.	(Boston, Cosby, Broady, Turner)	Nat'l Negro H. S. Meet, St. Louis
1946	880 sprint relay	1:37.9 s.	(Boston, Baucom, Broady, Turner)	Nat'l Negro H. S. Meet
1947	75 yards	7.8 s.	Marcellus Boston	S. A. A. A. U. (Indoors)
1947	440 relay	46.9 s.	(Boston, Norwood, Drummond, Yates)	S. A. A. A. U. Atlantic
1948	50 yards (B)	5.5 s.	Marcellus Boston	Middle A. A. U.
1948	50 yards (Open)	5.5 s.	Marcellus Boston	Middle Atlantic A. A. U.
1948	50 yards	5.4 s.	Marcellus Boston	Bd. of Educ. Invitation Meet, Philadelphia
1948	960 relay	1:42.7 s.	(Boston, Moon, Drummond, Walker)	Nat'l Prep and H. S. Meet
1948	Medley relay	5:12 s.	(Sibert, Walker, Boston, Sturdevant)	Middle Atlantic A. A. U., Camden
1948	Medley relay	5:12 s.	(Sibert, Walker, Boston, Sturdevant)	Middle Atlantic A. A. U. Baltimore
1948	One mile relay	3:43.7 s.	(Boston, Moon, Greene, Walker)	Middle Atlantic A. A. U.
1948	440 relay	44.6 s.	(Walker, McGoines, Greene, Walker)	Seton College Relays
1948	880 relay (Prep)	1:33.8 s.	(Boston, Drummond, Greene, Walker)	Seton College Relays
1948	880 relay	1:33.1 s.	(Boston, Drummond, Greene, Walker)	Bridgeton H. S. Relays

American Tennis Association Champions

MEN'S SINGLES

YEAR	PLACE OF PLAY	CHAMPION	STATE OR COUNTRY
1917	Baltimore, Md.	Talley Holmes	Washington, D. C.
1918	New York City, N. Y.	Talley Holmes	Washington, D. C.
1919	New York City, N. Y.	Dr. Sylvester Smith	Philadelphia, Pa.
1920	New York City, N. Y.	B. M. Clarke	Jamaica, B.W.I.
1921	Washington, D. C.	Talley Holmes	Washington, D. C.
1922	Philadelphia, Pa.	Edgar G. Brown	Indianapolis, Ind.
1923	Chicago, Ill.	Edgar G. Brown	Indianapolis, Ind.
1924	Baltimore, Md.	Talley Holmes	Washington, D. C.
1925	Bordentown, N. J.	Theodore Thompson	Washington, D. C.
1926	St. Louis, Mo.	Eyre Saitch	New York City, N. Y.
1927	Hampton Institute, Va.	Theodore Thompson	Washington, D. C.
1928	Bordentown, N. J.	Edgar G. Brown	Indianapolis, Ind.
1929	Bordentown, N. J.	Edgar G. Brown	Indianapolis, Ind.
1930	Indianapolis, Ind.	Douglas Turner	Chicago, Ill.
1931	Tuskegee Inst., Ala.	Reginald Weir	New York City, N. Y.
1932	Shady Rest, Scotch Plains, N. J.	Reginald Weir	New York City, N. Y.
1933	Hampton Institute, Va.	Reginald Weir	New York City, N. Y.
1934	Lincoln University, Pa.	Nathaniel Jackson	Laurinburg, N. C.
1935	West Va. State College Institute, West Va.	Franklyn Jackson	Laurinburg, N. C.
1936	Wilberforce University, Wilberforce, Ohio	Lloyd Scott	Prairie View, Texas
1937	Tuskegee Inst., Ala.	Dr. Reginald Weir	New York City, N. Y.
1938	Lincoln University, Pa.	Franklyn Jackson	Laurinburg, N. C.
1939	Hampton, Va.	Jimmie McDaniel	New Orleans, La.
1940	Wilberforce, Ohio	Jimmie McDaniel	New Orleans, La.
1941	Tuskegee, Ala.	Jimmie McDaniel	New Orleans, La.
1942	Lincoln Univ., Pa.	Dr. Reginald Weir	New York City
1943	NO NATIONAL TOURNAMENT HELD THIS YEAR ——		
1944	New York City	Pvt. Lloyd C. Scott	Prairie View, Texas
1945	New York City	Pvt. Lloyd C. Scott	Prairie View, Texas
1946	Wilberforce, Ohio	Jimmie McDaniel	Los Angeles, Calif.
1947	Tuskegee, Ala.	George Stewart	Panama

WOMEN'S SINGLES

1917	Baltimore, Md.	Lucy D. Slowe	Baltimore, Md.
1918	New York City, N. Y.	M. Rae	Jamaica, B.W.I.

WOMEN'S SINGLES—*Continued*

YEAR	PLACE OF PLAY	CHAMPION	STATE OR COUNTRY
1919	New York City, N. Y.	M. Rae	Jamaica, B.W.I.
1920	New York City, N. Y.	M. Rae	Jamaica, B.W.I.
1921	Washington, D. C.	Lucy D. Slowe	Baltimore, Md.
1922	Philadelphia, Pa.	Isadore Channels	Chicago, Ill.
1923	Chicago, Ill.	Isadore Channels	Chicago, Ill.
1924	Baltimore, Md.	Isadore Channels	Chicago, Ill.
1925	Bordentown, N. J.	Lula Ballard	Philadelphia, Pa.
1926	St. Louis, Mo.	Isadore Channels	Chicago, Ill.
1927	Hampton Inst., Va.	Lula Ballard	Philadelphia, Pa.
1928	Bordentown, N. J.	Lulu Ballard	Philadelphia, Pa.
1929	Bordentown, N. J.	Ora Washington	Philadelphia, Pa.
1930	Indianapolis, Ind.	Ora Washington	Philadelphia, Pa.
1931	Tuskegee Inst., Ala.	Ora Washington	Philadelphia, Pa.
1932	Shady Rest, Scotch Plains, N. J.	Ora Washington	Philadelphia, Pa.
1933	Hampton Inst., Va.	Ora Washington	Philadelphia, Pa.
1934	Lincoln University, Pa.	Ora Washington	Philadelphia, Pa.
1935	West Va. State College Inst., West Va.	Ora Washington	Philadelphia, Pa.
1936	Wilberforce University, Wilberforce, Ohio	Lula Ballard	Philadelphia, Pa.
1937	Tuskegee Inst., Ala.	Ora Washington	Philadelphia, Pa.
1938	Lincoln University, Pa.	Flora Lomax	Detroit, Mich.
1939	Hampton, Va.	Flora Lomax	Detroit, Mich.
1940	Wilberforce, Ohio	Agnes Lawson	Prairie View, Texas
1941	Tuskegee, Ala.	Flora Lomax	Detroit, Mich.
1942	Lincoln Univ., Pa.	Flora Lomax	Detroit, Mich.
1943	NO NATIONAL TOURNAMENT HELD THIS YEAR ——		
1944	New York City	Roumania Peters	Tuskegee, Ala.
1945	New York City	Kathryn Irvis	Pittsburgh, Pa.
1946	Wilberforce, Ohio	Roumania Peters	Tuskegee, Ala.
1947	Tuskegee, Ala.	Althea Gibson	Wilmington, N. C.

BOYS' SINGLES

YEAR	PLACE OF PLAY	CHAMPION	STATE OR COUNTRY
1937	Tuskegee Inst., Ala.	Marshall Arnold	Atlanta, Ga.
1938	Lincoln University, Pa.	Weldon Collins	Durham, N. C.
1939	Hampton, Va.	Robert Isaacs	Nassau, Bahamas
1940	Wilberforce, Ohio	Charles W. Lewis, Jr.	Prairie View, Texas
1941	Tuskegee, Ala.	John D. Rhodes, Jr.	Orangeburg, S. C.
1942	Lincoln Univ., Pa.	Matthew Branch	Tuskegee, Ala.
1943	NO NATIONAL TOURNAMENT HELD THIS YEAR ——		

YEAR	PLACE OF PLAY	CHAMPION	STATE OR COUNTRY
1944	New York City	Clyde Freeman, Jr.	Washington, D. C.
1945	New York City	Wilbert Davis	New York City
1946	Wilberforce, Ohio	Thomas Freeman	Washington, D. C.
1947	Tuskegee, Ala.	James Thompkins	Brooklyn, N. Y.

GIRLS' SINGLES

1935	West Va. State College Institute, West Va.	Mae Hamlin	Raleigh, N. C.
1936	Wilberforce University, Wilberforce, Ohio	Angeline Spencer	Bellevue, Va.
1937	Tuskegee Inst., Ala.	Mae Hamlin	Raleigh, N. C.
1938	Lincoln University, Pa.	Mamie Stanley	Brooklyn, N. Y.
1939	Hampton, Va.	Vivian Murphy	Buffalo, N. Y.
1940	Wilberforce, Ohio	Helen Hutchinson	Tuskegee, Ala.
1941	Tuskegee, Ala.	Thelma McDaniel	Tuskegee, Ala.
1942	Lincoln Univ., Pa.	Norma Davis	Elizabeth, N. J.
1943	NO NATIONAL TOURNAMENT HELD THIS YEAR ——		
1944	New York City	Althea Gibson	New York City
1945	New York City	Althea Gibson	New York City
1946	Wilberforce, Ohio	Gwendolyn Whitting-ton	New York City
1947	Tuskegee, Ala.	Wilma McGhee	Knoxville, Tenn.

JUNIOR SINGLES

1928	Bordentown, N. J.	Reginald Weir	New York City, N. Y.
1929	Bordentown, N. J.	Nathaniel Jackson	Laurinburg, N. C.
1930	Indianapolis, Ind.	Nathaniel Jackson	Laurinburg, N. C.
1931	Tuskegee Inst., Ala.	Franklyn Jackson	Laurinburg, N. C.
1932	Shady Rest, Scotch Plains, N. J.	Franklyn Jackson	Laurinburg, N. C.
1933	Hampton Inst., Va.	Hubert Eaton	Winston-Salem, N. C.
1934	Lincoln University, Pa.	Theodore Cousins	Montclair, N. J.
1935	West Va. State College Inst., West Va.	Ernest McCampbell	Tuskegee Inst., Ala.
1936	Wilberforce University, Wilberforce, Ohio	Johnson Wells	Buffalo, N. Y.
1937	Tuskegee Inst., Ala.	Johnson Wells	Buffalo, N. Y.
1938	Lincoln University, Pa.	Johnson Wells	Buffalo, N. Y.
1939	Hampton, Va.	Robert Ryland	Chicago, Ill.
1940	Wilberforce, Ohio	Joseph King	McIntosh, Ga.

JUNIOR SINGLES—*Continued*

YEAR	PLACE OF PLAY	CHAMPION	STATE OR COUNTRY
1941	Tuskegee, Ala.	Raymond Jackson	Brooklyn, N. Y.
1942	Lincoln Univ., Pa.	Richard Cunningham	Cleveland, Ohio
1943	NO NATIONAL TOURNAMENT HELD THIS YEAR		——
1944	New York City	Carl Williams	Orangeburg, S. C.
1945	New York City	Franklyn Bailey	Orangeburg, S. C.
1946	Wilberforce, Ohio	Clyde Freeman	Washington, D. C.
1947	Tuskegee, Ala.	Clyde Freeman	Washington, D. C.

VETERANS' SINGLES

YEAR	PLACE OF PLAY	CHAMPION	STATE OR COUNTRY
1933	Hampton Inst., Va.	John P. Wilkinson	Washington, D. C.
1934	Lincoln University, Pa.	Fred Johnson	New York City, N. Y.
1935	West Va. State College Institute, West Va.	Dr. C. W. Furlonge	Smithfield, N. C.
1936	Wilberforce University, Wilberforce, Ohio	Dr. C. W. Furlonge	Smithfield, N. C.
1937	Tuskegee Inst., Ala.	Fred Johnson	New York City, N. Y.
1938	Lincoln University, Pa.	Fred Johnson	New York City, N. Y.
1939	Hampton, Va.	John B. Garrett	Tuskegee, Ala.
1940	Wilberforce, Ohio	John B. Garrett	Tuskegee, Ala.
1941	Tuskegee, Ala.	John B. Garrett	Tuskegee, Ala.
1942	Lincoln Univ., Pa.	John B. Garrett	Tuskegee, Ala.
1943	NO NATIONAL TOURNAMENT HELD THIS YEAR		——
1944	New York City	John B. Garrett	Tuskegee, Ala.
1945	New York City	John B. Garrett	Tuskegee, Ala.
1946	Wilberforce, Ohio	John B. Garrett	Tuskegee, Ala.
1947	Tuskegee, Ala.	John B. Garrett	Tuskegee, Ala.

VETERANS' SINGLES (WOMEN)

YEAR	PLACE OF PLAY	CHAMPION	STATE OR COUNTRY
1947	Tuskegee, Ala.	Miss Blanche Winston	New York City

MEN'S DOUBLES

YEAR	PLACE OF PLAY	CHAMPION	STATE OR COUNTRY
1928	Bordentown, N. J.	Eyre Saitch	New York City, N. Y.
		Dr. Sylvester Smith	Philadelphia, Pa.
1929	Bordentown, N. J.	Eyre Saitch	New York City, N. Y.
		Dr. Sylvester Smith	Philadelphia, Pa.
1930	Indianapolis, Ind.	Dr. John Mc. Griff	Portsmouth, Va.
		Dr. Ellwood Downing	Roanoke, Va.
1931	Tuskegee Inst., Ala.	Nathaniel Jackson	Laurinburg, N. C.
		Franklyn Jackson	Laurinburg, N. C.
1932	Shady Rest, Scotch Plains, N. J.	Richard Hudlin	St. Louis, Mo.
		Douglas Turner	Chicago, Ill.

YEAR	PLACE OF PLAY	CHAMPIONS	STATE OR COUNTRY
1933	Hampton Inst., Va.	Nathaniel Jackson	Laurinburg, N. C.
		Franklyn Jackson	Laurinburg, N. C.
1934	Lincoln University, Pa.	Nathaniel Jackson	Laurinburg, N. C.
		Franklyn Jackson	Laurinburg, N. C.
1935	West Va. State College	Nathaniel Jackson	Laurinburg, N. C.
	Institute, West Va.	Franklyn Jackson	Laurinburg, N. C.
1936	Wilberforce University,	Nathaniel Jackson	Laurinburg, N. C.
	Wilberforce, Ohio	Franklyn Jackson	Laurinburg, N. C.
1937	Tuskegee Inst., Ala.	James Stocks	Pasadena, Calif.
		Thomas Walker	Chicago, Ill.
1938	Lincoln University	Nathaniel Jackson	Laurinburg, N. C.
		Franklyn Jackson	Laurinburg, N. C.
1939	Hampton, Va.	Jimmie McDaniel and	
		Richard Cohen	New Orleans, La.
1940	Wilberforce, Ohio	Clifford Russell and	
		Howard Minnis	Tuskegee, Ala.
1941	Tuskegee, Ala.	Jimmie McDaniel and	
		Richard Cohen	New Orleans, La.
1942	Lincoln Univ., Pa.	Clifford Russell and	
		Howard Minnis	Tuskegee, Ala.
1943	NO NATIONAL TOURNAMENT HELD THIS YEAR ——		
1944	New York City	Cpl. Howard Minnis	
		and Sgt. R. Fieulleteau	Tuskegee, Ala.
1945	New York City	Lloyd Scott and	
		Louis Graves	Texas and New York
1946	Wilberforce, Ohio	James Stocks and	
		Jimmie McDaniel	California
1947	Tuskegee, Ala.	John Chandler and	
		Harold Mitchell	N. J. and California

WOMEN'S DOUBLES

1928	Bordentown, N. J.	Lula Ballard	Philadelphia, Pa.
		Ora Washington	Philadelphia, Pa.
1929	Bordentown, N. J.	Lula Ballard	Philadelphia, Pa.
		Ora Washington	Philadelphia, Pa.
1930	Indianapolis, Ind.	Ora Washington	Philadelphia, Pa.
		Blanche Winston	New York City, N. Y.
1931	Tuskegee Inst., Ala.	Ora Washington	Philadelphia, Pa.
		Blanche Winston	New York City, N. Y.
1932	Shady Rest, Scotch	Lula Ballard	Philadelphia, Pa.
	Plains, N. J.	Ora Washington	Philadelphia, Pa.

WOMEN'S DOUBLES—*Continued*

YEAR	PLACE OF PLAY	CHAMPIONS	STATE OR COUNTRY
1933	Hampton Inst., Va.	Ora Washington	Philadelphia, Pa.
		Anita Gant	Washington, D. C.
1934	Lincoln University, Pa.	Ora Washington	Philadelphia, Pa.
		Lula Ballard	Philadelphia, Pa.
1935	West Va. State College	Ora Washington	Philadelphia, Pa.
	Institute, West Va.	Lula Ballard	Philadelphia, Pa.
1936	Wilberforce University,	Ora Washington	Philadelphia, Pa.
	Wilberforce, Ohio	Lula Ballard	Philadelphia, Pa.
1937	Tuskegee Inst., Ala.	Bertha Isaacs	Nassau, Bahamas
		Lilyan Spencer	Jacksonville, Fla.
1938	Lincoln University, Pa.	Margaret Peters	Washington, D. C.
		Roumania Peters	Washington, D. C.
1939	Hampton, Va.	Roumania Peters and	
		Margaret Peters	Tuskegee, Ala.
1940	Wilberforce, Ohio	Roumania Peters and	
		Margaret Peters	Tuskegee, Ala.
1941	Tuskegee, Ala.	Roumania Peters and	
		Margaret Peters	Tuskegee, Ala.
1942	Lincoln Univ., Pa.	Lillian Van Buren	
		and Flora Lomax	Detroit, Mich.
1943	NO NATIONAL TOURNAMENT HELD THIS YEAR ——		
1944	New York City	Roumania Peters and	
		Margaret Peters	Tuskegee, Ala.
1945	New York City	Roumania Peters and	
		Margaret Peters	Tuskegee, Ala.
1946	Wilberforce, Ohio	Roumania Peters and	
		Margaret Peters	Tuskegee, Ala.
1947	Tuskegee, Ala.	Roumania Peters and	
		Margaret Peters	Tuskegee, Ala.

JUNIOR DOUBLES

YEAR	PLACE OF PLAY	CHAMPIONS	STATE OR COUNTRY
1937	Tuskegee Inst., Ala.	Eugene Harrington	Durham, N. C.
		George Cox	Durham, N. C.
1939	Hampton, Va.	Joseph King and	
		Margaret Arnold	Georgia
1940	Wilberforce, Ohio	Robert Ashford and	
		Roland M. Daniel	Richmond, Va.
1941	Tuskegee, Ala.	Jack Points and	
		Richard Cunningham	Ohio
1942	Lincoln Univ., Pa.	DeWitt Willis and	
		Jefferson Craig	Plainfield, N. J.

YEAR	PLACE OF PLAY	CHAMPION	STATE OR COUNTRY
1943	NO NATIONAL TOURNAMENT HELD THIS YEAR ——		
1944	New York City	Carl Williams and Franklin Bailey	South Carolina
1945	New York City	Fred Wilson and Wilbert Davis	New York City
1946	Wilberforce, Ohio	Clyde Freeman and Thomas Freeman	Washington, D. C.
1947	Tuskegee, Ala.	Clyde Freeman and Thomas Freeman	Washington, D. C.

MIXED DOUBLES

YEAR	PLACE OF PLAY	CHAMPION	STATE OR COUNTRY
1928	Bordentown, N. J.	Blanche Winston W. A. Kean	New York City, N. Y. Kentucky
1929	Bordentown, N. J.	Anita Gant Dr. O. B. Williams	Washington, D. C. Chicago, Ill.
1930	Indianapolis, Ind.	Anita Gant Dr. O. B. Williams	Washington, D. C. Chicago, Ill.
1931	Tuskegee Inst., Ala.	Anne Roberts Theodore Thompson	Virginia Washington, D. C.
1932	Shady Rest, Scotch Plains, N. J.	Martha Davies Henry Williams	Elizabeth, N. J. Newark, N. J.
1933	Hampton Inst., Va.	Emma Leonard Dr. C. O. Hilton	New York City Newark, N. J.
1934	Lincoln University, Pa.	Emma Leonard Dr. C. O. Hilton	New York City Newark, N. J.
1935	This Event Suspended from Schedule		
1936	This Event Suspended from Schedule		
1937	Tuskegee Inst., Ala.	Flora Lomax W. H. Hall	Detroit, Mich. Louisville, Ky.
1938	Lincoln University, Pa.	Lula Ballard Gerald Norman, Jr.	Philadelphia, Pa. Flushing, N. Y.
1939	Hampton, Va.	Ora Washington and Dr. Sylvester Smith	Pennsylvania
1940	Wilberforce, Ohio	Flora Lomas, and Wm. Hall	Detroit Michigan and Penna.
1941	Tuskegee, Ala.	Eoline Thornton and Harold Mitchell	Los Angeles, Cal.
1942	Lincoln Univ., Pa.	Kathryn Jones, and Wm. Jones	Springfield Baltimore, Md.
1943	NO NATIONAL TOURNAMENT HELD THIS YEAR ——		

428 *The Negro in Sports*

MIXED DOUBLES—*Continued*

YEAR	PLACE OF PLAY	CHAMPION	STATE OR COUNTRY
1944	New York City	Lillian Van Buren and Delbert Russell	Detroit Detroit
1945	New York City	Lillian Van Buren and Delbert Russell	Detroit Detroit
1946	Wilberforce, Ohio	Ora Washington and George Stewart	Penna. and Panama
1947	Tuskegee, Ala.	Ora Washington and George Stewart	Penna. and Panama

AMERICAN TENNIS ASSOCIATION

NATIONAL INTER-COLLEGIATE CHAMPIONS—AMERICAN TENNIS ASSOCIATION

1931—Nathaniel Jackson . . . . Tuskegee Institute
1932—Nathaniel Jackson . . . . Tuskegee Institute
1933—Nathaniel Jackson . . . . Tuskegee Institute
1934—Harmon Fitch . . . . Johnson C. Smith University
1935—Harmon Fitch . . . . Johnson C. Smith University
1936—Lloyd Scott . . . . Prairie View College
1937—Ernest McCampbell . . . . Tuskegee Institute
1938—Richard Cohen . . . . Xavier University
1939—Jimmie McDaniel . . . . Xavier University
1940—Jimmie McDaniel . . . . Xavier University
1941—Jimmie McDaniel . . . . Xavier University
1942—Howard Minnis . . . . Tuskegee Institute
1943—No Contest
1944—Alva Taylor . . . . Tuskegee Institute
1945—No Contest
1946—Walter Austin . . . . Southern University
1947—Carl Williams . . . . Howard University

National Open Golf Tournaments

NATIONALS HELD SINCE 1926 AND WINNERS

YEAR	WINNER AND RUNNER UP	SCORE	WHERE PLAYED
1926	Harry Jackson, Washington, D. C.	295	Mapledale, Stow, Mass.
R.U.*	Porter Washington, Boston, Mass.	303	
1927	Robert P. Ball, Chicago, Ill.	293	Mapledale, Stow, Mass.
R.U.	John Shippen, Washington, D. C.	313	

* R.U.—Runner Up.

YEAR	WINNER AND RUNNER UP	SCORE	WHERE PLAYED
1928	Porter Washington, Boston, Mass.	286	Mapledale, Stow, Mass.
R.U.	Robert P. Ball, Chicago, Ill.	290	
1929	Robert P. Ball, Chicago, Ill.	290	Shady Rest, Westfield,
R.U.	Elmer Sout, Newark, N. J.	294	N. J.
1930	Edison Marshall, New Orleans, La.	288	Casa Loma, Powers Lake,
R.U.	Porter Washington, Boston, Mass.	294	Wis.
1931	Edison Marshall, New Orleans, La.	307	Sunset Hills, Kankakee,
R.U.	Robert P. Ball, Chicago, Ill.	313	Ill.
1932	Tie—Edison Marshal, John Dendy	283	Douglas Park, Indianap-
Play			olis, Ind.
Off	John Dendy, Asheville, N. C.	144	
R.U.	Edison Marshal, New Orleans, La.	147	
1933	Howard Wheeler, Atlanta, Ga.	294	Sunset Hills, Kankakee,
R.U.	Edison Marshal, New Orleans, La.	297	Ill.
1934	Robert P. Ball, Chicago, Ill.	296	Rackham Course, Detroit,
R.U.	Robert Seymore, Detroit, Mich.	305	Mich.
1935	Soloman Hughes, Gaston, Ala.	314	Mohansic Course, York-
R.U.	James McCoy, New York, N, Y.	315	town Heights, N. Y.
1936	John Dendy, Asheville, N. C.	302	Cobbs Creek Course,
R.U.	Howard Wheeler, Atlanta, Ga.	305	Philadelphia, Pa.
1937	John Dendy, Asheville, N. C.	294	Highland Park, Cleve-
R.U.	Howard Wheeler, Atlanta, Ga.	300	land, Ohio
1938	Howard Wheeler, Atlanta, Ga.	284	Palos Park, Chicago, Ill.
R.U.	John Roux	290	

NATIONAL OPEN GOLF TOURNAMENTS

1939	Cliff Strickland	296	Los Angeles
	Edison Marshall		
R.U.	Errol Strickland	305	Griffith Park
1940	High Smith	295	Chicago, Ill.
R.U.	Clyde Martin	297	Palos Park
1941	Robt. "Pat" Ball	302	Boston, Mass.
R.U.	Clyde Martin	303	Ponkapoag Golf
1942	No Tournaments		
1943	"		
1944	"		
1945	"		
1946	Howard Wheeler	292	Pittsburgh, Pa.
R.U.	Theodore Rhodes	195	South Park
1947	Howard Wheeler	283	Philadelphia, Pa.
R.U.	Charles Sifford	288	Cobbs Creek

NATIONAL AMATEUR CHAMPIONS

YEAR	WINNER AND RUNNER UP	SCORE	WHERE PLAYED
1928	Frank Gaskin, Philadelphia, Pa.	7–6	Mapledale, Stow, Mass.
R.U.	Bertram Barker, Washington, D. C.		
1929	Frank Gaskin, Philadelphia, Pa.	2–1	Shady Rest, Westfield,
R.U.	Elmer Brent, New York, N. Y.		N. J.
1930	George Roddy, Iowa City, Iowa	7–5	Casa Loma, Powers Lake,
R.U.	Harold Hunter, Chicago, Ill.		N. J.
1931	James McCoy, New York	1 Up	Sunset Hills, Kankakee,
R.U.	Lawrence Frierson, Chicago, Ill.	19 holes	Ill.
1932	Frank Gaskin, Philadelphia, Pa.	3–2	Douglas Park, Indianap-
R.U.	Warren Vinston, Philadelphia, Pa.		olis, Ind.
1933	Isaac Ellis, Chicago, Ill.	1 Up	Sunset Hills, Kankakee,
R.U.	Lawrence Frierson, Chicago, Ill		Ill.
1934	Percy Jones, Detroit, Mich.	4–3	Rackham Course, Detroit,
R.U.	William Herbert, New York, N. Y.		Mich.
1935	Frank Radcliff, New York, N. Y.	1 Up	Mohansic Course, York-
R.U.	Elmer E. Brent, New York, N. Y.		town Heights, N. Y.
1936	Clifford Taylor, New York, N. Y.	1 Up	Cobbs Creek, Philadel-
R.U.	Frank Gaskin, Philadelphia, Pa.	36 holes	phia, Pa.
1937	George Roddy, Greensboro, Ala.	4–2	Highland Park, Cleve-
R.U.	Clifford Taylor, New York, N. Y.		land, Ohio
1938	Remus G. Robinson, Detroit, Mich.	4–3	Palos Park, Chicago, Ill.
R.U.	John Lewis		
1939	Augustus Price	3–2	Los Angeles, Cal.
R.U.	Dr. Remus G. Robinson		Harding Course, Griffith Park
1940	Dr. Remus G. Robinson	4–3	Chicago, Ill.
R.U.	Alfred T. Holmes		Palos Park
1941	Cliff Taylor	1 Up	Boston, Mass.
R.U.	Dr. L. S. Terry		Ponkapoag Golf
1942	No tournaments		
1943	"		
1944	"		
1945	"		
1946	Bill Brown	2–1	Pittsburgh, Pa.
R.U.	Bill Spiller		South Park G. C.
1947	Alfred "Tupp" Holmes	2–1	Philadelphia, Pa.
R.U.	Euell Clark		Cobbs Creek

NATIONAL WOMEN CHAMPIONS

YEAR	WINNER AND RUNNER UP	SCORE	WHERE PLAYED
1930	Marie Thompson, Chicago, Ill.	104	Casa Loma, Powers Lake,
R.U.	Lucy Williams, Indianapolis, Ind.	120	Wis.
1931	Marie Thompson, Chicago, Ill.	172	Sunset Hills, Kankakee,
R.U.	Lucy Williams, Indianapolis, Ind.	178	Ill.
1932	Lucy Williams, Indianapolis, Ind.	99	Douglas Park, Indianap-
R.U.	Marie Thompson, Chicago, Ill.	105	olis, Ind.
1933	Julia Siles, St. Louis, Mo.	106	Sunset Hills, Kankakee,
R.U.	Lucy Williams, Indianapolis, Ind.	108	Ill.
1934	Ella C. Able, Indianapolis, Ind.	209	Rackham Course, Detroit
R.U.	Lucy Williams, Indianapolis, Ind.	218	Mich.
1935	Ella C. Able, Indianapolis, Ind.	218	Lake Mohansic, York-
R.U.	Laura Thoroughgood, New York, N. Y.		town Heights
1936	Lucy Williams, Indianapolis, Ind.	199	Cobbs Creek, Philadel-
R U.	Ella C. Able, Indianapolis, Ind.		phia, Pa.
1937	Lucy Williams, Indianapolis, Ind.	7–8	Highland Park, Cleve-
R.U.	Aileen Davis, Chicago, Ill.		land, Ohio
1938	Melnee Moyee, Atlanta, Ga.	5–4	Palos Park, Chicago, Ill.
R.U.	Cleo Ball		
1939	Geneva Wilson	1 Up	Los Angeles
	Aline Davis		Griffith Park
1940	Geneva Wilson	5–3	Chicago, Ill.
	Lucy W. Mitchem		Palos Park
1941	Cleo Ball	3–2	Boston, Mass.
	Vivian Pitts		Ponkapoag G. C.
1942	No tournaments		
1943	"		
1944	"		
1945	"		
1946	Lucy Williams Mitchem (1)	3–2	Pittsburgh, Pa.
	Hazel Foreman (2)		South Park
1947	(1) Thelma Cowans	2–1	Philadelphia, Pa.
	(2) Lorraine Sawyer		Cobbs Creek

UNITED GOLFERS ASSOCIATION, INC. ROSTER

St. Nicholas Golf Club
240 West 121st Street
New York, N. Y.

Monumental Golf Club
1725 Carey Street
Baltimore, Md.

UNITED GOLFERS ASSOCIATION, INC. ROSTER—*Continued*

Chicago Golfers Trophy Club
442 East 48th Street
Chicago, Illinois

Forest City Golf Club
2584 East 55th Street
Cleveland, 4, Ohio

Sunset Hills Golf Club
4216 Indiana Avenue
Chicago, Illinois

New Lincoln Country Club
91 West Lake Avenue, N. W.
Atlanta, Georgia

Douglas Park Golf Club
2024 North Capitol Avenue
Indianapolis, Indiana

Royal Golf Club
627 Kenyon Avenue, N. W.
Washington, D. C.

Fairview Golf Club
1322 North Alden Street
Philadelphia, Penna.

Quaker City Golf Club
Box 91
Devon, Penna.

Chicago Women's Golf Club
5430 Indiana Avenue
Chicago, Illinois

Bay State Golf Association
39 Jerome Street
West Medford, Mass.

Wake Robin Golf Club
1717 Euclid Street, N. W.
Washington, D. C.

Fairway Golf Club
112 Homestead Avenue
Dayton, Ohio

Yorkshire Golf Club
1104 Larimer Avenue
Pittsburgh, 6, Penna.

Buckeye Golf Club
1087 East 97th Street
Cleveland, Ohio

Pinehurst Colored Golf Association
Box 413
Pinehurst, N. C.

Green Acres Golf Club
109 Commonwealth Avenue
Boston, Mass.

Leisure Hour Golf Club
51 N. E. SanRafael
Portland, Oregon

Cosmopolitan Golf Club
712 East 122nd Street
Los Angeles, Cal.

Douglass Center Golf Club
719½ Pinewood Avenue
Toledo, Ohio

Sixth City Golf Club
2294 East 55th Street
Cleveland, Ohio

Flint Amateur Golf Club
1602 Clifford Street
Flint, Mich.

NATIONAL BOWLING ASSOCIATION RECORDS

N. B. A. NATIONAL TOURNAMENT WINNERS THROUGH THE YEARS

1939 MEN

FIVE-MAN—Woodlawn Alcumes, Chicago 2663
TWO-MAN—W. Harris and O. Houston, Chicago 1095

1939 MEN

SINGLES—J. Jones, Detroit 589
ALL EVENTS—M. Thomas, Chicago 1662

1940 MEN

FIVE-MAN—Log Cabin, Cleveland 2157
TWO-MAN—M. Thomas and G. Walker, Chicago 1156
SINGLES—P. Orr, Chicago 593
ALL EVENTS—G. Walker, Chicago 1747

1940 WOMEN

FIVE-MAN—Westerfield Beauty Salon, Detroit 2157
TWO-MAN—B. Miler and Sara Sturdivant, Cleveland 942
SINGLES—Edna Conner, Chicago 483
ALL EVENTS—Sara Sturdivant, Cleveland 1421

1941 MEN

FIVE-MAN—Woodlawn Alcumes, Chicago 2768
TWO-MAN—C. Hodo and E. Rollins, Chicago 1141
SINGLES—I. Thurman, Indianapolis 668
ALL EVENTS—G. Walker, Chicago 1698

1941 WOMEN

FIVE-MAN—Supreme Linen, Detroit 2247
TWO-MAN—M. Shannon, O'Neil, Detroit 1112
SINGLES—Hazel Lyman, Detroit 926
ALL EVENTS—Hazel Lyman, Detroit 1426

1942 MEN

FIVE-MAN—Henry C. Taylor, Chicago 2692
TWO-MAN—William Harris and O. Houston, Chicago 1230
SINGLES—Herbert Cross, Chicago 692
ALL-EVENTS—M. Thomas, Chicago 1722

1942 WOMEN

FIVE-MAN—Club Congo, Detroit 2324
TWO-MAN—Virginia Dolphin and Hazel Lyman, Detroit 1003
SINGLES—Virginia Dolphin, Detroit 550
ALL EVENTS—Virginia Dolphin, Detroit 1548

1946 MEN

FIVE-MAN—Bob's Tire and Supply, Chicago 2717
TWO-MAN—Arthur Plant and De Hart Hubbard, Cleveland 1210
SINGLES—Obra Houston, Chicago 649
ALL EVENTS—Thomas Washington, Chicago 1910

1946 WOMEN

FIVE-MEN—Gotham Hotel, Detroit 2216
TWO-MAN—Bessie Miller and Sara Sturdivant, Cleveland 975
SINGLES—Faye Johnson, Detroit 596
ALL EVENTS—Toni Taylor, Chicago 1520

NATIONAL BOWLING ASSOCIATION WINNERS SINCE 1939

1947 MEN

FIVE-MAN—The Termites, Cleveland 2891
TWO-MAN—Richard Williams and Calvin Thomas 1210
SINGLES—Andrew Sharpe, Indianapolis, Ind. 623
ALL-EVENTS—Roy Strickland, Cleveland 1868

1947 WOMEN

FIVE-MAN—Factory Furniture, Cleveland 2558
TWO-MAN—Maxine Webb and Isabell Baxter, Cincinnati 1136
SINGLES—Louise Horton, Chicago 561
ALL-EVENTS—Isabell Baxter, Cincinnati 1732

1948 MEN

FIVE-MAN—Porter Cleaners, Detroit 2762
TWO-MAN—Arthur Goodman and William Harris, Chicago 1191
SINGLES—John Williams, Chicago 634
ALL-EVENTS—A. Levins, Newark, N. J. 1773

1948 WOMEN

FIVE-MAN—Factory Furniture, Cleveland 2509
TWO-MAN—Doris Sargent and Carol Collins, Cleveland and Chicago . 1024
SINGLES—Connie Ware, Detroit 588
ALL-EVENTS—Ruth Coburn, Cleveland 1555

RECORD OF TUSKEGEE GIRL ATHLETES SINCE 1936

1936	Providence, R. I. (National Championships and Olympic Tryouts)	Tied for 2nd place	15 points
1937	Trenton, N. J. (National Senior Championships)	Won championship	33 points
1938	Naugatuck, Conn. (National Senior Championships)	Won championship	30 points
1939	Waterbury, Conn. (National Senior Championships)	Won championship	33 points

1940	Ocean City, N. J.		
	(National Senior Championships)	Won championship	85 points
1941	Atlantic City, N. J.		
	(National Senior Championships)	Won championship (indoor)	84 points
1941	Ocean City, N. J.		
	(National Senior Championships)	Won championship	100 points
1942	Ocean City, N. J.		
	(National Senior Championships)	Won championship	80 points
1943	Lakewood, Ohio		
	(National Senior Championships)	Second place	77⅓ points
1944	Harrisburg, Penn.		
	(National Senior Championships)	Won championship	110 points
1945	Buffalo, N. Y.		
	(National Senior Championships)	Won championship (indoor)	28 points
1945	Harrisburg, Penn.		
	(National Senior Championships)	Won championship	102 points
1946	Cleveland, Ohio		
	(National Senior Championships)	Won championship (indoor)	28 points
1946	Cleveland, Ohio		
	(National Junior Championships)	Won championship (indoor)	22 points
1946	Buffalo, N. Y.		
	(National Senior Championships)	Won championship	100 points
1947	San Antonio, Texas		
	(National Junior Championships)	Won championship	97 points
1947	San Antonio, Texas		
	(National Senior Championships)	Won championship	117 points
1948	Chicago, Ill.		
	(National Senior Championships)	Won championship (indoor)	61 points

TUSKEGEE GIRLS WIN A.A.U TITLE

September 24, 1937
Reprint from Afro-American   Trenton, N. J.
October 1, 1937

TEAM COPS A.A.U. CROWN WITH 33 POINTS: FIRST IN HISTORY

Aided by mid-summer climate to which they were accustomed, and scoring in ten of the eleven events, the Tuskegee Institute team romped off with the National A.A.U. Women's Track and Field Championships here Saturday afternoon at the Central High School Stadium. Led by Lula Hymes, the Institute's all-round star, the fleet-footed Alabama unit became the first colored team to win the crown in the fourteen years the women's meets have been held. No new marks were set. The 400-meter relay, for which a 20-inch trophy was awarded, developed into a thrilling duel between the two colored teams with the Mercury team winning by a scant six inches. Tuskegee won two firsts, seven second places and two fourth places. The Mercury A.C. obtained points by winning two firsts and two third places. The third colored unit, The West Philadelphia Athletic Club, which had two athletes scored one and a half points when Lucille Harris tied for third place in the high jump. Miss Hymes and Cora A. Gaines, both of Tuskegee, tied with eight points each for third place individual high point honors. Two white girls, Claire Isicson, and Margaret Bergman, by scoring eleven and ten points respectively, won first and second individual high point honors.

The only controversy during the entire meet came following the finals of the 50-meter dash when Miss Isicson was awarded a close decision over Miss Hymes. Judges were split over who was the winner when the two finished in what appeared to be a dead heat. Miss Hymes, whose ease at running is similar to that of Jesse Owens, from a slight angle, appeared to have broken the tape first, with the white girl a bare inch behind. The dispute arose when one of the judges ruled Miss Hymes winner and the other two selected the white girl. Coach Christine Petty of Tuskegee, declined to file a protest. Sol Goldstein, coach of the Eastern Women's Club which the white girl represented, stated he believed that Miss Hymes had broken the tape first.

The meet opened with the running of the three qualifying heats of the 50-meter dash. Miss Hymes ran the distance in :06.8 in the first heat to defeat Miss Ivy Wilson, colored defending champion, of the Mercury Club, by three yards. Misses Helen Hutchinson, of Tuskegee, and Ira Bynoe of Mercury, were disqualified in the second heat which was run in :06.6 by Miss Isicson to equal the record of Miss Louise Stokes, of Onteora, Mass., set in 1933.

The meet was marked by the absence of three outstanding former champions, Misses Tydie Pickett, of Chicago; Stokes, of Massachusetts, and Mabel Smith, of Newport, R. I. Only two of the 1936 champions, Miss Wilson, holder of the 50-meter crown, and Mabel Smith of Tuskegee, winner of the 1936 broad jump crown defended their titles. Both of the defending champions had their titles lifted. Miss Smith placed second in the jump to her teammate, Miss Hymes, who was recorded at 17 feet, 8¼ inches. Miss Wilson dropped her crown by placing fifth in the short dash.

In the broad jump, Miss Hymes missed a new record when she leaped 19 feet 2 inches on her third trial only to have a foul recorded when she fell backwards in the pit. Allowed another chance to break the record, she failed by stepping over the line on the take-off board. The young woman's leap bettered the mark of 18 feet 9⅜ inches set by Miss Stella Walsh, of Poland in

1930.   It was the only record nearly shattered by the 110 athletes competing in the championship contest.

In the featured relay, Miss Ivy Wilson, who had the pole, jumped four yards in front at the bark of the gun and had increased her lead to 6 yards when she had completed the first leg of the event.   Miss Celestine Birge, lead-off for Tuskegee, who was running from the fourth lane, led the remaining runners. Coming into the home stretch, Mrs. Gertrude Johnson, the lone matron competing who was running anchor for the Mercury Club and Miss Hymes, running for Tuskegee, were shoulder to shoulder until two yards from the finish.   The Alabaman, who had earlier competed in two other events, weakened slightly, giving the New York team victory in 51 seconds.

Jumping 4 feet 10½ inches in the high jump, Miss Gaines was awarded second place when a white girl, recently arrived from Germany, leaped an inch higher. Miss Lucille Harris of Philadelphia tied for third honors by clearing 4 feet 7 inches.   Leading the five white athletes by five yards, Miss Cora G. Gaines of Tuskegee won the 80-meter low hurdles in 12.7 seconds which was one-tenth of a second slower than the accepted American record for the event.   The world record for the event is held by Babe Didrickson, white, of Dallas, Texas, 12 seconds.   The broad jump, similar to that at male track meets, was dominated by the colored lassies.   Miss Hymes, who won the event, surpassed her teammate, Miss Smith, by four inches with Miss Esther Dennis of the Mercury Club copping third place with a leap of 16 feet 11 inches.   Miss Florence N. Wright, tall track, field and basketball star of Tuskegee, won second honors in the shot put and also in the discus.   She hurled the shot 37 feet 5 inches which was one inch shorter than the winner.   In the discus, she was short of winning by 1 foot 3 inches when she tossed 105 feet 1 inch.

The final of the 100-meter found Miss Esther Dennis of the Mercury Club winning second place and Miss Jessie Abbott, daughter of Coach and Mrs. Cleve Abbott of Tuskegee, receiving fourth honors.   Miss Celestine Birge, the third girl in the final running against three white girls did not place.   The 200-meter dash was won by Mrs. Gertrude Johnson of the Mercury Club in 26 seconds. She led two white girls by four yards as Mabel Smith, favorite to win the event, placed fourth after suffering a leg injury at the start.   Competing in her first national contest, Miss Melissa Fitzpatrick, a freshman at Tuskegee, won second place in the baseball throw with a hurl of 229 feet, 5½ inches.

80 mtr. hurdles—1. CORA GAINES, Tuskegee, 12.8s.

50 mtr. dash—2. LULA HYMES, Tuskegee, :06.8s.

Running high jump—2. CORA GAINES, Tuskegee, 4 ft., 10½ in.; 3. LUCILLE
    HARRIS, Philadelphia A. C.   (Tied).

Running broad jump—1. LULA HYMES, Tuskegee, 17 ft. 8½ in.; 2. MABEL B.
    SMITH, Tuskegee, (defending champion 2); 3. ESTHER DENNIS, Mercury
    A.C., New York.

100 mtr. dash—3. ESTHER DENNIS, Mercury A. C.; 4. JESSIE ABBOTT, Tuskegee;
12.8s.

Shot put—2. FLORENCE N. WRIGHT, Tuskegee, 37 ft. 5 in.

200 mtr. dash—1. GERTRUDE JOHNSON, Mercury A. C.; 4. MABEL SMITH,
Tuskegee. 26s.

400 mtr. relay—1. MERCURY A. C.; 2. TUSKEGEE INSTITUTE. 51s.

Discus throw—2. FLORENCE N. WRIGHT, Tuskegee. Distance 105 ft. 1 in.

WORLD RECORD TIED AS NINE NEW CHAMPIONS CROWNED AT WOMEN'S U. S. MEET

Naugatuck, August 7, 1938
by John A. Cluney

A world's record in the 50 meter run was tied while nine of eleven national
championships changed hands during the 1938 Women's National A. A. U.
Track and Field meet held at Recreation field here today under the auspices of
the Amateur Athletic Union and the New Haven County Sheriffs Association,
headed by High Sheriff J. Edward Slavin of New Haven. . . .

Scoring 30 points, the Tuskegee Institute Girls of Alabama retained national
team honors with LULA HYMES a double winner in the 100 meter run and broad
jump clinching team honors with a win over the able Polish Alliance team
of Chicago. Teams finishing behind the Tuskegee girls included the Eastern
Women's A. C. with 15½ points and the German-American A. C. 12 points.

50 mtr. run—1. Claire Isicson, Long Island University; 2. IVY WILSON, Mercury A. C., New York; 3. Olive Hasenfus, Boston Swimming Assoc.;
4. Josephine Warren, Boston Swimming Assoc. :06.6 s.

Shot put—1. Catherine Fellmeth, Dvorak Park, Chicago; 2. FLORENCE WRIGHT,
Tuskegee Institute, Alabama; 3. Mary Bergmann, Park Central A. C.;
4. Amy Dreyer, Brockton Girls A. A. of Providence, R. I. Distance
38 ft. 5¾ in.

80 mtr. hurdles—1. Marie Cotrel, German-American A. C., N. Y.; 2. CORA
GAINES, Tuskegee Institute; 3. Sylvia Rothenberg, New York, (unattached); 4. Sybil Cooper, German-American A. C., N. Y. 13 s.

Discus throw—1. Catherine Fellmeth, Dvorak Park, Chicago; 2. Frances
Sobczak, MacDonald A. C., Cleveland; 3. Elizabeth Lindsay, German-
American A. C., N. Y.; 4. Amy Dreyer, Brockton Girls' A. C. Dis-
tance 126 ft. ¼ in.

Javelin throw—1. Rose Auerbach, Eastern Women's A. C., N. Y.; 2. MAR-
GARET BARNES, Tuskegee Institute; 3. Rose Cea, Eastern Women's A. C.;
4. Sylvia Rothenberg, Eastern Women's A. C. Distance 121 ft. 6¾ in.

100 mtr. run—1. LULA HYMES, Tuskegee Institute: 2. Olive Hasenfus, Boston
Swimming Assoc.; 3. Claire Isicson, Long Island University; 4. Josephine Warren, Boston Swimming Assoc. 12.4 s.

Running broad jump—1. LULA HYMES, Tuskegee Institute; 2. Dorothy Caticco, German-American A. C., N. Y.; 3. ESTHER DENNIS, Mercury A. C., N. Y.; 4. LELIA PERRY, Tuskegee Institute. Distance 17 ft. 2 in.
Running high jump—1. Mary Bergmann, Park Central A. C., N. Y.; 2. Mildred Pufundt, Polish National Alliance, Chicago; 3. (tie) Beulah Clark, Crystal A. C., St. Louis; Frances Sobczak, MacDonald A. C., Cleveland; Mildred Kisick, Polish National Alliance, Chicago. Height 5 ft. 2 in.
200 mtr. run—1. Fanny Vitale, Park Central A. C., N. Y.; 2. HESTER BROWN, Tuskegee Institute; 3. Marie Cottrell, German-American A. C., N. Y.; 4. GERTRUDE JOHNSON, Mercury A. C., N. Y. 26.7 s.
Baseball throw—1. Betsy Jochum, Cincinnati, Ohio, unattached; 2. Rose Cea, Eastern Women's A. C., N. Y.; 3. Alicia Ordine, Eastern Women's Assoc., N. Y.; 4. Blanche Zabransky, Dvorak Park, Chicago. Distance 261 ft. 7 in.
400 mtr. relay—1. TUSKEGEE INSTITUTE, (CELESTINE BIRGE, JESSE ABBOTT, HESTER BROWN, LULA HYMES); 2. Polish National Alliance, Chicago; 3. TUSKEGEE INSTITUTE TEAM "B"; 4. Dvorak Park, Chicago. 52 s.

Waterbury American, Monday Evening, August 8, 1938

LULA HYMES, CATHERINE FELLMETH DOUBLE WINNERS IN WOMEN'S A. A. U. MEET

Six Titles Change Hands, World Mark Tied by Girls in Naugatuck Track Event
Tuskegee Institute Takes Team Title; Claire Isicson Retains 50-Meter Crown;
Roxy Atkin Injured.

Naugatuck, Aug. 8—A couple of "iron" girls, LULA HYMES of Tuskegee Institute and Catherine Fellmeth of Chicago, headed for their homes today sharing the heroine honors of the Women's National A. A. U. track and field meet. The two feminine stars stole the major honors in the championships held here yesterday being the only double winners. The meet was not without many other thrills, however, six titles changed, the 50-meter world's mark which has withstood assaults at it for 16 years, was tied and Tuskegee, last year's team champs, repeated. Tuskegee's HYMES won the broad jump for the second consecutive year, captured the 100-meter dash and ran the anchor leg on the institute's 400-meter relay championship team to be voted the outstanding individual athlete of the meet. Miss Fellmeth, representing the Dvorak Park A. C., was spectacular as she annexed the shot put and discus events. Tuskegee's 30 points which gave the team honors doubled the score of the runner-up Eastern Women's A. C. of New York.
In addition to the Misses HYMES, Isicson and Fellmeth, other champions and their titles included: Fanny Vitale of the Park Central A. C., New York, 200-meters; Betsy Jochum, Cincinnati, baseball throw; Marie Cotrell, New York, 80-meters. These were half of the titles that changed hands. The other three

were the 100-meter won by Miss HYMES and the shot put and discus captured by Miss Fellmeth.

The final team point totals were: TUSKEGEE INSTITUTE, 30; Eastern Women's A. C. of New York, 15; German-American A. C. of New York, 12½; Park Central A. C. of New York, 12; Dvorak Park A. C. of Chicago, 12; Polish National Alliance of Chicago, 7; Long Island University A. A., 7; Boston Swimming Association, 7; Mercury A. C. of New York, 6; McDonnell A. C. of Cleveland, 4; Brockton (Mass.) Girls' A. A. 2½; Crystal City A. C. of St. Louis, 1.

WOMEN'S OUTDOOR TRACK AND FIELD CHAMPIONSHIPS

Held at Waterbury, Conn., Sept. 3, 1939

50 mtrs. run—6.7s.—1. GERTRUDE JOHNSON Mercury A. C.; 2. IVY WILSON, Mercury A. C.; 3. JEANNETTE JONES, Harrisburg A. A. A.; 4. ERNESTINE ROGERS, Tuskegee Institute.

100 mtrs. run—12.6s.—1. Olive Hasenfus, Boston Swim Assn.; 2. LUCY NEWELL, Tuskegee Institute; 3. Elizabeth Kinnard, Missouri Racing Club; 4. LULA MAE HYMES, Tuskegee Institute.

200 mtrs. run—25.5 s.—1. Stella Walsh, Polish-American A. C.; 2. HESTER BROWN, Tuskegee Institute; 3. Hilda Plepis, Philadelphia Loyal Order of Moose; 4. JEWEL COLE, Prairie View College.

80 mtrs. hurdles—12.5s.—1. Marie Cottrell, German-American A. C.; 2. Sybil Cooper, German-American A. C.; 3. LEILA PERRY, Tuskegee Institute; 4. Sylvia Rothenberg, German-American A. C.

400 mtrs. relay—49.4s.—1. Tuskegee Institute; (CELESTINE BIRGE, JESSIE ABBOTT, ROWENA HARRISON, LULA MAE HYMES); 2. Mercury A. C.; 4. Chicago Park Hurricanes.

High jump—5 ft. 2 in.—1. ALICE COACHMAN, Tuskegee Institute; 2. Mary Haydon, Ottawa, Ontario; 3. Barbara Howe, Boston Swim Assn.; 4. Gerda Gottlieb, Park Central A. A.

Broad jump—19 ft. 4.8 in.—1. Stella Walsh, Polish-American A. C.; 2. LULA MAE HYMES, Tuskegee Institute; 3. LUCY NEWELL, Tuskegee Institute; 4. Thelma Lalumondier, Crystal City H. S.

Shot put—41 ft. 1¾ in.—1. Katherine Fellmeth, Chicago Park Hurricanes; 2. RAMONA HARRIS, Mercury A. C.; 3. FLORENCE WRIGHT, Tuskegee Institute; 4. Carolyn Yetter, Philadelphia Loyal Order of Moose.

Discus—113 ft. 7½ in.—1. Katherine Fellmeth, Chicago Hurricanes; 2. HATTIE HALL, Tuskegee Institute; 3. FLORENCE WRIGHT, Tuskegee Institute; 4. Betty McLaughlin, Unattached.

Javelin—130 ft. 9½ in.—1. Dorothy Dodson, Chicago Park Hurricanes; 2. Rose Auerbach, Eastern Women's A. C.; 3. Jean McGunnegle, Hope H. S.; 4. MARGARET BARNES, Tuskegee Institute.

Appendix   441

Baseball throw—233 ft. 3.1 in.—1. Catherine O'Connell, Boston Swim Assn.;
2. Jean McGunnegle, Hope H. S.; 3. Irene Romano, Eastern Women's
A. C.; 4. MARGARET MYERS, Harrisburg A. A. A.

Team scores—TUSKEGEE INSTITUTE 33; Chicago Park Hurricanes 16; MERCURY
A. C. (New York) 14; Boston Swimming Assn. 12; Polish-Olympic
A. C. (Cleveland) 12; German-American A. C. (New York) 9; East-
ern Women's A. C. (Brooklyn, N. Y.) 5; Hope H. S. (Providence) 5;
HARRISBURG (Pennsylvania) A. A. A. 3; Philadelphia Loyal Order of
Moose 3; Missouri Racing Club 2; Crystal City (Missouri) H. S. 1;
Park Central A. A. (New York) 1; PRAIRIE VIEW COLLEGE 1; Un-
attached 4.

TUSKEGEE GIRLS SET NEW RELAY RECORD
Ohio Lass Beats White Olympic Dash Champion

By Charles Campbell

Ocean City, N. J.   Afro-American, July 13, 1940
July 4, 1940

A slender, medium built lass from Wilberforce University broke the domina-
tion Stella Walsh, famed Polish sprinter, has held over the women of the world
here Saturday when JEAN LANE snatched victories from her opponents with
heart-pulsing triumphs in the 50- and 100-meter dashes in the National Women's
Track and Field Championships on Recreation Field.

The second highlight of the meet was the performance of the Tuskegee Institute's 400-meter relay team which successfully defended its title and set a new
record despite an exceedingly slow track. The Alabama institution's A team
composed of LUCY NEWELL, JESSIE ABBOTT, ROWENA HARRIS and LULA HYMES,
skirted the track in 0:49.3 to cut one-tenth of a second from their own mark of
0:49.4 set in 1939.

To completely dominate the event, Tuskegee's B team consisting of HATTIE
HALL, HESTER BROWN, LELIA PERRY and ALICE COACHMAN took second honors.
The Mercury A. C. team of New York and the famous New York German-
American quartet failed to give the competition expected. While the Tuskegee
Institute aggregation of eleven young women won but two first places, they
captured so many second and third place honors that for the fourth consecutive
year they won the team championship with 85 points. The Polish-American
girls, white, took second honors with 46½ and the Philadelphia Moose Club
took third with 24 points.

Miss LANE, the sensation from Wilberforce, Ohio, sped over the cinders like a
comet to win the 100 meters in 12 seconds from Stella Walsh, 1936 Olympic
champion, by a foot and copped the shorter distance by one-half step from LUCY
NEWELL of Tuskegee, in 6.6. After the heats of the century, it was obvious that
Miss Walsh was in for a hard time when four colored qualified for the finals in

remarkable time over the slow sandy track. Stella Walsh, JEAN LANE, Claire Isicson, white, JEANNETTE JONES, Harrisburg, and two Tuskegee flashes, LULA HYMES and ROWENA HARRISON, faced the starter. Before the echo of the gun had faded away Lula and Rowena were in the lead. At the fifty, Stella challenged the girls from Alabama and drew up to even terms with them. Then the long, even striding Jean began to pick up speed. And with knees rising and falling like pistons she began to overtake the leaders. With the same gargantuan stride, she flashed across the line the winner by a step, with the Olympic champion second. Lula taking a third and Rowena, fourth. JEANETTE JONES was in fifth place.

The 50-meter dash was a repetition of the longer dash, only this time it was LUCY NEWELL and JEANETTE JONES who fought it out with the Wilberforce sophomore. The finish of the shorter race was even closer than the century. Lucy, off with a burst of speed, took a short lead and kept it until she was some five yards from the tape. It was while they were taking the last four steps that JEAN LANE was barely able to nose out the lass from the South. Miss Jones finished third, the same spot she won last year.

ALICE COACHMAN, Tuskegee, won the high jump to become a repeat winner as she outjumped the field to win with a leap of 4 ft. 11 in. After winning, Alice tried to create a new record but the softness of the takeoff was too great a handicap to overcome. She missed getting over 5 feet 4 inches by hitting the bar at the very top.

In the 400-meter relay the Tuskegee girls won both first and second places, Team A coming in first and Team B romping in second. LUCY NEWELL led off for the winners but she found stern competition from a teammate in HATTIE HALL of Team B. Both girls touched off at the same time, Lucy to Jessie Abbott and Hattie to ALICE COACHMAN. It was on the second leg on the back stretch, that Team A began to roll. Miss Abbott picked up a yard on Miss Coachman and when Rowena Harrison took the baton for Team A she poured it on around the curve to give the stick to LULA HYMES three yards in front of Miss Brown. Miss Brown, Team B, tried to make a race of it with Lula but she was found wanting and had to take a second. The time was 49.3, one-tenth of a second off the winning time last year by the team from Alabama. The Mercury A. C. team, from New York, finished fourth in the relay with JAYNE MAYNARD, ESTHER DENNIS, Mrs. ISABELLA REYNOLDS and Mrs. GERTRUDE JOHNSON running in that order.

To keep the ball a-rolling, two Tuskegee young women grabbed off places in the 80-meter hurdles. LILLIE PURIFOY jumped into the lead at the start, but she was unable to stand the lightning fast finish of Sybil Cooper, 27-year-old white housewife from Brooklyn, who won in the time of 13.9. LEILA PERRY, of Tuskegee, was fourth in the hurdles. LUCY NEWELL, who was nosed out in the 50-meter race, was also nosed out on the last jump by Stella Walsh in the broad jump. Stella leaped 17 feet 7½ inches to win and Lucy went 17 feet

7 inches. Margaret Barnes of Tuskegee finished fourth in the jump. In the javelin throw, MISS BARNES also picked up a fourth. The winning distance was 126 feet, 1 inch.

WOMEN'S INDOOR TRACK AND FIELD CHAMPIONSHIPS

Atlantic City, N. J., April 12, 1941

50 mtrs.—6.8s.—1. JEAN LANE, Wilberforce; 2. JEANNETTE JONES, Harrisburg A. A.; 3. LUCY NEWELL, Tuskegee Institute; 4. ROWENA HARRISON, Tuskegee; 5. Mary DeShayes, Philadelphia Moose; 6. Betty Charters, Philadelphia Moose.

200 mtrs.—25.1s.—(Record disallowed—No border).—1. JEAN LANE, Wilberforce; 2. Stella Walsh, Polish Olympic Club; 3. HESTER BROWN, Tuskegee Institute; 4. JEANNETTE JONES, Harrisburg A. A.; 5. Olive Hasenfus, Boston Swim Assn.; 6. Elizabeth Peel, Philadelphia Moose.

50 mtrs. hurdles—8.1s.—1. LILLIE PURIFOY, Tuskegee Institute; 2. Hilda Plepis, Philadelphia Moose; 3. Nancy Cowperthwaite, German-American A. C.; 4. LEILA PERRY, Tuskegee Institute; 5. Ronnie Williams, Philadelphia Moose; 6. Helm McKee, Philadelphia Moose.

Standing broad jump—8 ft. 1⅞ in.—1. LUCY NEWELL, Tuskegee Institute; 2. LILLIE PURIFOY, Tuskegee Institute; 3. Jean M. Harvey, Philadelphia Moose; 4. Betty Charters, Philadelphia Moose; 5. Rita Corrigan, Polish Olympic; 6. Mary Campbell, York A. C.

Basketball throw—95 ft. 10¼ in.—1. Marian Twining, Philadelphia Moose; 2. Mildred Yetter, Philadelphia Moose; 3. Evelyn Taylor, Taylor A. C.; 4. Marie Sostar, Harrisburg A. A.; 5. Stella Walsh, Polish Olympic Club; 6. Elizabeth DeLone, Harrisburg A. A.

High jump—5 ft.—1. ALICE COACHMAN, Tuskegee Institute; 2. Jean M. Harvey, Philadelphia Moose; 3. Nancy Cowperthwaite, German-American; 4. Frances Gorn, Polish Olympic Club; 5. LEILA PERRY, Tuskegee Institute; 6. Elizabeth Clancy, German Olympic.

400 mtr. relay—50.1s.—1. Tuskegee Team A (LUCY NEWELL, LEILA PERRY, HESTER BROWN, ROWENA HARRISON); 2. Philadelphia Moose Team A; 3. Tuskegee Team B; 4. Philadelphia Moose Team B; 5. Polish Olympic Club. (New Worlds Indoor Record.)

8-lb. Shot put—35 ft. ⅝ in.—1. Dorothy Dodson, Chicago Hurricanes; 2. HATTIE HALL, Tuskegee Institute; 3. Frances Gorn, Polish Olympic; 4. Mildred Yetter, Philadelphia Moose; 5. Rose Przybylski, Polish Olympic A. C.; 6. Mary Twining, Philadelphia Moose.

Team Score—TUSKEGEE INSTITUTE, 84; Philadelphia Moose, 69; Polish Olympic Women's A. C., 26; WILBERFORCE UNIVERSITY, 20; HARRISBURG A. A., 17; German-American A. C., 13; Chicago Hurricanes, 10; Taylor A. C., Chicago, 6; Boston Swimming Association, 2; York A. C. 1.

NATIONAL SENIOR OUTDOOR TRACK AND FIELD CHAMPIONSHIPS

WOMEN

Held at Ocean City, N. J., July 5, 1941

50 mtr. dash—6.6s.—1. LUCY NEWELL, Tuskegee Institute; 2. JEANETTE JONES, Harrisburg A. A.; 3. Claire Isicson, Long Island University; 4. MAMIE TAYLOR, Tuskegee Institute; 5. Rita Corrigan, Polish Olympic Women's A. C.; 6. Margery Hall, Philadelphia Moose.

100 mtr. dash—12.4s.—1. JEAN LANE, Wilberforce University; 2. ALICE COACHMAN, Tuskegee Institute; 3. ROWENA HARRISON, Tuskegee Institute; 4. Margaret Wigeser, Eastern Women's A. C.; 5. Jeannette Ellicott, St. Clair A. C., Toronto; 6. Theresa Hanley, Red Diamond A. C., Boston.

200 mtr. dash—25.2s.—JEAN LANE, Wilberforce University; 2. Stella Walsh, Polish Olympic Women's A. C.; 3. HESTER BROWN, Tuskegee Institute: 4. BETSY CAREY, Tuskegee Institute; 5. Betty Charters, Philadelphia Moose; 6. Olive Hasenfus, Boston Swim. Assn.

80 mtr. hurdles—13.2s.—1. LEILA PERRY, Tuskegee Institute; 2. LILLIE PURIFOY, Tuskegee Institute; 3. Hilda Plepis, Philadelphia Moose; 4. Nancy Cowperthwaite, German-American A. C.; 5. Gladys Crisman, Rhode Island Cinder Lassies; 6. Helen McKee, Philadelphia Moose.

400 mtr. relay—50s.—1. TUSKEGEE INSTITUTE TEAM A (LUCY NEWELL, LEILA PERRY, ROWENA HARRISON, ALICE COACHMAN); 2. TUSKEGEE INSTITUTE TEAM B; 3. Philadelphia Moose Team A; 4. St. Clair A. C., Toronto; 5. Red Diamond A. C., Boston; 6. Philadelphia Moose Team B.

8-lb. shot put—37 ft. ⅜ in.—1. Catherine Fellmeth, Unattached, Chicago; 2. Dorothy Dodson, Unattached, Chicago; 3. HATTIE HALL, Tuskegee Institute; 4. Caroline Yetter, Philadelphia Moose; 5. Margaret Wigeser, Eastern Women's A. C., Brooklyn; 6. Kay Geary, Philadelphia Turners.

Running broad jump—5 ft. 2¾ in.—1. ALICE COACHMAN, Tuskegee Institute; 2. Norma Jeffrey, Chicago Park Hurricanes; 3. LEILA PERRY, Tuskegee Institute; 4. Jean M. Harvey, Philadelphia Moose; 5. tie between Elizabeth Clancy, German-American A. C., N. Y., and Claire Barcikowski, Polish Women's A. C.

Discus throw—113 ft. 10⅜ in.—1. Stella Walsh, Polish Olympic Women's A. C.; 2. Evelyn Taylor, Taylor A. C., LaGrange, Ill.; 3. Catherine Fellmeth, Unattached, Chicago; 4. HATTIE HALL, Tuskegee Institute; 5. Caroline Yetter, Philadelphia Moose; 6. Elizabeth DeLone, Harrisburg A. A.

Javelin throw—128 ft. 7⅛ in.—1. Dorothy Dodson, Unattached, Chicago; 2. Marion Twining, Philadelphia Moose; 3. Marie Sostar, Harrisburg

A. A.; 4. Angela Mica, St. Louis A. C.; 5. Katherine O'Connell, Boston Swim. Assn.; 6. Jean McGunnegle, Boston Swim. Assn.

Baseball throw— 260 ft. 10⅞ in.—1. Angela Mica, St. Louis A. C.; 2. Betsy Jochum, Unattached, Cincinnati; 3. Jean McGunnegle, Boston Swim. Assn.; 4. Margaret Wigeser, Eastern Women's A. C.; 5. Marion Twining, Philadelphia Moose; 6. Irene Romano, Eastern Women's A. C.

Team score—TUSKEGEE INSTITUTE, 100; Philadelphia Moose, 43; Polish Olympic Women's A. C., 31½; WILBERFORCE UNIVERSITY, 20; HARRISBURG A. A., 19; St. Louis A. C., 14; Eastern Women's A. C., 11; Boston Swim. Assn., 10; Chicago Park Hurricanes, 8; Taylor A. C., 8; St. Clair A. C., Toronto, 7; Long Island University, 6; German-American A. C., Brooklyn, 5½; Red Diamond A. C., 3; Rhode Island Cinder Lassies, 2; PHILADELPHIA TURNERS, 1; Unattached, 42.

WOMEN'S OUTDOOR TRACK AND FIELD CHAMPIONSHIPS

Held at Ocean City, N. J., July 4, 1942

50 mtr. dash—6.7s.—1. JEANNETTE JONES, Harrisburg A. A.; 2. Jeanette Ellicott, St. Clair A. C.; 3. MAMIE TAYLOR, Tuskegee Institute; 4. Rita Corrigan, Polish Olympic Women's A. C.; 5. Jean Woods, Toronto Laurel Ladies; 6. Betty Woods, Toronto Laurel Ladies.

100 mtr. dash—12.1s.—1. ALICE COACHMAN, Tuskegee Institute; 2. ROWENA HARRISON, Tuskegee Institute; 3. JEAN LOWE, Toronto Laurel Ladies; 4. JEANETTE JONES, Harrisburg A. A.; 5. Katherine Geary, Philadelphia Turners; 6. Betty Charters, Philadelphia Moose.

80 mtr. hurdles—12.6s.—1. LILLIE PURIFOY, Tuskegee Institute; 2. Nancy Cowperthwaite, German-American A. C.; 3. LEILA PERRY, Tuskegee Institute; 4. Roxy Campbell, Toronto Laurel Ladies; 5. Helen McKee, Philadelphia Moose; 6. Loretta Blaul, German-American A. C.

200 mtr. dash—25.4s.—1. Stella Walsh, Polish Olympic Women's A. C.; 2. Jean Kaplan, Chicago Park Hurricanes; 3. Katherine Geary, Philadelphia Turners; 4. Alice Jagus, Polish Olympic Women's A. C.; 5. Helen Busch, Philadelphia Moose; 6. Betty Charters, Philadelphia Moose.

400 mtr. relay—50.7s.—1. TUSKEGEE INSTITUTE, TEAM A (LILLIE PURIFOY, LEILA PERRY, ROWENA HARRISON, ALICE COACHMAN); 2. Toronto Laurel Ladies; 3. Philadelphia Moose, Team A; 4. Philadelphia Moose, Team B; 5. German-American A. C.; 6. TUSKEGEE INSTITUTE, TEAM B.

8-lb. shot put—37 ft. 10 in.—1. Romana Harris, Unattached, N. Y. C.; 2. Dorothy Dodson, Chicago Park Hurricanes; 3. Frances Gorn, Polish Olympic Women's A. C.; 4. Margaret Wigeser, Eastern Women's A. C.; 5. HATTIE HALL, Tuskegee Institute; 6. Mildred Yetter, Philadelphia Moose.

Running broad jump—17 ft. 11 in.—1. Stella Walsh, Polish Olympic Women's A. C.; 2. ROWENA HARRISON, Tuskegee Institute; 3. Betty Moore, Philadelphia Moose; 4. Betty Charters, Philadelphia Moose; 5. JEAN-ETTE JONES, Harrisburg A. A.; 6. Jean Kaplan, Chicago Park Hurricanes.

Running high jump—4 ft. 8 in.—1. ALICE COACHMAN, Tuskegee Institute; 2. Norma Jeffrey, Chicago Park Hurricanes; tie for third among Frances Gorn, Polish Olympic Women's A. C., CATHERINE BOLDEN, Tuskegee Institute, and LEILA PERRY, Tuskegee Institute; tie for sixth among Jean Walraven, Polish Olympic Women's A. C., Betty Woods, Toronto Laurel Ladies, Eleanor Millheiser, German-American A. C., Pauline Ruppeldt, Philadelphia Moose, and Alice Jagus, Polish Olympic Women's A. C.

Discus throw—110 ft. 11¾ in.—1. Stella Walsh, Polish Olympic W.A.C.; 2. Frances Gorn, Polish Olympic W.A.C.; 3. Anna Pallo, Polish Olympic W.A.C.; 4. Dorothy Dodson, Chicago Park Hurricanes; 5. Betty Weaver, Unattached, Bayonne, N. J.; 6. HATTIE HALL, Tuskegee Institute.

Javelin throw—122 ft. 10½ in.—1. Dorothy Dodson, Chicago Park Hurricanes; 2. Marie Sostar, Harrisburg A. A.; 3. Marion Twining, Philadelphia Moose; 4. Katherine Geary, Philadelphia Turners; 5. Mildred Yetter, Philadelphia Moose; 6. HATTIE HALL, Tuskegee Institute.

Baseball throw—259 ft. 7 in.—1. Irena Romano, Eastern Women's A. C.; 2. HATTIE TURNER, Tuskegee Institute; 3. Marion Twining, Philadelphia Moose; 4. Margaret Wigeser, Eastern Women's A. C.; 5. Ann Pallo, Polish Olympic W.A.C.

Team score—TUSKEGEE INSTITUTE, 80; Polish Olympic Women's A. C.; 64.5; Philadelphia Moose, 41.5; Chicago Park Hurricanes, 39; HARRISBURG A. A., 24; Toronto Laurel Ladies Club, 22.5; Eastern Women's A. C., 18; Philadelphia Turners, 12; German-American A. C., 11.5; St. Clair Athletic Club, 8; Unattached, 21.

NATIONAL SENIOR OUTDOOR TRACK AND FIELD CHAMPIONSHIPS

WOMEN

Held at Lakewood, Ohio, August 15, 1943

50 mtr. run—6.5s.—1. ALICE COACHMAN, Tuskegee Institute; 2. JEANETTE JONES, Harrisburg A. C.; 3. LILLIAN YOUNG, Chicago Central Assn.

100 mtr. run—11.6s.—1. Stella Walsh, Polish Olympic Women's A. C., Cleveland; 2. ALICE COACHMAN, Tuskegee Institute; 3. ROWENA HARRISON, Tuskegee Institute.

200 mtr. run—26.3—1. Stella Walsh, Polish Olympic Women's A. C., Cleveland; 2. Alice Jagus, Polish Olympic Women's A. C.; 3. Mary Cummins, Toronto Laurel Ladies A. C.

80 mtr. hurdles—12.3s.—1. Nancy Cowperthwaite, German-American A. C., N. Y.; 2. Joan Davis, St. Clair A. C., Toronto; 3. LEILA PERRY, Tuskegee Institute.

400 mtr. relay—50.6s.—1. Toronto Laurel Ladies A. C.; 2. TUSKEGEE INSTITUTE; 3. German-American A. C.

8-lb. shot put—37 ft. 11 in.—1. Frances Gorn, Polish Olympic Women's A. C.; 2. Dorothy Dodson, Unattached, Chicago; 3. Mildred Yetter, Philadelphia Moose.

Running high jump—5 ft.—1. ALICE COACHMAN, Tuskegee Institute; 2. ADRIENNE ROBINSON, Chicago Central Assn.; 3. BERNICE ROBINSON, Chicago Central Assn.

Running broad jump—19 ft. 1 in.—1. Stella Walsh, Polish Olympic Women's A. C.; 2. ROWENA HARRISON, Tuskegee Institute; 3. Betty Dummeldinger, Philadelphia Moose.

Discus throw—109 ft. 6¼ in.—1. Frances Gorn, Polish Olympic Women's A. C.; 2. Betty Weaver, Unattached; 3. Ann Pallo, Polish Women's A. C.

Javelin throw—111 ft. 3 in.—1. Dorothy Dodson, Unattached, Chicago; 2. Marian Twining, Philadelphia Moose; 3. Bessie Leick, Polish Olympic Women's A. C.

Baseball throw—260 ft. 6 in.—1. Elaine Grothe, Chicago Central Assn.; 2. Marian Twining, Philadelphia Moose Club; 3. HATTIE TURNER, Tuskegee Institute.

Team score—Polish Olympic Women's A. C., Cleveland, 87⅙; TUSKEGEE INSTITUTE, 77½; CHICAGO CENTRAL ASSN., 30; Moose Club, Philadelphia, 28; Toronto Laurel Ladies A. C., 16; German-American A. C., N. Y., 10; HARRISBURG A. C., 8; St. Clair A. C., Toronto 8; Unattached, 26.

NATIONAL SENIOR OUTDOOR TRACK AND FIELD CHAMPIONSHIPS

WOMEN

Held at Harrisburg, Pa., July 8, 1944

50 mtr. dash—6.4s.—1. ALICE COACHMAN, Tuskegee Institute; 2. LILLIAN YOUNG, Forestville Playground, Chicago; 3. Viola Myers, Laurel Ladies Club, Toronto. (This 6.4s. equals world record.)

100 mtr. dash—12s.—1. Stella Walsh, Unattached, Cleveland; 2. ALICE COACHMAN, Tuskegee Institute; 3. JEAN LOWE, Laurel Ladies Club, Toronto; 4. Kay Geary, Philadelphia Turners.

200 mtr. run—24.6s.—1. Stella Walsh, Unattached, Cleveland; 2. ROWENA HARRISON, Tuskegee Institute; 3. Mary Cummins, Laurel Ladies Club, Toronto; 4. Jean Walraven, Unattached, Cleveland; 5. GWENDOLYN TAYLOR, Harrisburg A.A.A.; 6. NELL JACKSON, Tuskegee Institute.

80 mtr. hurdles—12.8s.—1. LILLIE PURIFOY, Tuskegee Institute; 2. Jean Walraven, Unattached, Cleveland; 3. LEILA PERRY, Tuskegee Institute; 4. Dolores McElduff, Philadelphia Moose.

400 mtr. relay—52.8s.—1. Laurel Ladies Club, Toronto (Nancy McKay, Viola Myers, Doris Wright, JEAN LOWE); 2. TUSKEGEE INSTITUTE TEAM A; 3. German-American A. C., N. Y.; 4. Philadelphia Moose; 5. TUSKEGEE INSTITUTE TEAM B; 6. Harrisburg A.A.A.

8-lb. shot put—36 ft. ¼ in.—1. Dorothy Dodson, Unattached, Chicago; 2. Carolyn Yetter, Philadelphia Moose; 3. CLEO DAVIS, Tuskegee Institute; 4. Pauline Ruppeldt, Philadelphia Moose; 5. Eleanor Repinski, Cleveland.

Running broad jump—17 ft. 11⅛ in.—1. Stella Walsh, Unattached, Cleveland; 2. ROWENA HARRISON, Tuskegee Institute; 3. Jean Kaplan, Riis Park, Chicago; 4. LILLIAN YOUNG, Forestville Playground, Chicago; 5. LILLIE PURIFOY, Tuskegee Institute.

Running high jump—5 ft. 1⅝ in.—1. ALICE COACHMAN, Tuskegee Institute; 2. Nancy Cowperthwaite, German-American A. C., N. Y.; tie for third between NELLIE STAFFORD, Tuskegee Institute, and Clara Schroth, Philadelphia Turners; tie for fifth between LEILA PERRY, Tuskegee Institute and Edith Barber, German-American A. C., N. Y.

Discus—101 ft. 7¾ in.—1. HATTIE TURNER, Tuskegee Institute; 2. Betty Weaver, Unattached, Bayonne, N. J.; 3. Pauline Ruppeldt, Philadelphia Moose; 4. Mildred Yetter, Philadelphia Moose; 5. Marie Sostar, Harrisburg A.A.A.; 6. Dorothy Dodson, Chicago.

Javelin—123 ft. 1½ in.—1. Dorothy Dodson, Chicago; 2. Lillian Davis, Philadelphia Moose; 3. Marie Sostar, Harrisburg A.A.A.; 4. HATTIE TURNER, Tuskegee Institute; 5. Betty Weaver, Bayonne, N. Y.; 6. Elizabeth Yetter, Philadelphia Moose.

Baseball throw—214 ft. 6 in.—1. HATTIE TURNER, Tuskegee Institute; 2. Harriet Mitchell, Harrisburg A.A.A.; 3. Lillian Carrig, Harrisburg A.A.A.; 4. Lillian Davis, Philadelphia Moose.

Team score—TUSKEGEE INSTITUTE, 110; Philadelphia Moose, 51; Laurel Ladies Club, Toronto, 30; Harrisburg A.A.A., 29; German-American A. C., N. Y., 16; Forrestville Playground, Chicago, 11; Philadelphia Turners, 8; Riis Park, Chicago, 6; Unattached, 75.

Appendix 449

NATIONAL SENIOR INDOOR TRACK AND FIELD CHAMPIONSHIPS

WOMEN

Held at Buffalo, N. Y., March 31, 1945

50 yard run—6.1s.—1. ALICE COACHMAN, Tuskegee Institute; 2. LILLIAN YOUNG, Chicago Forrestville Playground; 3. ROWENA HARRISON, Tuskegee Institute; 4. Kay Geary, Philadelphia Turners. (New Indoor Record for this event.)

220 yard run—26.3s.—1. Stella Walsh, Polish Olympic A. C., Cleveland, Ohio; 2. NELL JACKSON, Tuskegee Institute; 3. GWENDOLYN TAYLOR, Harrisburg, A. A.; 4. Muriel Millheiser, German-American A. C., N. Y.

50 yard hurdles—7.6s.—1. Nancy Cowperthwaite, German-American A. C., N. Y.; 2. LILLIE PURIFOY, Tuskegee Institute; 3. Clara Schroth, Philadelphia Turners; 4. Edith Barber, German-American A. C., N. Y.

440 yard relay—53.6s.—1. TUSKEGEE INSTITUTE (NELL JACKSON, LILLIE PURIFOY, ROWENA HARRISON, ALICE COACHMAN); 2. German-American A. C., N. Y.; 3. Chicago Forrestville Playground; 4. Chicago Hurricanes.

Running high jump—1. ALICE COACHMAN, Tuskegee Institute—4 ft. 8 in.; 2. Pauline Ruppeldt, Philadelphia Moose; 3. tie between Clara Schroth, Philadelphia Turners and Nancy Cowperthwaite, German-American A. C., N. Y.

Standing broad jump—1. Clara Schroth, Philadelphia Turners—7 ft. 11¾ in.; 2. Lorraine Boesen, Chicago Hurricanes; 3. Corrine Winston, Chicago Forrestville Playground; 4. ROWENA HARRISON, Tuskegee Institute.

8-lb. shot put—Dorothy Dodson, Chicago Hurricanes—35 ft. 1⅝ in.; 2. Kay Geary, Philadelphia Turners; 3. HATTIE TURNER, Tuskegee Institute; 4. Pauline Ruppeldt, Philadelphia Moose.

Basketball throw—1. Marian Twining, Philadelphia Moose—94 ft. 10½ in.; 2. Dorothy Dodson, Chicago Hurricanes; 3. HATTIE TURNER, Tuskegee Institute; 4. Katherine Jones, Chicago Copernicus Playground.

Team score—TUSKEGEE INSTITUTE, 28; Philadelphia Turners, 12½; Chicago Hurricanes, 12; German-American A. C., N. Y., 11½; Philadelphia Moose, 9; Forrestville Playground, 7; Polish Olympic A. C., Cleveland, 5; Harrisburg A.A.A., 2; Copernicus Playground, Chicago 1.

WOMEN'S NATIONAL A.A.U., TRACK AND FIELD CHAMPIONSHIPS

Held at Harrisburg, Penn., June 30, 1945

200 mtr. run—1. Stella Walsh, Polish Olympic A. C., Cleveland; 2. NELL JACKSON, Tuskegee Institute; 3. GWEN TAYLOR, Harrisburg A. C.; 4. Alice Jagus, Polish A. C., Cleveland; 5. THERESA MANUEL, Tuskegee Institute; 6. WILLIE TYNER, Tuskegee Institute. Time 26.6 s.

50 mtr. run—1. ALICE COACHMAN, Tuskegee Institute; 2. LILLIAN YOUNG, Forrestville, Chicago; 3. ROWENA HARRISON, Tuskegee Institute; 4. Viola Myers, Laurel A. C., Toronto; 5. JEANNETTE JONES, Harrisburg A. C.; 6. BEATRICE BOOKER, Harrisburg A. C.; Time 6.5 s.

8-lb. shot put—1. Frances Kaszubski, Polish Olympic A. C., Cleveland; 2. HELEN STEWART, Harrisburg A. C.; 3. Dorothy Dodson, Hurricanes, Chicago; 4. Pauline H. Ruppeldt, Philadelphia Moose and Estelle Kasterbaum, German-American A. C., Brooklyn (tied); 6. Kay Geary, Philadelphia Turners. Distance: 37 ft. 9 ⅞ in.

80 mtr. hurdles—1. LILLIE PURIFOY, Tuskegee Institute; 2. Nancy Cowperthwaite, German-American A. C., Brooklyn; 3. Marie Wingo, Westside Country Club, Asbury Park; 4. Jean Walraven, Polish-American A. C., Cleveland; 5. Clara Schroth, Philadelphia Turners; 6. Helen McKee, Philadelphia Moose. Time: 12.5 s.

100 mtr. run—1. ALICE COACHMAN, Tuskegee Institute; 2. Stella Walsh, Polish Olympic A. C., Cleveland; 3. JEAN LOWE, Laurel A. C., Toronto; 4. LILLIAN YOUNG, Forrestville, Chicago; 5. LILLIAN JAMES, Forrestville, Chicago; 6. Ruth Harrigan, Laurel A. C., Toronto. Time: 12 s.

Discus throw—1. Frances Kaszubski, Polish Olympic A. C., Cleveland; 2. HATTIE TURNER, Tuskegee Institute; 3. Dorothy Dodson, Hurricanes, Chicago; 4. Marie Sostar, Harrisburg A. C.; 5. Pauline Ruppeldt, Philadelphia Moose; 6. Ann Pallo, Polish Olympic A. C. Distance: 103 ft. ¼ in.

400 mtr. relay—1. Laurel Athletic Club, Toronto, (Mackay, Myers, Wright, LOWE); 2. TUSKEGEE INSTITUTE TEAM A; 3. German-American Athletic Club, Brooklyn; 4. Harrisburg Athletic Club; 5. TUSKEGEE INSTITUTE TEAM B. Time: 51.4 s.

Running high jump—1. ALICE COACHMAN, Tuskegee Institute; 2. Marie Wingo, Westside A. C., Asbury Park, and Nancy Cowperthwaite, German-American A. C., Brooklyn, (tied); 4. Jean Walraven, Polish Olympic A. C., and Clara Schroth, Philadelphia Turners; 6. Frances Sobczak, Alice Jagus and Bessie Leich, Polish Olympic A. C. and Pauline Ruppeldt, Philadelphia Moose, (tied). Height: 5 ft.

Javelin throw—1. Dorothy Dodson, Chicago Hurricanes; 2. Marian Twining, Philadelphia Moose; 3. Marie Sostar, Harrisburg A. C.; 4. HATTIE TURNER, Tuskegee Institute; 5. Lillian Davis, Philadelphia Moose; 6. JAYNE BITNER, Harrisburg A. C. Distance: 124 ft. 10 in.

Baseball throw—1. Marion Twining, Philadelphia Moose; 2. HATTIE TURNER, Tuskegee Institute; 3. Peggie Anderson, Polish-American A. C.; 4. Pfc. Christine Long, Lincoln Air Field, Nebraska; 5. Bessie Leich, Polish-American A. C.; 6. Lillian Davis, Philadelphia Moose. Distance: 237 ft. 9 in.

Broad jump—1. Stella Walsh, Polish-American A. C., Cleveland; 2. ROWENA

Appendix

HARRISON, Tuskegee Institute; 3. LILLIAN YOUNG, Chicago Hurricanes; 4. ALICE CROWELL, Tuskegee Institute; 5. LILLIE PURIFOY, Tuskegee Institute; 6. Clara Schroth, Philadelphia Turners. Distance: 18 ft. 3 in. Team score—TUSKEGEE INSTITUTE, 102.

NATIONAL JUNIOR INDOOR TRACK AND FIELD CHAMPIONSHIPS

WOMEN

Under Auspices of the Ranger Athletic Club at Central Armory, Cleveland, Ohio, March 30, 1946

200 yard run—30.2s.—1. JUANITA WATSON, Tuskegee Institute; 2. NELL JACK-SON, Tuskegee Institute; 3. Marion Twining, Philadelphia Turners; 4. Nancy Cowperthwaite, German-American A. C.

50 yard hurdles—7.3s.—1. Jean Walraven, Polish Olympics; 2. THERESA MANUEL, Tuskegee Institute; 3. Loretta Blaul, German-American A. C.; 4. Bessie Leick, Polish Olympic; (New American Record)

50 yard run—6.3s.—1. Katherine Geary, Philadelphia Turners; 2. Nancy McLurken, Philadelphia Turners; 3. LILLIAN YOUNG, Bur. of Rec., Chicago; 4. Dorothy Jacobs, Chicago, unattached.

8-lb. shot put—34 ft.—1. HELEN STEWART, Harrisburg A.A.A.; 2. Katherine Geary, Philadelphia Turners; 3. Pauline Ruppeldt, Philadelphia Turners; 4. Rose Przybylski, Polish Olympic A. C.

High jump—4 ft. 7¾ in.—1. Nancy Cowperthwaite, German-American A. C.; 2. Eleanor Millheiser, German-American A. C., and Pauline Ruppeldt, Philadelphia Turners, (tied); 4. Jean Walraven, Polish Olympic W.A.C., and Loretta Blaul, German-American A. C., (tied)

440 yard relay—60.1s.—1. TUSKEGEE INSTITUTE TEAM B (MABEL WALKER, JEWEL JOHNSON, MARY CARTER, JUANITA WATSON); 2. Chicago Bur. of Rec. Team "A"; 3. TUSKEGEE INSTITUTE TEAM A; 4. German-American A. C.

Basketball throw—87 ft. 11½ in.—1. Peggy Anderson, Polish Olympic W.A.C.; 2. HARRIET MITCHELL, Harrisburg A.A.A.; 3. THERESA MANUEL, Tuskegee Institute; 4. Helen Lasch, Ranger A. C.

Standing broad jump—7 ft. 9½ in.—1. Lorraine Boesen, Unattached, Chicago; 2. Nancy Cowperthwaite, German-American A. C.; 3. ROWENA HARRI-SON, Tuskegee Institute; 4. Corrine Winston, Bur. of Rec., Chicago.

High point team—TUSKEGEE INSTITUTE, 22; Philadelphia Turners, 17½; 3. German-American A. C., 14⅚; 4. Polish Olympic W.A.C., 12⅔.

High point girl—1. Nancy Cowperthwaite, German-American A. C., 9; 2. Katherine Geary, Philadelphia Turners, 8; 3. Jean Walraven, Polish-Olympic W.A.C., 5⅓.

NATIONAL SENIOR INDOOR TRACK AND FIELD CHAMPIONSHIPS

WOMEN

Sponsored by the Polish Olympic Women's Athletic Club, Central Armory, Cleveland, Ohio, March 31, 1946

50 yard run—6.4 s.—1. ALICE COACHMAN, Tuskegee Institute; 2. Kay Geary, Philadelphia Turners; 3. LILLIAN YOUNG, Chicago Bur. of Rec.; 4. Eleanor Millheiser, German-American A. C.

220 yard run—28.6 s.—1. Stella Walsh, Polish Olympic W.A.C.; 2. JUANITA WATSON, Tuskegee Institute; 3. FANNIE JOHNSON, Tuskegee Institute; 4. GWENDOLYN TAYLOR, Harrisburg A.A.A.

8-lb. shot put—34 ft. 6½ in.—1. Dorothy Dodson, Unattached, Chicago; 2. HELEN STEWART, Harrisburg A.A.A.; 3. Stella Walsh, Polish Olympic; 4. Katherine Geary, Philadelphia Turners.

High jump—4 ft. 6⅞ in.—1. ALICE COACHMAN, Tuskegee Institute; 2. Jean Walraven, Polish Olympic W.A.C.; 3. Eleanor Millheiser, German-American A. C., and Bessie Lieck, Polish Olympic W.A.C., (tied).

Basketball throw—101 ft. 4¼ in.—1. Marion Twining, Philadelphia Turners; 2. HATTIE TURNER, Tuskegee Institute; 3. HARRIET MITCHELL, Harrisburg A.A.A.; 4. THERESA MANUEL, Tuskegee Institute.

Standing broad jump—8 ft. 1⅛ in.—1. Lorraine Boesen, Unattached, Chicago; 2. Stella Walsh, Polish Olympic W.A.C.; 3. Mildred Martin, Unattached, Chicago; 4. Nancy Cowperthwaite, German-American A. C.

50 yard hurdles—7.8 s.—1. LILLIE PURIFOY, Tuskegee Institute; 2. Nancy Cowperthwaite, German-American A. C.; 3. Jean Walraven, Polish Olympic W.A.C.; 4. THERESA MANUEL, Tuskegee Institute.

440 yard relay—59.8 s.—1. Philadelphia Turners (Helen McKee, Marion Twining, Katherine Geary, Nancy McClurken); 2. Chicago Bur. of Rec.; 3. TUSKEGEE INSTITUTE TEAM A; 4. TUSKEGEE INSTITUTE TEAM B.

Team score—TUSKEGEE INSTITUTE, 29; Polish Olympic, 16½; Philadelphia Turners, 14; German-American A. C., 6½.

Individual high score—1. ALICE COACHMAN, Tuskegee Institute, and Stella Walsh, Polish Olympic W.A.C., (tied) 10; Miss Coachman, having greatest number of first places was awarded the trophy.

NATIONAL SENIOR OUTDOOR TRACK AND FIELD CHAMPIONSHIPS

WOMEN

Auspices of Uniformed Firemen's Association at Buffalo, N. Y.
Sunday, August 4, 1946

50 mtr. dash—6.5 s.—1. ALICE COACHMAN, Tuskegee Institute; 2. Katherine Geary, Philadelphia Turners; 3. LILLIAN YOUNG, Forestville Playground, Chicago; 4. Shirley Eckel, Malvernette A. C., Toronto; 5. Eleanor

Millheiser, German-American A. C., N. Y.; 6. Verna Myers, Malvernette A. C., Toronto.

100 mtr. dash—12.3 s.—1. ALICE COACHMAN, Tuskegee Institute; 2. Stella Walsh, Cleveland Polish Olympic W.A.C.; 3. Nancy Mackay, Malvernette A. C., Toronto; 4. Katherine Geary, Philadelphia Turners.

220 yard dash—26.3 s.—1. Stella Walsh, Cleveland Polish Olympic W.A.C.; 2. NELL JACKSON, Tuskegee Institute; 3. JEANNETTE JONES, Harrisburg A.A.A.; 4. Mildred Martin, Unattached; 5. FANNIE JOHNSON, Tuskegee Institute.

80 mtr. hurdle—12.2 s.—1. Nancy Cowperthwaite, German-American A. C., N. Y.; 2. LILLIE PURIFOY, Tuskegee Institute; 3. Jean Walraven, Cleveland Polish Olympic W.A.C.; 4. THERESA MANUEL, Tuskegee Institute; 5. Joan M. Davis, Unattached; 6. Loretta M. Blaul, German-American A. C., N. Y.

440 yard relay—1. Malvernette A. C., Team A, Toronto, Canada, (Nancy Mackay, Ruth Harrigan, Viola Myers, Shirley Eckel); 2. German-American A. C., N. Y.; 3. TUSKEGEE INSTITUTE, TEAMA; 4. TUSKEGEE INSTITUTE, TEAM B; 5. Malvernette A. C., Team B, Toronto; 6. Cleveland Polish Olympic W.A.C. Time: 50 s.

Running broad jump—1. Stella Walsh, Cleveland Polish Olympic W.A.C., 17 ft. ¾ in.; 2. LILLIAN YOUNG, Forestville Playground, Chicago; 3. Jean Walraven, Cleveland Polish Olympic W.A.C.; 4. FANNIE JOHNSON, Tuskegee Institute; 5. Joan Davis, Unattached; 6. Mildred Martin, Unattached.

Running high jump—1. ALICE COACHMAN, Tuskegee Institute, 5 ft.; 2. Nancy Cowperthwaite, German-American A. C., N. Y. and Jean Walraven, Cleveland Polish W.A.C., (tied); 4. Verna Myers, Malvernette A. C., Toronto, and Bessie Leick, Cleveland Polish Olympic W.A.C., (tied).

Javelin throw—1. Dorothy Dodson, Unattached, 120 ft., 2 in.; 2. Marion Twining, Philadelphia Moose; 3. HATTIE TURNER PALMER, Tuskegee Institute; 4. Bessie Leick, Cleveland Polish Olympic W.A.C.; 5. Katherine Geary, Philadelphia Turners; 6. HARRIET MITCHELL, Harrisburg (Pa.) A.A.A.

8-lb. shot put—1. Dorothy Dodson, Unattached, Chicago, 38 ft. 10¾ in.; 2. ELAINE BRADFORD, Tuskegee Institute; 3. Florence Blasch, Unattached; 4. Josephine Wilkowski, Kay Daumet Hurricanes, Chicago; 5. Estelle Kastenbaum, German-American A. C., N. Y.; 6. Rose Przyblski, Cleveland Polish Olympic W.A.C.

Baseball throw—1. Marion Twining, Philadelphia Turners, 242 ft. 10¼ in.; 2. HATTIE TURNER PALMER, Tuskegee Institute; 3. Peggy Anderson, Cleveland Polish Olympic W.A.C.; 4. HARRIET MITCHELL, Harrisburg A.A.A.; 5. Bessie Leick, Cleveland Polish Olympic W.A.C.; 6. Estelle Kastenbaum, German-American A. C.

Discus throw—1. Dorothy Dodson, Unattached, Chicago, 102 ft. 6 in.;
2. HATTIE PALMER, Tuskegee Institute; 3. Estelle Kastenbaum, German-
American A. C., N. Y.; 4. ELAINE BRADFORD, Tuskegee Institute;
5. MILDRED BLOSSY, Harrisburg A.A.A.

Team score—1. TUSKEGEE INSTITUTE, 100; 2. Cleveland Polish Olympic
W.A.C., 64½; 3. German-American A. C., N. Y., 38½; 4. Malvernette A. C., Toronto, 32; 5. Philadelphia Turners, 29; 6. Forestville Playground, Chicago, 14; 7. Harrisburg (Pa.) A.A.A., 13; 8. Kay
Daumet Hurricanes, Chicago, 4; Unattached, 46.

WOMEN'S JUNIOR OUTDOOR TRACK AND FIELD CHAMPIONSHIPS
Held at San Antonio, June 28, 1947

200 mtr. run—1. AUDREY PATTERSON, Wiley College; 2. NELL JACKSON, Tuske-
gee Institute; 3. Nancy Cowperthwaite, German-American A. C.,
N. Y.; 4. GWENDOLYN TAYLOR, Tuskegee Institute; 5. FANNIE JOHNSON,
Tuskegee Institute.   Time 26.1 s.

Running broad jump—1. LILLIAN YOUNG, Chicago; 2. Shirley Stanley, Brook-
haven, Mississippi; 3. LILLIE PURIFOY, Tuskegee Institute; 4. FANNIE
JOHNSON, Tuskegee Institute; 5. Marion Barone, Philadelphia Turners
MARY HARDAWAY, Tennessee State (tied).   Distance: 16 ft. 2½ in.

8-lb. shot put—1. Katherine Geary, Philadelphia Turners; 2. VERDA CRAW-
FORD, Prairie View College; 3. Torchie Blasch, Chicago, Illinois;
4. Josephine Wilkowski, Chicago; 5. ELAINE BRADFORD, Tuskegee
Institute; 6. MELLIE MCKEE, Tuskegee Institute.   Distance: 34 ft. 1½ in.

Discus throw—1. VERDA CRAWFORD, Prairie View College; 2. ROSA NETTLES,
Tuskegee Institute; 3. Estelle Kestenbaum, German-American A. C.,
N. Y.; 4. MARVIA SMITH, Prairie View College; 5. Pauline Ruppeldt,
Philadelphia Turners; 6. Loretta Blaul, German-American A. C., N. Y.
Distance 102 ft. 5¾ in.

Running high jump—1. EMMA REED, Tennessee State; 2. Unar Martin,
Phoenix, Arizona; 3. GERTRUDE ORR, Tuskegee Institute; 4. Barbara
Mewes, St. Louis, Missouri; 5. Bessie Leick, Polish Olympic A. C.,
Cleveland.   Height 4 ft. 11 in.

50 mtr. dash—1. MABEL WALKER, Tuskegee Institute; 2. Elaine Burgess,
Brookhaven, Mississippi; 3. Nancy McClurken, Philadelphia Turners;
4. Eleanor Millheiser, German-American A. C., N. Y.; 5. BERDIE
EDMUNDSON, Prairie View College.   Time 6.9 s.

Baseball throw—1. Peggie Anderson, Cleveland Polish Olympic. (Peggy
Anderson was disqualified for first place, thereby causing each contestant to be moved up one place). 2. JUANITA WATSON, Tuskegee Institute; 3. Estelle Kastenbaum, German-American A. C., N. Y. Distance 238 ft. 7 in.

100 mtr. run— 1. MARY GRIGGS, Tuskegee Institute; 2. CLEO REESE, Prairie View; 3. AUDREY PATTERSON, Wiley College; 4. Nancy McKay, Toronto, Canada; 5. Viola Myers, Toronto, Canada; 6. Ruth Harrigan, Toronto, Canada. Time 13.2 s.

Javelin throw—1. Katherine Geary, Philadelphia Turners; 2. Bessie Leick, Cleveland Polish Olympic Club; 3. Bonnie Reed, San Antonio A. C.; 4. Torchi Blasch, Chicago Hurricanes; 5. Rose Przyblski, Cleveland Polish American A. C. Distance 103 ft. 11 in.

80 mtr. hurdles—1. THERESA MANUEL, Tuskegee Institute; 2. Loretta Blaul, German-American A. C., N. Y.; 3. Raynice Eads, Uvaldo, Texas; 4. Verna Myers, Toronto, Canada. Time 12.8 s.

400 mtr. relay—1. TUSKEGEE INSTITUTE TEAM A (WALKER, TAYLOR, JOHNSON, MANUEL); 2. TUSKEGEE INSTITUTE TEAM B; 3. German-American A. C., N. Y.; 4. Chicago Hurricanes. Time 51 s.

Team scores—TUSKEGEE INSTITUTE, 97; German-American A. C., 37; PRAIRIE VIEW, 33; Philadelphia Turners, 31½; Chicago Hurricanes, 23; Cleveland Polish Olympic Club, 22; Brookhaven, Mississippi, 18; WILEY COLLEGE, 16; Toronto, Canada, 11; TENNESSEE A. & I., 10; Forestville Playground, Chicago, 10; San Antonio A. C., 10; Phoenix, Arizona, 8; Uvaldo, Texas, 6; St. Louis, 4.

WOMEN'S SENIOR OUTDOOR TRACK AND FIELD CHAMPIONSHIPS

Held at San Antonio, June 29, 1947

Running high jump—1. ALICE COACHMAN, Albany, (Ga.) State College; 2. EMMA REED, Tennessee A. & I.; 3. GERTRUDE ORR, Tuskegee Institute; and Rebecca Oprea, Cleveland Polish Olympic A. C., (tied); 5. Frances Kaszubski, Cleveland Polish Olympic A. C.; 6. Jean Walraven, Cleveland Polish Olympic A. C. Height 5 ft. 1 in.

200 mtr. run—1. Stella Walsh, Cleveland Polish Olympic A. C.; 2. AUDREY PATTERSON, Wiley College, Marshall, Texas; 3. NELL JACKSON, Tuskegee Institute; 4. GWENDOLYN TAYLOR, Tuskegee Institute; 5. MARY WILSON, Tennessee State; 6. Wanda Field, Phoenix, Arizona. Time 26.2 s.

50 mtr. run—1. ALICE COACHMAN, Albany, (Ga.) State College; 2. Katherine Geary, Philadelphia Turners; 3. MABEL WALKER, Tuskegee Institute; 4. Shirley Eckels, Malvernette A. C., Toronto, Canada; 5. LILLIAN YOUNG, Chicago; 6. BETSY ABERNATHY, Tuskegee Institute. Time 6.8.

8-lb. shot put—1. Dorothy Dodson, Chicago Hurricanes; 2. Frances Kaszubski, Cleveland Polish Olympic A. C.; 3. Katherine Geary, Philadelphia Turners; 4. Josephine Wilowski, Chicago Hurricanes; 5. Torchi Blasch, Chicago Hurricanes; 6. ELAINE BRADFORD, Tuskegee Institute. Distance 37 ft. 11 in.

Running broad jump—1. LILLY PURIFOY, Tuskegee Institute; 2. Nancy Cowperthwaite, German-American A. C.; 3. LILLIAN YOUNG, Chicago Hurricanes; 4. Stella Walsh, Cleveland Polish Olympic A. C.; 5. Barbara Mewes, Ozark Sporting Club; St. Louis, Mo. Distance 17 ft. 6 in.

100 mtr. run—1. JUANITA WATSON, Tuskegee Institute; 2. ALICE COACHMAN, Albany (Ga.) State College; 3. MARY GRIGGS, Tuskegee Institute; 4. Elaine Burgess, Brookhaven, Mississippi; 5. AUDREY PATTERSON, Wiley College, Marshall, Texas; MARY HARDAWAY, Tennessee State College. Time 13.1 s.

Javelin throw—1. Dorothy Dodson, Chicago Hurricanes; 2. HATTIE PALMER, Tuskegee Institute; 3. Marion Barone, Philadelphia Turners; 4. Bessie Leick, Cleveland Polish Olympic A. C.; 5. Wynall Robinette, Lamesa, Texas; 6. Bonnie Reed, San Antonio Recreation. Distance 122 ft. 5 in.

400 mtr. relay—1. TUSKEGEE INSTITUTE TEAM A (WALKER, WATSON, HAYES, JACKSON); 2. Malvernette A. C., Toronto, Canada; 3. TUSKEGEE INSTITUTE TEAM B; 4. German-American A. C.; 6. Philadelphia Turners. Time 50.6 s.

80 mtr. hurdles—1. Nancy Cowperthwaite, German-American A. C.; 2. THERESA MANUEL, Tuskegee Institute; 3. LILLIE PURIFOY, Tuskegee Institute; 4. Jean Walraven, Cleveland Polish Olympic A. C.; 5. Loretta Blaul, German-American A. C.; 6. Clara Schroth, Philadelphia Turners. Time 12.6 s.

Discus throw—1. Frances Kaszubski, Cleveland Polish Olympic A. C.; 2. Dorothy Dodson, Chicago Hurricanes; 3. Pauline Ruppeldt, Philadelphia Turners; 4. HATTIE PALMER, Tuskegee Institute; 5. ROSIA NETTLES, Tuskegee Institute; 6. ELAINE BRADFORD, Tuskegee Institute. Distance 110 ft. 4¾ in.

Baseball throw—1. Marion Barone, Philadelphia Turners; 2. HATTIE PALMER, Tuskegee Institute; 3. Peggy Anderson, Cleveland Polish Olympic A. C.; 4. JUANITA WATSON, Tuskegee Institute; 5. Christine Long A.A.C., Columbus, Ohio. Distance 252 ft. 8 in.

Team score—TUSKEGEE INSTITUTE, 117; Cleveland Polish Olympic A. C., 49; Chicago Hurricanes, 40; Philadelphia Turners, 39; Albany State College, 28; Brooklyn German-American A. C., 24; Malvernette A. C., Toronto, Canada, 12; Texas A. & I., 10; WILEY COLLEGE, 10.

(Reprint from Chicago *Tribune*, Chicago, Ill., Sunday, Apr. 25, 1948)

2 RECORDS SET IN WOMEN'S A. A. U. INDOOR TRACK

By Robert Cromie

American indoor records in the 50 meter hurdles and the 50 meter dash were broken yesterday during the National Women's A. A. U. indoor track meet in the University of Chicago fieldhouse. The meet was the first such national event ever run in which all the judges were women.

In the hurdles event Theresa Manuel of Tuskegee Institute was clocked in 7.4 seconds, two-tenths of a second faster than the 15 year old record. Miss Manuel was hard pressed by Bernice Robinson, 21 year old flyer from Washington Park, Chicago, who was closing rapidly at the tape.

1935 MARK BROKEN

Juanita Watson, also of Tuskegee, set an American indoor dirt track record by clipping one-tenth of a second off the previous 6.6 mark, set in 1935. Miss Watson, who also won her semi-final heat in :06.5, took the lead in the final heat a few paces from the starting line and was never threatened. Another Chicagoan, Lillian Young of Forrestville playground, trailed her home.

The great Stella Walsh of Cleveland holds the American record in the 200 meter run, but since she was a Polish citizen when she covered the distance in :25.8 in 1941, the National A. A. U. also recognizes what is called the American record (citizen's). This latter mark of 26.8 was eclipsed by Audrey Patterson of Tennessee State college, who clocked in :26.4. Second place went to Nell Jackson, Tuskegee, who won her preliminary heat in 26.5, which made her the American (citizen's) record holder for approximately 15 minutes.

BERNICE GETS 20 POINTS

Miss Robinson who also took second in the high jump and fourth in the standing broad jump, was the meet's high point winner with 20 points. Second in total points were Frances Kaszubski of Cleveland, shot put winner and third in the basketball throw, and Nancy Cowperthwaite, German-American A. C., New York, with a first in the standing broad jump and third in the 50 meter hurdles.

Two defending champions were dethroned. Dorothy Dodson of the Chicago Hurricanes, defending the shot put, lost to Mrs. Kaszubski by less than 2 inches, and Lillie Purifoy, Tuskegee, hurdles queen, had to be content with fourth in her event.

Summaries:

200 METER DASH—Won by AUDREY PATTERSON, Tennessee State; NELL JACKSON, Tuskegee, second; JEAN LOWE, Tuskegee, third; KATHERINE GEARY, Philadelphia Turners, fourth. Time, :26.4.

50 METER DASH—Won by JUANITA WATSON, Tuskegee; LILLIAN YOUNG, Forrestville playground, Chicago, second; MABLE WALKER, Tuskegee, third; GEARY, Philadelphia Turners, fourth. Time, :06.5.

400 METER RELAY—Won by Tuskegee (HAYES, TAYLOR, WATSON, JACKSON); Tennessee State, second; German-American A. C., third; JOHN T. DEMPSEY Hurricanes, Chicago, fourth. Time, :51.8.

RUNNING HIGH JUMP—Won by EMMA REED, Tennessee State; MISS ROBINSON, Washington Park, second; REBECCA OPREA, North Olmsted-Westlake A. C., Cleveland, third; EVELYN LAWLER, Tuskegee, fourth. Height—4 feet, 11⅜ inches.

SHOT PUT—Won by FRANCES KASZUBSKI, North Olmsted-Westlake A. C.; DOROTHY DODSON, Chicago Hurricanes, second; GEARY, Philadelphia Turners, third; TORCHI BLASCH, Chicago Hurricanes, fourth. Distance, 38 feet 4⅜ inches.

STANDING BROAD JUMP—Won by COWPERTHWAITE, German-American A. C.; MILDRED MARTIN, Chicago Hurricanes, second; LAWLER, Tuskegee, third; ROBINSON, Washington Park, fourth. Distance, 7 feet 11½ inches.

BASKETBALL THROW—Won by STELLA GIRKS, Whittier playground, Chicago; EVA PIKAL, Gary playground, Chicago, second; KASZUBSKI, North Olmsted-Westlake A. C., third; MANUEL, Tuskegee, fourth. Distance, 93 feet 7 inches.

COACHMAN WON TITLE

Nor is the list of potential Olympic talent exhausted. Not to be overlooked, certainly is Alice Coachman, former Tuskegee athlete, who now teaches in Albany, Ga. Miss Coachman won the national women's high jump title last year with a leap of 5 feet 1 inch and also took the 50 meter dash, running the distance in 6.8 seconds.

These, and others, especially from Tuskegee, whose team has lost only one meet since 1936, will bear watching when the National A. A. U. outdoor championships for women are held July 6 in Grand Rapids, Mich., and the Olympic tryouts July 12 in the Brown University stadium in Providence, R. I.

IMPORTANT AMERICAN RACING STAKES WON BY NEGRO JOCKEYS

Compiled by

Buster Miller, Sports Editor of The New York Age

From

The American Racing Manual

Negroes have been identified with horse-racing in America from early Colonial times. In those days of slavery, it was only natural that the dirty and often dangerous work of grooming, feeding, breaking, exercising and training horses should be delegated to the slaves and it was in the great southern plantations that the knowledge of the peculiar ways of thoroughbreds was acquired which later was to make Negro jockeys and trainers the toasts of the American turf world.

The early races were all match affairs, with heavy wagering between owners and partisans of sectional favorites. In "The American Turf," by Lyman

Horace Weeks, these early matches are described and jockeys named "Pompey," "Scipio," "Cato," "Caesar," et al. are mentioned in descriptions of such famous turf duels as the American Eclipse-Sir Henty match in 1823, and the Post Boy-John Bascombe match in 1836. One such "Cato" received considerable credit for his fine performances in riding Wagner to two wins over Gray Eagle at Louisville in 1839. Since it was the custom among slave owners of that period to air their knowledge of the classics by bestowing the names of great Romans upon their human chattels, we may safely conclude that jockeys thus mentioned were all Negroes.

In spite of the fact that several abortive attempts were made to establish racing on a firm footing in Virginia, Maryland and Kentucky, the "Sport of Kings," as we know it today, began at Saratoga in 1864 and Belmont Park in 1866.

The first great Negro jockey on record survives only by the name of Abe. Practically nothing is known of him except that he rode Watson, winner of the inaugural Jerome Handicap at Belmont Park in 1866. In the same year, he also piloted Merrill to win the first Travers Stakes at Saratoga.

It was not the custom in those days to list the names of jockeys and trainers, probably owing to the fact that most of them were Negroes, and, as such of lesser importance than the animals they rode and trained. A program of the first Kentucky Derby in 1875 is an example. It is reproduced in Frank G. Menke's fine book, "The Story of Churchill Downs and the Kentucky Derby," and shows the name of the owner, horse, sex, color, age, pedigree and the colors worn by the jockey.

In spite of this handicap to the historian, it has been ascertained that fourteen of the fifteen starters in that first "Run for the Roses" were ridden by Negro jockeys and that the winner, Aristides, was guided by one Oliver Lewis. The Derby distance at that time was a mile and a half, instead of the present mile and a quarter, and Aristides' time of 2:37¾ was the fastest ever run by a three-year old in America up to that time.

Vagrant, the 1876 Derby winner, was trained by James Williams, a Negro.

The team of jockey Billy Walker and trainer Ed "Brown Dick" Brown sewed up the 1877 Derby with Baden-Baden. Walker was the top rider of that period. He rode the celebrated Ten Broeck in a race against time at Churchill Downs on May 27, 1877 and set a new record of 3:27½ for the mile and a half. California supporters of "Lucky" Baldwin's good mare, Mollie McCarthy, lost no time in challenging Ten Broeck to a two-mile match race at $5,000 a side. The race took place at Churchill Downs on July 4, 1878 and Ten Broeck, with Walker up, won by ten lengths.

Garrett or Garrison Lewis,—some doubt exists about his first name—piloted Fonso, winner of the 1880 Derby and Babe Hurd was up on Apollo, winner of the classic in 1882. Leonatus, winner of 1883, was trained by Raleigh Colston, a former jockey of great reputation.

The immortal Isaac Murphy made his first appearance in the Derby winning circle with Buchanan in 1884.   Buchanan was trained by William Bird, another Negro.

Murphy was born in Lexington, Ky., on Jan. 1, 1861.   He rode his first winner, Glentina, at the Crab Orchard track in 1875.   Not only did he establish a riding record of winning three Kentucky Derbies, a record that stood for forty years, until tied by Earl Sande in 1930, and recently eclipsed by Eddie Arcaro, he also rode the first four winners of the Latonia Derby and four of the first five winners of the American Derby at Washington Park.   Incidentally, Volante, Silver Cloud and Emperor of Norfolk, American Derby winners ridden by Murphy in 1885, 1886 and 1888 respectively, were trained by Albert Cooper.

In 1886, Murphy branched out as an owner, riding a colt, Playfellow, in his own colors at Lexington, October 20.   The horse finished third, but never amounted to much and Murphy never was as successful as an owner as he was in the saddle.

Probably Murphy's greatest personal triumph came in the celebrated match race between Salvator and Tenny at Sheepshead Bay on June 25, 1890. Murphy was up on Salvator while Tenny was ridden by the great "Snapper" Garrison.   The match between riders as well as that between horses attracted a record throng from New York and Philadelphia and Salvator won by a head. A colored lithograph of this famous race was used as an advertisement by a champagne company and used to adorn all the best bars in New York.

Ironically enough, Murphy's feat of riding three Kentucky Derby winners might never have happened if the little rider had had his own way.   He practically had to be forced to ride Buchanan, the 1884 winner.   Murphy had ridden Buchanan at Nashville a few weeks before the Derby and the horse was so wild he nearly unseated his rider at the post and then bolted all over the track. When the day came for him to ride Buchanan in the Derby, Murphy flatly refused to get into the saddle.   The owners, Cottrell and Guest, first flattered, cajoled and finally threatened Murphy with a suspension.   He finally gave in and went on to win the race.   Murphy died in Lexington, Feb. 13, 1896 of pneumonia.

Joe Cotton, 1885 winner, was ridden by Erskine Henderson and trained by Alex Perry.   Isaac Lewis, a brother of Garrett or Garrison Lewis, scored with Montrose in 1887.   Murphy took the Derby in 1890 with Riley and repeated in 1891 with Kingman to become the first jockey to ride two consecutive Derby winners.   Kingman was trained by Dud Allen.

A newcomer entered the ranks of the immortals when "Monk" Overton rode six winners out of six' mounts at Washington Park on July 10, 1891.   Although John Stoval twice rode four winners out of four mounts, Oct. 1, 1881 at Louisville and Oct. 28, 1882 at Memphis, and Pike Barnes had scored with four for four at Lexington on Oct. 25, 1887, Overton's feat overshadowed them all and stood as an all time record until duplicated by Jimmy Lee at Louisville, June 5, 1907.

The 1892 Derby had only three starters, all ridden by Negro jockeys. Azra, Alonzo Clayton up, was winner; Huron, with Tom Britton up, was second, and Phil Dwyer, with Overton up, was third.

James "Soup" Perkins, another native Lexingtonian, was a great little rider. He rode five winners out of six mounts at Lexington on Oct. 20, 1893, and did the same thing again at Saratoga, Aug. 23, 1894. Great as he was, Perkins had to wait until 1895 before riding his first Derby winner, Halma. He was a brother of the celebrated Bill Perkins who in 1926 was the leading American trainer.

The first Negro jockey to achieve international fame was Willie Simms. Born in Augusta, Ga. on Jan. 16, 1870, he rode five winners out of six mounts at Sheepshead Bay on June 23, 1893, and duplicated this feat at Jerome Park on August 24, 1894. Simms scored in the 1896 Derby with Ben Brush and again in 1898 with Plaudit. He was the turf idol of the day and engaged by Richard Croker and Michael F. Dwyer to accompany their horses to England where he became the first American Jockey to win an event on an English race-course with an American horse whose owner, trainer and complete outfit were all-American. Upon his return to this country, he was welcomed as one of the turf heroes of the day.

Another jockey to achieve international fame was Jimmy Winkfield. He won the Derby on His Eminence in 1901 and again in 1902 on Alan-a-Dale, thereby equalling Murphy's record of riding two Derby winners in a row. A chance to become immortal in turf history was muffed by Winkfield in 1903. He had the mount on Early and lengths in front going into the stretch when he decided to ease up and coast home. When he realized his mistake, it was too late, as the fast coming Judge Himes nipped him at the wire. He was the last Negro jockey to win a Kentucky Derby and left America to ride in France, where as late as 1923 he won the Prix du President de la Republique Stake at St. Cloud on a horse called Bahadur. He became a prominent trainer in France and only returned to this country in 1940 at the outset of World War II.

The last Negro jockey to have a mount in the Derby was Jess Conley. He finished third on Colston in 1911. Since that time, racing has had several good riders such as R. Simpson, C. Dishmon, Johnny Hudgins, Clarence Reed and Charlie Gregg. None of these, however, could compare with such old timers as Felix Carr, Pete Clay, Andy Hamilton, Billy Mitchell, Harry Ray, Linc Jones, Tommy Knight, Jim English, Spider Anderson, Jerry Chorn, Willie Penn, George Withers, Abram Walker, Ed West, Henry J. Harris, Bud Haggins, William Porter, Albert Clayton, John H. Jackson, Tom Britton, and Robert "Tiny" Williams, that incomparable rider of two-year olds. In fairness to the latter-day rider, it should be recorded that they never received the opportunities their predecessors did. The same thing is true of our present day trainers like Matt Smart, George R. Miller, Marshall Lilly and others who never had the chances afforded Ed Brown, Raleigh Colston, Charlie Anderson, Abe Terry, Bob Campbell, Henry B. Harris, Will Overton and G. H. Moton.

For many years, Pete Green has been one of the ablest trainers of steeple-chase horses. This dangerous form of the sport has had its fair share of great Negro riders, too. In the first rank will always be George and Charlie Smoot. Charlie was the leading steeplechase rider in 1927 with 10 winners out of 53 mounts. Paul McGinnis was the leading steeplechase jockey in 1936 with 9 winners out of 28 mounts. Other good riders over the sticks and brush were Nott Brooks, Angus Scott and Johnny Mason.

During the past ten years, some good riding on the flat has been done by G. Cardoza, R. Holland and Raymond Booker.

BIBLIOGRAPHY

The American Turf by Lyman Horace Weeks.
The Story of Churchill Downs and the Kentucky Derby by Frank G. Menke.
The History of the American Derby by Ted Williams.
Famous American Jockeys by F. W. Vosburgh.
The American Racing Manual.

ALABAMA STAKES
(originated Saratoga in 1872)

YEAR	WINNER	JOCKEY
1882	Belle of Runnymede	John Stoval
1885	Ida Hope	Isaac Murphy
1887	Grisette	Ed West
1889	Princess Bowling	Isaac Murphy
1890	Sinaloa	Pike Barnes
1891	Sallie McClelland	Spider Anderson
1892	Ignite	Alonzo Clayton

AMERICAN DERBY
(originated Washington Park in 1884)

1884	Modesty	Isaac Murphy
1885	Volante	Isaac Murphy
1886	Silver Cloud	Isaac Murphy
1887	C. H. Todd	Anthony Hamilton
1892	Carlsbad	Tiny Williams

ANNUAL CHAMPION STAKES
(originated Sheephead Bay in 1900)

| 1901 | Maid of Harlem | Willie Simms |

BASHFORD MANOR STAKES
(originated Churchill Downs 1902)

YEAR	WINNER	JOCKEY
1902	Von Rouse	Jimmy Winkfield
1918	Billy Kelly	R. Simpson

BELMONT STAKES
(originated Jerome Park 1867; run at Morris Park 1890–1905; at Belmont Park since)

1890	Burlington	Pike Barnes
1893	Comanche	Willie Simms
1894	Henry of Navarre	Willie Simms

BRIGHTON HANDICAP
(originated Brighton Beach in 1896)

1897	Ben Brush	Willie Simms
1898	Ornament	Willie Simms

BROOKLYN HANDICAP
(originated Gravesend 1887; run at Aqueduct since 1914)

1889	Exile	Anthony Hamilton
1891	Tenny	Pike Barnes
1895	Hornpipe	Anthony Hamilton

BURNS HANDICAP
(originated Oakland, Cal. in 1894)

1894	Lissak	Jerry Chorn
1895	Hawthorne	Felix Carr

CALIFORNIA DERBY
(originated Oakland, Cal., 1897)

1898	Traverser	Alonzo Clayton
1909	High Private	Jimmy Lee

CHAMPAGNE STAKES
(originated Jerome Park 1867; run at Belmont Park since 1905)

1889	June Day	Pike Barnes
1891	Azra	Alonzo Clayton
1895	Ben Brush	Willie Simms
1903	Stalwart	Willie Hicks

CHICAGO DERBY
(originated Hawthorne, Ill. in 1890)

1890	Prince Fonso	Monk Overton
1892	Lew Weir	Monk Overton

CHRISTMAS HANDICAP
(originated Jefferson Park 1919; Fair Grounds since 1934)

YEAR	WINNER	JOCKEY
1920	Eddie Rickenbacker	H. King

CINCINNATI TROPHY
(originated Latonia, Ky., 1902)

| 1903 | Paris | Tommy Knight |
| 1909 | The Fad | Dale Austin |

CLARK HANDICAP
(originated Churchill Downs 1875)

1879	Falsetto	Isaac Murphy
1833	Ascender	John Stoval
1884	Buchanan	Isaac Murphy
1885	Bersan	Isaac Murphy
1887	Jim Gore	Linc Jones
1890	Riley	Isaac Murphy
1891	High Tariff	Monk Overton
1892	Azra	Alonzo Clayton
1895	Halma	James Perkins
1896	Ben Eder	Willie Simms
1897	Ornament	Alonzo Clayton
1898	Plaudit	Tiny Williams
1901	His Eminence	Jimmy Winkfield

CLIPSETTA STAKES
(originated Latonia, Ky. in 1883)

1883	Eva S.	John Stoval
1886	Jennie T.	Isaac Murphy
1888	Kee-Vee-Na	Pike Barnes
1889	Flyaway	John Stoval
1891	Ignite	Monk Overton
1892	Issie O.	Tom Britton
1894	Kitty Olive	Monk Overton
1895	Myrtle Harkness	Tiny Williams
1903	Stumpy	Tiny Williams
1906	La Velta	Dale Austin
1907	Grand Dame	Jimmy Lee

CRESCENT CITY DERBY
(originated New Orleans in 1898)

| 1902 | Lord Quex | Jimmy Winkfield |

DIXIE HANDICAP
(originated Pimlico in 1870)

YEAR	WINNER	JOCKEY
1877	King Fargo	Billy Walker
1884	Loftin	John Stoval

DOUBLE EVENT—First Part
(originated Sheepshead Bay 1889)

| 1889 | Torso | Spider Anderson |
| 1896 | Ornament | Alonzo Clayton |

DOUBLE EVENT—Second Part

| 1908 | Sir Martin | Jimmy Lee |

DWYER STAKES
(originated Aqueduct 1887)

1888	Emperor of Norfolk	Isaac Murphy
1890	Burlington	Pike Barnes
1894	Dobbins	Willie Simms

ECLIPSE STAKES
(originated Morris Park 1889; run at Belmont Park 1905)

| 1890 | Sallie McClelland | Spider Anderson |

FIRST SPECIAL
(originated Gravesend in 1886)

1887	Volante	Isaac Murphy
1888	Kingston	Isaac Murphy
1889	Kingston	Isaac Murphy
1891	Tenny	Pike Barnes
1892	Lamplighter	Willie Simms
1894	Banquet	Willie Simms
1897	Ben Brush	Willie Simms
1899	Imp	Pete Clay

FLASH STAKES
(originated Saratoga in 1869)

1888	Princess Bowling	Pike Barnes
1889	Protection	Don Allen
1895	Onaretto	Alonzo Clayton
1903	Tippecanoe	Willie Hicks
1918	Billy Kelly	R. Simpson

FLATBUSH STAKES
(originated Sheepshead Bay 1884)

YEAR	WINNER	JOCKEY
1885	Charity	Tiny Williams
1888	Salvator	Pike Barnes
1889	Torso	Anthony Hamilton
1890	Potomac	Anthony Hamilton
1892	Lady Violet	Willie Simms
1896	Ornament	Alonzo Clayton

FUTURITY STAKES
(originated Sheepshead Bay 1888; run at Belmont Park since 1915)

| 1888 | Proctor Knott | Pike Barnes |
| 1890 | Potomac | Anthony Hamilton |

GAZELLE STAKES
(originated Gravesend 1887; run at Aqueduct since 1915)

1887	Firenze	Anthony Hamilton
1890	Amazon	Anthony Hamilton
1892	Yorkville Belle	Isaac Murphy
1893	Naptha	Willie Simms

GREAT AMERICAN STAKES
(originated Aqueduct in 1889)

| 1908 | Sir Martin | Jimmy Lee |

GRAND TRIAL STAKES
(originated Sheepshead Bay in 1891)

| 1892 | Chiswick | Anthony Hamilton |
| 1908 | Sir Martin | Jimmy Lee |

GREAT WESTERN HANDICAP
(originated Washington Park 1884)

1884	Boatman	George Withers
1886	Jim Guest	Ed West
1888	Montrose	Isaac Lewis
1889	Elyton	Pike Barnes
1891	Verge d'Or	Tiny Williams
1894	Sabin	Alonzo Clayton
1900	Jolly Roger	Jimmy Winkfield
1902	Six Shooter	Tommy Knight

HYDE PARK STAKES
(originated Washington Park in 1884)

| 1887 | Emperor of Norfolk | Isaac Murphy |
| 1888 | Caliente | Pike Barnes |

YEAR	WINNER	JOCKEY
1891	Curt Gunn	Isaac Lewis
1901	Sir Oliver	Tommy Knight
1902	Dick Welles	Tommy Knight

JEROME HANDICAP
(originated Jerome Park 1866; run at Belmont Park since 1905)

1866	Watson	Abe
1889	Longstreet	Isaac Murphy
1891	Picknicker	Alonzo Clayton
1895	Counter Tenor	Willie Simms

JUVENILE STAKES
(originated Jerome Park 1874; run at Belmont Park since 1905)

1890	St. Charles	Anthony Hamilton
1894	Prince of Monaco	Willie Simms
1898	Glenheim	Willie Simms

KENNER STAKES
(originated Saratoga 1870)

1870	Enquirer	Raleigh Colston
1879	Falsetto	Isaac Murphy
1882	Boatman	Billy Walker
1884	Powhatan III	John Stoval
1885	Irish Pat	Ed West
1887	Swarthmore	Tiny Williams
1888	Los Angeles	Isaac Murphy
1889	Long Dance	Pike Barnes
1891	Valera	Tiny Williams

KENTUCKY DERBY
(originated Churchill Downs in 1875)

1875	Aristides	Oliver Lewis
1877	Baden-Baden	Billy Walker
1880	Fonso	G. Lewis
1882	Apollo	Babe Hurd
1884	Buchanan	Isaac Murphy
1885	Joe Cotton	Erskine Henderson
1887	Montrose	Isaac Lewis
1890	Riley	Isaac Murphy
1891	Kingman	Isaac Murphy
1892	Azra	Alonzo Clayton
1895	Halma	James Perkins
1896	Ben Brush	Willie Simms
1898	Plaudit	Willie Simms
1901	His Eminence	Jimmy Winkfield
1902	Alan-a-Dale	Jimmy Winkfield

KENTUCKY OAKS
(originated Churchill Downs 1875)

YEAR	WINNER	JOCKEY
1882	Katie Creel	John Stoval
1883	Vera	John Stoval
1884	Modesty	Isaac Murphy
1889	Jewel Ben	John Stoval
1891	Miss Hawkins	Tom Britton
1892	Miss Dixie	Harry Ray
1894	Selika	Alonso Clayton
1895	Voladora	Alonso Clayton
1900	Etta	Monk Overton
1905	Janeta	Dale Austin
1907	Wing Ting	Jimmy Lee

LADIES' HANDICAP
(originated Jerome Park 1868; run at Belmont Park since 1905)

1890	Sinaloa II	Pike Barnes
1892	Yorkville Belle	Isaac Murphy
1893	Naptha	Willie Simms

LATONIA CUP
(originated Latonia, Ky. 1884)

1884	Harry Gilmore	Isaac Murphy
1885	Bob Miles	George Withers
1887	Fosteral	John Stoval

LATONIA DERBY
(originated Latonia, Ky. 1883)

1883	Leonatus	Isaac Murphy
1884	Bersan	Isaac Murphy
1886	Silver Cloud	Isaac Murphy
1887	Libretto	Isaac Murphy
1888	White	Pike Barnes
1890	Bill Letcher	Don Allen
1891	Kingman	Isaac Murphy
1892	Newton	Alonso Clayton
1896	Ben Brush	Willie Simms
1897	Ornament	Alonso Clayton
1898	Han d'Or	Jess Conley
1901	Hernando	Jimmy Winkfield
1907	The Abbott	Jimmy Lee

LATONIA OAKS
(originated Latonia, Ky. 1887)

YEAR	WINNER	JOCKEY
1888	Lavinia Belle	John Stoval
1889	Retrieve	Pike Barnes
1891	Ida Pickwick	Tiny Williams
1892	Lake Breeze	Alonso Clayton
1894	Orinda	James Perkins
1898	Sardonic	Alonso Clayton
1900	Anthracite	Monk Overton
1906	Content	Dale Austin
1907	Lillie Turner	Jimmy Lee

LAWRENCE REALIZATION
(originated Sheepshead Bay 1889; run at Belmont Park since 1913)

1891	Potomac	Anthony Hamilton
1893	Daily America	Willie Simms
1894	Dobbins	Willie Simms
1896	Requital	Alonso Clayton

LOUISVILLE CUP
(originated Douglas Park, Ky. in 1913)

1913	Clubs	M. Dishmon

MATRON STAKES
(originated Morris Park 1892; run at Belmont Park since 1905)

1903	Armenia	Willie Hicks

METROPOLITAN HANDICAP
(originated Morris Park 1891; run at Belmont Park since 1905)

1896	Counter Tenor	Anthony Hamilton
1898	Bowling Brook	Pete Clay

NATIONAL STALLION STAKES
(originated Morris Park 1898; run at Belmont Park since 1905)

1908	Sir Martin	Jimmy Lee

SARATOGA CUP
(originated Saratoga in 1865)

1881	Checkmate	Isaac Murphy
1886	Volante	Isaac Murphy
1891	Los Angeles	Isaac Lewis

SECOND SPECIAL
(originated Gravesend in 1886)

YEAR	WINNER	JOCKEY
1888	Kingston	Isaac Murphy
1890	Los Angeles	Pike Barnes
1892	Lamplighter	Willie Simms
1894	Clifford	Willie Simms
1895	Clifford	Willie Simms
1897	Ben Brush	Willie Simms
1899	Imp	Pete Clay

SPINAWAY STAKES
(originated Saratoga 1881)

1882	Miss Woodford	John Stoval
1887	Los Angeles	Ed West
1890	Sallie McClelland	Don Allen
1891	Promenade	Willie Simms
1903	Raglan	Jimmy Hicks

ST. LOUIS DERBY
(originated St. Louis 1882)

1882	Monogram	Billy Walker
1883	Bondholder	John Stoval
1887	Terra Cotta	Isaac Murphy
1888	Falcon	Anthony Hamilton
1890	Bill Letcher	Don Allen
1896	Prince Lief	James Perkins
1897	Ornament	Alonso Clayton

SUBURBAN HANDICAP
(originated Sheepshead Bay 1884; run at Belmont Park since 1913)

1890	Salvator	Isaac Murphy
1895	Lazzarone	Anthony Hamilton
1897	Ben Brush	Willie Simms
1898	Tillo	Alonso Clayton

SWIFT STAKES
(originated Sheepshead Bay 1885; run at Belmont Park since 1911)

1888	Emperor of Norfolk	Isaac Murphy
1892	Vestibule	Anthony Hamilton
1893	Ajax	Marlo Thompson
1894	Discount	Willie Simms
1896	Requital	Alonso Clayton

TENNESSEE DERBY
(originated Memphis 1884)

YEAR	WINNER	JOCKEY
1885	Joe Cotton	Erskine Henderson
1891	Valera	Tom Britton
1892	Tom Elliott	Tom Britton
1897	Buckvedere	Tiny Williams
1901	Royal Victor	Jimmy Winkfield

TENNESSEE OAKS
(originated Memphis 1884)

1885	Ida Hope	Ed West
1895	Handspun	Alonso Clayton
1896	Lady Inez	James Perkins
1903	Olefiant	Jimmy Winkfield

TIDAL STAKES
(originated Sheepshead Bay 1880)

1890	Burlington	Isaac Murphy
1891	Portchester	Anthony Hamilton
1892	Charade	Willie Simms
1894	Dobbins	Willie Simms
1897	Buddha	Willie Simms
1898	Handball	Tiny Williams

TOBOGGAN HANDICAP
(originated Belmont Park 1890)

1890	Fides	Anthony Hamilton
1898	Octagon	Willie Simms

TRAVERS STAKES
(originated Saratoga 1864)

1866	Merrill	Abe
1879	Falsetto	Isaac Murphy
1889	Long Dance	Pike Barnes
1891	Valera	Tiny Williams
1892	Azva	Alonso Clayton
1908	Dorante	Jimmy Lee

TREMONT STAKES
(originated Gravesend 1887; run at Aqueduct since 1914)

1897	Handball	Willie Simms

UNITED STATES HOTEL STAKES
(originated Saratoga 1880)

YEAR	WINNER	JOCKEY
1884	Kosciusko	John Stoval
1889	Retrieve	Isaac Lewis
1890	Sinaloa II	Pike Barnes
1891	Bermuda	Spider Anderson
1895	Axiom	Alonso Clayton
1918	Billy Kelly	R. Simpson

WITHERS STAKES
(originated Jerome Park 1874; run at Belmont Park since 1905)

1896	Handspring	Willie Simms
1897	Octagon	Willie Simms

BEVERWYCK STEEPLECHASE HANDICAP
(originated Saratoga 1897)

1901	The Bachelor	George Green
1916	Weldship	Charlie Smoot
1926	Brightness	Charlie Smoot
1933	Crumpler	Charlie Smoot

BROAD HOLLOW STEEPLECHASE HANDICAP
(originated Belmont Park 1915)

1930	Rooney	Charlie Smoot
1937	Route One	Charlie Smoot
1939	Satilla	Angus Scott

BROOK STEEPLECHASE
(originated Belmont Park 1905)

1917	Skibbereen	Lester Franklin
1919	Skibbereen	Charlie Smoot

CHARLES L. APPLETON MEMORIAL CUP STEEPLECHASE
(originated Belmont Park 1922)

1925	Tassel	Charlie Smoot
1936	Rock Lad	Paul McGinnis

CHEVY CHASE STEEPLECHASE HANDICAP
(originated Laurel, Md. 1911)

1920	St. Charlcote	Sammy Bush
1921	Flying Cloud	A. Simms
1932	Rideaway	George Smoot

Appendix 473

Corinthian Steeplechase Handicap
(originated Belmont Park 1902)

YEAR	WINNER	JOCKEY
1915	Swish	Lester Franklin
1917	St. Charlcote	Charlie Smoot
1932	Beacon Hill	George Smoot

Grand National Steeplechase
(originated Morris Park 1899; run at Belmont Park since 1905)

1918	St. Charlcote	Charlie Smoot
1925	Moseley	Charlie Smoot

Harbor Hill Steeplechase
(originated Aqueduct 1905)

1906	T. S. Martin	Jimmy Dupee
1926	Flyman	Charlie Smoot
1933	Wyandanch	Angus Scott
1934	Black Bean	Paul McGinnis
1935	Driver	Angus Scott

Indian River Steeplechase Handicap
(originated Delaware Park in 1938)

1939	Rioter	Johnny Mason

International Steeplechase Handicap
(originated Morris Park 1897; run at Belmont Park since 1905)

1908	Sanctus	Jimmy Dupee
1916	Brentwood	Lester Franklin
1917	Belle of Bryn Mawr	Sammy Bush
1918	Belle of Bryn Mawr	Sammy Bush
1922	Belle of Bryn Mawr	A. Sims
1932	Beacon Hill	George Smoot
1936	Rock Lad	Paul McGinnis
1937	Rioter	Angus Scott

Manly Steeplechase Handicap
(originated Pimlico 1916)

1921	Flyi	A. Sims

North American Steeplechase Handicap
(originated Saratoga 1904)

1916	Weldship	Charlie Smoot
1917	Weldship	Charlie Smoot
1939	Cottesmore	Angus Scott

SARATOGA STEEPLECHASE HANDICAP
(originated Saratoga 1906)

YEAR	WINNER	JOCKEY
1917	St. Charlcote	Charlie Smoot
1918	St. Charlcote	Charlie Smoot
1931	Beacon Hill	George Smoot

SHILLELAH STEEPLECHASE
(originated Saratoga 1902)

1916	Weldship	Charlie Smoot
1933	Lord Johnson	Charlie Smoot
1939	Saluda	Johnny Mason

YEAR	FOOTBALL	BASKETBALL	BASEBALL	TRACK	TENNIS	BOXING	WRESTLING
1922–23	Hampton				Howard—Singles Howard—Doubles		
1923–24	Virginia Union	Hampton	Va. Normal	Hampton	Va. Normal and Shaw—S		
1924–25	Lincoln	Hampton	Va. Union	Hampton	Va. Normal—D Va. Seminary—S		
1925–26	Hampton	Hampton	Va. Normal	Hampton	Shaw—D		
1926–27	Hampton	Hampton	Va. State	Hampton	Hampton—S Va. Seminary—D		
1927–28	A. and T. College	Va. Seminary	Va. State	Lincoln	Va. Seminary—S		
1928–29	Hampton	Va. Seminary	Va. State	Hampton	Shaw—D		
1929–30	Va. State	Lincoln	Lincoln	Morgan	Hampton—S Shaw—D		
1930–31	Morgan	Morgan	Va. State	Hampton	Hampton—S Union—D		
1931–32	Hampton	Morgan	Va. State	St. Paul	Howard—S Va. State—D		
1932–33	Morgan	Morgan	Va. State	Morgan	Howard—S		
1933–34	Morgan	Howard	Va. State and Hampton	Union	Hampton—D		
1934–35	Morgan	Howard	No champion	Hampton	Smith—S Smith—D	Lincoln and Hampton	Lincoln
1935–36	Morgan	Hampton	No champion	Va. State and Morgan	Smith—S Smith—D	Hampton	Hampton
1936–37	Va. State	A. and T.	No champion	Hampton	Morgan—S Morgan—D	Hampton	Hampton and Lincoln
1937–38	Morgan	Va. State	No champion	Va. State	St. Augustine—S St. Augustine—D	Hampton	Lincoln
1938–39	Va. State	Union	No champion	Va. State	St. Augustine—S St. Augustine—D	Smith	Lincoln
1940–41	Morgan	None	Union	Hampton	Smith	Smith	Lincoln
1941–42	None	None	N. C. State	None	Smith	Smith	Va. State* and Lincoln
1945	Va. State	None	Morgan	Morgan			
1946	Morgan	None	N. C. State†	Howard	Lincoln		
1947	Shaw U.	A. and T.	Va. State‡	Howard	Howard	Howard	Hampton

*Tied †Visitation tournament at Lincoln. ‡Visitation tournament at N. C. State.

475

S.I.A.C. CHAMPIONSHIPS

YEAR	FOOTBALL	BASKETBALL	TRACK AND FIELD	BASEBALL	TENNIS
1916	Morehouse	Morehouse	Tuskegee		
1917	Tuskegee	Morehouse		Morehouse—Morris Brown	
1918	Talladega	Morehouse		Morehouse—Morris Brown	
1919	Fisk	Morehouse		Talladega	
1920	Morehouse	Morehouse		Morehouse	
1921	Morehouse	Morehouse		Atlanta University	
1922	Morehouse	Morehouse		Morehouse	
1923	Morehouse—Fisk	Morehouse		Morehouse	
1924	Tuskegee	Morehouse		Atlanta University	
1925	Tuskegee	Morehouse		Morehouse	
1926	Tuskegee	Morehouse		Morehouse—Alabama	
1927	Tuskegee	Clark		Alabama	Tuskegee
1928	Tuskegee	Clark		Atlanta University	Tuskegee
1929	Talladega	Morehouse—Clark		Alabama	Tuskegee
1930	Tuskegee	Knoxville			Tuskegee
1931	Tuskegee	Morris Brown			Tuskegee
1932	Tuskegee	Morris Brown			Tuskegee
1933	Tuskegee	Tuskegee			Tuskegee
1934	Morris Brown	Tuskegee			Tuskegee
1935	Alabama State	Alabama State			Tuskegee
1936	Tuskegee	Alabama State			Tuskegee
1937	Florida A. and M.	Morehouse			Tuskegee
1938	Florida A. and M.	Xavier	Xavier		Tuskegee
1939	Alabama	Clark	Xavier		Tuskegee
1940	Florida A. and M.	Clark			Tuskegee
1941		Xavier			Tuskegee
1942		Florida A. and M.			Tuskegee
1943	Tuskegee	S. C. State			Tuskegee
1944		Tuskegee			Tuskegee
1945		Florida A. and M.			Tuskegee
1946		Morehouse	Tuskegee	Tuskegee	Tuskegee
1947	Florida A. and M.	Florida A. and M.	Tuskegee	Tuskegee	Tuskegee
1948	Florida A. and M.	Tuskegee	Xavier	Tuskegee	Tuskegee

MID-WESTERN ATHLETIC ASSOCIATION—CHAMPIONS

YEAR	FOOTBALL	BASKETBALL	BASEBALL	TRACK	TENNIS	BOXING	WRESTLING
1932–33	Wilberforce			Wilberforce			
1933–34	Wilberforce	Wilberforce		Wilberforce			
1934–35	Ky. State*	Wilberforce		Wilberforce			
1935–36	Ky. State	Wilberforce		Wilberforce			
1936–37	W. Va. State*	Lincoln Univ.		No meet	Wilberforce		
1937–38	Ky. State	W. Va. State		Wilberforce	W. Va. State		
1938–39	Ky. State*	W. Va. State		Lincoln Univ.	W. Va. State		
1939–40		Ky. State		Lincoln Univ.	W. Va. State		
1940–45	No awards						
1946–47		Tenn. State		Lincoln Univ.	Lincoln Univ.	Tenn. State	
1947–	Tenn. State			Lincoln Univ.			

*National Champions.

477

SOUTHWESTERN ATHLETIC CONFERENCE

YEAR	FOOTBALL	BASKETBALL	BASEBALL	TRACK	TENNIS	BOXING	WRESTLING
1921	Wiley						
1922	Paul Quinn						
1923	Wiley						
1924	Paul Quinn						
1925	Bishop						
1926	Sam Houston						
1927	Wiley						
1928	Wiley						
1929	Wiley						
1930	Wiley						
1931	Prairie View						
1932	Wiley						
1933	Langston and Pr. V.						
1934	Texas College						
1935	Texas College						
1936	Langston and Texas						
1937	Texas						
1938	Langston—Southern	Wiley		Bishop			
1939	Langston	Langston		Prairie View			
1940	Langston—Southern	Bishop		Southern			
1941	Prairie View	Bishop		Southern			
1942	Texas College	Langston		Prairie View	Southern		
1943	None	Southern		Wiley	Southern		
1944	Lang. Texas—Wiley	Langston					
1945	Wiley	Langston					
1946	Southern	Langston		Southern	Southern		
1947	Southern	Langston		Wiley	Prairie View		

SOUTH CENTRAL ATHLETIC CONFERENCE

YEAR	FOOTBALL	BASKETBALL	BASEBALL	TRACK	TENNIS	BOXING	WRESTLING
1927			Alcorn				
1928			Alcorn				
1929			Alcorn				
1930	Tougaloo		No award				
1931	No award		Alcorn				
1932	Alcorn		No award				
1933	Alcorn		No award				
1934	Alcorn	Alcorn	No award				
1935	Tougaloo	Alcorn	Okolona				
1936	Tougaloo	Alcorn	Piney Woods				
1937	Alcorn	Alcorn	Okolona				
1938	Alcorn	Alcorn					
1939	Leland	Alcorn		Alcorn			
1940	Alcorn	Alcorn		Dillard	Tougaloo		
1941	Leland	Tougaloo		Alcorn	Tougaloo		
1942	Leland	Tougaloo		No award	Tougaloo		
1943	No award	M. I. College		Tougaloo	No award		
1944	No award	M. I. College		Okolona	Okolona		
1945	No award	S. Christian		Okolona	No award		
1946	Leland	M. I. College		Alcorn	Tougaloo		

479

EASTERN INTERCOLLEGIATE ATHLETIC CONFERENCE

YEAR	FOOTBALL	BASEBALL	BASKETBALL	TRACK	TENNIS	BOXING	WRESTLING
1939	Conference organized						
1940	Fayetteville S. T. College		Miner T. College				
1941	Winston-Salem T. College		Fayetteville				
1942	Norfolk Unit, Va. State College						
1947	Elizabeth City State Teachers College						

480

C.I.A.A. COLLEGIATE TRACK AND FIELD RECORDS

Relays

EVENTS	HOLDER	COLLEGE	YEAR PLACE	TIME
440-yard	Virginia State		1939—Hampton	43.3 s.
880-yard	Virginia State		1939—Hampton	1 m. 31.5 s.
One mile	Hampton		1939—Hampton	3 m. 23.5 s.
Two miles	Hampton		1939—Hampton	8 m. 16.7 s.
Sprint medley	Morgan		1939—Hampton	3 m. 40.6 s.
480-yard shuttle hurdle	Virginia State		1938—Hampton	1 m. 10.6 s.
				HEIGHT
High jump	Milby	Virginia State	1938—Hampton	5 ft. 11 in.
Pole vault	Perkins	Hampton	1939—Hampton	11 ft.
				DISTANCE
Broad jump	Smith	Hampton	1938—Hampton	22 ft. 11½ in.
Shot put	Dismond	Hampton	1939—Hampton	41 ft. 10⅞ in.
Discus	Mosby	Morgan	1938—Hampton	137 ft. 9¾ in.
Javelin	Hall	Virginia State	1939—Hampton	175 ft.

Open Meets

EVENTS	HOLDER	COLLEGE	YEAR PLACE	TIME
100-yard dash	Hall	Virginia State	1939—Virginia State	9.6 s.
220-yard dash (turn)	Singletary	St. Augustine's	1937—Howard	21.1 s.
440-yard dash	Tyler	Morgan	1947—Hampton	49.2 s.
880-yard run	Staten	St. Paul	1933—Hampton	1 m. 59.4 s.
One mile run	Lee	Howard	1937—Hampton	4 m. 29.6 s.
Two mile run	Lee	Union	1933—Hampton	9 m. 51.4 s.
120-yard high hurdles	Boyd	Virginia State	1933—Hampton	15 s.
220-yard low hurdles	Morris	Morgan	1947—Hampton	24.2 s.
Mile relay	Hampton		1940—A. and T.	3 m. 21.4 s.
Medley relay (440, 220, 220, 880)	St. Paul		1940—A. and T.	3 m. 38.4 s.

481

EVENTS	HOLDER	COLLEGE	YEAR	PLACE	DISTANCE
Javelin	Williams	Hampton	1932—Hampton		196 ft. 10½ in.
Broad jump	Davis	Lincoln	1935—Howard		22 ft. 6½ in.
Shot put	Simpson	Morgan	1937—Howard		44 ft. 7 in.
Discus throw	Mosby	Morgan	1938—Virginia State		143 ft.
					HEIGHT
High jump	Luvenda	Lincoln	1939—Virginia State		6 ft. 4 in.
Pole vault	Bailey	Virginia State	1939—Virginia State		12 ft. 5 in.

CHAMPIONSHIPS

EVENTS	HOLDER	COLLEGE	YEAR	PLACE	TIME
100-yard dash	Hall	Virginia State	1940—Hampton		9.6 s.
220-yard dash (straightaway)	Singletary	St. Augustine's	1937—Hampton		21.0 s.
440-yard dash	Early	Hampton	1930—Howard		49.0 s.
880-yard run	Byrd	Lincoln	1931—Hampton		1 m. 59.1 s.*
One mile relay	Hampton		1940—Hampton		3 m. 20.2 s.
One mile run	Lipscombe	Hampton	1935—Hampton		4 m. 25.1 s.
Two miles run	Lee	Union	1932—Hampton		9 m. 51.4 s.
220-yard low hurdles (turn)	Cottman	Morgan	1932—Howard		25.2 s.
220-yard low hurdles (straightaway)	Borican	Virginia State	1936—Hampton		24.4 s.
120-yard high hurdles	Wilson	Delaware	1947—A. and T.		14.9 s.
Medley relay (440, 220, 220, 880)	Howard		1930—Howard		3 m. 32.7 s.
					DISTANCE
Javelin throw	Sturgis	Morgan	1934—Howard		202 ft. 11.5 in.
Broad jump	Cromwell	Bowie	1934—Howard		24 ft. 3 in.
Hop- step- jump	Cottman-Troupe	Morgan	1933—Hampton		43 ft. 10.25 in.
Discus	Mosby	Morgan	1937—Howard		136 ft. 3 in.
Shot put	Simpson	Morgan	1937—Howard		44 ft. 4¾ in.
					HEIGHT
Pole vault	Jones	Union	1935—Hampton		12 ft.
High jump	Luyanda	Lincoln	1939—Morgan		6 ft. 4⅝ in.

*This record was equalled by Furcron (Hampton) in 1940.

C.I.A.A. SCHOLASTIC TRACK AND FIELD RECORDS

OPEN MEETS

EVENTS	HOLDER	SCHOOL	YEAR—PLACE	TIME
100-yard dash	Bellows	Armstrong	1936—Hampton	10.1 s.
220-yard dash	Tucker	Bordentown	1937—Hampton	22.5 s.
440-yard dash	Willis	Bordentown	1936—Hampton	51.6 s.
880-yard dash	Reynolds	Phenix	1936—Hampton	2 m. 4.8 s.
One mile run	Washington	Bordentown	1937—Hampton	4 m. 47.3 s.
120-yard low hurdles	Lomax	Douglass	1934—Hampton	14.4 s.
220-yard low hurdles	Higgins	Bordentown	1937—Hampton	26.6 s.
One mile relay	Bordentown		1934—Hampton	3 m. 32.1 s.
Medley relay	Bordentown		1936—Hampton	3 m. 44.6 s.
				HEIGHT
Pole vault	Courtney	Roosevelt	1934—Hampton	11 ft. 5 in.
High jump	Boyd	Phenix	1934—Howard	48 ft. 3 in.
				DISTANCE
Broad jump	Courtney	Roosevelt	1934—Hampton	22 ft. 2½ in.
Shot put (12 lbs.)	Kenner	Armstrong	1935—Howard	48 ft. 3 in.
Javelin throw	Johnson	Bordentown	1937—Hampton	144 ft. 2½ in.

CHAMPIONSHIPS

EVENTS	HOLDER	COLLEGE	YEAR—PLACE	TIME
100-yard dash	Richardson	Dunbar (Washington)	1925—Hampton	9.9 s.
220-yard dash (straightaway)	Richardson	Dunbar (Washington)	1925—Hampton	22 s.
440-yard dash	Cary	St. Paul	1940—Hampton	50.4 s.
880-yard run	Henderson	Bordentown	1930—Howard	2 m. 1.8 s.
One mile run	Price	Ga. T. and A. Hi.	1933—Hampton	4 m. 40 s.
220-yard low hurdles (straightaway)	Watkins	Bordentown	1933—Hampton	26.5 s.
One mile relay	Bordentown		1931—Hampton	3 m. 35 s.

				HEIGHT
High jump	Tolson	Cardoza	1934—Howard	6 ft.
Pole vault	Courtney	Roosevelt	1931—Hampton	10 ft. 7 in.

				DISTANCE
Broad jump	Harrod	Armstrong	1935—Hampton	21 ft. 11 in.
Shot put (12 lbs.)	Kenner	Armstrong	1935—Hampton	47 ft. 3½ in.
Javelin throw	Ballard	D. Webster Davis	1940—Hampton	158 ft. ½ in.
Discus	Stevenson	Douglass	1939—Morgan	110 ft. 8 in.

C.I.A.A. ALL TIME RECORDS IN BASKETBALL

INDIVIDUAL RECORDS

I. Highest in Individual Scoring for Single Season (Total games)—Rudolph Roberson, 1943—19 games Field Goals Free Throws.
415 Tol. Points average of 21 points per game.

II. Highest in Individual Scoring in a Single Conference Game—Rudolph Roberson, February 20, 1943—North Carolina College 92—Shaw University 42.
25 Field goals, 8 Free Throws, 58 Points.
(National Record of 1943-1944)

III. Highest in Individual Scoring in a Single Non-conference Game— Hutchinson Hart, February 9, 1947—Delaware State 115; Princess Anne 35.
18 Field goals, 0 Free Throws, 36 Points.

IV. Highest in Individual Free Throws in one game (10 or more)—Rudolph Roberson, February 17, 1947, 12 F.T. out of 13 FTA Pct. .923.

V. Highest in Individual Free Throws in Consecutive games (2 or more games and 10 or more free throws)
Elmer McDougal, North Carolina College, 1946.

	FTA	FTM	TFT
1. North Carolina College vs. Virginia State, February 2, 1946	11	10	10
2. North Carolina College vs. Morgan State, February 5, 1946	5	5	5
3. North Carolina College vs. Shaw University, February 6, 1946	4	4	4

Percentage—.950

TEAM RECORDS

I. Highest Single Conference Game Score
North Carolina College 119; St. Augustine 34, February 18, 1944.
North Carolina College, 52 FG—15 FT—119 Pts.

II. Highest Single Non-conference Game Score
Delaware State 115; Princess Anne 35, February 8, 1947.
Delaware State, 55 FG—5 FT—115 Pts.

III. Highest number of Points Scored in the First Half of Game.
North Carolina College 57; Bluefield Teachers 15, January 28, 1944.
Final: North Carolina College 95; Bluefield Teachers 24.

IV. Highest number of Points Scored in the Second Half of Game.
North Carolina College 63; Shaw University 21.
Final Score: North Carolina College 87; Shaw University 44.

V. Highest Games Scoring Average for a Season (Conference and non-conference) 1944.

North Carolina College 1186 pts. in 18 games—Average 65.8 per game.

VI. Highest Games Scoring Average for a Season (Conference Games) 1944.

North Carolina College 907 pts. in 13 games—Average 69.76 pct. per game.

VII. Leading Defensive Scoring Average (Conference and non-conference) 1944.

Johnson C. Smith opponents 651 pts. in 22 games—Average 29 points per game.

VIII. Leading Defensive Average (Conference) 1944.

Johnson C. Smith's opponents 454 pts. in 15 games—Average 30.26 points per game.

LETTER OF PROFESSOR J. FRANCIS GREGORY ON BASEBALL

"Mr. Samuel Lacy, Sports Editor,
The Washington Tribune,
Washington, D. C.

My dear Mr. Lacy:

I am writing to express my appreciation for your temerity and restraint in initiating this campaign for the admission of Negro players into big-league baseball in this country, 'a consummation devoutly to be wished' and the ultimate accomplishment of which has always seemed to me to be inevitable.

At the outset I wish to affirm without reservation my unshakable confidence in the superior performing skill of the Negro in the national game, covering the entire range of our players from the masterful Grant, who, we might say, 'jest grow'd' into the game, on to the equally superb Matthews, who was polished on the campus of Phillip's Andover and the playing fields of Harvard University. However, not to encroach upon the territory of the many illuminating contributions which have been made to this column, I am venturing to approach the problem from a comparatively untouched aspect—that of the potential availability of the college player as the entering wedge or spearhead of these thrusts into an untried field.

Those of us who have kept in intimate contact with the game of baseball outside of the schools have noted the steady elevation of the tone of the game during the past half century. I can always picture the striking contrast my brother drew between the two types of players back in the early nineties, when he compared the St. Louis team of the National League, with their shaved skulls, their crude manners and their flashy clothes—resembling a gang of ex-convicts—to the polished, well-groomed gentlemen of the Harvard University baseball team, both nines the box guests one evening of a large theatre in Boston. It is true that we find the uncouth and the vicious in all races and in all sports;

but it is also true that these objectionable types are rapidly being weeded out of professional sports, and all new performers must meet a higher and a more wholesome standard.

My contribution to this symposium is not that of a second-guessing bleacherite, nor of a speculative theorist, nor of a professional agitator, but rather that of a Negro whose baseball experience has been largely in association with players of the other group and before spectators of the other race. I simply offer this first-hand experience to drive home my point.

A glimpse of my baseball background will serve to give some authority to my comments. My brother and I were born into a baseball atmosphere, our father being one of the early players who delivered the ball underhand from the pitcher's box, and saw the scores soaring to the baffling heights of modern basketball contests, being often as high as 75 to 60. He was a very enthusiastic fan, and we youngsters must have learned a great deal through the psychological principle of empathy as we sat on the edges of our seats in the various Washington League baseball parks.

We went through the customary experiences of the youngsters of our day on the Saturday sandlots, and later with the more mature clubs who finally formed a league in the District of some six teams, of which I recall the Eclipse team and the famous Market House nine. A composite club drawn from these teams engaged in more pretentious contests with strong visiting teams, among which was the sensational Cuban Giant Club. I recall very vividly the elephantine catcher, Williams, driving a home-run far into the tall trees which shaded the old buildings of the Freedman's Hospital.

My last appearance on a team of my own race was that during the season of 1894, when, though a senior in the preparatory department, I played first base on the varsity nine of Howard University. I am venturing to refer to this club as one of the greatest ball clubs in Howard's history. Charlie Cook, the Sir Galahad of Howard athletes, played second base on this team, demonstrating that a man can play baseball skillfully and still be a gentleman. It was during this season that we played Trinity College on the old Howard campus, Columbia University in the Washington ball park, then on Capitol Hill, and Gallaudet College at Kendall Green. I think this was the first and the last time that Howard played baseball with clubs of the other group.

My baseball career proper began in Amherst College, where I played for four years, being the captain of the varsity nine in my senior year. I was never made unpleasantly conscious of my race during all these years, but, on the other hand, had many delightful personal contacts and other cordial associations. My relations with players at Amherst and on the campuses of Bowdoin, the University of Vermont, Williams, Dartmouth, Tufts, Harvard, Holy Cross, Brown, Wesleyan, Trinity, and Yale were invariably comrade-like. I recall especially the cordial sportsmanship of Lewis of Williams, Crolius of Dartmouth, Jimmie Dean and Percy Haughton of Harvard, and Billy Lauder and Dave

Fultz of Brown. Perhaps the most striking evidence of this unalloyed fellow-ship during that season of my captaincy in traveling around New England, was the unobtrusive but firm insistence—contrary to the somewhat pointed hint of hotel proprietors—of our manager, that the captain and manager, as had been the custom, occupy the same bed. That manager, by the way, is now a judge of the Superior Court of Massachusetts.

The same friendly attitude characterized the spectators at these games. No slighting remark or taunting slur ever reached my ear from the crowded stands on those far-flung fields. On the contrary, the reaction to my presence was always enthusiastically favorable. One incident at Holy Cross, the famous Catholic College at Worcester, Mass., is significant. When I stepped to the plate as captain to lead off the Amherst batting order in a game with that notable team, the stands burst forth in a spontaneous cheer, which only died down when I had lifted my cap in response. This experience is one of my most cherished recollections, not so much because of the personal element, but be-cause of the expression of sincere fairness to a visiting athlete regardless of race.

During those years at Amherst we played the Cuban Giants in two successive seasons. They played excellently at Amherst, although their shabby appearance and their tendency to overclown detracted somewhat from their skillful per-formance. It was at this time that I met the great Grant, the peerless second-basement—Lajoie and Collins not excepted. On this team were also Jordan, White and Howard, the pitcher. This was before the days of the brilliant Rube Foster.

These congenial relationships continued later at Yale, where I captained the Divinity School nine, a team composed of graduates of the leading colleges of the country. Among the prominent athletes studying in the Divinity School at this time was George B. Cutten, the great Yale center, now the president of Colgate University.

Of the players from college diamonds of my day who afterwards became outstanding professionals, I might mention Powers of Holy Cross, afterwards a brilliant backstop for Connie Mack; Sockalexis of the same college, the speedy Indian outfielder of the Cleveland team; Kellogg of Amherst, who played second base for Brooklyn; Crolius of Dartmouth, who played right field for the Pitts-burgh Pirates; Lewis of Williams, the mainstay in the pitcher's box for the Boston Nationals for many years; Billy Lauder and Dave Fultz of Brown, who played in the infield and the outfield for the Philadelphia Athletics and the New York Yankees. Dave Fultz later became president of the International League. I consider this Brown team of 1897 as one of the greatest college baseball teams of all time.

A word might be said here of the professional coaches who worked with Amherst during these years. For two seasons the coach at Amherst was Roy Thomas, the versatile center-fielder for the University of Pennsylvania and later the invaluable middle gardener of the Phillies for ten years. He was another rare gentleman who carried his gentility onto the diamond. During the season of my captaincy, Jimmy Callahan, the foxy shortstop and captain of the Chicago White Sox, was the coach and consequently my daily associate. He often spoke of Clark Griffith and demonstrated to our box candidates some of the deceptive pitching methods of the present president of the Washington Baseball Club. The older fans in Washington will recall that Griffith brought his old pal to Washington some seasons ago as a coach for the home team. Above all, it is interesting to know that Callahan, on his retirement from the White Sox, became an enthusiastic promoter of semi-professional baseball on the sandlots of Chicago, especially from the standpoint of interracial games. Jimmy Callahan judged a baseball player by his ability to perform, and being a gentleman, attracted similar associates.

As a transitional period between my college and professional experience, with my brother, a pitcher on the Harvard University team, I played on the Eaglesmere baseball team, playing visiting teams on that famous mountain-top resort in Northern Pennsylvania and journeying to the towns in that general area. This team was composed of college players, largely the sons of the resident cottagers representing some of the leading families in Williamsport, Pittsburgh and Philadelphia. Among the players were the Young brothers, a famous athletic family of Cornell, White of Lehigh, Bucky Vail of the University of Pennsylvania, Gregory of Harvard and the writer, of Amherst. We played for two seasons under the most delightful conditions. One game I particularly recall was in Williamsport against that city's Tri-State team, on which Schreckengast, who afterwards caught so effectively for Connie Mack, played. We won this game, to our great delight. I might add that my grandmother had a cottage in Eaglesmere and was an electrical physician. My brother and I therefore were invited to join this team on the same basis as the sons of other residents.

My purely professional career started with a notice to report at the Hotel Albion in Atlantic City to play on the baseball team of that summer resort. If I had accepted this summons, I feel that an opening into a wider field in professional baseball might have been opened to our young players, as this was the only instance when a Negro was invited to play on this particular club. A trip to Europe, planned months before, precluded the acceptance of this inviting offer. My son-in-law, Dr. Charles West, formerly of Washington and Jefferson, told me the other day that Honus Wagner, the Pittsburgh shortstop, scouted him one day on a high school diamond with the intention of persuading him to enter Carnegie Tech to play on the baseball team of that school as a stepping-stone to a later career in the professional field. When West told him that there was little hope for a Negro in professional baseball, the famous Pirate shortstop made the very significant statement, 'You may be the first one to break into this field.'

Later, with my brother, I joined the Whitehill baseball team of the Burlington County League in New Jersey. After two seasons with this team, we were signed by the Bordentown team of this same league and played around the circuit, including Bordentown, Whitehill, Florence, Burlington, Mt. Holly, Delanco, Riverton, Riverside and Palmyra, for nearly ten years. My brother pitched or played third base and I played second base or centerfield. During all these years we never met with any embarrassing experience from players or spectators. In fact, we were often spared some of the inevitable razzing and jibing which the average ball player expects as a part of the game. And even in the heated clashes which suddenly arise between players on opposing teams, no racial slur was ever passed. Indeed, in one of the towns where we had heard no colored person was permitted to tarry our experiences were invariably pleasant. As an illustration of the fairness of this attitude, I recall that after a tie game at Mt. Holly where we had faced the renowned Indian pitcher, Bruce, later with Connie Mack's Athletics, the Bordentown manager paid my way back from New Haven, where I had returned to Yale University, and advertised my personal return with mammoth posters.

Now, Mr. Lacy, I feel that this sheer recital of actual experiences with the other group, better than a layman's theoretical tirade, drives home my message that the school man may be the one to blaze the way for the entrance of the Negro into big-league baseball. I might add that my brother and I conducted ourselves in a far more exemplary manner than our white associates on the professional field, and that is the only reason we remained there.

Might I add that we are confronted, however, with the distressing fact that our college boys do not know how to play baseball. The high schools do not sufficiently encourage the game, and many of our larger universities have eliminated it completely from their athletic programs. Perhaps it is largely a matter of sentiment, but I have always regretted the shortsightedness of a great institution like Howard University in dropping this national sport from its program of physical education.

I learned to play baseball at Howard, and later was able to hold my own in the great athletic centers of New England and elsewhere. I am the only Negro who ever made an Amherst baseball team in all the years of its history, and you can count on the fingers of one hand, the outstanding Negro baseball players in all the colleges of the other group in the East. Baseball is the American game; American boys love the game; they crave skill in its playing; they make all sorts of sacrifices—sitting up all night on a box outside the gates of a ball park to be able to witness a world series game from some remote perch far up in the corner of the bleachers. And yet we make no provision for them to learn to play the game.

The craze for softball has worked against the development of legitimate baseball players. Softball may have democratic value, but it is not the proper approach to so-called hard ball. I have always felt that a hard-ball player could readily adapt himself to softball; but not so easily can a softball player adjust himself to the legitimate game.

Modern professional baseball offers a lucrative career for an ambitious young man, and more and more as the standards of the game are lifted, the aspirants for admission to this field of sport must present evidence not only of playing excellence, but also of alert intelligence and wholesome character.

It is true that the opening has not yet been made, but as the old Pirate Wizard put it, 'Perhaps the college player will be the first to break in.'

Keep a stout heart, my young pioneer; the approach to the goal may be slow, but its final attainment is sure!

Sincerely yours,

J. FRANCIS GREGORY."

STORY OF THE CARDOZO HIGH SCHOOL TRACK TEAM SINCE 1943

Cardozo High School Track Team. Billy Mathis on February 24, 1944, won the 60 yards dash in 6.5 seconds over the favored Tom Bartzos of George Washington High in New York City, becoming national scholastic champion. In the Penn Relays of 1944, Cardozo's mile relay team won a class mile relay championship over the New Utrecht team from Brooklyn in 3:34.4 seconds. In the annual track and field carnival at Schenectady, New York of 1944, the Cardozo track team tied St. Michael's High School of Jersey City for the Class "B" championship with 18 points. (Class B schools have less than 700 boys enrolled.) Billy Mathis won the 100 yards dash in the amazing school boys' time of 9.8 seconds. He shattered the existing records of 10.2 seconds by .4 of a second. He also anchored the winning Cardozo 880 yards relay team which set a new record of 1:33.8 seconds. On May 30, 1944, Cardozo won the Eastern Championship team trophy in Providence, R. I. with 24 points and a five man squad. Mathis won the 100 lowering the record from 10.2 seconds to 9.9 seconds, broke the 220 yards record of 23.6 by a time of 22.1 seconds, and helped lower the 880 yards relay record of 1:36.2 seconds to 1:34.2 seconds. A team mate, Roland Morgan won the 440. On June 18–19, at Randall Island in New York, Mathis was second in 100 meters to the sensational high school sprinter, Charley Parker from Texas. In 1945 Mathis finished second to Barney Ewell in two 60 yards dashes. In the national preparatory and high school indoor meet on February 24, 1945, Mathis met Perry Samuels from San Antonio, Texas, and won by two strides, setting a new national scholastic record of 6.3 seconds for the 60 yard dash. Mathis was awarded a gold Hamilton wrist watch and adjudged the most outstanding athlete of this meet. At the Bridgeton Relay Carnival in 1945 the Cardozo distance medley team (Holmes, McCaskill, Mathis and Hansford) lowered the distance medley relay

492   *The Negro in Sports*

meet record from 8:53 seconds to 8:35.1 seconds; also the 880 yards relay team set a new meet record of 1:34.9 in this event. At the Penn Relay Games in 1945 the Cardozo 440 relay team won the quarter mile high school championship of America from a field of 78 schools in 44.3. This gave Cardozo High School its second national title, the second straight year. Cardozo's mile relay team also won a "class" championship in 3:31.2 seconds and scored fourth in the high school one mile relay championship of America. In June, 1945, Mathis was graduated from Cardozo and matriculated at the University of Illinois where he went on to become a national sprint champion. But Hall had two more boys of promise—David Clark and Marcellus Boston. In the National Indoor Meet at Madison Square Garden, Coach Hall's six lap's relay team (Cosby, Boston, Yates, Turner) established a new meet record of 1:47.2 seconds. This was the second record held by Cardozo in Madison Square Garden. In the Philadelphia Interscholastic Convention Hall meet in 1946 David Clark won the 50 yards in 5.5 seconds and Cardozo's mile relay team won over Mercersburg and Haverford. Cosby's injury in this meet weakened Cardozo's teams, but at the Penn Relays the Cardozo mile relay team won a class mile championship for the third consecutive year. This team was comprised of Turner, Yates, Holmes and Baucom.

Travelling to St. Louis, Missouri in May the six man Cardozo team won the National Negro High School Track and Field Championship by scoring 37 points. The wearers of the Purple and White captured three individual and three relay titles; two second places and one third. Boston in the 100; Turner the 220; and Baucom in the 440 were the individual titlists. Queen in the discus and Boston in the broad jump were second while Broady placed third in the broad jump. The 440 team tied the national record of 45 seconds to win, the 880 yards sprint medley relay team lowered the record from 1:39.2 to 1:37.9. The 880 yards team won the third of the relay championships. Freshman Marcellus Boston won the high point trophy with 11¼ points.

In 1947 Cardozo's six laps relay team of Boston, Norwood, Drummond and Yates set a new record of 1:47.0 in this event at the National Preparatory and High School Indoor Meet at Madison Square Garden in February. Boston also captured the National Preparatory School indoor 60 yards dash title in 6.5 seconds. At the South Atlantic Athletic Association Union's indoor meet held at the 5th Regiment Armory in Baltimore in March, Boston won the 75 yards dash title in 7.8 seconds. The Cardozo 440 relay team won this event in 46.9. Boston received the award for being voted the most outstanding high school athlete of the meet. To open the 1947 outdoor season Cardozo athletes won the team trophy of the scholastic division of the Howard University Relay Carnival on April 12th with 31 points. Boston was first in the 100 yards dash, anchored the winning 440 and 880 yards relays, ran a 220 leg on the victorious sprint medley team, and finished second in the running broad jump. The team went on to finish third in the 440 relay at the Penn Relays;

second in the city championships and won the South Atlantic High School Athletic Association crown.

The team began its 1948 season by participating in the Washington Evening Star Games held at the National Guard Armory on January 3rd. Marcellus Boston was the sole high school athlete in the star-studded sprint series (70, 80, 100 yards dashes). He ran second to the ex-Cardozo sprint champion Billy Mathis in the 70, was fourth in the 80 and second in the 100 yards dash. He placed third behind Cianciabella of Manhattan College and Mathis in the final point score for the series. At an indoor meet jointly sponsored by the Philadelphia *Inquirer Charities*, Inc. and the Philadelphia Board of Education at Convention Hall on January 23rd Boston won the 50 yards dash and set a new record of 5.4 seconds. The old record of 5.5 was held by ex-team mate David Clark. Henry Johnson placed second in the 50 yards high hurdles and the one mile relay team ran third. On February 21st at the National Preparatory and High School indoor meet at Madison Square Garden Cardozo athletes finished second in the preparatory school division with 23 points. This was the highest number of points ever scored at this meet by a Cardozo team. Freshman Joseph Walker, barely 16 years old, dethroned Marcellus Boston in the 60 yards dash. Boston was second in this event and in the running broad jump. Henry Johnson placed fourth in the 60 yards high hurdles as did DeReef Green in the 440 yards dash. George Sibert finished fifth in the one mile run. The six laps relay team of Boston, Lorenzo Moon, William Drummond and Walker set a *new world record* for the 960 yards by negotiating the distance in 1:42.7. The former record was 1:46.8 held by St. Peters High School of Jersey City, N. J. At the Middle Atlantic Indoor Meet sponsored by the Camden Board of Education at Convention Hall, Camden, N. J., March 19th and 20th, Cardozo went on a record breaking rampage by creating four new standards and tieing the fifth. Moreover, it also won the Class B team title with 26 points. Class A was made up of all schools in the state of New Jersey, Class B all schools outside the state. The open class was comprised of those teams or athletes who finished first, second and third in Class A and B. The first record was set in the medley relay (440, 220, 220, 880). The former Class B record was 5:13.8 until the Cardozo quartet of George Sibert, Joe Walker, Boston and William Sturdevant lowered it to 5:12.0. Second was the one mile relay record lowered from 3:46.0 to 3:43.7 by Boston, Lorenzo Moon, De Reef Greene and Walker. Third, the open class medley relay with a former record of 5:13.7 lowered by Cardozo to 5:09.0. Boston accounted for the other two. He won the open class 50 yards dash in 5.5 seconds automatically setting a record because this was a new event. He also won the Class B 50 yards dash and tied the existing record of 5.5 seconds made by Billy Mathis in 1945.

The outdoor season began with the Seton Hall College Relay Carnival held at the City Stadium, Newark, N. J., April 16th. Cardozo High School's 440 relay team of Walker, Rudolph McGoines, De Reef Greene and Boston set a new record in the preparatory school division, winning in 44.6 seconds. The former record was 44.9 held by Seton Hall Preparatory School. The Purple and White 880 yards team automatically became possessor of a new record of 1:33.8 when it won this new event. This team was made up of Boston, William Drummond, Greene and Walker. The following day, April 17th, the team participated in the Bridgeton High School Relay Carnival in Bridgeton, N. J. Cardozo athletes won the Group 3 team title with 30 points. Group 3 was composed of all schools having a boys' enrollment from 301 to 500. The 880 yards relay team of Boston, Drummond, Greene and Walker covered the distance in 1:33.1. This was the fastest time ever recorded on the Bridgeton track. The one mile relay team won this event while the two mile and distance medley teams finished third and second respectively.

INDEX

Index

497

502

Index

CPSIA information can be obtained
at www.ICGtesting.com
Printed in the USA
BVHW031227060222
PP13112600001B/3